Learning With Technology

You will be making many exciting journeys across time and place in *World Studies*. Technology will help make what you learn come alive.

For: An activity on the Renaissance
Visit: PHSchool.com
Web Code: lgd-8601

For a complete list of features for this book, use Web Code **lgk-1000.**

Go Online at PHSchool.com

Use the Web Codes listed below and in each Go Online box to access exciting information or activities.

How to Use the Web Code:
1. Go to **www.PHSchool.com**.
2. Enter the Web Code.
3. Click Go!

Medieval Times to Today Activities

Web Code	Activity
	History Interactive
lgp-8900	Explore the Hagia Sofia
lgp-8901	Learn more about the 5 Pillars of Islam
lgp-8902	Travel with Mansa Musa
lgp-8903	Travel Along the Inca Roads
lgp-8904	Tour a Maya City
lgp-8905	Explore a Chinese Ship
lgp-8906	Tour a Japanese Castle
lgp-8907	Explore Two Feudal Societies
lgp-8908	Explore the Magna Carta
lgp-8909	Explore Luther's Legacy
lgp-8910	Trade between Europe, Africa and Asia About 1700
lgp-8911	Transforming the World: The Columbian Exchange
lgp-8922	Triangular Trade
lgp-8924	Explore the Scientific Method
lgp-8925	Spreading the Word of Revolution
lgp-8929	Jazz Age
	Geography Interactive
lgp-8923	Expansion of Russia
lgp-8926	Imperialism in Africa to 1914
lgp-8927	Independent Nations of Latin America, 1844
lgp-8928	The Western Front and the Eastern Front, 1914-1918
lgp-8930	World War II in Europe and North Africa, 1942-1945
lgp-8941	The Cold War World
lgp-8942	Latin America: Economic Activity
lgp-8943	World Oil Resources and Consumption
	MapMaster
lgp-8944	The Seasons

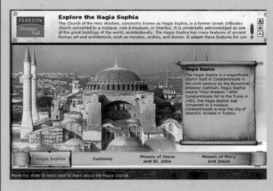

World Desk Reference Online

There are more than 190 countries in the world. To learn about them, you need the most up-to-date information and statistics. The **DK World Desk Reference Online** gives you instant access to the information you need to explore each country.

PRENTICE HALL

WORLD STUDIES

MEDIEVAL TIMES TO TODAY

In association with
DK

Discovery
CHANNEL
SCHOOL

PEARSON

Prentice
Hall

Boston, Massachusetts
Upper Saddle River, New Jersey

Program Consultants

Heidi Hayes Jacobs

Heidi Hayes Jacobs has served as an education consultant to more than 1,000 schools across the nation and abroad. Dr. Jacobs serves as an adjunct professor in the Department of Curriculum on Teaching at Teachers College, Columbia University. She has written two best-selling books and numerous articles on curriculum reform. She received an M.A. from the University of Massachusetts, Amherst, and completed her doctoral work at Columbia University's Teachers College in 1981. The core of Dr. Jacobs's experience comes from her years teaching high school, middle school, and elementary school students. As an educational consultant, she works with K–12 schools and districts on curriculum reform and strategic planning.

Michal L. LeVasseur

Michal LeVasseur is the Executive Director of the National Council for Geography Education. She is an instructor in the College of Education at Jacksonville State University and works with the Alabama Geographic Alliance. Her undergraduate and graduate work were in the fields of anthropology (B.A.), geography (M.A.), and science education (Ph.D.). Dr. LeVasseur's specialization has moved increasingly into the area of geography education. Since 1996 she has served as the Director of the National Geographic Society's Summer Geography Workshops. As an educational consultant, she has worked with the National Geographic Society as well as with schools and organizations to develop programs and curricula for geography.

Senior Reading Consultants

Kate Kinsella

Kate Kinsella, Ed.D., is a faculty member in the Department of Secondary Education at San Francisco State University. A specialist in second-language acquisition and adolescent literacy, she teaches coursework addressing language and literacy development across the secondary curricula. Dr. Kinsella earned her M.A. in TESOL from San Francisco State University, and her Ed.D. in Second Language Acquisition from the University of San Francisco.

Kevin Feldman

Kevin Feldman, Ed.D., is the Director of Reading and Early Intervention with the Sonoma County Office of Education (SCOE) and an independent educational consultant. At the SCOE, he develops, organizes, and monitors programs related to K–12 literacy. Dr. Feldman has an M.A. from the University of California, Riverside in Special Education, Learning Disabilities and Instructional Design. He earned his Ed.D. in Curriculum and Instruction from the University of San Francisco.

Acknowledgments appear on page 297, which constitutes an extension of this copyright page.

Copyright © 2008 by Pearson Education, Inc., publishing as Pearson Prentice Hall, Boston, Massachusetts 02116.
All rights reserved. Printed in the United States of America. This publication is protected by copyright, and permission should be obtained from the publisher prior to any prohibited reproduction, storage in a retrieval system, or transmission in any form or by any means, electronic, mechanical, photocopying, recording, or likewise. For information regarding permission(s), write to: Rights and Permissions Department, One Lake Street, Upper Saddle River, New Jersey 07458.

MapMaster™ is a trademark of Pearson Education, Inc.
Pearson Prentice Hall™ is a trademark of Pearson Education, Inc.
Pearson® is a registered trademark of Pearson plc.
Prentice Hall® is a registered trademark of Pearson Education, Inc.
Discovery Channel School® is a registered trademark of Discovery Communications, Inc.

 is a registered trademark of Dorling Kindersley Limited.
Prentice Hall World Studies is published in collaboration with DK Designs, Dorling Kindersley Limited, 80 Strand, London WC2R 0RL. A Penguin Company.

ISBN 0-13-251659-4
12345678910   10 09 08 07 06

Cartography Consultant
 **Andrew Heritage**

Andrew Heritage has been publishing atlases and maps for more than 25 years. In 1991, he joined the leading illustrated nonfiction publisher Dorling Kindersley (DK) with the task of building an international atlas list from scratch. The DK atlas list now includes some 10 titles, which are constantly updated and appear in new editions either annually or every other year.

Academic Reviewers

Africa
Barbara B. Brown, Ph.D.
African Studies Center
Boston University
Boston, Massachusetts

Ancient World
Evelyn DeLong Mangie, Ph.D.
Department of History
University of South Florida
Tampa, Florida

Central Asia and the Middle East
Pamela G. Sayre
History Department,
    Social Sciences Division
Henry Ford Community College
Dearborn, Michigan

East Asia
Huping Ling, Ph.D.
History Department
Truman State University
Kirksville, Missouri

Eastern Europe
Robert M. Jenkins
Center for Slavic, Eurasian and
    East European Studies
University of North Carolina
Chapel Hill, North Carolina

Latin America
Dan La Botz
Professor, History Department
Miami University
Oxford, Ohio

Medieval Times
James M. Murray
History Department
University of Cincinnati
Cincinnati, Ohio

North Africa
Barbara E. Petzen
Center for Middle Eastern Studies
Harvard University
Cambridge, Massachusetts

Religion
Charles H. Lippy, Ph.D.
Department of Philosophy
    and Religion
University of Tennessee
    at Chattanooga
Chattanooga, Tennessee

Russia
Janet Vaillant
Davis Center for Russian
    and Eurasian Studies
Harvard University
Cambridge, Massachusetts

South Asia
Robert J. Young
Professor Emeritus
History Department
West Chester University
West Chester, Pennsylvania

United States and Canada
Victoria Randlett
Geography Department
University of Nevada, Reno
Reno, Nevada

Western Europe
Ruth Mitchell-Pitts
Center for European Studies
University of North Carolina
    at Chapel Hill
Chapel Hill, North Carolina

Reviewers

Sean Brennan
Brecksville-Broadview Heights City
    School District
Broadview Heights, Ohio

Stephen Bullick
Mt. Lebanon School District
Pittsburgh, Pennsylvania

William R. Cranshaw, Ed.D.
Waycross Middle School
Waycross, Georgia

Dr. Louis P. De Angelo
Archdiocese of Philadelphia
Philadelphia, Pennsylvania

Paul Francis Durietz
Social Studies
    Curriculum Coordinator
Woodland District #50
Gurnee, Illinois

Gail Dwyer
Dickerson Middle School,
    Cobb County
Marietta, Georgia

Michal Howden
Social Studies Consultant
Zionsville, Indiana

Rosemary Kalloch
Springfield Public Schools
Springfield, Massachusetts

Deborah J. Miller
Office of Social Studies,
    Detroit Public Schools
Detroit, Michigan

Steven P. Missal
Newark Public Schools
Newark, New Jersey

Catherine Fish Petersen (Retired)
East Islip School District
Islip Terrace, New York

Joe Wieczorek
Social Studies Consultant
Baltimore, Maryland

MEDIEVAL TIMES TO TODAY

Develop Skills

Use these pages to develop your reading, writing, and geography skills.

Focus on History

Learn about the geography, history, and cultures from medieval times to today.

- Learn map skills with the MapMaster Skills Handbook.
- Practice your skills with every map in this book.
- Interact with every map online and on CD-ROM.

DK

Maps and illustrations created by DK help build your understanding of the world. The DK World Desk Reference Online keeps you up to date.

The World Studies Video Program takes you on field trips to study countries around the world.

i*nteractive* Textbook

The *World Studies* Interactive Textbook online and on CD-ROM uses interactive maps and other activities to help you learn.

Special Features

Literature

A selection from the tales of King Arthur brings to life the age of knights and chivalry.

Focus On

Learn more about how the people of different places and eras lived their daily lives.

Skills for Life

Learn skills that you will use throughout your life.

Links

See the fascinating links between social studies and other disciplines.

Eyewitness Technology

Detailed drawings show how technology shapes places and societies.

Target Reading Skills

Chapter-by-chapter reading skills help you read and understand social studies concepts.

Citizen Heroes

Meet people who have made a difference in their country.

Maps and Charts

MAP MASTER™

MAP MASTER™ Interactive

Go online to find an interactive version of every MapMaster map in this book. Use the Web Code provided to gain direct access to these maps.

How to Use Web Codes:

1. Go to **www.PHSchool.com**.
2. Enter the Web Code.
3. Click Go!

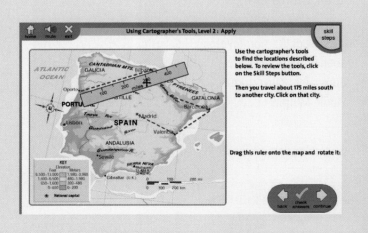

Charts, Graphs, and Tables

Building Geographic Literacy

Learning about a country often starts with finding it on a map. The MapMaster™ system in *World Studies* helps you develop map skills you will use throughout your life. These three steps can help you become a MapMaster!

The MAP★MASTER™ System

1 Learn

You need to learn geography tools and concepts before you explore the world. Get started by using the MapMaster Skills Handbook to learn the skills you need for success.

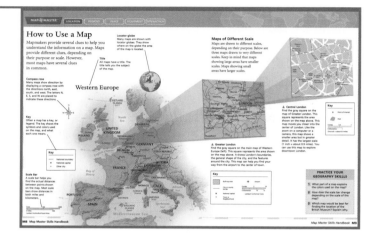

MAP★MASTER™ Skills Activity

Location The Equator runs through parts of Latin America, but it is far from other parts of the region.

Locate Find the Equator on the map. Which climates are most common in Latin America, and how far is each climate region from the Equator?

Draw Conclusions How do climates change as you move away from the Equator?

Go Online
PHSchool.com Use Web Code **lfp-1142** for step-by-step **map skills practice**.

2 Practice

You need to practice and apply your geography skills frequently to be a MapMaster. The maps in *World Studies* give you the practice you need to develop geographic literacy.

3 Interact

Using maps is more than just finding places. Maps can teach you many things about a region, such as its climate, its vegetation, and the languages that the people who live there speak. Every MapMaster map is online at **PHSchool.com,** with interactive activities to help you learn the most from every map.

Learning With Technology

You will be making many exciting journeys across time and place in *World Studies*. Technology will help make what you learn come alive.

Go Online PHSchool.com

For: An activity on the Renaissance
Visit: PHSchool.com
Web Code: lgd-8601

Go Online at PHSchool.com

Use the Web Codes listed below and in each Go Online box to access exciting information or activities.

How to Use the Web Code:
1. Go to **www.PHSchool.com**.
2. Enter the Web Code.
3. Click Go!

For a complete list of features for this book, use Web Code **lgk-1000**.

Medieval Times to Today Activities

Web Code	Activity
	History Interactive
lgp-8900	Explore the Hagia Sofia
lgp-8901	Learn more about the 5 Pillars of Islam
lgp-8902	Travel with Mansa Musa
lgp-8903	Travel Along the Inca Roads
lgp-8904	Tour a Maya City
lgp-8905	Explore a Chinese Ship
lgp-8906	Tour a Japanese Castle
lgp-8907	Explore Two Feudal Societies
lgp-8908	Explore the Magna Carta
lgp-8909	Explore Luther's Legacy
lgp-8910	Trade between Europe, Africa and Asia About 1700
lgp-8911	Transforming the World: The Columbian Exchange
lgp-8922	Triangular Trade
lgp-8924	Explore the Scientific Method
lgp-8925	Spreading the Word of Revolution
lgp-8929	Jazz Age
	Geography Interactive
lgp-8923	Expansion of Russia
lgp-8926	Imperialism in Africa to 1914
lgp-8927	Independent Nations of Latin America, 1844
lgp-8928	The Western Front and the Eastern Front, 1914-1918
lgp-8930	World War II in Europe and North Africa, 1942-1945
lgp-8941	The Cold War World
lgp-8942	Latin America: Economic Activity
lgp-8943	World Oil Resources and Consumption
	MapMaster
lgp-8944	The Seasons

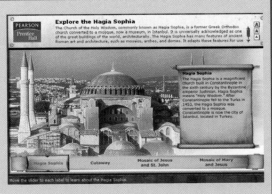

PEARSON Prentice Hall

Explore the Hagia Sophia
The Church of the Holy Wisdom, commonly known as Hagia Sophia, is a former Greek Orthodox church converted to a mosque, now a museum, in Istanbul. It is universally acknowledged as one of the great buildings of the world, architecturally. The Hagia Sophia has many features of ancient Roman art and architecture, such as mosaics, arches, and domes. It adapts these features for use

Hagia Sophia
The Hagia Sophia is a magnificent church built in Constantinople in the sixth century by the Byzantine emperor Justinian. Hagia Sophia means "Holy Wisdom." After Constantinople fell to the Turks in 1453, the Hagia Sophia was converted to a mosque. Constantinople is now the city of Istanbul, located in Turkey.

Hagia Sophia | Cutaway | Mosaic of Jesus and St. John | Mosaic of Mary and Jesus

Move the slider to each label to learn about the Hagia Sophia.

World Desk Reference Online

There are more than 190 countries in the world. To learn about them, you need the most up-to-date information and statistics. The **DK World Desk Reference Online** gives you instant access to the information you need to explore each country.

Reading Informational Texts

Reading a magazine, an Internet page, or a textbook is not the same as reading a novel. The purpose of reading nonfiction texts is to acquire new information. On page M18 you'll read about some 🎯 **Target Reading Skills** that you'll have a chance to practice as you read this textbook. Here we'll focus on a few skills that will help you read nonfiction with a more critical eye.

Analyze the Author's Purpose

Different types of materials are written with different purposes in mind. For example, a textbook is written to teach students information about a subject. The purpose of a technical manual is to teach someone how to use something, such as a computer. A newspaper editorial might be written to persuade the reader to accept a particular point of view. A writer's purpose influences how the material is presented. Sometimes an author states his or her purpose directly. More often, the purpose is only suggested, and you must use clues to identify the author's purpose.

Distinguish Between Facts and Opinions

It's important when reading informational texts to read actively and to distinguish between fact and opinion. A fact can be proven or disproven. An opinion cannot—it is someone's personal viewpoint or evaluation.

For example, the editorial pages in a newspaper offer opinions on topics that are currently in the news. You need to read newspaper editorials with an eye for bias and faulty logic. For example, the newspaper editorial at the right shows factual statements in blue and opinion statements in red. The underlined words are examples of highly charged words. They reveal bias on the part of the writer.

> More than 5,000 people voted last week in favor of building a new shopping center, but the opposition won out. The margin of victory is irrelevant. Those radical voters who opposed the center are obviously self-serving elitists who do not care about anyone but themselves.

> This month's unemployment figure for our area is 10 percent, which represents an increase of about 5 percent over the figure for this time last year. These figures mean unemployment is getting worse. But the people who voted against the mall probably do not care about creating new jobs.

Identify Evidence

Before you accept an author's conclusion, you need to make sure that the author has based the conclusion on enough evidence and on the right kind of evidence. An author may present a series of facts to support a claim, but the facts may not tell the whole story. For example, what evidence does the author of the newspaper editorial on the previous page provide to support his claim that the new shopping center would create more jobs? Is it possible that the shopping center might have put many small local businesses out of business, thus increasing unemployment rather than decreasing it?

Evaluate Credibility

Whenever you read informational texts, you need to assess the credibility of the author. This is especially true of sites you may visit on the Internet. All Internet sources are not equally reliable. Here are some questions to ask yourself when evaluating the credibility of a Web site.

- ❑ Is the Web site created by a respected organization, a discussion group, or an individual?
- ❑ Does the Web site creator include his or her name as well as credentials and the sources he or she used to write the material?
- ❑ Is the information on the site balanced or biased?
- ❑ Can you verify the information using two other sources?
- ❑ Is there a date telling when the Web site was created or last updated?

Writing for Social Studies

Writing is one of the most powerful communication tools you will ever use. You will use it to share your thoughts and ideas with others. Research shows that writing about what you read actually helps you learn new information and ideas. A systematic approach to writing—including prewriting, drafting, revising, and proofing—can help you write better, whether you're writing an essay or a research report.

Narrative Essays

Writing that tells a story about a personal experience

1 Select and Narrow Your Topic

A narrative is a story. In social studies, it might be a narrative essay about how an event affected you or your family.

2 Gather Details

Brainstorm a list of details you'd like to include in your narrative.

3 Write a First Draft

Start by writing a simple opening sentence that conveys the main idea of your essay. Continue by writing a colorful story that has interesting details. Write a conclusion that sums up the significance of the event or situation described in your essay.

4 Revise and Proofread

Check to make sure you have not begun too many sentences with the word *I*. Replace general words with more colorful ones.

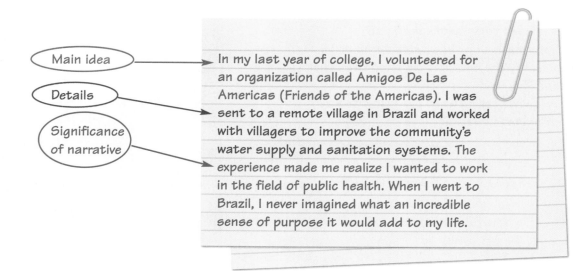

Main idea → In my last year of college, I volunteered for an organization called Amigos De Las Americas (Friends of the Americas). I was

Details → sent to a remote village in Brazil and worked with villagers to improve the community's water supply and sanitation systems. The

Significance of narrative → experience made me realize I wanted to work in the field of public health. When I went to Brazil, I never imagined what an incredible sense of purpose it would add to my life.

Persuasive Essays

Writing that supports an opinion or position

1 Select and Narrow Your Topic

Choose a topic that provokes an argument and has at least two sides. Choose a side. Decide which argument will appeal most to your audience and persuade them to understand your point of view.

2 Gather Evidence

Create a chart that states your position at the top and then lists the pros and cons for your position below, in two columns. Predict and address the strongest arguments against your stand.

3 Write a First Draft

Write a strong thesis statement that clearly states your position. Continue by presenting the strongest arguments in favor of your position and acknowledging and refuting opposing arguments.

4 Revise and Proofread

Check to make sure you have made a logical argument and that you have not oversimplified the argument.

Main Idea
Supporting (pro) argument
Opposing (con) argument
Transition words

> It is vital to vote in elections. When people vote, they tell public officials how to run the government. Not every proposal is carried out; however, politicians do their best to listen to what the majority of people want. Therefore, every vote is important.

Expository Essays

Writing that explains a process, compares and contrasts, explains causes and effects, or explores solutions to a problem

① Identify and Narrow Your Topic

Expository writing is writing that explains something in detail. It might explain the similarities and differences between two or more subjects (compare and contrast). It might explain how one event causes another (cause and effect). Or it might explain a problem and describe a solution.

② Gather Evidence

Create a graphic organizer that identifies details to include in your essay.

Cause 1	Cause 2	Cause 3
Most people in the Mexican countryside work on farms.	The population in Mexico is growing at one of the highest rates in the world.	There is not enough farm work for so many people.

Effect

As a result, many rural families are moving from the countryside to live in Mexico City.

③ Write Your First Draft

Write a topic sentence and then organize the essay around your similarities and differences, causes and effects, or problem and solutions. Be sure to include convincing details, facts, and examples.

④ Revise and Proofread

Research Papers

Writing that presents research about a topic

① Narrow Your Topic

Choose a topic you're interested in and make sure that it is not too broad. For example, instead of writing a report on Panama, write about the construction of the Panama Canal.

② Acquire Information

Locate several sources of information about the topic from the library or the Internet. For each resource, create a source index card like the one at the right. Then take notes using an index card for each detail or subtopic. On the card, note which source the information was taken from. Use quotation marks when you copy the exact words from a source.

Source #1
McCullough, David. *The Path Between the Seas: The Creation of the Panama Canal, 1870-1914.* N.Y., Simon and Schuster, 1977.

③ Make an Outline

Use an outline to decide how to organize your report. Sort your index cards into the same order.

Outline
I. Introduction
II. Why the canal was built
III. How the canal was built
   A. Physical challenges
   B. Medical challenges
IV. Conclusion

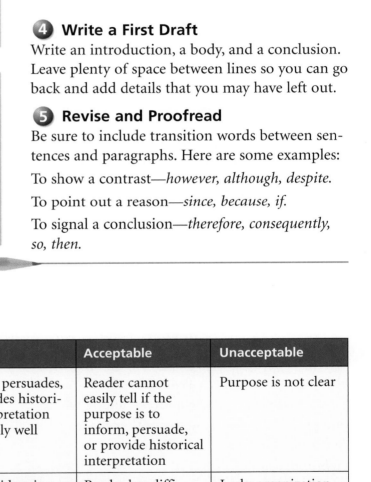

Introduction

Building the Panama Canal

Ever since Christopher Columbus first explored the Isthmus of Panama, the Spanish had been looking for a water route through it. They wanted to be able to sail west from Spain to Asia without sailing around South America. However, it was not until 1914 that the dream became a reality.

Conclusion

It took eight years and more than 70,000 workers to build the Panama Canal. It remains one of the greatest engineering feats of modern times.

4 Write a First Draft

Write an introduction, a body, and a conclusion. Leave plenty of space between lines so you can go back and add details that you may have left out.

5 Revise and Proofread

Be sure to include transition words between sentences and paragraphs. Here are some examples:

To show a contrast—*however, although, despite.*

To point out a reason—*since, because, if.*

To signal a conclusion—*therefore, consequently, so, then.*

Evaluating Your Writing

Use this table to help you evaluate your writing.

	Excellent	Good	Acceptable	Unacceptable
Purpose	Achieves purpose—to inform, persuade, or provide historical interpretation—very well	Informs, persuades, or provides historical interpretation reasonably well	Reader cannot easily tell if the purpose is to inform, persuade, or provide historical interpretation	Purpose is not clear
Organization	Develops ideas in a very clear and logical way	Presents ideas in a reasonably well-organized way	Reader has difficulty following the organization	Lacks organization
Elaboration	Explains all ideas with facts and details	Explains most ideas with facts and details	Includes some supporting facts and details	Lacks supporting details
Use of Language	Uses excellent vocabulary and sentence structure with no errors in spelling, grammar, or punctuation	Uses good vocabulary and sentence structure with very few errors in spelling, grammar, or punctuation	Includes some errors in grammar, punctuation, and spelling	Includes many errors in grammar, punctuation, and spelling

MAP✦MASTER™ SKILLS HANDBOOK

CONTENTS

Go Online PHSchool.com Use Web Code lap-0000 for all of the maps in this handbook.

Five Themes of Geography

Studying the geography of the entire world is a huge task. You can make that task easier by using the five themes of geography: location, regions, place, movement, and human-environment interaction. The themes are tools you can use to organize information and to answer the where, why, and how of geography.

▲ **Location**
This museum in England has a line running through it. The line marks its location at 0° longitude.

LOCATION

1 Location answers the question, "Where is it?" You can think of the location of a continent or a country as its address. You might give an absolute location such as 40° N and 80° W. You might also use a relative address, telling where one place is by referring to another place. *Between school and the mall* and *eight miles east of Pleasant City* are examples of relative locations.

REGIONS

2 Regions are areas that share at least one common feature. Geographers divide the world into many types of regions. For example, countries, states, and cities are political regions. The people in any one of these places live under the same government. Other features, such as climate and culture, can be used to define regions. Therefore the same place can be found in more than one region. For example, the state of Hawaii is in the political region of the United States. Because it has a tropical climate, Hawaii is also part of a tropical climate region.

MOVEMENT

4 Movement answers the question, "How do people, goods, and ideas move from place to place?" Remember that what happens in one place often affects what happens in another. Use the theme of movement to help you trace the spread of goods, people, and ideas from one location to another.

PLACE

3 Place identifies the natural and human features that make one place different from every other place. You can identify a specific place by its landforms, climate, plants, animals, people, language, or culture. You might even think of place as a geographic signature. Use the signature to help you understand the natural and human features that make one place different from every other place.

INTERACTION

5 Human-environment interaction focuses on the relationship between people and the environment. As people live in an area, they often begin to make changes to it, usually to make their lives easier. For example, they might build a dam to control flooding during rainy seasons. Also, the environment can affect how people live, work, dress, travel, and communicate.

◄ **Interaction**
These Congolese women interact with their environment by gathering wood for cooking.

PRACTICE YOUR GEOGRAPHY SKILLS

1 Describe your town or city, using each of the five themes of geography.

2 Name at least one thing that comes into your town or city and one that goes out. How is each moved? Where does it come from? Where does it go?

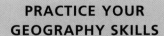

Understanding Movements of Earth

The planet Earth is part of our solar system. Earth revolves around the sun in a nearly circular path called an orbit. A revolution, or one complete orbit around the sun, takes 365 ¼ days, or one year. As Earth orbits the sun, it also spins on its axis, an invisible line through the center of Earth from the North Pole to the South Pole. This movement is called a rotation.

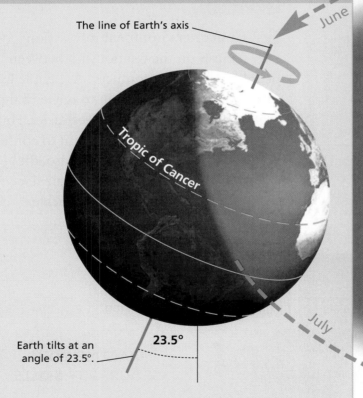

How Night Changes Into Day

The line of Earth's axis

Tropic of Cancer

Earth tilts at an angle of 23.5°.

23.5°

Earth takes about 24 hours to make one full rotation on its axis. As Earth rotates, it is daytime on the side facing the sun. It is night on the side away from the sun.

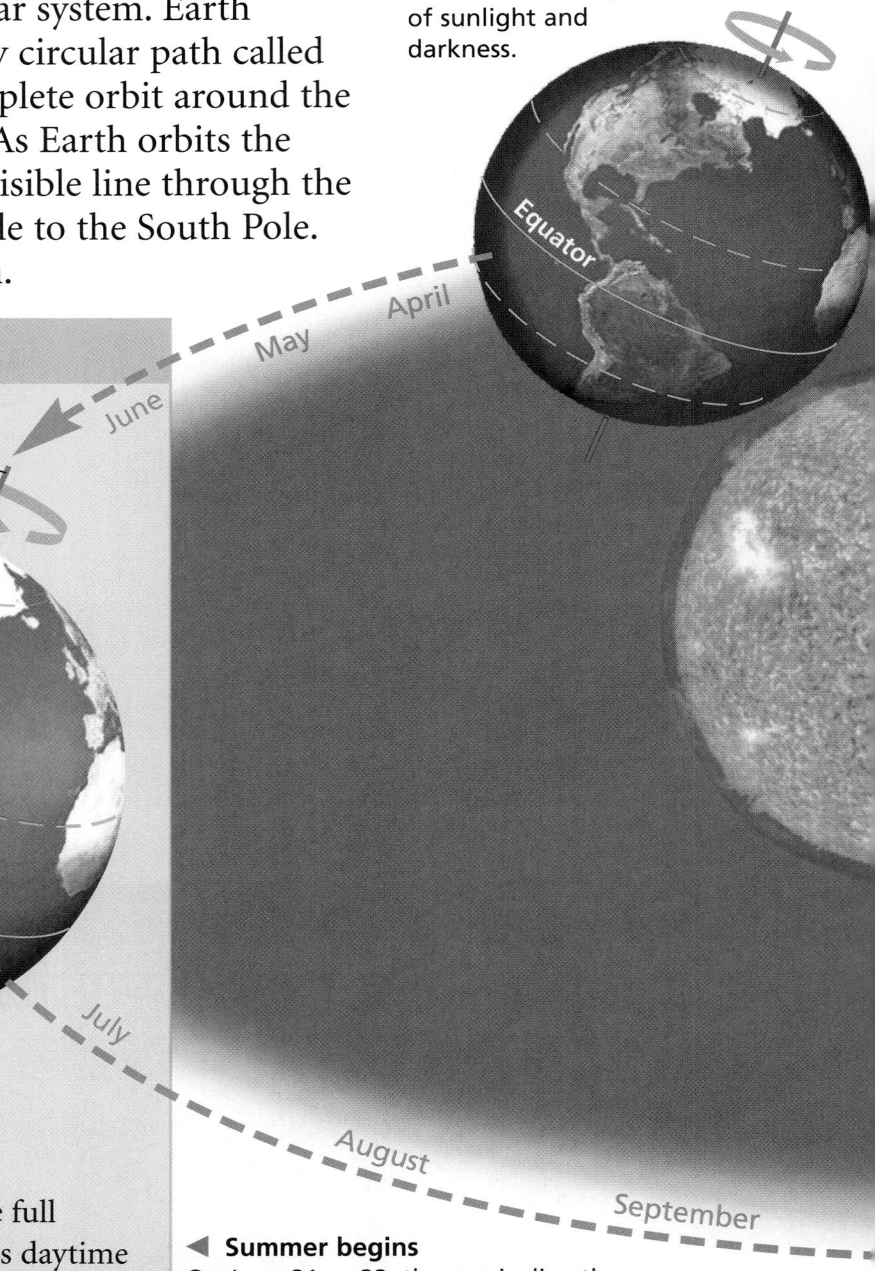

▼ **Spring begins**
On March 20 or 21, the sun is directly overhead at the Equator. The Northern and Southern Hemispheres receive almost equal hours of sunlight and darkness.

Equator

April
May
June
July
August
September

◄ **Summer begins**
On June 21 or 22, the sun is directly overhead at the Tropic of Cancer. The Northern Hemisphere receives the greatest number of sunlight hours.

The Seasons

Earth's axis is tilted at an angle. Because of this tilt, sunlight strikes different parts of Earth at different times in the year, creating seasons. The illustration below shows how the seasons are created in the Northern Hemisphere. In the Southern Hemisphere, the seasons are reversed.

PRACTICE YOUR GEOGRAPHY SKILLS

1. What causes the seasons in the Northern Hemisphere to be the opposite of those in the Southern Hemisphere?
2. During which two days of the year do the Northern Hemisphere and Southern Hemisphere have equal hours of daylight and darkness?

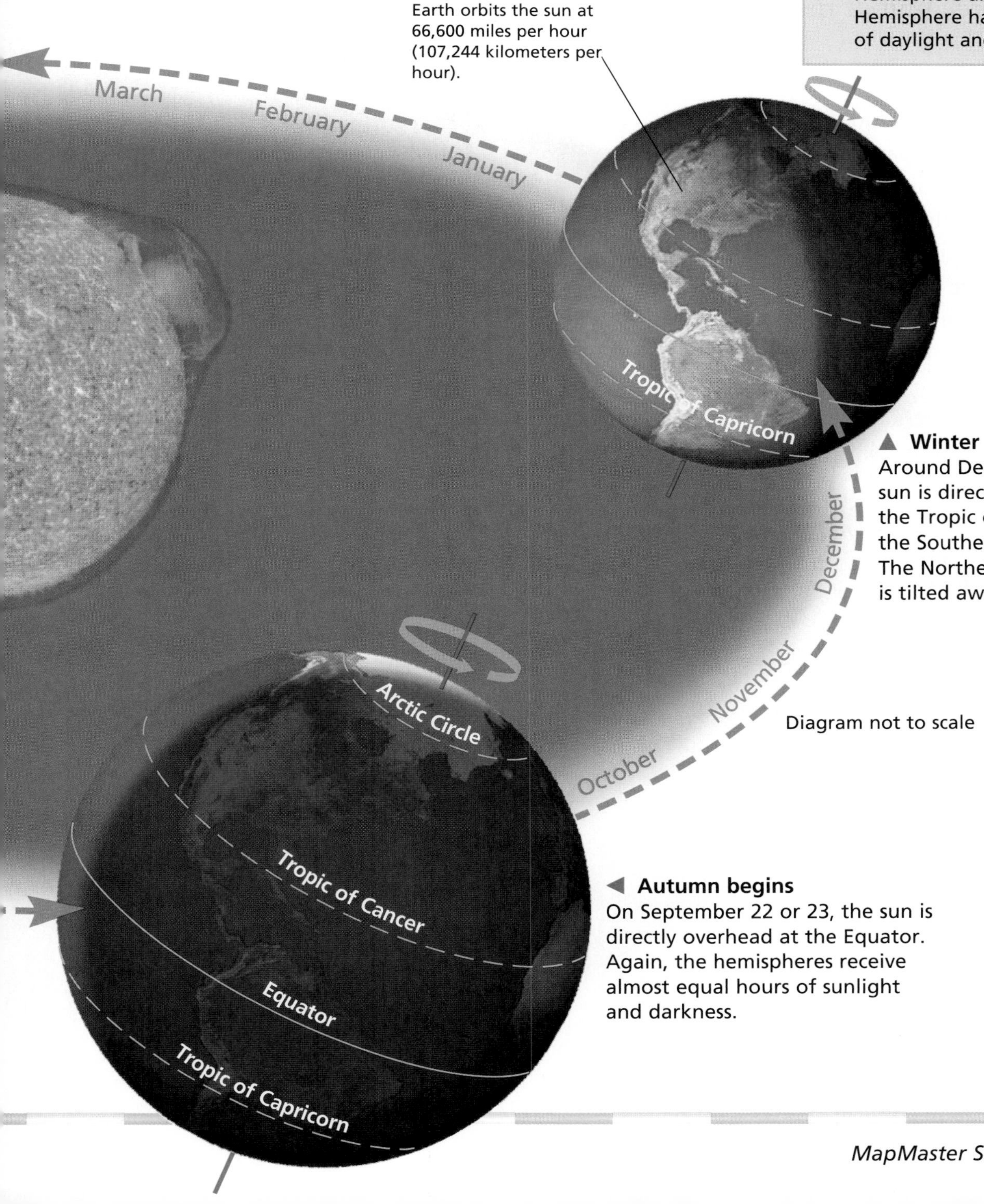

Earth orbits the sun at 66,600 miles per hour (107,244 kilometers per hour).
March
February
January
Tropic of Capricorn
December
November
October
Diagram not to scale
Arctic Circle
Tropic of Cancer
Equator
Tropic of Capricorn

▲ **Winter begins**
Around December 21, the sun is directly overhead at the Tropic of Capricorn in the Southern Hemisphere. The Northern Hemisphere is tilted away from the sun.

◀ **Autumn begins**
On September 22 or 23, the sun is directly overhead at the Equator. Again, the hemispheres receive almost equal hours of sunlight and darkness.

Understanding Globes

A globe is a scale model of Earth. It shows the actual shapes, sizes, and locations of all Earth's landmasses and bodies of water. Features on the surface of Earth are drawn to scale on a globe. This means that a small unit of measure on the globe stands for a large unit of measure on Earth.

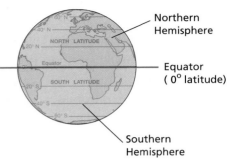

Northern Hemisphere

Equator (0° latitude)

Southern Hemisphere

Parallels of Latitude

Geographers divide the globe along imaginary horizontal lines called parallels of latitude. One of these latitude lines is the Equator, located halfway between the North and South Poles. Parallels of latitude are measured in degrees (°). One degree of latitude represents a distance of about 69 miles (111 kilometers).

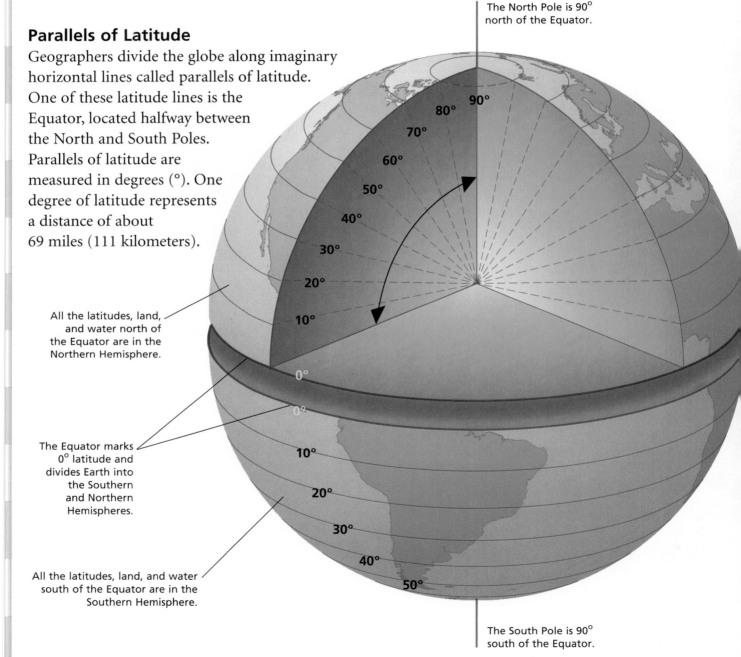

The North Pole is 90° north of the Equator.

All the latitudes, land, and water north of the Equator are in the Northern Hemisphere.

The Equator marks 0° latitude and divides Earth into the Southern and Northern Hemispheres.

All the latitudes, land, and water south of the Equator are in the Southern Hemisphere.

The South Pole is 90° south of the Equator.

Meridians of Longitude

Geographers also divide the globe along imaginary vertical lines called meridians of longitude, which are measured in degrees (°). The longitude line called the Prime Meridian runs from pole to pole through Greenwich, England. All meridians of longitude come together at the North and South Poles.

PRACTICE YOUR GEOGRAPHY SKILLS

1 Which continents lie completely in the Northern Hemisphere? In the Western Hemisphere?

2 Is there land or water at 20° S latitude and the Prime Meridian? At the Equator and 60° W longitude?

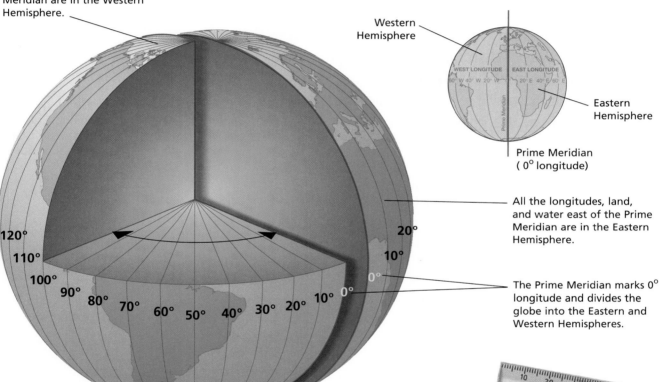

All the longitudes, land, and water west of the Prime Meridian are in the Western Hemisphere.

Western Hemisphere

WEST LONGITUDE   EAST LONGITUDE
60° W 40° W 20° W   20° E 40° E 60° E

Eastern Hemisphere

Prime Meridian
(0° longitude)

All the longitudes, land, and water east of the Prime Meridian are in the Eastern Hemisphere.

The Prime Meridian marks 0° longitude and divides the globe into the Eastern and Western Hemispheres.

120° 110° 100° 90° 80° 70° 60° 50° 40° 30° 20° 10° 0°   0° 10° 20°

The Global Grid

Together, the pattern of parallels of latitude and meridians of longitude is called the global grid. Using the lines of latitude and longitude, you can locate any place on Earth. For example, the location of 30° north latitude and 90° west longitude is usually written as 30° N, 90° W. Only one place on Earth has these coordinates—the city of New Orleans, in the state of Louisiana.

▲ **Compass**
Wherever you are on Earth, a compass can be used to show direction.

Map Projections

Maps are drawings that show regions on flat surfaces. Maps are easier to use and carry than globes, but they cannot show the correct size and shape of every feature on Earth's curved surface. They must shrink some places and stretch others. To make up for this distortion, mapmakers use different map projections. No one projection can accurately show the correct area, shape, distance, and direction for all of Earth's surface. Mapmakers use the projection that has the least distortion for the information they are presenting.

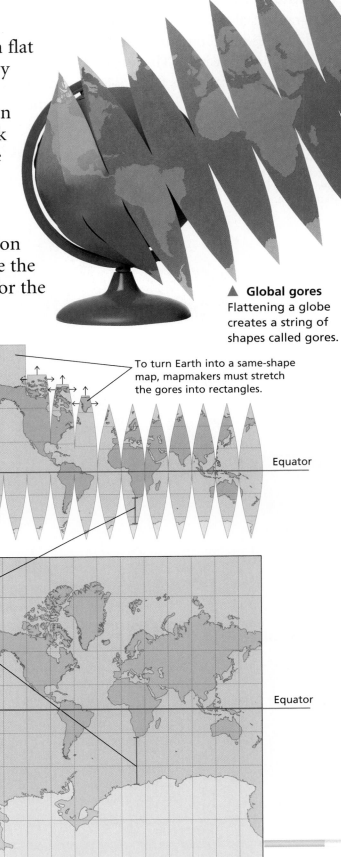

▲ **Global gores**
Flattening a globe creates a string of shapes called gores.

Same-Shape Maps

Map projections that accurately show the shapes of landmasses are called same-shape maps. However, these projections often greatly distort, or make less accurate, the size of landmasses as well as the distance between them. In the projection below, the northern and southern areas of the globe appear more stretched than the areas near the Equator.

To turn Earth into a same-shape map, mapmakers must stretch the gores into rectangles.

Equator

Stretching the gores makes parts of Earth larger. This enlargement becomes greater toward the North and South Poles.

Mercator projection ▶
One of the most common same-shape maps is the Mercator projection, named for the mapmaker who invented it. The Mercator projection accurately shows shape and direction, but it distorts distance and size. Because the projection shows true directions, ships' navigators use it to chart a straight-line course between two ports.

Equator

Equal-Area Maps

Map projections that show the correct size of landmasses are called equal-area maps. In order to show the correct size of landmasses, these maps usually distort shapes. The distortion is usually greater at the edges of the map and less at the center.

PRACTICE YOUR GEOGRAPHY SKILLS

1 What feature is distorted on an equal-area map?

2 Would you use a Mercator projection to find the exact distance between two locations? Tell why or why not.

To turn Earth's surface into an equal-area map, mapmakers have to squeeze each gore into an oval.

Equator

The tips of all the gores are then joined together. The points at which they join form the North and South Poles. The line of the Equator stays the same.

North Pole

Equator

South Pole

Robinson Maps

Many of the maps in this book use the Robinson projection, which is a compromise between the Mercator and equal-area projections. The Robinson projection gives a useful overall picture of the world. It keeps the size and shape relationships of most continents and oceans, but distorts the size of the polar regions.

The entire top edge of the map is the North Pole.

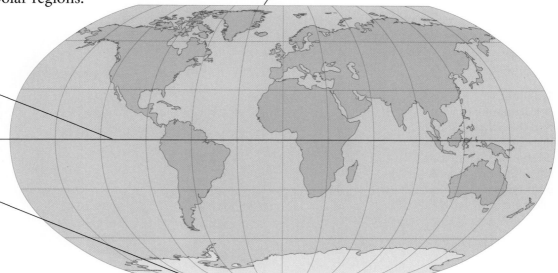

The map is least distorted at the Equator.

Equator

The entire bottom edge of the map is the South Pole.

How to Use a Map

Mapmakers provide several clues to help you understand the information on a map. Maps provide different clues, depending on their purpose or scale. However, most maps have several clues in common.

Locator globe
Many maps are shown with locator globes. They show where on the globe the area of the map is located.

Title
All maps have a title. The title tells you the subject of the map.

Compass rose
Many maps show direction by displaying a compass rose with the directions north, east, south, and west. The letters N, E, S, and W are placed to indicate these directions.

Key
Often a map has a key, or legend. The key shows the symbols and colors used on the map, and what each one means.

Scale bar
A scale bar helps you find the actual distances between points shown on the map. Most scale bars show distances in both miles and kilometers.

Western Europe

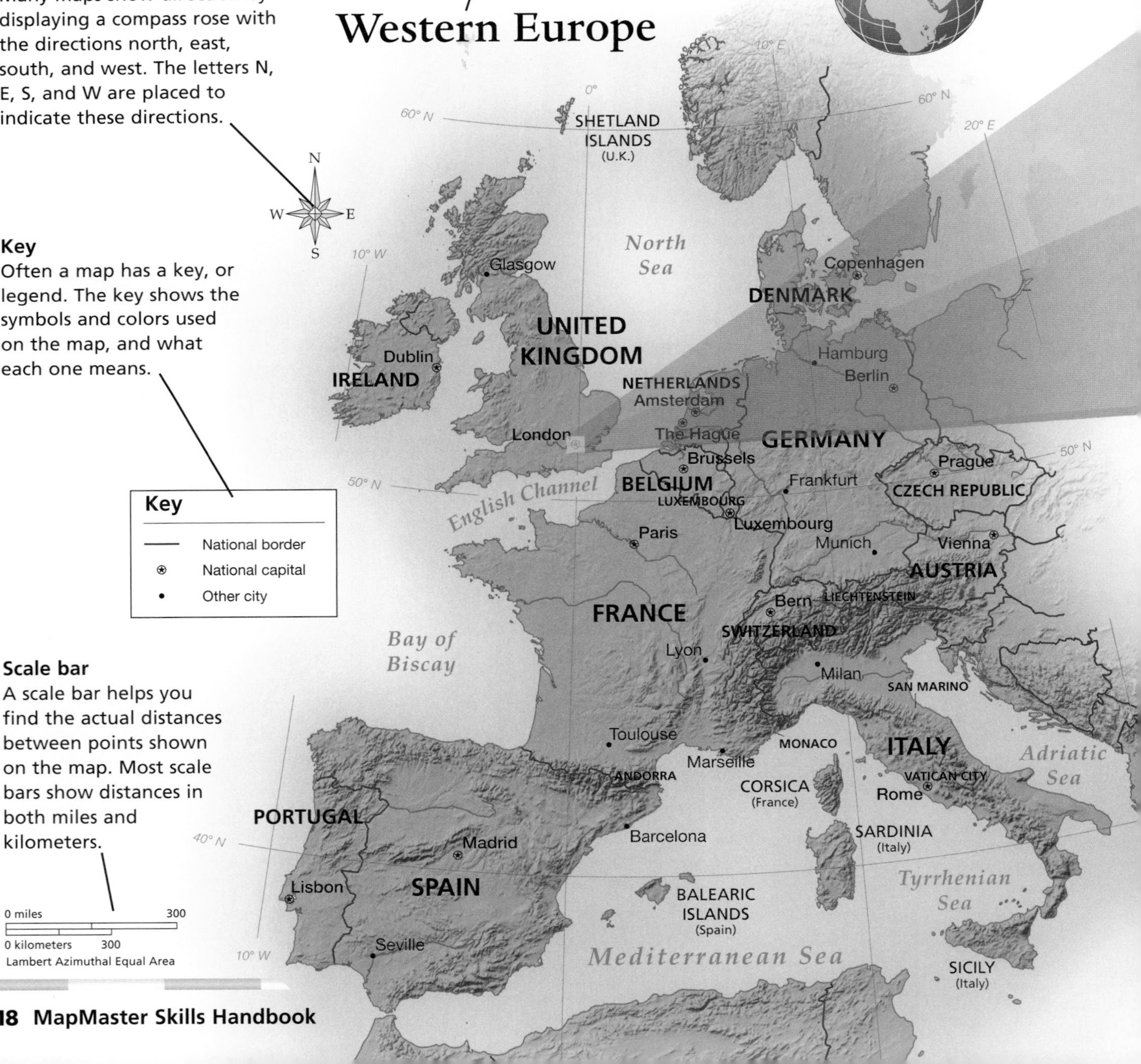

N
W — E
S

Key

——	National border
⊛	National capital
•	Other city

0 miles — 300
0 kilometers — 300
Lambert Azimuthal Equal Area

SHETLAND ISLANDS (U.K.)

North Sea

Glasgow
Copenhagen
DENMARK

Dublin
IRELAND
UNITED KINGDOM
Hamburg
Berlin

London
The Hague
NETHERLANDS
Amsterdam
GERMANY

Brussels
BELGIUM
Frankfurt
Prague
CZECH REPUBLIC

LUXEMBOURG
Luxembourg
Munich
Vienna

Paris
AUSTRIA

English Channel

FRANCE
Bern
LIECHTENSTEIN
SWITZERLAND
Lyon
Milan
SAN MARINO

Bay of Biscay

Toulouse
MONACO
ITALY
Adriatic Sea

Marseille
ANDORRA
CORSICA (France)
VATICAN CITY
Rome

PORTUGAL
Madrid
Barcelona
SARDINIA (Italy)

Lisbon
SPAIN
BALEARIC ISLANDS (Spain)
Tyrrhenian Sea

Seville
Mediterranean Sea
SICILY (Italy)

10° E
0°
60° N
20° E
60° N
10° W
50° N
50° N
40° N
10° W

Maps of Different Scales

Maps are drawn to different scales, depending on their purpose. Here are three maps drawn to very different scales. Keep in mind that maps showing large areas have smaller scales. Maps showing small areas have larger scales.

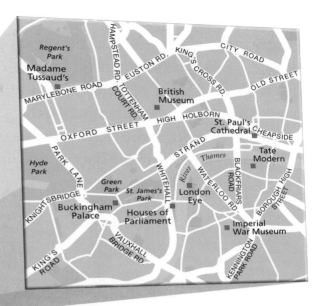

▲ **Greater London**
Find the gray square on the main map of Western Europe (left). This square represents the area shown on the map above. It shows London's boundaries, the general shape of the city, and the features around the city. This map can help you find your way from the airport to the center of town.

▲ **Central London**
Find the gray square on the map of Greater London. This square represents the area shown on the map above. This map moves you closer into the center of London. Like the zoom on a computer or a camera, this map shows a smaller area but in greater detail. It has the largest scale (1 inch represents about 0.9 mile). You can use this map to explore downtown London.

Key

■ Point of interest

▰ Park

0 miles   0.5   1

0 kilometers   1

Key

▨ Built-up area

—— City or county border

⊛ National capital

• Town or neighborhood

✈ Airport

0 miles   10   20

0 kilometers   20

Lambert Conformal Conic

PRACTICE YOUR GEOGRAPHY SKILLS

1 What part of a map explains the colors used on the map?

2 How does the scale bar change depending on the scale of the map?

3 Which map would be best for finding the location of the British Museum? Explain why.

Political Maps

Political maps show political borders: continents, countries, and divisions within countries, such as states or provinces. The colors on political maps do not have any special meaning, but they make the map easier to read. Political maps also include symbols and labels for capitals, cities, and towns.

PRACTICE YOUR GEOGRAPHY SKILLS

1 What symbols show a national border, a national capital, and a city?

2 What is Angola's capital city?

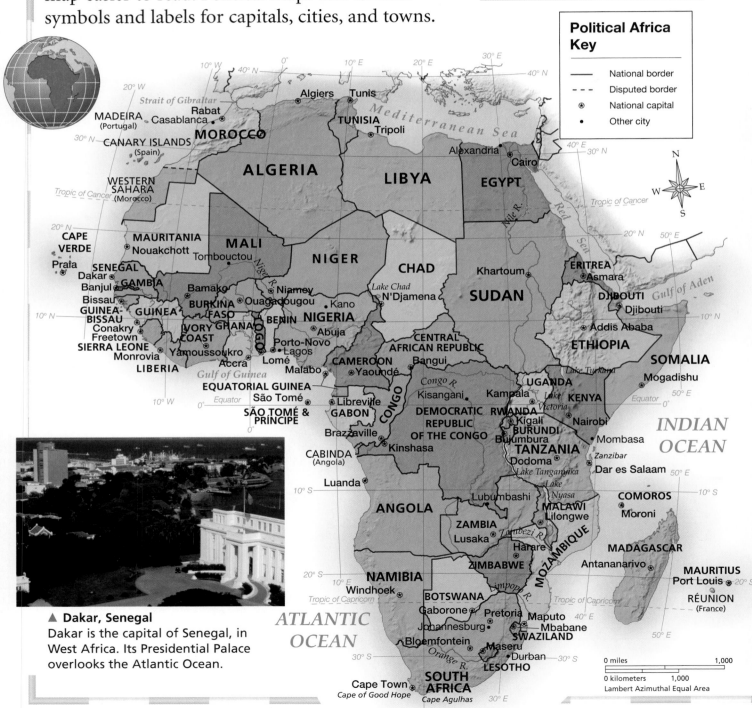

Political Africa Key

——	National border
- - -	Disputed border
⊛	National capital
•	Other city

▲ **Dakar, Senegal**
Dakar is the capital of Senegal, in West Africa. Its Presidential Palace overlooks the Atlantic Ocean.

Physical Maps

Physical maps represent what a region looks like by showing its major physical features, such as hills and plains. Physical maps also often show elevation and relief. Elevation, indicated by colors, is the height of the land above sea level. Relief, indicated by shading, shows how sharply the land rises or falls.

PRACTICE YOUR GEOGRAPHY SKILLS

1 Which areas of Africa have the highest elevation?

2 How can you use relief to plan a hiking trip?

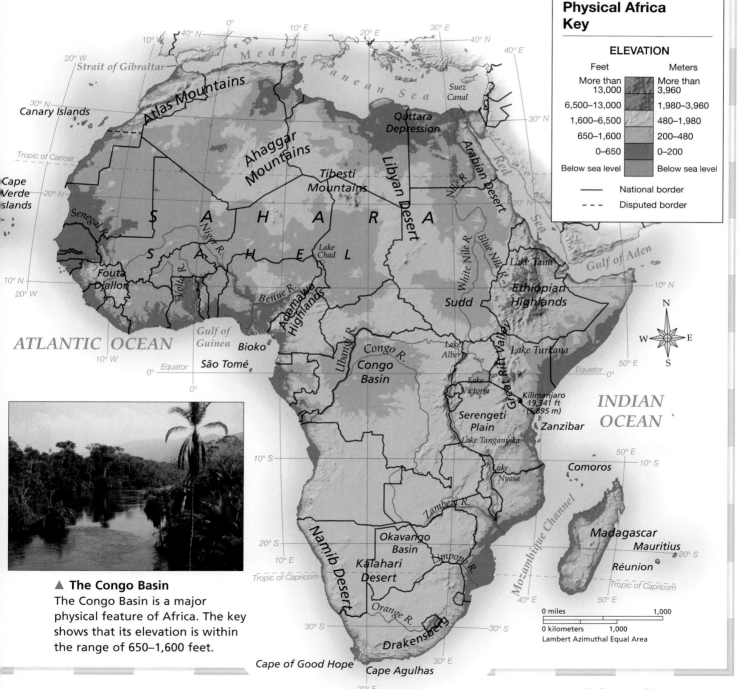

Physical Africa Key

ELEVATION

Feet	Meters
More than 13,000	More than 3,960
6,500–13,000	1,980–3,960
1,600–6,500	480–1,980
650–1,600	200–480
0–650	0–200
Below sea level	Below sea level

—— National border
- - - Disputed border

Kilimanjaro 19,341 ft (5,895 m)

0 miles 1,000
0 kilometers 1,000
Lambert Azimuthal Equal Area

▲ **The Congo Basin**
The Congo Basin is a major physical feature of Africa. The key shows that its elevation is within the range of 650–1,600 feet.

Special-Purpose Maps: Climate

Unlike the boundary lines on a political map, the boundary lines on climate maps do not separate the land into exact divisions. For example, in this climate map of India, a tropical wet climate gradually changes to a tropical wet and dry climate.

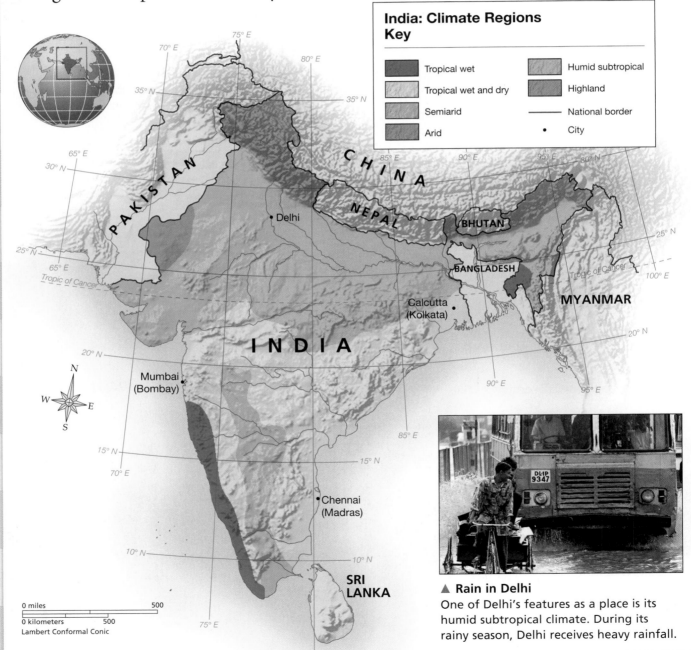

India: Climate Regions Key

- Tropical wet
- Tropical wet and dry
- Semiarid
- Arid
- Humid subtropical
- Highland
- ——— National border
- • City

▲ **Rain in Delhi**
One of Delhi's features as a place is its humid subtropical climate. During its rainy season, Delhi receives heavy rainfall.

0 miles   500
0 kilometers   500
Lambert Conformal Conic

Special-Purpose Maps: Language

This map shows the official languages of India. An official language is the language used by the government. Even though a region has an official language, the people there may speak other languages as well. As in other special-purpose maps, the key explains how the different languages appear on the map.

PRACTICE YOUR GEOGRAPHY SKILLS

1 What color represents the Malayalam language on this map?

2 Where in India is Tamil the official language?

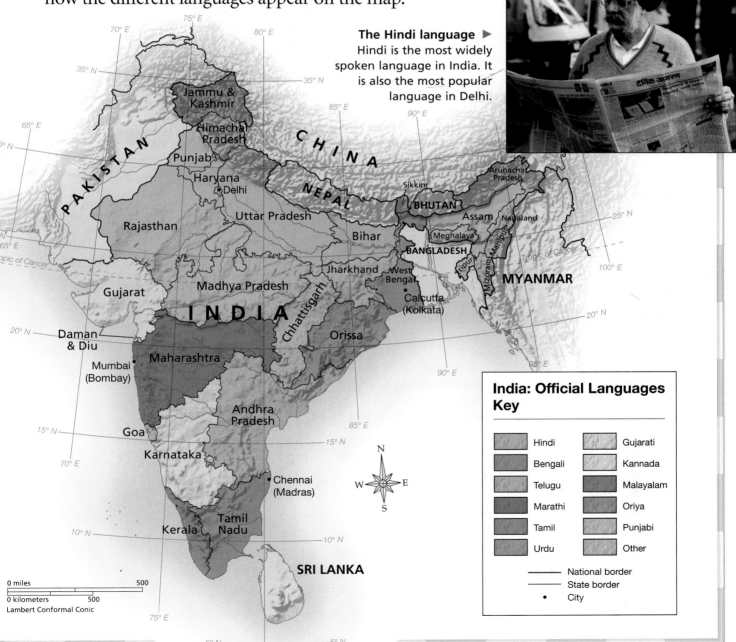

The Hindi language ▶
Hindi is the most widely spoken language in India. It is also the most popular language in Delhi.

India: Official Languages Key

	Hindi		Gujarati
	Bengali		Kannada
	Telugu		Malayalam
	Marathi		Oriya
	Tamil		Punjabi
	Urdu		Other

—— National border
—— State border
• City

0 miles 500
0 kilometers 500
Lambert Conformal Conic

Human Migration

Migration is an important part of the study of geography. Since the beginning of history, people have been on the move. As people move, they both shape and are shaped by their environments. Wherever people go, the culture they bring with them mixes with the cultures of the place in which they have settled.

Explorers arrive ▼
In 1492, Christopher Columbus set sail from Spain for the Americas with three ships. The ships shown here are replicas of those ships.

▲ **Native American pyramid**
When Europeans arrived in the Americas, the lands they found were not empty. Diverse groups of people with distinct cultures already lived there. The temple-topped pyramid shown above was built by Mayan Indians in Mexico, long before Columbus sailed.

Migration to the Americas, 1500–1800

A huge wave of migration from the Eastern Hemisphere began in the 1500s. European explorers in the Americas paved the way for hundreds of years of European settlement there. Forced migration from Africa started soon afterward, as Europeans began to import African slaves to work in the Americas. The map to the right shows these migrations.

ATLANTIC OCEAN

NEW SPAIN
(Spain)
Mexico City

Caribbean Sea

DUTCH GUIANA
(Netherlands)

Panama City

NEW GRENADA
(Spain)

FRENCH GUIANA
(France)

Amazon R.

PERU
(Spain)
Lima
Cuzco

BRAZIL
(Portugal)

Potosí

RIO DE LA PLATA
(Spain)

Concepción

Buenos Aires

0 miles 1,000
0 kilometers 1,000
Wagner VII

SCOTLAND
IRELAND ENGLAND
NETHERLANDS
FRANCE
EUROPE
PORTUGAL SPAIN
MOROCCO

N
W E
S

WALO AFRICA
Saint-Louis
Fort James
Cacheu
AKAN STATES
Niger R.
Elmina
Axim Accra BENIN
Congo R.
Congo Basin
KONGO
Luanda
Benguela

ATLANTIC OCEAN

Migration to Latin America, 1500–1800
Key

← European migration	Spain and possessions
← African migration	Portugal and possessions
— National or colonial border	Netherlands and possessions
···· Traditional African border	France and possessions
African State	England and possessions

PRACTICE YOUR GEOGRAPHY SKILLS

1 Where did the Portuguese settle in the Americas?

2 Would you describe African migration at this time as a result of both push factors and pull factors? Explain why or why not.

"Push" and "Pull" Factors

Geographers describe a people's choice to migrate in terms of "push" factors and "pull" factors. Push factors are things in people's lives that push them to leave, such as poverty and political unrest. Pull factors are things in another country that pull people to move there, including better living conditions and hopes of better jobs.

▲ **Elmina, Ghana**
Elmina, in Ghana, is one of the many ports from which slaves were transported from Africa. Because slaves and gold were traded here, stretches of the western African coast were known as the Slave Coast and the Gold Coast.

World Land Use

People around the world have many different economic structures, or ways of making a living. Land-use maps are one way to learn about these structures. The ways that people use the land in each region tell us about the main ways that people in that region make a living.

World Land Use Key

	Nomadic herding
	Hunting and gathering
	Forestry
	Livestock raising
	Commercial farming
	Subsistence farming
	Manufacturing and trade
	Little or no activity
——	National border
- - - -	Disputed border

▲ **Wheat farming in the United States**
Developed countries practice commercial farming rather than subsistence farming. Commercial farming is the production of food mainly for sale, either within the country or for export to other countries. Commercial farmers like these in Oregon often use heavy equipment to farm.

Levels of Development

Notice on the map key the term *subsistence farming*. This term means the production of food mainly for use by the farmer's own family. In less-developed countries, subsistence farming is often one of the main economic activities. In contrast, in developed countries there is little subsistence farming.

▲ **Growing barley in Ecuador**
These farmers in Ecuador use hand tools to harvest barley. They will use most of the crop they grow to feed themselves or their farm animals.

NORTH AMERICA

SOUTH AMERICA

0 miles 2,000
0 kilometers 2,000
Robinson

▲ **Growing rice in Vietnam**
Women in Vietnam plant rice in wet rice paddies, using the same planting methods their ancestors did.

PRACTICE YOUR GEOGRAPHY SKILLS

1. In what parts of the world is subsistence farming the main land use?

2. Locate where manufacturing and trade are the main land use. Are they found more often near areas of subsistence farming or areas of commercial farming? Why might this be so?

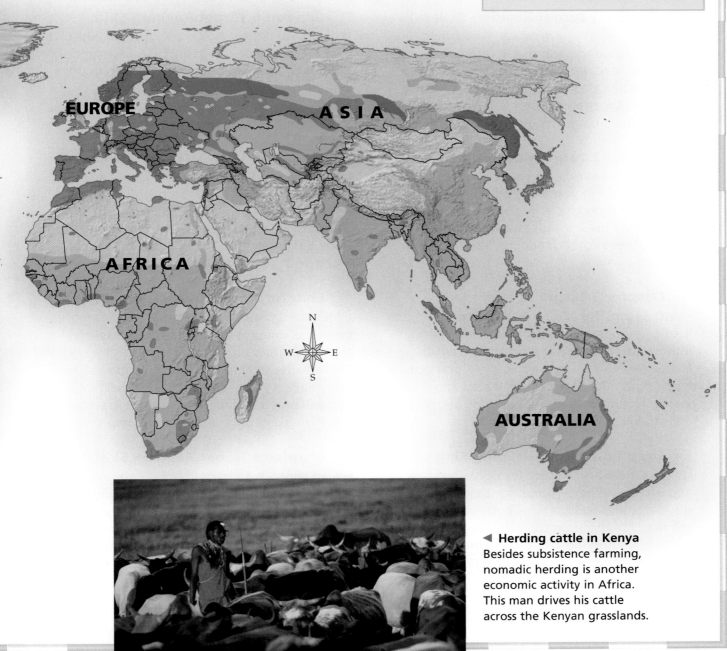

EUROPE

ASIA

AFRICA

AUSTRALIA

◀ **Herding cattle in Kenya**
Besides subsistence farming, nomadic herding is another economic activity in Africa. This man drives his cattle across the Kenyan grasslands.

How to Read Social Studies

 ## Target Reading Skills

The Target Reading Skills introduced on this page will help you understand the words and ideas in this book and in other social studies reading you do. Each chapter focuses on one of these reading skills. Good readers develop a bank of reading strategies, or skills. Then they draw on the particular strategies that will help them understand the text they are reading.

Chapter 1 Target Reading Skill

Using the Reading Process Previewing can help you understand and remember what you read. In this chapter you will practice using these previewing skills: setting a purpose for reading, predicting, and asking questions before you read.

Chapter 2 Target Reading Skill

Clarifying Meaning If you do not understand something you are reading, you can use several skills to clarify the meaning of the word or idea. In this chapter you will practice these skills: rereading, paraphrasing, and summarizing.

Chapter 3 Target Reading Skill

Identifying the Main Idea The main idea of a section or paragraph is the most important point and the one you want to remember. In this chapter you will practice these skills: identifying both stated and implied main ideas and identifying supporting details.

Chapter 4 Target Reading Skill

Using Cause and Effect Recognizing cause and effect will help you understand relationships among the situations and events you are reading about. In this chapter you will practice identifying cause and effect, understanding effects, and recognizing cause-and-effect signal words.

Chapter 5 Target Reading Skill

Using Sequence Noting the order in which events take place can help you understand how the events relate to one another. In this chapter you will practice recognizing sequence signal words, identifying sequence, and making a sequence chart.

Chapter 6 Target Reading Skill

Using Context Context—the words and sentences surrounding a word—can help you understand the word's meaning. In this chapter you will practice using these context clues: definitions, synonyms, and explanations, along with your own general knowledge.

Chapter 7 Target Reading Skill

Comparing and Contrasting Comparing means examining the similarities between things. Contrasting is looking at differences. These skills can help you sort out and analyze information you are reading. In this chapter you will practice comparing and contrasting, identifying contrasts, and making comparisons.

Chapter 8 Target Reading Skill

Using Word Analysis Breaking an unfamiliar word into its parts can help you understand and pronounce it. In this chapter you will practice using prefixes and suffixes—word parts that attach to a word root and change its meaning—as well as your knowledge of word origins.

MEDIEVAL TIMES TO TODAY

To understand today's world, we must learn about its past. Ancient civilizations laid many of the foundations for modern cultures. The people who lived in medieval times—the years between ancient and modern times—built upon those foundations but also made contributions of their own. Advances in science, technology, and the arts; new belief systems; migrations of people and ideas; developments in government and economic systems—all of these helped to shape our modern world.

Guiding Questions

The text, photographs, maps, and charts in this book will help you discover answers to these Guiding Questions.

1. **Geography** How did physical geography affect the development of societies around the world?
2. **History** How have societies around the world been shaped by their history?
3. **Culture** What were the belief systems and patterns of daily life in those societies?
4. **Government** What types of government were formed in those societies?
5. **Economics** How did each society organize its economic activities?

Project Preview

You can also discover answers to the Guiding Questions by working on projects. Several project possibilities are listed on page 246 of this book.

Investigate Medieval Times to Today

The fall of the Western Roman Empire in A.D. 476 marked the end of the ancient world and the beginning of medieval times. Civilizations developed in separate regions of the world. Then new methods of travel and the ambitions of powerful leaders led to exploration and huge migrations of people.

▲ **The Sahara, Algeria**
The Sahara is the largest desert in the world. Deserts—dry areas receiving little rainfall—cover about one fifth of the world's land surface.

▲ **Amazon Basin, Venezuela**
The mighty Amazon River runs through the Amazon basin, a region that contains the world's largest tropical rain forest.

LOCATION

1 Investigate the Continents of Earth

Look at the map at the right. Find the Equator. Is most of the land on the map north or south of the Equator? How many continents are there? Which continents are entirely north of the Equator? Which continents are entirely south of it? Which two continents are part of the same landmass? How do you think being part of one landmass might have affected the history of these two continents?

The World: Physical

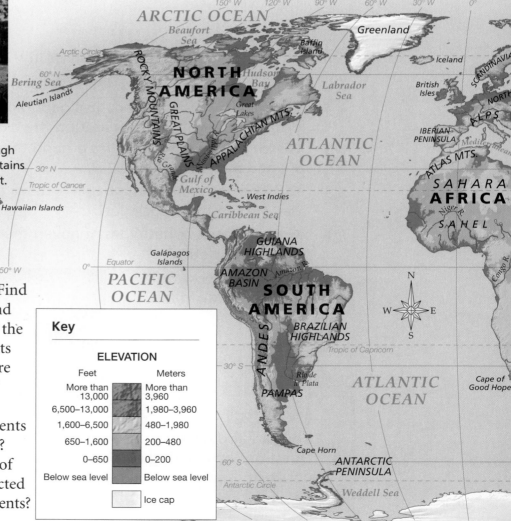

Key

ELEVATION

Feet	Meters
More than 13,000	More than 3,960
6,500–13,000	1,980–3,960
1,600–6,500	480–1,980
650–1,600	200–480
0–650	0–200
Below sea level	Below sea level
Ice cap	

PLACE

2 Examine Elevation

As you study the map key, remember that elevation is the height of land above sea level. What color indicates the highest elevation? Where are areas of high elevation found? What effect do you think mountain ranges might have had on human settlement and travel?

▲ **The Himalayas, Nepal**
The Himalayas contain the world's tallest peaks. This mountain range formed millions of years ago when the Indian and Eurasian landmasses collided.

PLACE

3 Explore Earth's Oceans

Does the map show more land or more water? What does that tell you about Earth? Which ocean lies between South America and Africa? Which ocean is west of the Americas? Which ocean is east of Asia? Why do you think some people say that there is just one ocean, the "world ocean"?

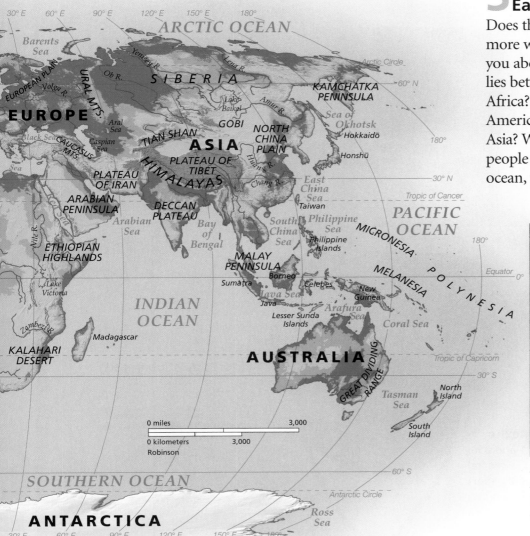

▲ **Kayangel Atoll, Micronesia**
Atolls, small ring-shaped coral islands that surround lagoons, dot the Pacific Ocean.

Human Settlement: A.D. 500 to Today

MOVEMENT

4 Investigate Where People Live

The black dots on this map show where people lived in A.D. 500, when the population was much smaller than it is now. The colors show where people live today. What parts of the world were most densely populated in A.D. 500? What parts of the world are most densely populated today? Describe the change in population density in a sentence or two. Why do you think this change has occurred?

▲ **Pueblo Cave Painting, Arizona**
People who lived in the cliffs of the present-day southwestern United States left paintings like this one, which dates from around A.D. 1200.

▲ **Mayan Ruins, Guatemala**
The Mayas flourished in Mexico and Central America from about A.D. 300 to 900. Today, ruins of towns and temples provide clues to this rich civilization.

Stone Mask, Mexico ▶
Between around A.D. 1 and 650, a civilization flourished in central Mexico. Its people were expert mask makers and built a huge, planned city called Teotihuacán.

World: Population Density Key

Population per sq. mile	Population per sq. kilometer
More than 259	More than 100
52–259	21–100
24–51	5–20
Less than 24	Less than 5

• 1 Million people in A.D. 500
— National border
- - Disputed border

◀ **Hagia Sophia, Istanbul, Turkey**
The Hagia Sophia was first built as
a Christian church in A.D. 537. Its
architecture is a classic example of
Byzantine architecture.

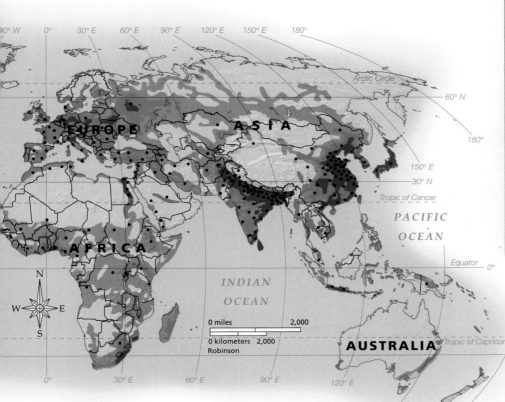

▲ **Songshan Pagoda, China**
Built in A.D. 520, this is the
oldest Buddhist temple in China.
Buddhism spread to China from
India in the century after A.D. 1.

INTERACTION

5 Consider Why People Live Where They Do

Study the map on this page, and then look back at the
physical map of the world on the previous page.
Identify at least three types of places where people
settled in A.D. 500. For example, did they tend to settle
along the seacoasts or in the middle of continents?
What natural features seem to attract human
settlement? Why might these natural features be
less important today than in 500?

▲ **Alice Springs, Australia**
Aborigines, or native peoples, had
lived in this area long before European
settlers arrived in the late 1800s.

The World Around 1500

PLACE

6 Explore Changes in Political Geography

Look at the map below and then at the World: Political map in the Atlas. What is the major difference that you see? Notice that some areas on this map have no boundaries representing major civilizations or nations, but they do have the names of different peoples. Where are civilizations or nations close to one another? Which civilizations are isolated? What effect might nearness to other civilizations have on a culture?

▲ **Carcassonne, France**
Built in the 1200s, Carcassonne is a classic example of a medieval walled town. People still live in the town today.

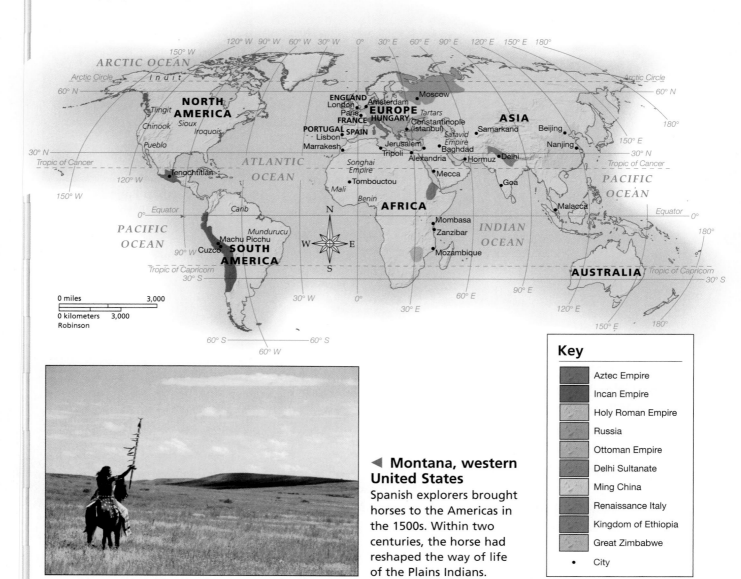

◄ **Montana, western United States**
Spanish explorers brought horses to the Americas in the 1500s. Within two centuries, the horse had reshaped the way of life of the Plains Indians.

Key

	Aztec Empire
	Incan Empire
	Holy Roman Empire
	Russia
	Ottoman Empire
	Delhi Sultanate
	Ming China
	Renaissance Italy
	Kingdom of Ethiopia
	Great Zimbabwe
•	City

MOVEMENT

7 Investigate the Columbian Exchange

When Europeans explored and settled the Americas, they brought many things with them. They also brought things from the Americas back to Europe. This movement of plants, animals, and diseases is called the Columbian Exchange. Because of trade with Africa, including the transport of enslaved Africans to the Americas, Africa also became part of the Columbian Exchange. Study the diagram at the right. Name three items from Europe that you think had an important effect on the Americas.

FROM AFRICA, ASIA, AND EUROPE TO THE AMERICAS

Coffee	Honeybee
Banana	Chicken
Citrus fruit	Sheep, Cattle
Watermelon	Horse
Peach, Pear	Chickenpox
Lettuce, Onion	Measles
Grains (wheat, barley, oats)	Scarlet fever
Sugar cane	Smallpox
	Malaria

FROM THE AMERICAS TO AFRICA, ASIA, AND EUROPE

Pumpkin	Pineapple
Avocado	Quinine, Corn
Peanut, Beans (lima, pole, navy, kidney)	Wild rice
	Tomato
	Alpaca
Peppers (bell, chili)	Turkey, Llama
	Guinea pig

PRACTICE YOUR MAP SKILLS

1. A map that shows Alexandria and Tombouctou as important settlements would most likely be a map of the world in which of the following: 500, 1500, or today?

2. If you wanted to visit a densely populated area in Asia today, where might you go? Where in North America would you find a sparsely populated area?

3. If you were in Tenochtitlán in about 1400, which of the following might you find: corn, bananas, beans, tomatoes, or chickenpox?

▲ A Latin American vendor sells bananas.

Byzantine and Muslim Civilizations

Chapter Preview

This chapter will introduce you to the Byzantine Empire, the religion of Islam, and the golden age of Muslim civilization.

**Target
Reading Skill**

Reading Process In this chapter you will focus on the reading process by using previewing to help you understand and remember what you read.

▶ Interior of a Byzantine church in present-day Turkey

The Byzantine Empire and Islamic World

MAP★MASTER™
Skills Activity

Kiev

Dnieper R.

Volga R.

ATLANTIC OCEAN

50° N

Venice

40° N

Danube R.

Black Sea

Bosporus

Caspian Sea

40° N

Rome

Córdoba

Constantinople

Asia Minor

Aegean Sea

Antioch

Tigris R.

Euphrates R.

Baghdad

Indus R.

30° N

Crete

Cyprus

Mediterranean Sea

Jerusalem

Persian Gulf

Tropic of Cancer

20° N

Alexandria

Tropic of Cancer

Arabian Sea

20° N

Nile R.

Medina

Red Sea

INDIAN OCEAN

Mecca

Arabian Peninsula

10° N

KEY

    Byzantine Empire, about A.D. 1000

    Islamic rule, about A.D. 1000

    Roman Empire, about A.D. 120

    • City

0 miles   1,000

0 kilometers   1,000

Lambert Azimuthal Equal Area

10° N

0°   10° E   20° E   30° E   40° E   50° E   60° E

Regions Notice the three political regions on this map.
Identify Which empire was the earliest? The largest? **Conclude** Find
Constantinople. How do you think its location contributed to its
growth and importance?

Go Online
PHSchool.com Use Web Code
lgp-8111 for step-by-step
map skills practice.

1 The Byzantine Empire

Prepare to Read

Objectives

In this section you will
1. Find out how Constantinople and the Byzantine Empire became powerful.
2. Discover the achievements of the Age of Justinian.
3. Learn about the later years of the Byzantine Empire.

Taking Notes

As you read this section, take notes about the Byzantine Empire's capital and rulers. Copy the concept web below and record your data in it.

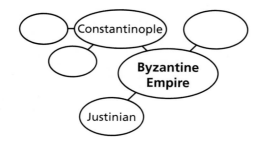

Target Reading Skill

Preview and Set a Purpose
When you set a purpose for reading, you give yourself a focus. Before you read this section, look at the headings, photos, and illustrations to see what the section is about. Then set a purpose for reading, such as finding out about the city of Constantinople or the Byzantine Empire. Now read to meet your purpose.

Key Terms

- **Constantinople** (kahn stan tuh NOH pul) *n.* the capital of the eastern Roman Empire and later of the Byzantine Empire
- **Constantine** (KAHN stun teen) *n.* an emperor of the Roman Empire and the founder of Constantinople
- **Justinian** (jus TIN ee un) *n.* one of the greatest Byzantine emperors
- **Justinian's Code** (jus TIN ee unz kohd) *n.* an organized collection and explanation of Roman laws for use by the Byzantine Empire
- **schism** (SIZ um) *n.* a split, particularly in a church or religion

Greek fire being used in battle, as shown in a Byzantine manuscript

Prince Igor (EE gawr) of Kiev, which was then an important city in Russia, watched as a large force of his warships sailed across the Black Sea in A.D. 941. The prince was sure that **Constantinople,** capital of the Byzantine (BIZ un teen) Empire, would soon be his.

As his fleet drew close to the city, the prince's excitement turned to horror. Byzantine ships shot "Greek fire" at the invaders. Anything this "fire" touched burst into flames. Soon, most of Igor's fleet was ablaze. Water could not put out the flames.

Greek fire was made from a formula so secret that it was never written down. Even today, no one knows exactly how it was made, except that it contained petroleum. But this deadly weapon gave the Byzantines tremendous power throughout the Mediterranean area.

Constantinople at a Crossroads

At its height, the ancient Roman Empire controlled the lands surrounding the Mediterranean Sea. It also ruled parts of northern Europe and the region we now call the Middle East. In the centuries after Rome's power faded, these lands went through a tug of war. Two groups—the Christian Byzantines and the Muslim Arabs and Turks—developed powerful civilizations at this time. These two groups sometimes shared control and sometimes fought over the region.

Constantine and His Capital The emperor **Constantine** began his rule of the enormous Roman Empire in A.D. 306. His reign was marked by two important changes. First, Constantine became a Christian and stopped the persecution of Christians in the empire. Second, after 20 years of ruling from the city of Rome, Constantine decided to build a new imperial capital.

Constantine chose Byzantium, an ancient city founded by the Greeks, at the eastern end of the empire. He spared no expense building and fortifying his capital. In A.D. 330, Byzantium was renamed Constantinople (kahn stan tuh NOH pul), the "city of Constantine." By the early 500s, Constantinople had large markets, forums or public squares, paved roads, a cathedral, a palace, public baths, and a hippodrome or circus. An estimated half a million people lived there. Although the name of their city had changed, the people who lived there were still called Byzantines.

Fortress City
Notice the walls that protect Constantinople in the medieval painting and in the diagram of the city. The photo shows ruins of a city wall. **Infer** *Why would the aqueduct, which carried water, and the cisterns, which stored water, also be important if the city were attacked?*

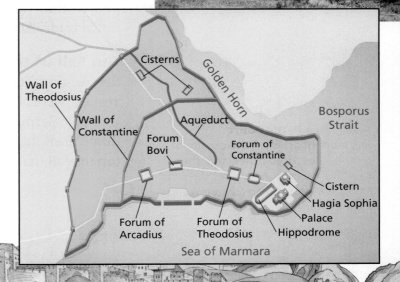

Explore Constantinople, the Byzantine capital.

Gold coin from Constantinople ▶

The emperors who followed Constantine continued to rule from Constantinople, in the eastern part of the empire. Over time, the Roman Empire split in two. The eastern half was by far the stronger. One reason for its strength was military. The Byzantines had the strongest army in the world. Another reason for the Byzantines' strength was trade.

Trade Constantinople was built at a major crossroads of land and sea trade routes. Find it on the map on page 9. Notice that it is located on the Bosporus. The Bosporus is a strait, or narrow passage that links two bodies of water. It connects the Black Sea and the Sea of Marmara, which flows into the Mediterranean Sea. The Bosporus also links two continents, Europe and Asia.

Goods came to Constantinople from Kiev in the north, from Egypt in the south, and across Central Asia from as far away as China. The Byzantines charged taxes on all goods that went through the city. The diverse people, goods, and ideas that poured into Constantinople made it a major center of international trade. And over time, the Byzantine Empire grew rich.

The Fall of the Western Empire Meanwhile, by A.D. 350, the western Roman Empire was already in decline. Roman armies were having difficulty holding back invaders from Europe. Germanic groups were coming closer and closer to Rome itself. In 476, a Germanic leader ousted the emperor. Historians call that event the fall of the Roman Empire.

✓ **Reading Check** Why did Constantinople become rich and powerful?

The Age of Justinian

As Rome was falling to invaders, strong fortifications and an excellent army protected Constantinople. But these were not the city's only strengths. The early Byzantine Empire had many excellent rulers who were wise as well as popular. They encouraged education and made reforms to laws and government. This kind of leadership also contributed to the strength of their empire.

The Emperor Justinian One of the greatest Byzantine emperors was **Justinian** (jus TIN ee un), whose rule began in 527. Justinian was an energetic ruler who rarely gave up on a task until it was completed. He had been born into a poor family, and he listened to the ideas of all his subjects—whether they were wealthy nobles or poor peasants.

Justinian and His Court
This work of art is a mosaic made of ceramic tiles fitted closely together.
Analyze Images *How does the artist indicate that Justinian (center) is the most important person?*

Justinian's Code One of Justinian's most lasting contributions was a system of laws. When he became emperor, the empire was using a disorganized system of old Roman laws. Some laws even contradicted others. It was difficult to make sense of them—or to enforce them. Justinian appointed a team to collect and summarize centuries of Roman laws. The result was **Justinian's Code,** an organized collection and explanation of Roman laws for use by the Byzantine Empire. Eventually, this code became the basis for the legal systems of most modern European countries.

Byzantine Culture In addition to preserving the principles of Roman law, Byzantine scholars also kept and copied the works of the ancient Greeks. At its peak, Byzantine civilization blended Greek, Roman, and Christian influences. Later, when the empire was in decline, scholars took the ancient manuscripts and their knowledge of the rich Byzantine culture to the newly powerful city-states of Italy. In Chapter 6 you will read how these influences helped to spark the Renaissance.

✓ **Reading Check** **What cultures influenced Byzantine civilization?**

Citizen Heroes

Empress Theodora
Theodora (thee uh DAWR uh), empress of the Byzantine Empire, came from humble beginnings. Her father was a bearkeeper at Constantinople's Hippodrome, or circus. Theodora's marriage to Justinian gave her great power. Many of Justinian's decisions were made with her advice. Theodora worked to improve women's rights, and helped change divorce laws to protect women.

Hagia Sophia
It took 10,000 workers five years to build the Hagia Sophia cathedral in Constantinople. Since the fall of the empire, it has been used as a mosque. **Infer** *Why do you think Justinian built such a majestic church?*

If your purpose is to learn about the Byzantine Empire, how does the paragraph at the right help you meet your purpose?

The Importance of Icons
This icon shows the Virgin Mary and the baby Jesus. The ban on icons was finally lifted in A.D. 843, and they are important in Eastern Orthodox Christianity to this day. **Identify Frame of Reference** *Why might medieval Christians have valued icons?*

The Empire's Later Years

After Justinian's death in 565, the Byzantine Empire began to decline. Later emperors had to fight wars against many neighboring enemies—including Persians and Turks to the east, Arabs to the south, and Germanic peoples to the north and west. The Byzantine Empire was shrinking in both size and power. As the Byzantines struggled to keep nearby enemies from invading Constantinople, religious and political arguments were weakening the empire from within.

A Religious Dispute Although most Byzantines were Christians, they did not practice Christianity the same way as the people in Western Europe did. Byzantine Christians rejected the authority of the pope, the leader of the church in Rome. The Byzantine emperor had to approve the choice of the patriarch, or highest church official in Constantinople. Greek was the language of the Byzantine church, while Latin was the language of the Roman church. The two branches of Christianity began to grow apart.

At that time, many Christians prayed to saints or holy people, represented by icons, or paintings of these people. In the 700s, a Byzantine emperor outlawed the use of icons, saying that they violated God's commandments. The pope disagreed, and banished the emperor from the church.

Byzantines felt that the pope did not have the authority to banish the emperor from the church. These disputes led to a **schism,** or split, in the Christian church in 1054. Now there were two distinct forms of Christianity: the Roman Catholic Church in the west and the Eastern (Greek) Orthodox Church in the east.

A Second Golden Age From about 900 until the mid-1000s, the Byzantine Empire experienced a final period of greatness. Trade increased and merchants came to Constantinople from as far away as Venice and Russia. Once again the population of the city grew in size and diversity.

As the economy grew in strength, so did the government. The long reign of Basil II—from 976 until 1025—was the most exceptional period of Byzantine history since the rule of Justinian. The empire regained some of the land it had lost. There was a burst of creativity in the arts.

The Fall of Constantinople During the 1000s, however, Muslim peoples to the east were also gaining power. By the late 1100s, Turks had taken the inland areas of Asia Minor away from the weakening Byzantine Empire.

The Byzantines were also threatened by Europeans. In 1171, disagreements over trade led to a war with Venice. And in the early 1200s, Constantinople was attacked by Christian crusaders. Western Christians ruled the city for 50 years. In 1261, the Byzantines regained their capital, but little was left of their empire.

In 1453, a force of about 70,000 Turks surrounded Constantinople. They came both by sea and by land, and they brought cannons to attack the city's walls. The defending force, which numbered about 7,000, held out for two months. Then the Byzantine capital—which had been a defensive fortress for more than 1,000 years—finally fell.

However, like Constantine before them, the new rulers would rebuild the city and make it an imperial capital. Renamed Istanbul, the city at the crossroads became a great center of Muslim culture and the capital of the Ottoman Empire.

 **Reading Check** **Why did Constantinople finally fall?**

The Turks Take Constantinople
The Turks dragged some of their ships overland and launched them into Constantinople's harbor. **Synthesize** *From what you know about the city's fortifications, why was this a good strategy?*

Section 1 Assessment

Key Terms
Review the key terms at the beginning of this section. Use each term in a sentence that explains its meaning.

Target Reading Skill
What was your purpose for reading this section? Did you accomplish it? If not, what might have been a better purpose?

Comprehension and Critical Thinking
1. (a) Locate Where was Constantinople located?

(b) Identify Effects How did its location contribute to its growth and to the strength of the Byzantine Empire?

2. (a) Recall What qualities made Justinian a good and successful ruler?

(b) Draw Conclusions Why was Justinian's Code so important?

3. (a) Explain What was the dispute that split the medieval Christian church?

(b) Draw Conclusions Why might that split have weakened the empire?

Writing Activity
Write a letter to a friend or family member from the point of view of a foreign merchant traveling to Constantinople during the reign of Justinian. Describe the city and its location as well as what you have heard about the emperor.

For: An activity on the Byzantines
Visit: PHSchool.com
Web Code: lgd-8101

Using a Table to Write a Paragraph

Mr. Perez's students have just finished studying the Byzantine Empire. Now they are studying modern Turkey, which occupies some of the same land. They have learned that Istanbul is the modern name of Constantinople. Mr. Perez has asked the students to use a table of information about Istanbul and Constantinople to write a paragraph that compares the two cities.

Byzantine cup

Information—words or numbers—presented in graphs, charts, or tables is called data. When you use this type of data to write a paragraph, you are transferring information from one medium to another.

Learn the Skill

Follow these steps to write a paragraph based on data from a table.

1. **Identify the topic of the table.** First read the title. Then look at the table to get a general idea of its purpose.

2. **Identify the key pieces of information.** Headings tell the main topics. Read both across and down to understand how the data relate to the headings.

Modern Istanbul

3. **Look for similarities and differences in data.** The columns of a table often compare and contrast information.

4. **Analyze the meaning of the information.** What information seems most important? List several conclusions you can draw from the data.

5. **Write a paragraph that states and supports your conclusions.** Your main conclusion can be your topic sentence. Support it with examples from the data.

Istanbul Past and Present

Characteristic	Constantinople in A.D. 540	Istanbul Today
Importance	Capital of Byzantine Empire, largest city in Byzantine Empire	Turkey's largest city
Population	About 500,000	About 10 million
Major Religion	Christianity	Islam
Sources of Wealth	Trade	Textiles, manufacturing, tourism
Language	Greek	Turkish
Challenges	Overpopulation, disease, earthquakes, attacks by foreigners	Overpopulation, earthquakes, pollution

Practice the Skill

Use the steps in Learn the Skill to transfer the information in the table above into a paragraph.

1 What is the title of the table? In your own words, state what the table is about.

2 What are the important headings? How do you find key information, such as the major religion of present-day Istanbul?

3 Note how Istanbul is similar to Constantinople and how it is different.

4 Which headings or topics represent the most important information? Are the similarities or the differences more important?

5 What is the most important thing you've learned about the two cities? Use your conclusion as the topic sentence, and support it with data from the table.

Apply the Skill

Study the table at the right, and draw a conclusion about the information in it. Write a paragraph that uses data from the table to support your conclusion.

The Christian Church Divides, A.D. 1054

Characteristic	Eastern Orthodox	Roman Catholic
Head of Church	Patriarch	Pope
Had Most Power Over Church	Emperor	Pope
Main Location	Eastern Europe	Western Europe
Language	Greek	Latin
Practices	• Priests could marry • Pope's authority was not recognized	• Priests could not marry • Pope had supreme authority

Section 2

The Beginnings of Islam

Prepare to Read

Objectives

In this section you will

1. Learn about the Arabian Peninsula, its nomadic people, and its centers of trade.
2. Find out about the life and mission of the Muslim prophet Muhammad.
3. Learn about Muslim beliefs.

Taking Notes

As you read this section, keep track of the most important ideas about the beginnings of Islam. Copy the outline started below, and add to it as you read.

> I. The Arabian Peninsula
>   A. Nomadic Bedouins
>   1.
>   2.
>   B. Mecca: A center of trade

 **Target Reading Skill**

Preview and Predict
Making predictions about your text helps you set a purpose for reading and remember what you read. Before you begin, look at the headings, photos, and anything else that stands out. Then predict what the text might be about. For example, you might predict that this section will tell about the origins of Muslim beliefs. As you read, if what you learn doesn't support your prediction, revise your prediction.

Key Terms

- **Muhammad** (muh HAM ud) *n.* the prophet and founder of Islam
- **nomads** (NOH madz) *n.* people with no permanent home, who move from place to place in search of food, water, or pasture
- **caravan** (KA ruh van) *n.* a group of traders traveling together for safety
- **Mecca** (MEK uh) *n.* an Arabian trading center and Muhammad's birthplace
- **Muslim** (MUZ lum) *n.* a follower of Islam
- **mosque** (mahsk) *n.* a Muslim house of worship
- **Quran** (koo RAHN) *n.* the holy book of Islam

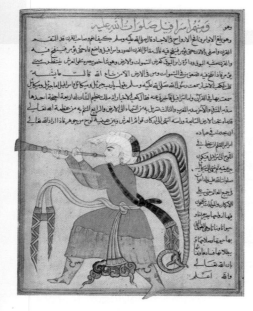

In this miniature painting, an angel's announcement is symbolized by the blowing of a horn.

The religion of Islam (IS lahm) teaches that in about 610, the prophet **Muhammad** (muh HAM ud) went into a cave in the Arabian mountains to pray. (A prophet is a person who is regarded as speaking for God.) It is said that while Muhammad was inside the cave, he heard the voice of an angel. God told Muhammad through the angel that people had abandoned the true faith. Instead of worshiping only God, they worshiped many false gods. Muhammad was to share this message.

According to Islamic teaching, Muhammad was frightened and unsure that he was worthy of such an important mission. But he obeyed. God continued to send Muhammad messages, which Muhammad shared with the people of the Arabian Peninsula. These teachings became a religion that brought great changes to the region. And in the centuries after Muhammad's death, the new religion spread to many parts of the world.

The Arabian Peninsula

In Muhammad's time, as today, much of the Arabian Peninsula was covered by desert. Although surrounded by water, the peninsula has no major rivers and receives little rainfall. Trade with neighboring peoples supported the growth of towns along trade routes. And many groups of Bedouins (BED oo inz) made their homes among the shifting sand dunes of the desert.

Nomadic Bedouins The Bedouins were **nomads,** or people who have no permanent home but move from place to place in search of food, water, and pasture. The Arabian desert yielded little food for the Bedouins or for their herds of sheep, camels, and goats. Water was also scarce—for people as well as for animals.

To make their way across the desert, the Bedouins followed traditional routes from one oasis to another. An oasis is a green area within a desert, fed by underground water. These all-important oases provided plenty of water for the nomads and their animals.

Because of their knowledge of the desert and its oases, the Bedouins also worked as guides for traders. They helped traders travel across the desert in large groups called **caravans.** These desert caravans depended on camels, which carried both people and their goods. Camels are sturdy animals with a special ability to store water for long periods.

Bedouins Today
These Bedouins in the Sinai desert of Egypt are still nomads like their ancestors. **Predict** *What kinds of events and conditions might prevent the Bedouins from continuing their traditional way of life?*

Mecca: A Center of Trade The oases on the Arabian Peninsula became busy trading centers. One of the most important was Mecca (MEK uh). From Mecca, great caravans traveled northwest to markets in what is now Syria. From Syria, goods could be shipped across the Mediterranean Sea to Europe. Other caravans traveled northeast from Mecca. They made a dangerous journey across the desert to markets in the area now known as Iraq. Trade was also conducted with Yemen to the south. Precious goods traded along these routes included perfume and spices, incense, expensive cloth, elephant tusks, and gold.

✓ **Reading Check** Why did Bedouins make good guides for traders?

Links to Economics

New Business Methods
From 750 to 1350, Muslims like the Arab traders shown above dominated the trade routes in Arabia and far beyond. They not only found new goods to trade, they also developed new *ways* to trade. Muslim merchants bought and sold goods on credit and set up locations for exchanging currency. To avoid carrying large sums of cash across thousands of miles, they developed a way to transfer money from one location to another—a forerunner to today's checks. Merchants could deposit funds at one location and use a letter of credit to withdraw those funds at a different location.

The Prophet Muhammad

Muhammad was born and grew up in the trading center of Mecca. His great-grandfather had been a wealthy merchant. However, by the time Muhammad was born in about 570, his family was poor. As a young man, Muhammad worked on caravans. His job took him to distant places, including Syria, which was then part of the Byzantine Empire.

Muhammad's Mission Muhammad liked to walk in the mountains outside Mecca. Troubled by problems he saw in society, he liked to be alone to pray and think. When Muhammad was 40 years old, he first heard God speak to him through the angel in the cave. God told him that people would submit to, or agree to obey, the one true God. In time, a person who accepted the teachings of Muhammad came to be known as a **Muslim** (MUZ lum), "a person who submits." The religion of Muslims is called Islam.

Muhammad preached God's message—that all people were brothers and sisters in a community established by God—but few people in Mecca listened. They thought Muhammad's teachings threatened their old gods. They feared that abandoning their old gods would end Mecca's importance as a religious center. Many Arabs traveled to Mecca in order to pray at an ancient shrine called the Kaaba (KAH buh). People in Mecca also feared that Muhammad might gain political power.

Muhammad in Medina In 622, Muhammad and his followers were invited to Yathrib (yah THREEB), a city north of Mecca. The people there regarded Muhammad as a prophet. This movement of early Muslims is known as the hijra (hih JY ruh), or "the migration." The year of the hijra—622 in the calendar used in the United States—became year 1 on the Muslim calendar.

After the hijra, the name of Yathrib was changed to Medina. This name means "city" and is short for "city of the prophet." Medina quickly became an important Islamic center. But Islam did not remain limited to Medina. In 630, Muhammad returned to Mecca—this time in triumph. By the time Muhammad died two years later, the new religion of Islam had spread all across the Arabian Peninsula.

✓ Reading Check **Why did Muhammad go to Yathrib?**

Muslim Belief

A muezzin (myoo EZ in), a man who calls Muslims to worship, looks out over the city and begins his loud call. The muezzin's voice echoes in all directions: "There is no god but God, and Muhammad is the messenger of God." In Arabic, the word for God is *Allah*. Five times each day, Muslims are called to worship in this way. And five times a day, every faithful Muslim stops whatever he or she is doing to pray.

Some Muslims gather in a house of worship called a **mosque** (mahsk). Others kneel outside. Wherever Muslims are in the world—in the Arabian Peninsula, in North Africa, or in the United States—they kneel in a direction that faces toward Mecca. "There is no god but God," the faithful respond, "and Muhammad is the messenger of God."

The Five Pillars of Islam Basic Muslim beliefs are expressed in the Five Pillars of Islam. These practices, shown in the table above, are the foundations of Islam. Muslims regard these pillars as sacred duties. The fifth pillar—the hajj (haj), or pilgrimage to the Kaaba—is required only of those who are able to travel to Mecca.

The Five Pillars of Islam

Pillar	Description
Declaration of Faith	Muslims must regularly declare the belief that there is only one God and Muhammad is God's messenger.
Prayer	Muslims must pray five times each day, facing in the direction of the holy city of Mecca.
Almsgiving	Muslims must give alms, or money that goes to the needy.
Fasting	Muslims must fast during daylight hours in the month of Ramadan.
Pilgrimage	Muslims must make a pilgrimage to Mecca at least one time in their lives if they are able.

■ **Chart Skills**

The photo above shows Muslim men and boys worshiping at a mosque in Brunei, in Southeast Asia. **Identify** Which pillar of Islam are they fulfilling? **Analyze Information** Which one of the five pillars would it be most difficult to fulfill? Explain why.

The Hajj
Muslims making a hajj to the Kaaba wear special white, seamless garments. The large photo shows a modern hajj. The small painting is from a 1410 manuscript. **Compare** *What can you conclude about this tradition by comparing the two pictures?*

Preview and Predict
Based on what you have read so far, is your prediction on target? If not, revise or change your prediction now.

The Quran The holy book of Islam is called the **Quran** (koo RAHN). It contains the messages God revealed to Muhammad, including the rules of Islam. Many Muslims have memorized the Quran. Muslims believe that the meaning and beauty of the Quran are best appreciated in its original language. Therefore, many converts to Islam learn Arabic. This shared language has helped unite Muslims from many regions.

Like the Torah (TOH ruh), the Jewish holy book, and the Christian Bible, the Quran contains many kinds of writing, including stories, promises, warnings, and instructions. There is a reason for the similarity of the Quran to Jewish and Christian holy books. Muslims, like Jews and Christians, believe in one God. They regard Adam, Noah, Abraham, and Moses as important people in their religious history. Muhammad saw himself as the last prophet in a long line of prophets that included all these men. Muhammad felt respect for Jews and Christians, whom he called "people of the Book."

The Role of Women Before Islam, in most of Arab society, women were not regarded as equal to men, and female children were not valued. The Quran, however, taught that men and women were spiritually equal. It also gave women more rights under the law, such as the right to inherit property and to get an education. Muslim women could not be forced to marry against their will, and they had the right to divorce.

A Split Among Muslims You have already read about a schism that split the Christian church at the time of the Byzantine Empire. A schism, or split, also occurred among followers of Islam.

In 656, Uthman (OOTH mahn), the leader of the Muslim community, was assassinated. His death split the Muslim world in two. Muslims disagreed over who should be their rightful leader. Over the next several decades, two main groups gradually emerged on opposite sides of this disagreement.

The smaller group, called Shiites (SHEE yts), argued that the ruler should be a man who was a direct descendant of Muhammad. They believed that Muhammad's descendants would be inspired by God, just as Muhammad had been. They felt that their leader should explain the meanings of the messages Muhammad received from God, which are found in the Quran.

The larger group, called Sunnis (SOO neez), argued that any truly religious Muslim man of Muhammad's tribe could lead the community. They believed that no one man, not even the leader of Islam, should tell Muslims what God's messages meant. The Sunnis argued that a group of Muslim scholars could best explain the Quran. Today, about 85 percent of all Muslims are Sunnis.

Illustrated manuscript pages from a 1500s Quran

✓ **Reading Check** **What issues split the Shiites and Sunnis?**

Section 2 Assessment

Key Terms
Review the key terms at the beginning of this section. Use each term in a sentence that explains its meaning.

Target Reading Skill
What did you predict about this section? How did your prediction guide your reading?

Comprehension and Critical Thinking
1. (a) Note What geographic feature covers most of the Arabian Peninsula?

(b) Identify Effects How did geography affect trade and settlement there?
(c) Conclude Why do you think the Bedouins became nomads?
2. (a) Recall What were the main events of Muhammad's life?
(b) Synthesize What are the main beliefs of Islam?
(c) Compare and Contrast What beliefs do Sunnis and Shiites share? Which beliefs separate them?

Writing Activity
Write a poem or a paragraph describing what it might have been like to travel in a caravan. How would it feel to ride a camel? To cross the desert? To stop for a rest at an oasis?

> **Writing Tip** Review the illustrations in this section. Then think about the sights, sounds, and smells you would expect to experience as part of caravan life. Use vivid descriptive words and phrases to describe what you see and feel.

Focus On
Bedouin Life

The air is hot and dry. A blinding, bright sun scorches the sand. At times, a screaming wind sweeps across the land, blowing clouds of sand that block the sun. These are the desert lands of the Arabian Peninsula. By the time of the prophet Muhammad in the A.D. 600s, the Bedouins of Arabia had been thriving in the desert for hundreds of years. These nomadic peoples lived in tents and moved camp frequently in their search for water. Some of their descendants still live in the desert today.

Surviving in the Desert The ancient Bedouins depended upon the desert, the camel, their fellow tribe members, and the family tent. Plants gathered from the desert were used for food and medicine. Camels provided transportation, as well as milk, meat, and hides. Family members worked together to search for water and to herd their camels, goats, and sheep. The family tent sheltered the Bedouins in the harsh desert climate.

Women were responsible for the tents. They spun goats' hair into yarn to make the tent panels. When it was time to move their camp, the women took down the tents and then pitched them at the new campsite.

It was the men's job to herd camels and other livestock. Sometimes Bedouin men would raid villages or other tribes for goats, sheep, camels, and other goods.

The illustration at the right shows a Bedouin family in their tent. Bedouin women created jewelry, like the necklace shown at the top of this page.

Goatskin Bag
Bags made from goatskin carried precious water.

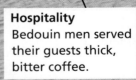

Hospitality
Bedouin men served their guests thick, bitter coffee.

Bedouin Coffee Pot
The Bedouins served coffee from copper or brass pots.

Water
Carried in goatskin bags, water came from oases and wells.

Cooking
Fires were fueled by camel dung, twigs, and dry plants.

Assessment

Identify Name the four things the Bedouins depended upon most.

Analyze How did the Bedouins survive in the desert?

Section 3
The Golden Age of Muslim Civilization

Prepare to Read

Objectives
In this section you will
1. Find out how the religion of Islam spread.
2. Learn about the golden age of Islam under the rule of the caliphs.

Taking Notes
As you read this section, jot down key events of early Muslim history and when they occurred. Copy the timeline below and use your data to complete it.

Muslim History, 632–1180

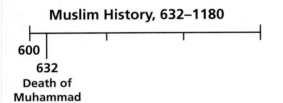

600
632
Death of Muhammad

Target Reading Skill
Preview and Ask Questions Before you read this section, preview the headings and illustrations to see what the section is about. Then write two questions that will help you understand or remember something important in the section. For example, you might ask, "How did Islam spread beyond the Arabian Peninsula?" Then read to answer your question.

Key Terms
- **Omar Khayyam** (OH mahr ky AHM) *n.* a Muslim poet, mathematician, and astronomer
- **caliph** (KAY lif) *n.* a Muslim ruler
- **Sufis** (SOO feez) *n.* a mystical Muslim group that believed they could draw closer to God through prayer, fasting, and a simple life

The cover of a book of verses by Omar Khayyam

Almost one thousand years ago, Persia boasted great scientists, mathematicians, and poets. One man was all three. **Omar Khayyam** (OH mahr ky AHM) was a skilled Muslim astronomer, one of the most famous mathematicians in the world, and a great poet. The poems he wrote in the Persian language are still read today. This is one of his poems:

> **When I was a child, I sometimes went to a teacher. And sometimes I taught myself, but eventually I learned The limits to all knowledge: we come into this world upon the waters, we leave it on the wind.**
>
> —*Omar Khayyam*

Although Khayyam writes of limits to knowledge, his was a time when mathematics, science, and poetry were all making new breakthroughs and expanding the boundaries of knowledge. It was called the golden age of Muslim civilization, and it took place across a wide geographic area.

The Spread of Islam

Within 150 years after Muhammad's death in 632, Islam spread west to North Africa, and into present-day Spain. It also spread north into Persia and east to the borders of northern India and China.

Many New Converts Arab merchants traveled to many parts of Asia and North Africa and along the Mediterranean coast. Many of these traders were Muslims, and they helped to spread their new religious beliefs. Arab armies also conquered neighboring regions. This was another way that Islam spread.

In 717, the Arabs attacked Constantinople, but they were unable to take the great fortress. Even so, most Christians who lived along the eastern and southern Mediterranean converted to Islam in the 700s and 800s. By the 700s, Muslims had also crossed from North Africa into Spain. In 732, Arab forces were defeated by European soldiers at the Battle of Tours, in present-day France. This battle halted the Muslim advance into Christian Europe.

The Battle of Tours

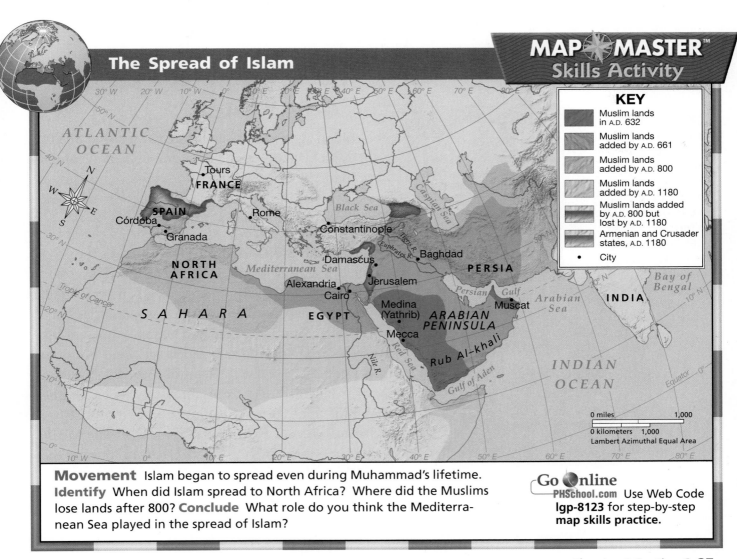

The Spread of Islam

MAP★MASTER™
Skills Activity

KEY

- Muslim lands in A.D. 632
- Muslim lands added by A.D. 661
- Muslim lands added by A.D. 800
- Muslim lands added by A.D. 1180
- Muslim lands added by A.D. 800 but lost by A.D. 1180
- Armenian and Crusader states, A.D. 1180
- • City

0 miles 1,000
0 kilometers 1,000
Lambert Azimuthal Equal Area

Movement Islam began to spread even during Muhammad's lifetime. **Identify** When did Islam spread to North Africa? Where did the Muslims lose lands after 800? **Conclude** What role do you think the Mediterranean Sea played in the spread of Islam?

Go Online PHSchool.com Use Web Code **lgp-8123** for step-by-step map skills practice.

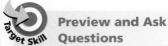
Preview and Ask Questions

Ask a question that will help you learn something important from the paragraph at the right. Now read the paragraph, and answer your question.

Reasons for Success In the centuries before Muhammad, Arab peoples had not been able to conquer neighboring regions. The strong Roman Empire made invasions of these lands nearly impossible. And the later Byzantine and Persian empires successfully blocked Arabs from advancing north. So why were the Muslims successful after Muhammad's death?

By that time, the three empires that might have stopped the Arab expansion north and east were either defeated or weakened. Also, a shared religion now united the Arab peoples into one community. And once they began to work together, the Muslims quickly grew powerful.

Under Muslim Rule Unlike Byzantine leaders of the time—who did not accept different religions—Muslims tolerated other faiths. Muslim rulers allowed Christians and Jews to practice their own religions and pursue their own business affairs. Non-Muslim citizens did have fewer rights than Muslims, however. For example, they were forbidden to carry weapons and could not serve in the military. They also paid a special tax, which helped support the government.

✓ **Reading Check** **Compare Muslim rulers and Byzantine rulers.**

A Royal Gift
The caliph Harun ar-Rashid presented this water jug to Charlemagne, the ruler of a Christian empire in Europe. He hoped to form an alliance with Charlemagne. **Infer** *What can you infer about Harun from this gift?*

The Golden Age

The golden age of Muslim culture from about 800 to 1100 was a brilliant period of history. Great advances were made in mathematics and science, and lasting works of literature and architecture were created. Why did so much happen at that time?

The Age of the Caliphs One reason was the great wealth of the Arab world. Under Muslim rulers called caliphs (KAY lifs), an empire developed and grew rich. Its wealth came both from the many lands it controlled and from trade. Baghdad was the capital of the Muslim empire during the golden age. Find it on the map titled The Spread of Islam on page 27. You can see that Baghdad, like Constantinople, was a natural center for trade. With your finger, trace a route from India to Baghdad. Now trace a route from the Mediterranean Sea to Baghdad. Traders from all over the world brought their goods to the caliph's court. The caliph was considered to be Muhammad's successor, or the next person who had the right to rule.

Harun ar-Rashid: A Powerful Caliph

Harun ar-Rashid (hah ROON ar rah SHEED) became caliph of Baghdad in 786. His rule was a time of prosperity. For 23 years, Harun ruled the world's most glamorous court. He and his favorite subjects ate off gold plates and drank from goblets studded with jewels.

Harun did not use the riches of Baghdad just for his own pleasure. He was also a great patron, or supporter, of the arts. Harun paid many skilled writers, musicians, dancers, and artists to live in Baghdad. And he lavishly rewarded those whose works pleased him. One musician is said to have received a gift of 100,000 silver pieces for a single song.

Achievements of the Golden Age

Arab scholars not only created new works but also studied history and ideas from other cultures. One scholar wrote,

> **"We should not be ashamed to acknowledge truth from whatever source it comes to us, even if it is brought to us by former generations and foreign peoples."**
>
> —al-Kindi

This approach led Muslim scholars to make great advances in mathematics, in science, and in literature.

Mathematics and Science Arab scholars studied both Greek and Indian mathematics. They learned about the idea of zero from Indian scholars. And they borrowed the use of the so-called Arabic numerals that we use today from India, too. The Muslim mathematician al-Khwarizme (al KWAHR iz mee) wrote a book explaining Indian arithmetic. He also made significant contributions to the development of algebra. The word *algebra* comes from the Arabic word "al-jabr." These contributions enabled later scientists to make great discoveries in astronomy, physics, and chemistry.

The famous Islamic scientist and philosopher Ibn Sina (IB un SEE nah) lived from 980 to 1037. Also known as Avicenna (ahv ih SEN uh), he organized the medical knowledge of the Greeks and Arabs into the *Canon of Medicine.*

Arab Contributions to Mathematics and Science

Medicine
The Arabs were the first to organize separate pharmacies, which sold spices, herbs, and other medicines to the public.

Mathematics
Arab mathematicians made important contributions to algebra. They studied formulas like this one. It explains how to find the length of one side of a right triangle when you know the length of the other sides.

Machines
Water-driven machines fascinated Arab scientists. Here, water falling into the cups causes the globe at the top to turn.

Explorations of Faith Moses Maimonides (my MAHN uh deez) was a Jewish scholar, doctor, and philosopher. He lived in the Muslim-controlled lands of Spain, North Africa, and Southwest Asia. In 1180, he completed *The Torah Reviewed,* which classified and explained all the laws of Judaism. His *Guide for the Perplexed,* written in Arabic, tried to resolve reason and faith by exploring how people could believe in both science and religion at the same time. The Latin translation of the *Guide* influenced the Christian writers of the Scholastic movement of medieval Europe.

Literature Muslim writers created many lasting works of literature. Poetry was particularly important in the Islamic world. Poets were treated as popular musicians are today. One group of Muslims used poetry to teach their ideas and beliefs.

This group, called the **Sufis** (soo feez), were mystics who believed that they could draw close to God through prayer, fasting, and a simple life. They taught that the world will reveal its mysteries to careful observers. Sufi missionaries also helped spread Islam to Central Asia, India, and Africa south of the Sahara.

The most famous Sufi poet, Rumi (ROO mee), founded a religious group known to Europeans as the Whirling Dervishes. This group used music and dance to communicate with God. Rumi composed these verses:

> ❝Never think the earth [empty] or dead—
> It's a hare, awake with shut eyes:
> It's a saucepan, simmering with broth—
> One clear look, you'll see it's in [motion].❞
>
> —*Rumi*

✓ **Reading Check** What did the Sufis teach?

Section 3 Assessment

Key Terms
Review the key terms at the beginning of this section. Use each term in a sentence that explains its meaning.

Target Reading Skill
What questions helped you learn something important from this section? What are the answers to your questions?

Comprehension and Critical Thinking
1. (a) Recall Describe the two main ways that Islam spread beyond the Arabian Peninsula.

(b) Predict How might the culture of Europe be different today if the Arabs had won the Battle of Tours in 732?

2. (a) Locate Where is Baghdad located?

(b) Synthesize Information What made it a good choice for the capital of an empire?

(c) Generalize How do geography and trade contribute to a city's prosperity and power?

3. (a) Identify Name three Arab contributions to mathematics and science.

(b) Analyze How do these contributions combine borrowed knowledge and new ideas?

Writing Activity
Write a newspaper editorial either for or against the use of government money to support the arts. Use Harun ar-Rashid as one example in your argument. Begin with a statement of your position and then support it with reasons and facts.

For: An activity on Islam's golden age
Visit: PHSchool.com
Web Code: lgd-8103

Chapter 1 Review and Assessment

◆ Chapter Summary

Justinian

Section 1: The Byzantine Empire

- The Roman emperor Constantine established a new capital in the eastern part of the Roman Empire. Later, Constantinople became the capital of the rich and powerful Byzantine Empire.
- Justinian, one of the greatest Byzantine emperors, organized a system of laws called Justinian's code.
- After Justinian's death, the Byzantine Empire shrank in size and power. It later enjoyed a second golden age. A schism split the Christian church into eastern and western branches.

Section 2: The Beginnings of Islam

- Although much of the Arabian Peninsula is covered by desert, important cities, such as Mecca, grew up on trade routes.
- The Muslim prophet Muhammad preached in Mecca and Medina. His teachings became the religion of Islam.
- The Five Pillars of Islam and the Quran are the basis of Muslim beliefs. A dispute among Muslims led to the split between Shiites and Sunnis.

Section 3: The Golden Age of Muslim Civilization

- After the death of Muhammad, the religion of Islam spread to many neighboring regions by both trade and conquest.
- The golden age of Islam occurred under wealthy Muslim rulers called caliphs.
- The golden age was marked by great achievements in mathematics, science, literature, and art.

Caliph's water jug

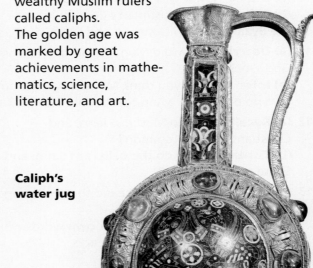

◆ Key Terms

Match each key term with its definition from the list at the right.

1. mosque
2. Constantine
3. nomads
4. caliph
5. Justinian
6. caravan
7. schism
8. Omar Khayyam

A a Muslim ruler

B a group of traders traveling together for safety

C emperor of the Byzantine Empire

D emperor of the Roman Empire

E Muslim house of worship

F a Muslim astronomer, mathematician, and poet

G people with no permanent home, who move from place to place

H a split, particularly in a church or religion

◆ Comprehension and Critical Thinking

9. (a) **Recall** In what part of the old Roman Empire was Constantinople located?
(b) **Identify Cause and Effect** How did Constantinople's location affect the culture that developed there?
(c) **Compare and Contrast** What enabled the eastern part of the Roman Empire to survive after the western Roman Empire "fell"?

10. (a) **Define** What was Justinian's Code?
(b) **Infer** How did Justinian's Code help make the Byzantine Empire strong and successful?

11. (a) **Describe** How did Muhammad first receive God's message?
(b) **Infer** Why do you think Muhammad did not give up preaching when few people listened?

12. (a) **Recall** What do Muslims, Jews, and Christians have in common?
(b) **Contrast** How do the beliefs of Sunni and Shiite Muslims differ?

13. (a) **Recall** When and where did the golden age of Muslim civilization occur?
(b) **Synthesize** Explain in your own words why these years are called a golden age.

◆ Skills Practice

Using a Table to Write a Paragraph In the Skills for Life activity in this chapter, you learned how to use the data in a table to write a paragraph. Review the steps you followed to learn the skill.

Now review the table The Five Pillars of Islam on page 21. Use the data in the table to draw a conclusion about the topic. Write a paragraph that states your conclusion and that uses data from the table as supporting details.

◆ Writing Activity: Language Arts

A monologue is a speech by one person. In drama, a monologue is spoken directly to the audience. Choose one of the rulers you have read about in this chapter. Write a monologue that this ruler might speak in a theatrical performance. It can be about the person's whole life or about one important event. Do further research on the ruler if you wish. You may want to perform your monologue for your class.

MAP MASTER™
Skills Activity

Place Location For each place or feature listed below, write the letter from the map that shows its location.

1. Rome
2. Mecca
3. Constantinople
4. Mediterranean Sea
5. Bosporus
6. Baghdad
7. Arabian Peninsula

Go Online
PHSchool.com Use Web Code **lgp-8133** for an interactive map.

The Byzantine Empire and the Spread of Islam

Standardized Test Prep

Test-Taking Tips

Some questions on standardized tests ask you to evaluate a source for a research assignment. Read the passage below. Then use the tip to help you answer the sample question.

> Vera is writing a research paper about Justinian's Code. At the school library, she found four books that she might use.

Think It Through Even if you don't know about Justinian's Code, you can eliminate A because it is fiction—an invented story. You can also rule out C because it is about a merchant's travels, not about Justinian's Code. That leaves B and D. Justinian's Code refers to laws, not to copying Roman and Greek books. The correct answer is B.

Pick the letter that best answers the question.

Which one of the following books would be best for Vera's topic?

A ~~*Justinian's Bride*—a novel about the Empress Theodora~~

B *The Birth of Law*—a nonfiction book about the Byzantine legal system

C ~~*The Journal of Ignatius*—a firsthand account of a merchant's travels during the time of Justinian~~

D *The Rescue of Knowledge*—the story of how Byzantine scholars copied and cared for books of ancient Rome and Greece

TIP Rule out choices that don't make sense. Then choose the best answer from the remaining choices.

Practice Questions

Use the tip above and other tips in this book to help you answer the following questions.

1. Miguel's history class has been studying the Byzantine Empire. Miguel has decided to write a research paper about the empire's capital, Constantinople. He would like to find out the population of Constantinople at the time of Justinian's rule.

   Which one of the following would be the best choice for this information?

   A *An Atlas of Modern Turkey*—a nonfiction book that includes maps and factual data

   B *Our Trip to Istanbul*—a new Web site that tells about a family's vacation to the city formerly called Constantinople

   C *An Atlas of the Ancient World*—a nonfiction book that includes historical maps and other historical data

   D *Population Growth of Major U.S. Cities*—a nonfiction book that includes charts and maps

Pick the letter of the word or phrase that best completes each sentence.

2. Muslims are called to worship _____.

   A once a day   B four times a month

   C five times a day   D once a year

3. Constantine was the first _____ to rule the Roman Empire.

   A Muslim   B Jew

   C Sufi   D Christian

4. The _____ links the Black Sea and the Sea of Marmara, which flows into the Mediterranean Sea.

   A Bosporus   B Arabian Peninsula

   C Mecca   D hijra

Use Web Code **lga-8103** for a **Chapter 1 self-test.**

Chapter Preview

This chapter will introduce you to the early history of Africa and to some of its great civilizations.

Target Reading Skill

Clarifying Meaning In this chapter, you will focus on clarifying meaning by learning how to reread, how to paraphrase, and how to summarize.

▶ Ruins of the Great Mosque of Kilwa, in present-day Tanzania, East Africa

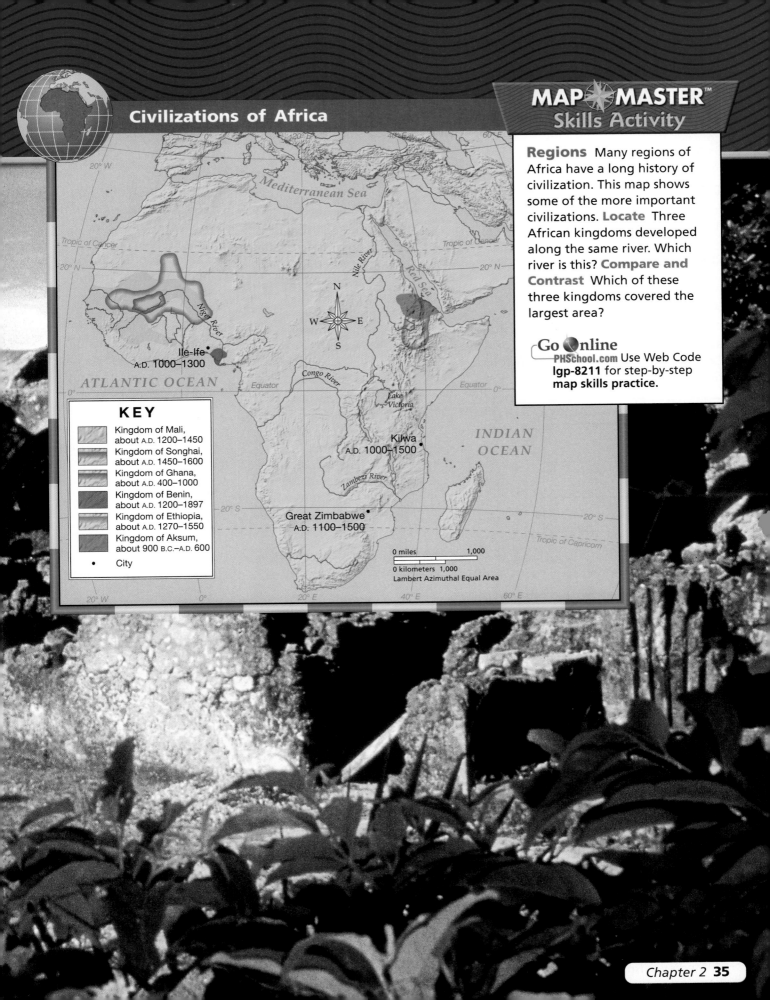

Civilizations of Africa

Regions Many regions of Africa have a long history of civilization. This map shows some of the more important civilizations. **Locate** Three African kingdoms developed along the same river. Which river is this? **Compare and Contrast** Which of these three kingdoms covered the largest area?

Go Online
PHSchool.com Use Web Code **lgp-8211** for step-by-step **map skills practice**.

Mediterranean Sea

Tropic of Cancer

20° W

0°

20° E

60° E

20° N

Nile River

Red Sea

Niger River

N
W   E
S

Ile-Ife
A.D. 1000–1300

ATLANTIC OCEAN

Equator

Congo River

Lake Victoria

Equator

INDIAN OCEAN

Kilwa
A.D. 1000–1500

KEY

- Kingdom of Mali, about A.D. 1200–1450
- Kingdom of Songhai, about A.D. 1450–1600
- Kingdom of Ghana, about A.D. 400–1000
- Kingdom of Benin, about A.D. 1200–1897
- Kingdom of Ethiopia, about A.D. 1270–1550
- Kingdom of Aksum, about 900 B.C.–A.D. 600
- • City

Zambezi River

Great Zimbabwe
A.D. 1100–1500

20° S

Tropic of Capricorn

0 miles   1,000
0 kilometers 1,000
Lambert Azimuthal Equal Area

20° W   0°   20° E   40° E   60° E

1 Africa and the Bantu

Prepare to Read

Objectives

In this section, you will
1. Learn about the physical geography of Africa.
2. Find out about the Bantu and their movement across the continent.

Taking Notes

As you read this section, look for information about the major physical features of Africa. Copy the table below, and record your findings in it.

Physical Features of Africa	
Deserts	• •
Savannas	• •
Rain Forests	• •

Target Reading Skill

Reread or Read Ahead If you do not understand a passage, reread it to look for connections among the words and sentences. Reading ahead can also help. Words and ideas may be clarified further on.

Key Terms

- **migration** (my GRAY shun) *n.* the movement from one country or region to settle in another
- **Bantu** (BAN too) *n.* a large group of central and southern Africans who speak related languages
- **savanna** (suh VAN uh) *n.* an area of grassland with scattered trees and bushes
- **Sahara** (suh HA ruh) *n.* a huge desert stretching across most of North Africa
- **oral history** (AWR ul HIS tuh ree) *n.* accounts of the past that people pass down by word of mouth
- **clan** (klan) *n.* a group of families who trace their roots to the same ancestor

Zulu women in traditional dress in South Africa

About 4,000 years ago, many families left the places where they lived in West Africa. They would never return to their homeland. Some families had to climb over rocky hills. Others journeyed through forests or across lands baked by the sun. Mothers, fathers, and children carried everything they owned with them. After traveling for many miles, these people settled somewhere new.

No one knows exactly why they first moved. The population may have grown very quickly. If so, there may not have been enough land and resources to support all of the people. Over many years, later generations moved farther away from their original homes. They kept searching for better land for farming. Over time, their **migration** (my GRAY shun), or movement from one region to settle in another, took them across most of Africa south of the Equator. Today, their descendants number more than 200 million. The name **Bantu** (BAN too) describes both this large group of Africans and the related languages they speak.

Africa's Physical Geography

Look at the map titled Africa: Natural Vegetation. Notice the tropical rain forests that are located on either side of the Equator. They have hot, moist climates.

Surrounding these forests are bands of **savanna,** areas of grassland with scattered trees and bushes. Much of Africa is savanna. Africa's lions, zebras, and elephants live mainly on the savannas. Deserts stretch north and south of the savannas. The **Sahara** (suh HA ruh) is a desert stretching across most of North Africa. It is the world's largest desert. The Sahara is a hot, dry place of sand dunes and rocky mountains. A band of lakes, deep valleys, and rugged mountains runs north to south through East Africa.

Africa's physical geography has affected its people's ways of life. For example, there is little farming in Africa's deserts, because there is too little water. People herd cattle on the savannas, but cattle cannot survive in the rain forests. Flies and other pests in the rain forests carry diseases that are deadly for cattle.

An Oasis in the Sahara
An oasis (oh AY sis) is an area of vegetation within a desert, fed by springs and underground water. **Infer** *How might oases help travelers crossing a desert?*

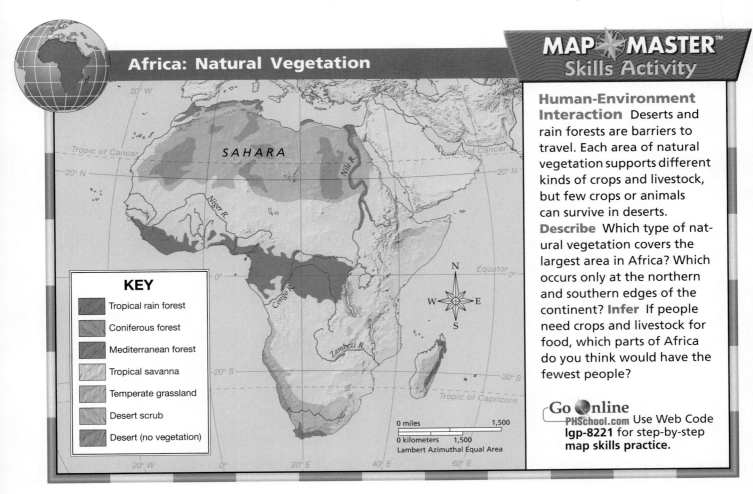

Africa: Natural Vegetation

KEY
- Tropical rain forest
- Coniferous forest
- Mediterranean forest
- Tropical savanna
- Temperate grassland
- Desert scrub
- Desert (no vegetation)

SAHARA

Tropic of Cancer
20° W
20° N
Niger R.
Nile R.
Congo R.
Equator
0°
Zambezi R.
20° S
Tropic of Capricorn
60° E
40° E
20° E

0 miles 1,500
0 kilometers 1,500
Lambert Azimuthal Equal Area

MAP MASTER™ Skills Activity

Human-Environment Interaction Deserts and rain forests are barriers to travel. Each area of natural vegetation supports different kinds of crops and livestock, but few crops or animals can survive in deserts. **Describe** Which type of natural vegetation covers the largest area in Africa? Which occurs only at the northern and southern edges of the continent? **Infer** If people need crops and livestock for food, which parts of Africa do you think would have the fewest people?

Go Online
PHSchool.com Use Web Code lgp-8221 for step-by-step map skills practice.

Groups that share the same environment may live differently. For example, Mbuti (em BOO tee) people of Africa's rain forest live mainly by hunting animals and gathering plants, but neighboring peoples live mainly by farming.

✓ Reading Check **How do Africa's physical features affect people's ways of life?**

The Bantu Migrations

The physical barriers formed by lakes, forests, mountains, and rivers did not stop the movement of people across Africa. The map titled Bantu Migrations, on page 39, traces the major routes of the Bantu people. These migrations continued for more than 1,000 years. They are among the largest population movements in all of human history.

The History of Sub-Saharan Africa Historians know a great deal about North Africa's history. But they have only a sketchy knowledge of the history of Africa south of the Sahara. That area is called sub-Saharan Africa. Until modern times, the Sahara cut off this larger part of Africa from Europe. European historians have found it difficult to study sub-Saharan Africa. Today, scientists and historians are working to piece together the history of this area. In many ways, it is like solving a puzzle.

Reread Reread the last four paragraphs, under the heading Africa's Physical Geography, to understand how Africa's physical features might have been a barrier to movement.

The Zambezi River plunges over Victoria Falls, on the Zambia-Zimbabwe border.

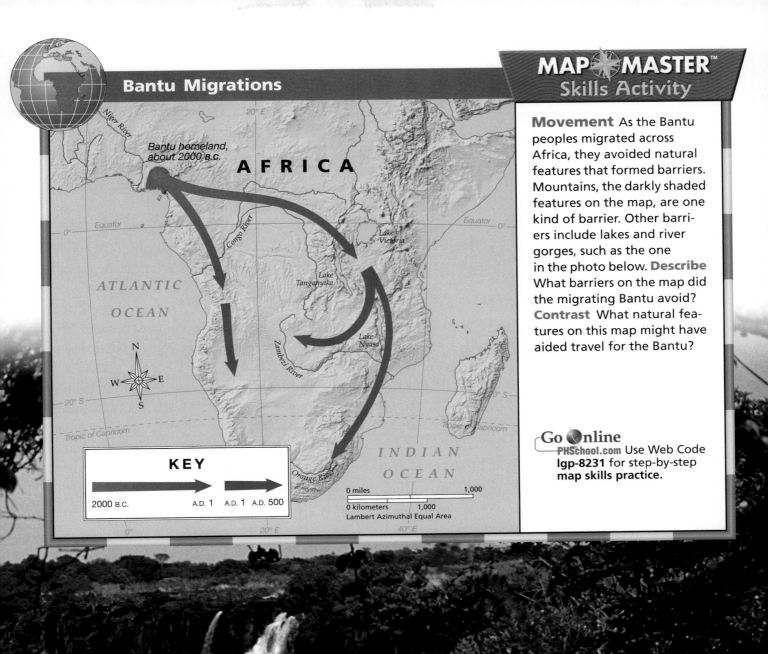

Bantu Migrations

Niger River

Bantu homeland, about 2000 B.C.

A F R I C A

20° E

Equator

Congo River

Lake Victoria

Equator

ATLANTIC OCEAN

Lake Tanganyika

Lake Nyasa

Zambezi River

N
W   E
S

20° S

20° S

Tropic of Capricorn

Tropic of Capricorn

INDIAN OCEAN

Orange River

KEY

2000 B.C.   A.D. 1   A.D. 1   A.D. 500

0 miles   1,000
0 kilometers   1,000
Lambert Azimuthal Equal Area

0°   20° E   40° E

Movement As the Bantu peoples migrated across Africa, they avoided natural features that formed barriers. Mountains, the darkly shaded features on the map, are one kind of barrier. Other barriers include lakes and river gorges, such as the one in the photo below. **Describe** What barriers on the map did the migrating Bantu avoid? **Contrast** What natural features on this map might have aided travel for the Bantu?

Go Online
PHSchool.com Use Web Code **lgp-8231** for step-by-step **map skills practice.**

Bantu Languages As the Bantu speakers moved through Africa, they also spread their languages. Today, more than 200 million Africans speak Bantu languages. In fact, about 500 of the languages spoken in Africa south of the Sahara belong to the Bantu language family.

One reason this puzzle is difficult is that the wood and clay that many African peoples used for building have disintegrated. Even iron tools and weapons have not lasted, because iron rusts fairly quickly. However, modern techniques and inventions have helped scientists uncover new information. Stories told by traditional African storytellers have led to new areas of exploration. That is because these stories are often **oral history,** accounts of the past that people pass down by word of mouth.

The Bantu In early times, most Bantu-speaking peoples were fishers, farmers, and herders. Their villages were made up of families from the same **clan** (klan), or group of families who traced their roots to the same ancestor. Many of these clans traced their ancestry through mothers rather than fathers. For this reason, property and positions of power were passed down through the mother's side of the family.

The Bantu-speaking peoples moved slowly from their traditional homelands. Each generation moved a fairly short distance in their search for better farmland and better grazing. As the Bantu migrated, they entered different environments. In many places, they had to change the way they lived. For example, they learned to raise different crops or different kinds of animals.

These women in Windhoek, Namibia, belong to a present-day Bantu group, the Herero.

The Spread of Bantu Culture Often, Bantu people moved into areas where other people already lived. When this happened, they sometimes joined the groups living there. The older cultures then usually adapted to Bantu culture. For example, the Bantu introduced crops such as yams to other parts of Africa. At other times, however, the Bantu forced the people already living there to leave their homes.

As the Bantu migrated, they also carried a knowledge of metalworking with them. Iron tools gave the Bantu more control over their environment than older cultures had. With hard axes, they could cut down trees and clear the land. Their sharp, iron-headed spears and arrows were powerful weapons for hunting and for warfare.

These migrations continued over many generations, with groups moving whenever an area became crowded. In time, the Bantu had settled throughout Central and Southern Africa.

✓ **Reading Check** What kinds of skills did the Bantu carry with them?

Making Iron Tools
Bantu peoples heated rocks containing iron in furnaces to produce a lump of iron, shown above at the far left. They then gradually hammered it to shape a useful tool, such as the hoe above at the right. **Draw Conclusions** *How might iron tools have given the Bantu an advantage over people who lacked metal tools?*

Section 1 Assessment

Key Terms
Review the key terms at the beginning of this section. Use each term in a sentence that explains its meaning.

Target Reading Skill
What were you able to clarify about Africa's physical features by rereading?

Comprehension and Critical Thinking
1. (a) Identify Describe the main physical features of Africa.

(b) Synthesize Information How do Africa's physical features affect people's ways of life?
2. (a) Recall Over how many years did the Bantu migrations occur?
(b) Summarize Tell what happened when the Bantu met other African peoples.
(c) Conclude Why are the Bantu migrations an important part of African history?

Writing Activity
Consider the Bantu people's long history of migration and adaptation to new environments. Write a paragraph to answer the following question: What does this history suggest about the kind of people the Bantu were?

For: An activity on the Bantu migration
Visit: PHSchool.com
Web Code: lgd-8201

Using Reliable Information

Grace was writing a paper about the Nok culture, the earliest known Iron Age culture in West Africa. She found this passage in a book called *Great Civilizations of Ancient Africa,* published in 1971. It was written by the historian Lester Brooks. Was this passage a good source for Grace's paper?

"The Nok peoples are known to have had a sophisticated agricultural society and . . . the ability to produce weapons of iron at this early time. They undoubtedly must have had relations—peaceful or otherwise—with other peoples over a wide expanse of the African interior. . . .

"But the truth . . . is that we just do not know who the Nok peoples were or how they lived. We have no written records, we have no legends or myths that explain them."

All books are not equally reliable. Use the skill below to help you determine how reliable a piece of writing is.

Nok statue

Learn the Skill

To decide whether a piece of writing is reliable, use the following steps:

1 Look at the date of the source. A source might have been written near the time of an event or many years later. Eyewitness accounts can tell you how an event was understood at the time it happened. Later writing may be based on respected research. New discoveries might have been made since the passage above was written.

2 Identify the author's qualifications and purpose. A "historian" should be a reliable source. But think about the sentence beginning, "The Nok peoples are known to have had a . . ." Who is it who *knows?* Where might this author have gotten his information?

3 Decide whether the author has a bias. Look for opinions, beliefs that cannot be proved. "They undoubtedly must have had relations . . ." is an opinion, not a fact. Also look for loaded words and phrases. The word *sophisticated* gives a positive impression that may or may not be accurate. Sometimes biased writers leave out information that does not support their bias.

4 Decide how reliable the source is and why. Consider your purpose: Are you writing about how an event seemed to the people who experienced it? Or, do you need the latest research to support your conclusions about the event?

42 Medieval Times to Today

The following passage is from *Travels in Asia and Africa 1325–1354*, written by a North African merchant named Ibn Battutah. He describes a journey through the Sahara.

"[W]e passed ten days of discomfort because the water there is bitter and the place is plagued with flies. . . . We passed a caravan on the way and they told us that some of their party had become separated from them. We found one of them dead under a shrub of the sort that grows in the sand. . . ."

Practice the Skill

Read the passage above. Then follow the steps in Learn the Skill to decide if it is a reliable source.

1 When was the passage written? Would this information be more reliable if it had been written more recently? Explain why or why not.

2 What qualifies the author to describe the Sahara? Do you think he was an accurate observer?

3 Identify an example of loaded language in the passage. Could this statement be proved true or false? Is it possible that the writer has left important information out of his account?

4 Do you consider this passage a reliable source? How might your purpose in using the passage affect your decision?

Sand dunes in the Sahara

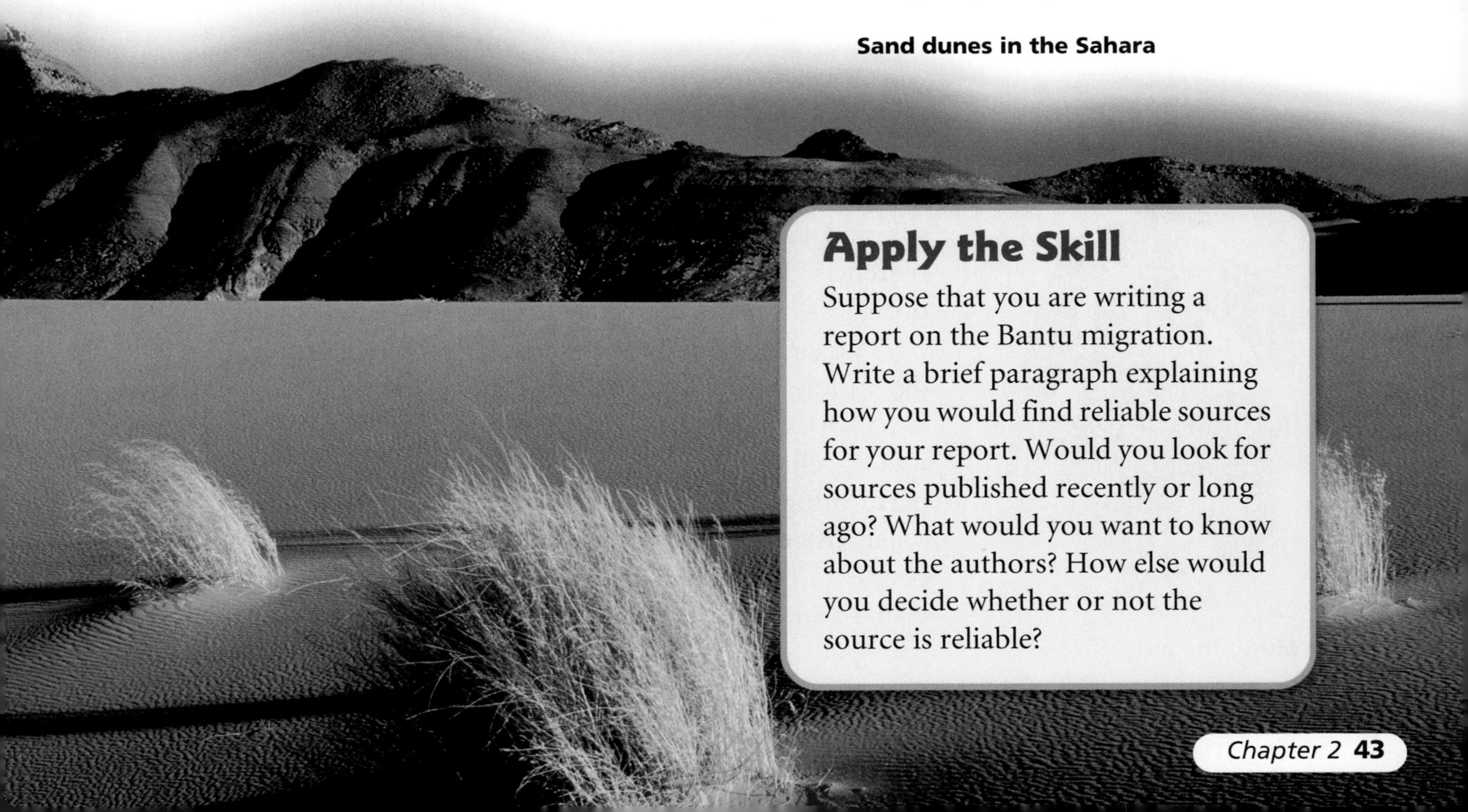

Apply the Skill

Suppose that you are writing a report on the Bantu migration. Write a brief paragraph explaining how you would find reliable sources for your report. Would you look for sources published recently or long ago? What would you want to know about the authors? How else would you decide whether or not the source is reliable?

Section 2
Kingdoms of West Africa

Prepare to Read

Objectives

In this section, you will
1. Learn about the trading kingdoms of the West African savanna.
2. Investigate the kingdoms of the West African rain forests.

Taking Notes

As you read this section, look for the main ideas and details about different African cultures. Create an outline of the section using the example below as a model.

> I. Kingdoms of the savanna
>   A. Ghana
>   1.
>   2.
>   B.
> II.

Target Reading Skill

Paraphrase When you paraphrase, you restate what you have read in your own words. For example, you could paraphrase the first paragraph below this way: "Thousands of people and dozens of camels carrying gold marched in a group."

As you read this section, paraphrase the information after each red or blue heading.

Key Terms

- **Mansa Musa** (MAHN sah MOO sah) *n.* a king of Mali in the 1300s
- **Mali** (MAH lee) *n.* a rich kingdom of the West African savanna
- **Ghana** (GAH nuh) *n.* the first West African kingdom based on the gold and salt trade
- **Songhai** (SAWNG hy) *n.* a powerful kingdom of the West African savanna
- **Ile-Ife** (EE lay EE fay) *n.* the capital of a kingdom of the West African rain forest
- **Benin** (beh NEEN) *n.* a kingdom of the West African rain forest

Mansa Musa, the king of Mali

Soldiers whose swords hung from gold chains rode horses decorated with gold. Hundreds of government officials marched along with the soldiers. Thousands of slaves, each one dressed in silk and carrying a staff made of gold, also accompanied the marchers. The procession included more than 60,000 people and dozens of camels, each camel loaded with many pounds of gold.

This sight greeted the astonished people of Cairo, Egypt, one day in July 1324. It was the caravan of **Mansa Musa** (MAHN sah MOO sah), the powerful king of Mali, in West Africa. The caravan was traveling from Mali across North Africa. Mansa Musa was performing his duty as a Muslim by traveling to the Southwest Asian city of Mecca, the holiest city of Islam. Many years later, people in Egypt were still talking about Mansa Musa's amazing visit—and about the amount of gold that he and his officials had spent.

Kingdoms of the Savanna

Mansa Musa ruled **Mali** (MAH lee), a rich kingdom of the West African savanna. The kingdoms of the savanna controlled important trade routes across the Sahara. The Niger River, which flows through the region, was another important trade route. Traders traveling through these lands had to pay taxes on all their goods. This made the kingdoms rich. In return, the rulers kept peace and order throughout the land. Thus, merchants— and their caravans of valuable goods—could travel safely from one place to another.

Ghana, a Kingdom Built on Trade Salt and gold were the basis of West African trade. Most of the salt came from mines in the central Sahara. Salt was very valuable. People needed it to flavor food, to preserve meat, and to maintain good health. Salt was scarce in the rain forest region. So people from the forest region of West Africa sold gold in exchange for salt. Some gold was sold to traders on their way to North Africa. These traders returned with glass and other precious North African goods. Traders could travel hundreds of miles across the dry Sahara because their camels could travel for days without water.

The first West African kingdom to be based on the wealth of the salt and gold trade was **Ghana** (GAH nuh). By about A.D. 400, the people of Ghana took control of the trade routes across the Sahara. Ghana's location was ideal. Find Ghana on the map titled Civilizations of Africa, on page 35. Ghana was just north of the rich gold fields. Land routes south from the Sahara went through Ghana. By about A.D 800, Ghana was a major trading kingdom.

The Salt Trade in Africa
Camel caravans like the one shown at the bottom of the page carried slabs of salt from salt mines in the Sahara. Slabs of salt were traded in markets like the one below, in Mopti, Mali.
Apply Information *When traders from the forest region bought salt, what might they have offered in exchange?*

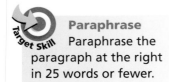
Paraphrase
Paraphrase the paragraph at the right in 25 words or fewer.

Ghana's capital, Kumbi Saleh, was divided into two cities. One was the center of trade. The other was the royal city, where the king had his court and handed down his decisions. Around A.D. 1000, the power of Ghana began to weaken. Invaders from the north overran the capital and other cities. By the 1200s, Ghana had broken into small, independent states. Soon, most of the trade in the area was controlled by a powerful new kingdom, the kingdom of Mali.

The Powerful Kingdom of Mali Mali was centered in the Upper Niger Valley. Under the leadership of Sundiata (sun JAH tah), who united the kingdom about 1230, Mali took control of the salt and gold trade. Sundiata conquered surrounding areas and increased the size of the kingdom. By 1255, when Sundiata died, Mali had grown rich from trade. It had become the most powerful kingdom in West Africa. Mali continued to grow in the years after Sundiata's death.

In 1312, Mansa Musa became ruler of Mali. By this time, traders from North Africa had brought a new religion, Islam, to West Africa. Muslims, or people who practice Islam, worship one god. Mansa Musa greatly expanded his kingdom and made Islam the official religion. Mansa Musa's trip to the holy city of Mecca created new ties between Mali and the Muslim peoples of North Africa and Southwest Asia.

The Great Mosque at Djenné
The mosque below is in the city of Djenné, an important trading center in the kingdoms of Mali and Songhai. A mosque is a Muslim place of worship. **Analyze Images** *What does the scale of this mosque suggest about the importance of Islam to people in this region?*

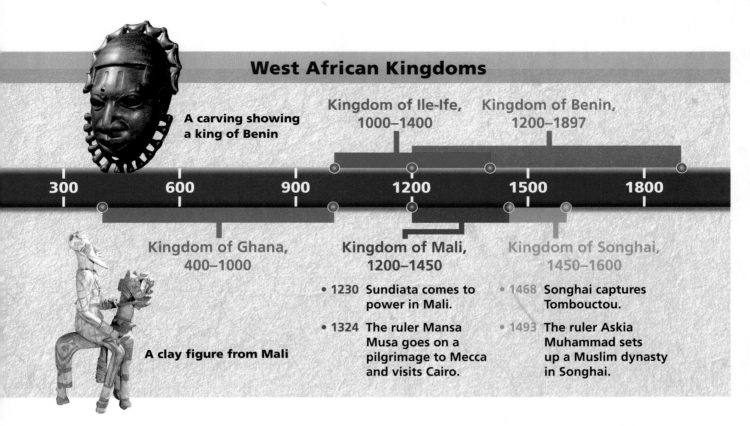

West African Kingdoms

A carving showing a king of Benin

Kingdom of Ile-Ife, 1000–1400

Kingdom of Benin, 1200–1897

300   600   900   1200   1500   1800

Kingdom of Ghana, 400–1000

A clay figure from Mali

Kingdom of Mali, 1200–1450

- 1230 Sundiata comes to power in Mali.
- 1324 The ruler Mansa Musa goes on a pilgrimage to Mecca and visits Cairo.

Kingdom of Songhai, 1450–1600

- 1468 Songhai captures Tombouctou.
- 1493 The ruler Askia Muhammad sets up a Muslim dynasty in Songhai.

During his 25-year rule, Mansa Musa used his new ties to these Muslim peoples to make Mali a center of learning. Scholars came to teach religion, mathematics, medicine, and law. In the late 1300s, however—about 50 years after Mansa Musa died—Mali's power began to fade. Raiders attacked from the north, and fighting broke out within the kingdom. Several provinces broke away and became independent. One of these former provinces became an empire in its own right. It was called Songhai (SAWNG hy).

The Rise and Fall of Songhai Songhai became the leading kingdom of the West African savanna during the 1400s. Like the rulers of Ghana and Mali, Songhai's leaders controlled trade routes and the sources of salt and gold. Songhai's wealth and power grew when it conquered the rich trading city of Tombouctou in 1468. Find Songhai on the map titled Civilizations of Africa on page 35.

In less than 100 years, however, the kingdom of Songhai began to lose power. In the late 1500s, the people of Songhai began fighting among themselves. The kingdom became weaker. And it easily fell to the guns and cannons of an army from Morocco, in North Africa. The era of the rich and powerful trading empires of West Africa was at an end.

✔ Reading Check   **Name the two most important trade items in West Africa.**

Timeline Skills

This timeline shows five West African kingdoms. Vertical lines mark specific dates. Horizontal bars show periods of time. The kingdoms of the savanna are at the bottom of the timeline. The forest kingdoms are at the top. **Identify** Which kingdom lasted the longest? Which lasted the shortest time? **Analyze** Which forest kingdoms overlapped in time with the kingdom of Mali?

Kingdoms of the Forest

Ghana, Mali, and Songhai developed on West Africa's savanna. At the same time, other kingdoms arose in the rain forests to the south of these grasslands. The peoples of the rain forests were not Muslim. They practiced religions with hundreds of different gods.

Two of the most important kingdoms of the West African forests were centered around the cities of **Ile-Ife** (EE lay EE fay) and **Benin** (beh NEEN). Both of these cities were located in the present-day nation of Nigeria. As with the kingdoms of the savanna, trade made these forest kingdoms powerful and wealthy. With their wealth and stability, these kingdoms supported larger populations than other African rain forest regions could support.

Ile-Ife: A Center of Culture and Trade

About A.D. 1000, Ile-Ife became a major cultural and trading center. The powerful leaders of this kingdom were called onis (OH neez). Traditional stories told by these people described Ile-Ife as "the place where the world was created," but historians know little about the early city or the people who lived there.

One of the reasons that we know little about Ile-Ife is that the modern town of Ife is located on top of the earlier city. Also, the region is thickly forested and damp. Trees have covered old sites outside the town, and rains have washed away old mud buildings. Dampness has also rusted iron and long since rotted wood and fabrics.

Among the most important artifacts that have survived are sculptures. Many were discovered only in the last 100 years. Scientists have dated these works of art to the years between the 1100s and the 1300s. Many of these sculptures are lifelike and may be portraits of the powerful onis of Ile-Ife.

The rain forests of West Africa have a damp climate and lush vegetation.

Benin Rules an Empire The city of Benin dates to the 1200s. At that time, workers in the region mined copper, iron, and gold. Benin's leaders, called obas (OH buz), also sold slaves to African traders. Many of these slaves were forced to work as servants for rich families on the savanna. Others joined slaves from Europe and Asia to work in North Africa.

By the 1500s, Benin reached its greatest strength and size. The oba controlled a large army, priests, government workers, and less important local chiefs. The city of Benin ruled the trade routes along the rivers to the north and south. It became immensely rich. It ruled much of present-day southern Nigeria. Benin remained strong until the late 1600s, when the kingdom began to lose its power over the region.

Like Ile-Ife, the city of Benin also became a center of art. The obas hired skilled artists to make many beautiful objects from bronze, brass, ivory, and copper. These artists may have borrowed some cultural traditions from Ile-Ife, but the exact relationship between the two kingdoms is unclear. The artists of Benin and other West African kingdoms have in turn influenced modern artists in Europe and the Americas.

 Reading Check **What were the leaders of Ile-Ife and Benin called?**

Bronze Plaques Benin artists made bronze plaques and sculptures for the royal palaces of the obas. For example, one sculpture shows a man playing a flute and wearing an animal-skin skirt. After 1897, the British ruled this region and removed many objects. Today, hundreds of Benin plaques can be seen in museums in Europe and the United States. This plaque is about 300 years old.

 Section 2 Assessment

Key Terms
Review the key terms at the beginning of this section. Use each term in a sentence that explains its meaning.

Target Reading Skill
Find the second paragraph under the heading Kingdoms of the Forest, on page 48. Paraphrase this paragraph by rewriting it in your own words.

Comprehension and Critical Thinking
1. (a) List What were the names of the three major kingdoms of the West African savanna?

(b) Identify Causes What made each of the three kingdoms rich?
(c) Apply Information What do the powerful countries of today have in common with these kingdoms?
2. (a) Recall Describe some of the art objects that the people of Ile-Ife and Benin left behind.
(b) Identify Cause and Effect Why are these objects among the few things that have survived from these cultures?

Writing Activity
Suppose that you are a foreign visitor who has traveled to the kingdom of Benin in the late 1500s. You will be allowed to meet briefly with the current oba. Write a list of five or six questions that you would like to ask him about his daily life, his kingdom, and the people he rules.

Writing Tip Be sure that your questions are worded in a way that shows respect for the powerful ruler and his kingdom. Also be sure to include a brief introduction identifying yourself and the purpose of your visit.

From the salt mines of the Sahara, caravan leaders drove their camels through the hot desert sand. Heavily weighted with slabs of salt, the camel train headed south. Meantime, trade caravans from West Africa's gold mines traveled north. They met in the West African city of Tombouctou (tohm book TOO). In the 1500s, salt was as valuable as gold in the city's markets.

A Marketplace of Goods and Ideas Business was brisk in Tombouctou's markets. Buyers and sellers traded for metal wares and wood; grains and nuts; fish, camel meat, milk, water, and dates; rugs and linen; precious ivory, gold, salt, and even slaves.

By the mid-1500s, about 60,000 people lived in Tombouctou. Artisans such as weavers, dyers, and metalsmiths had shops in the busy city.

More than just a marketplace, this city drew scholars from all over the Islamic world to study and exchange ideas. Many people within the city spoke Arabic. Muslims could pray at three impressive dried-mud mosques.

The illustration at the right shows a market scene in Tombouctou with a mosque in the background. The illustration at the top of the page is of an ancient manuscript that was found in the city.

The Salt and Gold Trade

Salt from mines in the Saharan desert was traded in the markets of Tombouctou. At one time, about 25,000 camels traveled from Taoudenni in the Sahara to Tombouctou yearly. Gold came from the southern areas of West Africa.

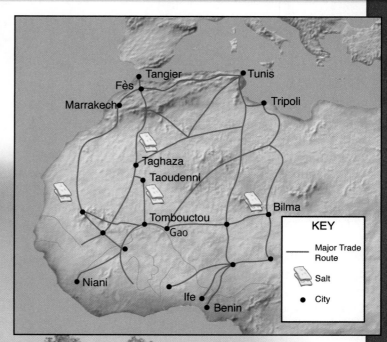

Tangier
Fès
Marrakech
Tunis
Tripoli
Taghaza
Taoudenni
Bilma
Tombouctou
Gao
Niani
Ife
Benin

KEY

― Major Trade Route

▱ Salt

● City

Weights for Gold Dust
Merchants and traders in medieval Africa used the metal pieces at the right to measure the weight of gold dust.

Assessment

Describe What was Tombouctou like in the 1500s?

Conclude What was the importance of salt and gold in Tombouctou?

East Africa's Great Trading Centers

Prepare to Read

Objectives

In this section, you will

1. Learn about powerful East African civilizations whose cities included Aksum and Lalibela.
2. Find out why the coastal cities of East Africa were important.

Taking Notes

As you read this section, look for the major events in this period of East Africa's history. Copy the timeline below, and add events and dates in the proper places on it.

A.D. **100** ─────────────────── A.D. **1600**

 Target Reading Skill

Summarize When you summarize, you review and state, in the correct order, the main points you have read. Summarizing can help you understand and study. As you read, pause occasionally to summarize what you have read.

Key Terms

- **Kilwa** (KEEL wah) *n.* one of many trading cities on the East African coast
- **Aksum** (AHK soom) *n.* an important East African center of trade

- **city-state** (SIH tee stayt) *n.* a city that is also a separate, independent state
- **Swahili** (swah HEE lee) *n.* a Bantu language with Arabic words, spoken along the East African coast
- **Great Zimbabwe** (grayt zim BAHB way) *n.* a powerful southeast African city

The ruins of the Great Mosque of Kilwa in Tanzania

The port was full of hurrying people, bobbing ships, and bundles of goods. The bright sun reflected off the water. Some traders were unloading glass beads, rice, spices, and expensive jewels carried from India. Others were bringing honey and wheat from Southwest Asia. Rich silks and fragile porcelains were also arriving after the long voyage from faraway China.

This was the bustling scene at **Kilwa** (KEEL wah), one of many trading cities along the coast of East Africa. Find Kilwa on the map titled Civilizations of Africa on page 35. Located in present-day Tanzania, Kilwa was an Islamic city with a royal palace and lush orchards and gardens. Kilwa's rulers charged taxes on all goods that entered their port. These taxes made Kilwa rich. Ibn Battutah (IB un bat TOO tah)—a famous Muslim traveler from North Africa—visited in the 1330s. He wrote that Kilwa was "one of the most beautiful and best-constructed towns in the world."

Ancient Ethiopia

Thousands of years ago, rich civilizations began to develop in southern Arabia and northeastern Africa along the Red Sea. By A.D. 1, the city of **Aksum** (AHK soom), located in present-day Ethiopia, was an important East African center of trade.

Aksum, a Center of Trade and Christianity Although the city of Aksum was located in the mountains about 100 miles (160 kilometers) inland, it controlled a trading port at Adulis (AD oo lis) on the Red Sea. Over time, Aksum conquered much of modern Ethiopia and southwestern Arabia. It grew steadily in strength and wealth.

The merchants of Aksum traded goods at ports as far away as India. One of the main trade goods they controlled was ivory. Ivory, the white material from elephant tusks, was highly valued for carving. As they traded goods with foreign merchants, the people of Aksum also exchanged ideas and beliefs with them.

During the A.D. 300s, King Ezana (ay ZAH nuh) of Aksum learned about a new religion—Christianity. Soon, the king became a Christian himself and made Christianity the official religion of his kingdom. Over time, most people under Aksum's rule converted to Christianity.

For several hundred years, Aksum kept its control of the major trade routes linking Africa with Europe and Asia. Then in the A.D. 600s, Muslims fought with the rulers of Aksum for control of the Red Sea trade routes. Eventually, the Muslims conquered the coastal ports. The Muslim conquest of the coast ended the trade that had given Aksum its power and wealth.

Christianity in Ethiopia
The city of Aksum, at top, remains an important religious center today. The St. Mary of Zion Church is at the right. The young priest above is holding a Coptic cross, a symbol of Ethiopian Christianity. **Compare and Contrast** *How do these images of Christianity compare to Christian imagery in the United States?*

St. George's Church, Lalibela
At top, worshipers surround St. George's Church, one of the churches that King Lalibela had carved into the rock about A.D. 1200. Above, a priest at the church's entrance.
Apply Information *How long has this church been in use?*

Lalibela and the Spread of Christianity

After Aksum had lost power, the Christian kings of the region built churches and monasteries. But these kings did not build a new capital. Instead, they moved from place to place around the kingdom. They lived in royal tents and were accompanied by thousands of citizens and servants.

Many neighboring lands converted to Islam, but present-day Ethiopia remained Christian. Cut off in their mountainous home, the Ethiopians had little direct contact with other Christian peoples. In time, their churches developed unique customs and traditions. In one such tradition, churchgoers rest their foreheads against the outside wall of a church and kiss it to show respect.

Another unique feature of the region's Christianity is a group of churches built about A.D. 1200 under King Lalibela (lah lee BAY lah). The king had his people build new churches—but not from the ground up. Instead, the people were to carve the churches down into the solid red rock. The flat rooftops of the buildings are level with the surrounding land. The churches are in a town named Lalibela in honor of the king. These fascinating churches are still used today by the Christians of Ethiopia.

√ **Reading Check** **Describe the churches of Lalibela.**

Rich Centers of Trade

After Muslims gained control of Indian Ocean trade, trade centers developed along the east coast of Africa. Each of these ports was a **city-state** (SIH tee stayt), a city with its own government that controls much of the surrounding land. By 1400, there were about 30 such city-states along Africa's Indian Ocean coast.

Trade thrived in East Africa because the region supplied goods such as gold and ivory that were very scarce outside Africa. In return, Muslim traders brought luxury goods that could not be found in Africa. Muslim traders from Arabia also brought their religion and language to these African city-states.

The City-State of Kilwa The merchants of Kilwa traded goods from inland regions of Africa for the foreign goods that traders brought to the port by sea. Contact between Africans and Arabs in Kilwa and other coastal city-states led to a new culture and language. Called **Swahili** (swah HEE lee), this Bantu language has words borrowed from Arabic. Swahili was spoken all along the East African coast. Most people on this coast converted to Islam.

In the 1500s, Portuguese troops sailing from Europe captured and looted Kilwa and the other coastal city-states. Portugal took over the prosperous trade routes. But the influence of Swahili culture remained. Today, Swahili is an official language in Kenya and Tanzania, and most East Africans use Swahili for business. Islam is still an important religion in the region.

Great Zimbabwe Much of the gold traded at Kilwa was mined in an inland area to the south, between the Zambezi and Limpopo rivers. This was the region controlled by the powerful southeastern African city of **Great Zimbabwe** (grayt zim BAHB way). Like other medieval African centers that you have read about, Great Zimbabwe grew rich and powerful through trade.

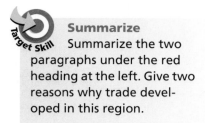
Summarize Summarize the two paragraphs under the red heading at the left. Give two reasons why trade developed in this region.

DISCOVERY CHANNEL
SCHOOL Video
Learn about Great Zimbabwe and explore its ruins.

Mombasa Harbor, Kenya
Like Kilwa, the port of Mombasa on the Indian Ocean has a long history of trade. Wooden sailing ships like the ones below carried the trade of these city-states. **Infer** Why were the East African city-states located along the coast?

Stone-walled ruins at Great Zimbabwe, in the present-day nation of Zimbabwe

Historians believe that the city of Great Zimbabwe had been founded by about 1100. Its Bantu-speaking people were the ancestors of today's Shona (SHOHN uh) people. Most people in this area were poor farmers. For those who were better off, large herds of cattle were an important form of wealth. Richest of all were the leaders who controlled the gold trade. These powerful leaders and their families lived among impressive stone-walled structures.

Great Zimbabwe thrived for hundreds of years. Historians believe that the city reached its peak before the early 1400s. By 1500, the city had fallen. Trade routes may have moved to favor other centers. Farmers also may have worn out the soil. In either case, the glory of Great Zimbabwe was not entirely lost. Its stone ruins still stand, and its history is a source of pride for the present-day nation of Zimbabwe.

 **Reading Check** **What were two possible causes for the collapse of Great Zimbabwe?**

Section 3 Assessment

Key Terms

Review the key terms at the beginning of this section. Use each term in a sentence that explains its meaning.

 **Target Reading Skill**

Write a summary of the two paragraphs at the top of this page.

Comprehension and Critical Thinking

1. (a) Recall What change did King Ezana of Aksum make in the A.D. 300s?

(b) Identify What are some of the most famous sites in Ethiopia today?

(c) Synthesize Information How are these famous sites related to the changes made by King Ezana?

2. (a) Explain What connection was there between Great Zimbabwe and Kilwa?

(b) Analyze Information How did the locations of Kilwa and Great Zimbabwe make them powerful and rich?

Writing Activity

Study the photo of the rock-cut church of Lalibela on page 54. Write a description of this unusual church to a friend or relative. Where is it located? What does the building look like? How was it built? In what ways is it similar to or different from other buildings?

For: An activity on historic Ethiopia
Visit: PHSchool.com
Web Code: lgd-8203

Review and Assessment

◆ Chapter Summary

Section 1: Africa and the Bantu

- The physical geography and natural vegetation of Africa are diverse, from tropical rain forests along the Equator to the world's largest desert.
- More than 2,000 years ago, the Bantu-speaking people of West Africa began migrating across central and southern Africa, carrying their culture wherever they went.

Section 2: West African Kingdoms

- Powerful trading kingdoms, including Ghana, Mali, and Songhai, controlled the savannas of West Africa for hundreds of years.
- The cities of Ile-Ife and Benin were important centers of trade and art in the West African rain forests.

Section 3: East Africa's Great Trading Centers

- Strong kings built lasting monuments and brought changes to the lands they ruled in present-day Ethiopia.
- City-states along the East African coast and the inland city of Great Zimbabwe grew rich from trade.

A bronze plaque from Benin

◆ Key Terms

Each statement below includes a key term from this chapter. If the statement is true, write *true*. If it is false, rewrite the statement to make it true.

1. Swahili is a language based on Portuguese, with Bantu words, that is spoken in West Africa.

2. Movement from one country or region to settle in another is called migration.

3. Mansa Musa ruled the kingdom of Mali.

4. A city-state is a city with its own government that controls much of the surrounding land.

5. The Sahara is the world's longest river.

6. Oral history is an account of the past that is passed down from generation to generation by word of mouth.

◆ Comprehension and Critical Thinking

7. (a) **Locate** Where are Africa's tropical rain forests located?
(b) **Describe** What are some important features of Africa's savannas?
(c) **Compare and Contrast** In what ways are Africa's rain forests and savannas alike? In what ways are they different?

8. (a) **List** Name two things that have helped modern historians study the history of Africa south of the Sahara.
(b) **Explain** Why is studying this history "like solving a puzzle"?

9. (a) **Summarize** When and why did African Muslims fight the rulers of Aksum?
(b) **Analyze** Why was this fight important?

10. (a) **Recall** In which two rain forest kingdoms did artists make bronze sculptures?
(b) **Generalize** Why might an artist depict a powerful king in his or her work?

11. (a) **Identify** Where did Mansa Musa and his caravan stop in July 1324?
(b) **Infer** Why might a large caravan need to stop in the middle of a very long journey?

◆ Skills Practice

Using Reliable Information In the Skills for Life activity in this chapter, you learned how to judge whether information is reliable. Review the steps for this skill. Suppose you found the text below in a recent travel guide to Africa. Use the steps for this skill to decide whether the information is reliable. Write a sentence that explains why or why not.

"The mosque at Djenné is the most magnificent building in all of Africa. It must have been built by a powerful ruler with a strong religious faith. Every traveler to Africa should visit this mosque."

◆ Writing Activity: Science

You have read about the importance of iron tools and weapons to early peoples. Do research, using reliable sources, to find out how Africans made these early iron tools. What were the different steps in the process? What equipment did they use? What kind of tools did they make? Write a short report on your findings.

MAP MASTER™ Skills Activity

Place Location For each place or feature listed below, write the letter from the map that shows its location.
1. Great Zimbabwe
2. Sahara
3. Kilwa
4. Kingdom of Ghana
5. Equator
6. Kingdom of Benin
7. Kingdom of Mali

Go Online PHSchool.com Use Web Code **lgp-8214** for an **interactive map**.

Sub-Saharan Africa

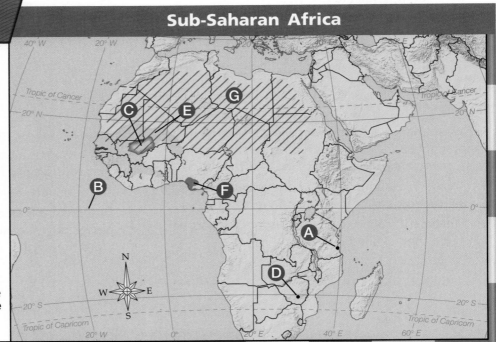

Standardized Test Prep

Test-Taking Tips

Some questions on standardized tests ask you to find main ideas. Read the paragraph below. Then follow the tips to answer the sample question.

> Imagine trading a pound of salt for a pound of gold. At today's prices, a pound of salt costs only about 50 cents, but a pound of gold is worth thousands of dollars. That has not always been true everywhere. In parts of Africa, salt was as scarce as gold in medieval times. People needed salt to preserve their food. They needed it to stay healthy, too. So they traded their gold for nearly the same weight of salt.

TIP As you read the paragraph, try to identify its main idea, or most important point. In some cases, the main idea may be stated. In other cases, such as this one, you have to add up the details to find the main idea.

Pick the letter that best answers the question.

The main idea of this paragraph is that

A today, a pound of salt costs only about 50 cents.

B in medieval Africa, salt was nearly as valuable as gold because it was needed and scarce.

C people need salt to stay healthy.

D in medieval Africa, gold was easier for traders to carry than salt.

TIP Look for key words in the answer choices or question that connect to the paragraph. In this case, two key words are *salt* and *gold*.

Think It Through The paragraph's main idea is that Africans traded gold for salt long ago, when salt was hard to get. Look at all four choices. A and C both just give details about salt. They do not compare the values of salt and gold. That leaves B and D. D gives information that is not in the paragraph. So, the correct answer is B, which is the main idea of the paragraph.

Practice Questions

Use the tips above and other tips in this book to help you answer the following questions.

1. In Africa, tropical rain forests lie along
   A Madagascar.
   B the Equator.
   C an oasis.
   D the Nile.

2. The kingdom of Mali rose to power after this West African kingdom weakened.
   A Songhai
   B Benin
   C Ghana
   D Nigeria

3. Which Christian king of East Africa had his people carve underground churches?
   A Sundiata
   B Ezana
   C Mansa Musa
   D Lalibela

Read the paragraph below, and answer the question that follows.

Medieval traders sold East African ivory in India. Ivory comes from elephant tusks. India has its own elephants, so why did Indians buy East African ivory? East African elephants have softer tusks. East African ivory is better for carving.

4. The main idea of this paragraph is that
   A ivory comes from elephant tusks.
   B Indians bought East African ivory because it was good for carving.
   C trading elephant tusks is illegal today.
   D East African elephants have softer tusks than Indian elephants.

Use Web Code **lga-8201** for a **Chapter 2 self-test.**

Chapter

3

Early Civilizations of the Americas

Chapter Preview

This chapter will introduce you to the civilizations that existed in the Americas before the arrival of Europeans.

Section 1
South America and the Incas

Section 2
Cultures of Middle America

Section 3
Cultures of North America

 **Target
Reading Skill**

Main Idea In this chapter you will focus on finding and remembering the main idea, or the most important point, of sections and paragraphs.

▶ Temple of the Cross,
Palenque, Mexico

Civilizations of the Americas

MAP MASTER™
Skills Activity

NORTH AMERICA

Northwest Coast

PACIFIC OCEAN

Tropic of Cancer

20° N

Chaco Canyon

Southwest

Great Plains

Mississippi R.

Cahokia

Eastern Woodlands

Gulf of Mexico

Tenochtitlán

ATLANTIC OCEAN

Tropic of Cancer

20° N

Caribbean Sea

MIDDLE AMERICA

N
W   E
S

Equator

0°

PACIFIC OCEAN

Equator

0°

Amazon R.

SOUTH AMERICA

ANDES

Cuzco

20° S

Tropic of Capricorn

ANDES

40° S

40° S

160° W   140° W   120° W   100° W   80° W   60° W   40° W   20° W
140° W   120° W   100° W   80° W   60° W   40° W   20° W   0°   20° E

KEY

	Mayas, about A.D. 250–900
	Aztecs, A.D. 1400s–1521
	Incas, A.D. 1400s–1535
	Mound Builders, about 700 B.C.–A.D. 1250
	Anasazi, about A.D. 100–1200
	Pueblo, 1200–present
	Peoples of the Northwest Coast, about A.D. 500–1800
	Iroquois League, 1500s–1784
•	City

0 miles   1,500
0 kilometers 1,500
Lambert Azimuthal Equal Area

Regions The term *Middle America* is often used to describe the region of Mexico and Central America, even though this region is also part of the continent of North America. In this chapter, *North America* describes what is now the United States and Canada.
Identify Which two civilizations were located in Middle America? **Predict** Notice the end dates for these two civilizations. What events might have contributed to their ending?

Go Online
PHSchool.com Use Web Code **lgp-8321** for step-by-step **map skills practice.**

Section 1

South America and the Incas

Prepare to Read

Objectives

In this section, you will
1. Find out about the geography of the Americas.
2. Learn about the empire established by the Incas of South America.

Taking Notes

As you read this section, record key points about the Incan Empire. Copy the start of the outline below, and then add more information to complete it.

> I. The mountain empire of the Incas
>   A. Growth of an empire
>   1.
>   2.
>   B.
> II.

Target Reading Skill

Identify Main Ideas Good readers identify the main idea in every written passage. The main idea is the most important, or the biggest, point of the section. It includes all of the other points made in the section. As you read, note the main idea of each paragraph or written passage.

Key Terms

- **Incas** (ING kuhz) *n.* people of a powerful South American empire during the 1400s and 1500s
- **Andes** (AN deez) *n.* a mountain chain of western South America
- **Cuzco** (KOOS koh) *n.* the capital city of the Incan Empire, located in present-day Peru
- **census** (SEN sus) *n.* an official count of people in a certain place at a certain time
- **quipu** (KEE poo) *n.* a group of knotted strings used by the Incas to record information
- **terraces** (TEHR us iz) *n.* steplike ledges cut into mountains to make land suitable for farming

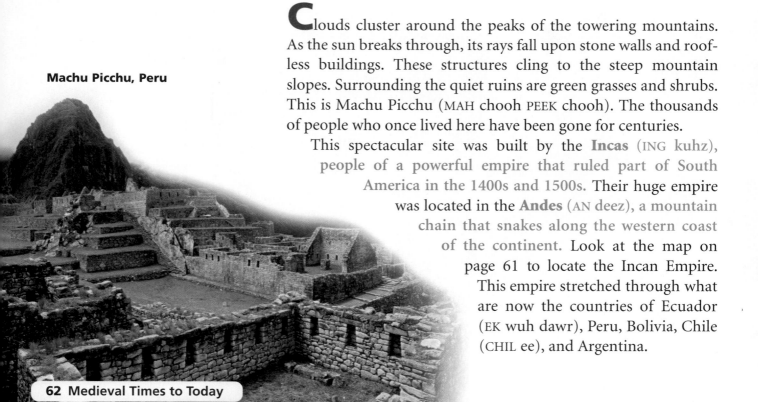

Machu Picchu, Peru

Clouds cluster around the peaks of the towering mountains. As the sun breaks through, its rays fall upon stone walls and roofless buildings. These structures cling to the steep mountain slopes. Surrounding the quiet ruins are green grasses and shrubs. This is Machu Picchu (MAH chooh PEEK chooh). The thousands of people who once lived here have been gone for centuries.

This spectacular site was built by the **Incas** (ING kuhz), people of a powerful empire that ruled part of South America in the 1400s and 1500s. Their huge empire was located in the **Andes** (AN deez), a mountain chain that snakes along the western coast of the continent. Look at the map on page 61 to locate the Incan Empire. This empire stretched through what are now the countries of Ecuador (EK wuh dawr), Peru, Bolivia, Chile (CHIL ee), and Argentina.

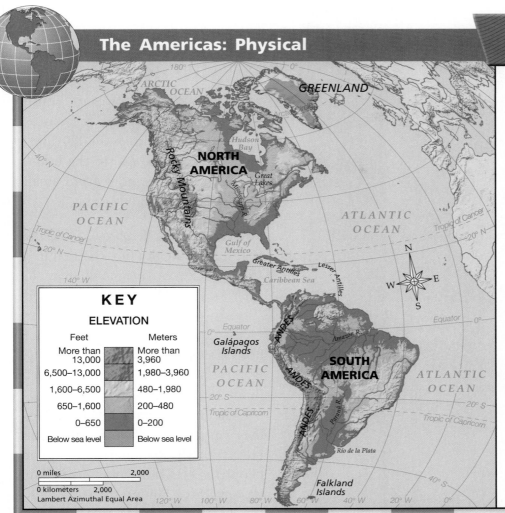

MAP MASTER™
Skills Activity

Place A wide variety of geographical features can be found throughout the Americas. **Locate** Compare this map with the map on page 61. What is the geography of the area in which the Incas lived? **Contrast** How does this geography compare with the geography of the area in which the Anasazi lived?

KEY
ELEVATION

Feet	Meters
More than 13,000	More than 3,960
6,500–13,000	1,980–3,960
1,600–6,500	480–1,980
650–1,600	200–480
0–650	0–200
Below sea level	Below sea level

0 miles 2,000
0 kilometers 2,000
Lambert Azimuthal Equal Area

Go Online
PHSchool.com Use Web Code **lgp-8311** for step-by-step map skills practice.

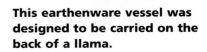

This earthenware vessel was designed to be carried on the back of a llama.

Geography of the Americas

The Incas were not the first culture to develop in the Americas. Many groups had lived in the region for thousands of years. Individual cultures developed different ways of life to fit their geographic settings. Some peoples made their homes in dense forests or fertile river valleys. Other peoples lived among rocky cliffs in areas that were dry for much of the year.

Locate the mountain ranges on the map above. See which parts of the Americas are covered by plains, highland plateaus, and deserts. Also, locate the Mississippi and Amazon rivers, two of the largest river systems in the world. In North America, temperatures range from extreme cold in the far north to hot and tropical in the southern region. In South America, mountain regions are cold. Areas near sea level are hot near the Equator but much cooler in the far south.

✓ **Reading Check** Which two river systems in the Americas are among the largest in the world?

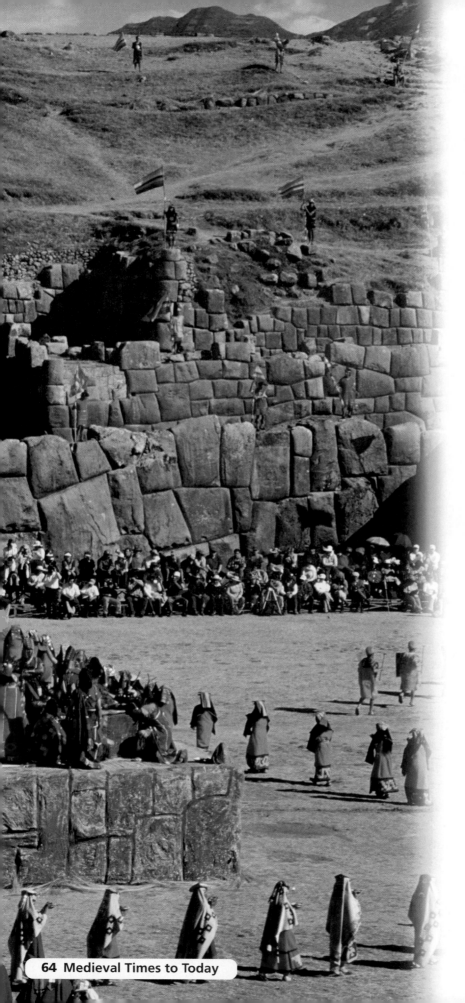

The Mountain Empire of the Incas

At its peak, the powerful South American empire of the Incas measured 2,500 miles (4,020 kilometers) from one end to the other. This great empire grew from small beginnings over many years.

Growth of an Empire About the year A.D. 1200, the Incas settled in a small village on a high plateau in the Andes. This village, named **Cuzco** (KOOS koh), became the Incas' capital city and a center of both government and religion. In fact, the word *cuzco* means "center" in the Incan language.

The Incas extended their control over nearby lands through conquests, or the conquering of other peoples. Over time, many different groups came under their rule. By the 1400s, the lands ruled by the Incas had grown into an empire. At its height, the Incan Empire included as many as 12 million people.

Even when the empire included millions of people, it was run in an orderly way. Incan rulers had a complex system of gathering knowledge about events that happened hundreds of miles away from their capital city.

Festival of the Sun
Thousands of people gather at the ruins of an Incan fortress in Cuzco for the yearly Festival of the Sun, which celebrates the winter solstice.
Infer *How can you tell which people are part of the festival and which are just watching?*

Quipus in Incan Life
In the drawing below, dating from the 1500s, an official gives a noble a quipu like the one at left. The quipu may have been created hundreds of miles away. **Analyze Images** *What details in the drawing tell which person is the noble?*

Incan Government The Incan ruler was called Sapa Inca, or "the emperor." The people believed that their emperor was related to the sun-god. The emperor, and only he, owned all the land and divided it among those under his rule. Under the Sapa Inca was the noble class. Nobles oversaw government officials, who made sure the empire ran smoothly.

Officials used a **census,** or an official count of the people, to keep track of everyone's responsibilities. The census helped to make sure that everyone paid taxes. It recorded which men worked as soldiers or on public projects such as gold mining and road building. Farmers had to give the government part of their crops, while women had to weave cloth. In return, the empire took care of the poor, the sick, and the elderly.

The official spoken language of the empire was Quechua (KECH wuh), but the Incas did not have a written language. Instead, they invented a complex system for keeping detailed records. Information such as births, deaths, and harvests was recorded on a group of knotted strings called a **quipu** (KEE poo). Each quipu had a main cord with several colored strings attached. The colors represented different items, and knots of varying sizes recorded numbers.

Incan relay runners carried quipus across vast networks of roads and bridges to keep the government informed about distant parts of the empire. These roads also carried the Incan armies and trade caravans, both of which helped to unify the vast empire.

Links Across Time

Rope Bridges This rope bridge, strung across a gorge in the Andes, is similar to those used by the Incas. A gorge is a narrow pass between steep cliffs or walls. Incan bridges were made with strong cords of braided vines and reeds. Some peoples in the Andes still make bridges from vines and reeds today. Modern steel suspension bridges in other parts of the world use the engineering principles developed by the Incas hundreds of years ago when they built their rope-and-vine bridges.

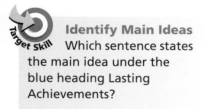

Identify Main Ideas Which sentence states the main idea under the blue heading Lasting Achievements?

Lasting Achievements The achievements of the Incas still amaze people today. They constructed thousands of miles of paved roads, massive walls, and mountaintop buildings. And they did all this with only stone hammers and bronze chisels. Remarkably, much of what the Incas built hundreds of years ago with only primitive tools still stands today.

The Incas took advantage of their environment. They used stone—plentiful in the Andes—for many purposes. Sometimes they used enormous stones whole. At other times, they carefully broke stones into smaller blocks. First they cut a long groove into a rock's surface. Then they drove stone or wooden wedges into the groove until the rock split.

When Incan stonemasons made a wall, they made sure its large, many-sided stones fit together perfectly. After a wall was complete, the fit was so tight that not even a very thin knife blade could be slipped between two blocks. Construction without mortar, or cement, also allowed the massive stones to move and resettle during earthquakes without damaging the wall.

Among their many ingenious uses of stone was a method to increase farm production. The Andes are steep, dry, and rocky. There is little natural farmland. By building **terraces,** or steplike ledges cut into the mountains, the Incas could farm on slopes that would otherwise have been too steep. Stone terraces held the soil in place so it would not be washed away by rain. A complex system of aqueducts, or stone-lined channels, carried water to these farms. One of these aqueducts was 360 miles (579 kilometers) long.

The Decline of the Incan Empire The power of the Incan Empire peaked in the 1400s. After that, it lasted for less than 100 years. A number of factors contributed to the fall of the empire. Members of the ruling family began to fight among themselves for control. Also, many workers started to rebel against the strict government.

Then, in the 1530s, a Spanish conquistador (kahn KEES tuh dawr), or conqueror, named Francisco Pizarro arrived in South America. Pizarro had heard of the wealthy Incan Empire. He wanted to explore the region and conquer its peoples. The Incan emperor welcomed Pizarro. But when he and his unarmed men met the conquistador, they walked into a trap. Pizarro captured the emperor and killed his men.

The Spanish had superior weapons. They also carried diseases, such as smallpox and measles, to which the Incas had never been exposed. These diseases killed much of the Incan population. The Spanish quickly gained control of the vast Incan Empire. For decades, the Incas tried to regain rule of their land, but they never succeeded.

A wooden cup made for Pizarro shows Spanish and Incan figures.

✔ Reading Check **Which Spanish conquistador conquered the Incas?**

Section 1 Assessment

Key Terms
Review the key terms at the beginning of this section. Use each term in a sentence that explains its meaning.

Target Reading Skill
State the main idea of the first paragraph on this page.

Comprehension and Critical Thinking
1. (a) Identify Name two geographic settings in which peoples of the Americas lived.
(b) Synthesize Information What are the climates of those two regions?

(c) Infer How might the people who lived in these regions have adapted to their geography and climate?
2. (a) Recall How much land did the Incan Empire cover at its greatest extent?
(b) Explain How did the government in Cuzco keep track of distant parts of the empire?
(c) Draw Conclusions What do you think were the major problems of keeping such a large empire running smoothly? Explain your answer.

Writing Activity
If you could interview a stonemason from the Incan Empire, what would you ask? Make a list of questions you would ask in order to learn how these skilled workers accomplished so much so long ago. Then write a paragraph explaining why you want to ask the questions.

For: An activity on the Incas
Visit: PHSchool.com
Web Code: lgd-8301

Skills for Life ✓

Identifying Cause and Effect

Wondering why things happen is something every human being does. Why does the sun rise in the east? Why does the United States have a president and not a king? Why did the Incas build Machu Picchu? This curiosity has driven people to ask how history has shaped our world. When we ask "why" about something, we are really trying to figure out causes and effects.

A cause is something that makes an event or a situation happen. An effect is a result of a cause. When you identify cause and effect, you understand how an action or several actions led to a particular result. Causes and effects can be short term or long term.

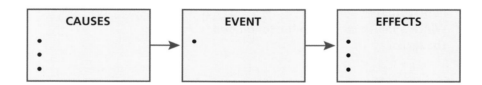

CAUSES	EVENT	EFFECTS
• • •	•	• • •

Learn the Skill

Use these steps to understand cause-and-effect relationships.

1 **Choose one event or condition as a starting point.** Determine whether in this case it is a cause or an effect.

2 **Look at earlier events or conditions for possible causes.** Also look for clue words that signal cause, such as *because*, *so*, and *since*. Words such as *therefore*, *then*, *reason*, and *as a result* signal effects.

3 **Make a cause-and-effect diagram.** A diagram like the one above can help you understand cause-and-effect relationships. Remember that sometimes an effect becomes a cause for another effect.

4 **Summarize the cause-and-effect relationships.** Be sure to include all of the causes and effects.

An Incan woman weaving

Incan Taxes

The Incas did not use money. Even so, villages had to pay taxes on their harvest and herds. To do so, they gave one third of their crops and animals to the empire. Villages could also pay their taxes by having their people do special work.

For this reason, every village sent a few young men and women to work for the empire. Some made jewelry, textiles, or pottery for nobles. Many men worked as soldiers or miners. Others built buildings or inspected roads or bridges.

In return, the government gave something back to the villages. The poor, the old, and the sick received government help.

Practice the Skill

Follow the steps in Learn the Skill to look for causes and effects in the passage above.

1. Read the passage. Find one event or condition that can serve as your starting point. Decide if it is a cause or an effect. How might the title help you?

2. What facts or conditions led to the way Incas paid taxes? What clue words in the second paragraph signal cause and effect?

3. Make a cause-and-effect diagram. Check for effects that in turn become causes for other effects. Expand your diagram if you need to.

4. Summarize the cause-and-effect relationships you have discovered.

Incan men building a fortress

Apply the Skill

Reread the two paragraphs under the heading The Decline of the Incan Empire on page 67. Use the steps in this skill to identify the causes and effects described in the passage. Make a cause-and-effect diagram or write a paragraph explaining the cause-and-effect relationships you find.

Cultures of Middle America

Prepare to Read

Objectives

In this section, you will
1. Learn about the Mayan culture of Middle America.
2. Find out about the powerful Aztec Empire.

Taking Notes

As you read this section, look for the characteristics of the Mayan and Aztec civilizations. Copy the web diagram below and record your findings for the Mayas. Then make a similar diagram for the Aztecs.

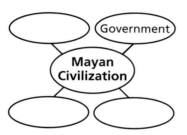

Target Reading Skill

Identify Supporting Details Sentences in a paragraph may give further details that support the main idea. These details may give examples, explanations, or reasons. In the first paragraph on page 71, this sentence states the main idea: "Thousands of years before the Aztecs built Tenochtitlán, other cultures thrived in Middle America." Note three details that support this main idea.

Key Terms

- **Aztecs** (AZ teks) *n.* a people who lived in the Valley of Mexico
- **Tenochtitlán** (teh nawch tee TLAHN) *n.* capital city of the Aztecs
- **Mayas** (MAH yuhz) *n.* a people who established a great civilization in Middle America
- **slash-and-burn agriculture** (slash and burn AG rih kul chur) *n.* a farming technique in which trees are cut down and burned to clear and fertilize the land
- **maize** (mayz) *n.* corn
- **hieroglyphics** (hy ur oh GLIF iks) *n.* the signs and symbols that made up the Mayan writing system

This page dating from the 1500s illustrates the Aztec legend. A version of it forms part of the Mexican flag today.

In about 1325, the **Aztecs** (AZ teks), a people who lived in the Valley of Mexico, began looking for a place to build a new capital. According to legend, the Aztecs asked their god of war where they should build this capital. He replied, "Build at the place where you see an eagle perched on a cactus and holding a snake in its beak."

When the Aztecs found the sign their god had described, they were surprised. The cactus on which the eagle perched was growing on a swampy island in the center of Lake Texcoco. It was an unlikely setting for an important city. But they believed their god had given them this sign, and so this was the place where the Aztecs built **Tenochtitlán** (teh nawch tee TLAHN), their capital. It would become one of the largest and finest cities of its time.

The Culture of the Mayas

Thousands of years before the Aztecs built Tenochtitlán, other cultures thrived in Middle America. One of these ancient peoples, called the Olmec (AHL mek), lived along the Gulf Coast from about 1200 B.C. until about 600 B.C. The Olmec are known for their pyramid-shaped temples and huge carved stone heads.

Somewhat later, an important culture developed in parts of Central America and the Yucatán Peninsula to the north. The Yucatán Peninsula is located at Mexico's southeastern tip. These people, called the **Mayas** (MAH yuhz), established a great civilization and built many cities in this region of Middle America. The Mayas may have been influenced by Olmec culture. The Mayan way of life lasted for many centuries. Its greatest period was from about A.D. 250 until 900.

Olmec statues like this one were usually several feet tall.

A Farming Culture Mayan life was based on farming. To grow crops, Mayan farmers used a technique called **slash-and-burn agriculture.** They first cleared the land by cutting down trees. They then burned the tree stumps, saving the ash to use as fertilizer. Finally, they planted seeds. After a few years, however, the soil would be worn out. The farmers would then have to clear and plant a new area.

Mayan farmers grew a variety of crops, including beans, squash, peppers, papayas (puh PY uz), and avocados. But their most common crop was **maize** (mayz), or corn. In fact, maize was so important to the Mayas that one of the gods they worshiped was a god of corn. And since the corn needed the sun and rain to grow, it is not surprising that the Mayas also worshipped a rain god and a sun god.

Tikal—Ruins of a Great City
Tikal, located in Guatemala, was once a thriving Mayan city. The city and its surrounding areas had a population of nearly 100,000. **Infer** *Judging from the photo, what challenge probably faced Mayan farmers who lived in this region?*

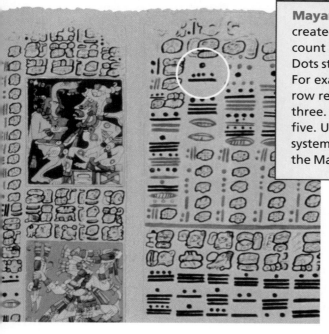

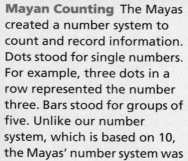

Links to
Math

Mayan Counting The Mayas created a number system to count and record information. Dots stood for single numbers. For example, three dots in a row represented the number three. Bars stood for groups of five. Unlike our number system, which is based on 10, the Mayas' number system was based on 20. So, to record a number larger than 19, they used one large dot standing alone to represent the number 20, and more large dots for larger numbers divisible by 20. Dots and bars were used to make up the rest of the number. In the Mayan book at left, the number 29 is circled in white.

Centers of Religion and Government Mayan cities were religious and governmental centers. A different ruler commanded each city. Priests and nobles were also important community leaders. These leaders lived in large palaces within the city. Ordinary people lived on the edges of the city. Each city held great festivals to honor the many Mayan gods. The most important religious events took place at large temple-pyramids. Some of the ceremonies included human sacrifice.

Skilled mathematicians, Mayan priests developed a calendar to plan when to hold religious celebrations. The Mayas also created a system of writing using signs and symbols called hieroglyphics. They used these hieroglyphics to record information in books made from the bark of fig trees.

A Mayan Game Cities also had outdoor courts where a special ball game called pok-ta-tok was played. A court was about the size of a football field, and the game was a bit like soccer and basketball combined. The ball was made of hard rubber. Players tried to knock it through a stone hoop set on a wall. They could hit the ball with their elbows, knees, or hips—but not with their hands or feet. The ball could not touch the ground.

The Mayas Abandon Their Cities Around A.D. 900, the Mayas abandoned their cities, and their civilization declined. No one knows the exact reason they left. Crop failures, war, disease, or overuse of natural resources may have altered the Mayan way of life. Or people may have rebelled against their leaders. Today, descendants of the Mayas still live in Middle America. Many continue some of the cultural traditions of their Mayan ancestors.

✓ **Reading Check** **What did Mayan priests do?**

Target Skill **Identify Supporting Details**
What details in the paragraph at right support the main idea that the Mayas had an important culture?

The Aztec Empire

You have already read that the Aztecs built their new capital, Tenochtitlán, in the middle of a lake in about 1325. They had first settled in the Valley of Mexico in the 1100s. By the 1470s, the Aztecs had conquered the surrounding lands. Their large empire stretched from the Gulf of Mexico in the east to the Pacific Ocean in the west. A single powerful leader, the Aztec emperor, ruled these lands. All the people he conquered were forced to pay him tribute, or heavy taxes, in the form of food, gold, or slaves.

Find out how Cortés defeated the Aztecs.

Waterways and Gardens In spite of its swampy origins, Tenochtitlán became a magnificent capital city. At its center were an open plaza and one or more towering pyramid-temples. There were schools for the sons of the nobles and large stone palaces. Raised streets of hard earth, called causeways, connected the city to the surrounding land. To supply the city with enough fresh water, the Aztecs also built aqueducts. These special channels carried spring water from distant sources to storage areas in the city.

As the population of Tenochtitlán grew, the Aztecs realized they needed more farmland. Their solution was to build many island gardens in the shallow lakes around the capital. These raised fields, called chinampas (chih NAM puz), were made from rich soil dredged up from the lake bottom. Trees planted along the edges prevented soil from washing away. Between the fields were canals. Farmers used the canals to transport produce by boats to a huge marketplace near the capital.

Floating Gardens Today
A man poles a boat among the chinampas on the outskirts of Mexico City. **Draw Conclusions** *List some advantages and disadvantages of growing crops on chinampas.*

Religion and Learning To bring about good harvests, Aztec priests held ceremonies that would win the favor of their gods. Their most important god was the sun god. Aztec religion taught that the sun would not have the strength to rise and cross the sky every day without human blood. Of course, if the sun did not rise, crops could not grow, and the people would starve. Therefore, Aztec religious ceremonies included human sacrifice. The Aztecs also prayed to their gods for victory in war. Prisoners captured in war often served as human sacrifices.

To schedule their religious festivals and farming cycles, Aztec priests created a calendar based on the Mayan calendar and their own knowledge of astronomy. The calendar had 13 periods, like months, of 20 days each. The Aztecs also kept records using hieroglyphs similar to those used by the Mayas.

Tenochtitlán had schools and a university. Boys from noble families attended these schools. They studied to be government officials, teachers, or scribes.

Aztec Society Aztec society had a strict class structure. The emperor, of course, was most important. Next were members of the royal family, nobles, priests, and military leaders. Soldiers were next in importance. Below soldiers came artisans—skilled creators of jewelry, pottery, sculpture, and other goods—and merchants. Then came the farmers. They made up the largest class of people. The lowest position in Aztec society was held by slaves, most of whom were prisoners captured in battle.

War was a part of life in the Aztec Empire, as new territory was conquered. Most young men over the age of 15 served as soldiers for a period of time. They were well trained and well equipped. Soldiers had swords and bows and arrows. For protection, they had special armor made from heavy quilted cotton. Priests and government officials did not serve in the military.

Aztec Gods and Goddesses
The Aztec God Quetzalcoatl (top) was the god of priests, and was believed to have invented the Aztec calendar. Above is the Aztec maize goddess. Both figures appear often in Aztec art.
Make Generalizations *What does the worship of gods and goddesses such as these tell you about Aztec society?*

Aztec women were not allowed to work as soldiers or military leaders, though they could train to be priestesses. Most women—even women from noble families—had to be skilled at weaving. Some of the cloth they wove was used for trade. Some was used to decorate temples. The finest cloth was used to make clothing for the Aztec royal family and nobles. Before teenage girls learned to weave, they were expected to grind flour, make tortillas, and cook meals.

The End of an Empire In 1519, Spanish conquistadors invaded the Aztec Empire. Some of the peoples whose lands the Aztecs had conquered joined forces with the Spanish. Together, they fought the Aztecs and tried to overthrow the Aztec emperor, Moctezuma. The two sides waged fierce battles. Diseases carried by the Spanish spread to the Aztecs and killed many of them. In 1521, the Aztecs surrendered to the Spanish. The once-powerful Aztec Empire was at an end.

✓ Reading Check **Describe the levels of Aztec society.**

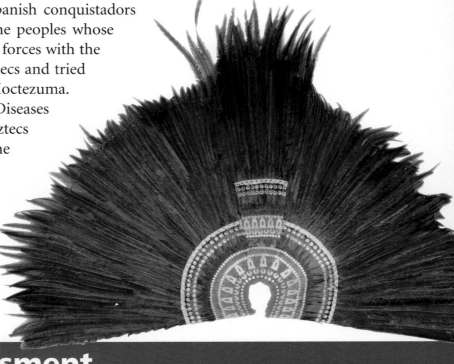

Aztec Feather Headdress
Moctezuma's head covering was decorated with feathers—an important symbol in the Aztec religion.

Section 2 Assessment

Key Terms
Review the key terms at the beginning of this section. Use each term in a sentence that explains its meaning.

Target Reading Skill
State three details that support the main idea of the first paragraph under the heading Aztec Society.

Comprehension and Critical Thinking
1. (a) Recall What activity was the basis of Mayan life?

(b) Explain How did Mayan religion reflect the importance of this activity?
(c) Infer What do you think is the most likely reason the Mayas abandoned their cities? Explain your choice.
2. (a) Describe How did the Aztec Empire expand?
(b) Synthesize How did the Aztecs treat the peoples they conquered in war?
(c) Draw Conclusions Why might some of the peoples conquered by the Aztecs have wanted to overthrow the emperor?

Writing Activity
The Mayas and the Aztecs created great civilizations. How were their cultures alike? How were they different? Write a paragraph comparing and contrasting the two civilizations.

Writing Tip First take notes on the similarities and differences. You may want to use a chart to help you organize. Be sure to write a topic sentence for your paragraph, and then support it with details from your notes.

In 1521, the Spanish conquered the Aztecs and began to destroy the Aztec capital of Tenochtitlán. On the site of the ruined Aztec city, they built a new capital: Mexico City. For many years, an important piece of Mexico's past—the Great Temple of the Aztecs—remained buried under this new city. Scholars were not sure where the site of the Great Temple lay. Then in 1978, electrical workers dug up an old stone carving. Experts who studied the carving knew that it had been made by the Aztecs. The site of the Great Temple had been found.

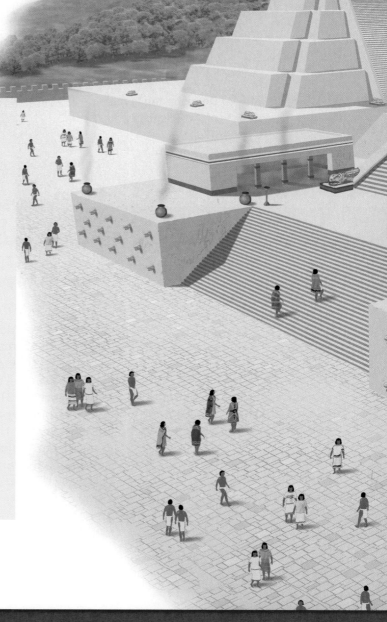

Building the Temple The Great Temple honored two Aztec gods: Tlaloc (tlah LOHK), the god of earth and rain, and Huitzilopochtli (weets eel oh POHCH tlee), the god of sun and sky. The Aztecs first built the temple about 1325. A solid, earth-filled pyramid, the heavy temple soon began to sink into the soft soil of Tenochtitlán. To save their sinking monument, the Aztecs rebuilt it six times within the next 200 years.

The Aztecs rebuilt each new temple over the previous temple. After rebuilding, they honored their gods with human sacrifices in the temple's shrines. A figure called a chacmool, at the top left, was used to hold offerings to the gods.

The illustration at the right shows some of the temple layers. By the time the Spanish began to destroy Tenochtitlán in 1521, the Great Temple had been built seven times.

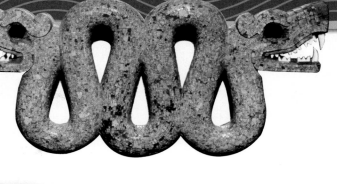

Sacred Ornament
The double-headed serpent was a symbol of Tlaloc, the god of earth and rain. A high priest probably wore this ornament on his chest.

Shrines
The shrine at the left honored the god Tlaloc. The shrine at the right honored the god Huitzilopochtli.

Stone Disk
A stone carving of Huitzilopochtli's sister Coyolxauhqui (koh yohl SHAH kee) was part of the sixth temple layer.

Assessment

Identify Name the two main gods the Aztecs honored at the Great Temple.

Infer Why were these gods so important to the Aztecs?

Cultures of North America

Prepare to Read

Objectives

In this section, you will

1. Find out about the Mound Builders who lived in eastern North America.
2. Learn about the cultures of the Southwest and the Great Plains.
3. Find out about the Woodland peoples of North America.

Taking Notes

As you read this section, look for information about three major Native American cultures. Copy the table below and record your findings in it. Add categories as needed.

Culture	Location	Source of Food	Type of Dwelling

Target Reading Skill

Identify Implied Main Ideas Identifying main ideas can help you remember what you read. Even if a main idea is not stated directly, the details in a paragraph add up to the main idea. For example, the details in the paragraph under the heading The Eastern Mound Builders add up to this main idea: The Mound Builders, hunters and gatherers who relied on the land's resources, became settled farmers over time.

Key Terms

- **Mound Builders** (mownd BIL durz) *n.* Native American groups who built earthen mounds
- **Anasazi** (ah nuh SAH zee) *n.* one of the ancient Native American peoples of the Southwest
- **pueblo** (PWEB loh) *n.* a Native American stone or adobe dwelling, part of a cluster of dwellings built close together
- **kiva** (KEE vuh) *n.* a round room used by the pueblo people for religious ceremonies
- **Great Plains** (grayt playnz) *n.* a mostly flat and grassy region of western North America

A Mississippian copper sculpture dating from the 1000s

Seen from above, a huge snake seems to twist and turn across the landscape. A mysterious shape—perhaps an egg?—is at its mouth. This enormous earthwork was created hundreds of years ago in what is now Ohio. Called the Great Serpent Mound, it is the largest image of a snake anywhere in the world. Uncoiled, the serpent would be about 1,349 feet (411 meters) long.

Archaeologists have found more than 1,000 earthen mounds across eastern North America. They were made by thousands of workers moving baskets of earth by hand. There are small mounds and large ones. Some contain graves, but others—like the Great Serpent Mound—do not. Most were constructed between around 700 B.C. and A.D. 1250. Today, we call the different Native American groups who built these curious and long-lasting mounds the **Mound Builders**.

The Eastern Mound Builders

The Mound Builders lived in eastern North America. They occupied the region roughly between Minnesota and Louisiana, and between the Mississippi River and the Atlantic Ocean. The Mound Builders lived along the area's many rivers, which provided them with plenty of fish and fresh water. They hunted wild animals for food, including deer, turkeys, bears, and even squirrels. They also gathered nuts such as acorns, pecans, and walnuts to supplement their diet. Over time, these communities began to grow their own food. This meant they did not have to move as much in search of food and could form settlements.

Early Mound Builders: The Adena Archaeologists have discovered evidence of early Mound Builders who lived about 600 B.C. in the Ohio Valley. Called the Adena (uh DEE nuh), these people constructed mounds that are usually less than 20 feet high. Certain mounds were tombs that contained weapons, tools, and decorative objects in addition to bodies. Some items were made from materials not found locally, such as copper and seashells. Thus, historians believe that the Adena must have taken part in long-distance trade. Little is known about the daily life of the Adena, but they seem to have declined about 100 B.C.

Great Serpent Mound
The Great Serpent Mound snakes across Ohio's countryside.
Infer *What about the mound suggests that it may have had religious importance?*

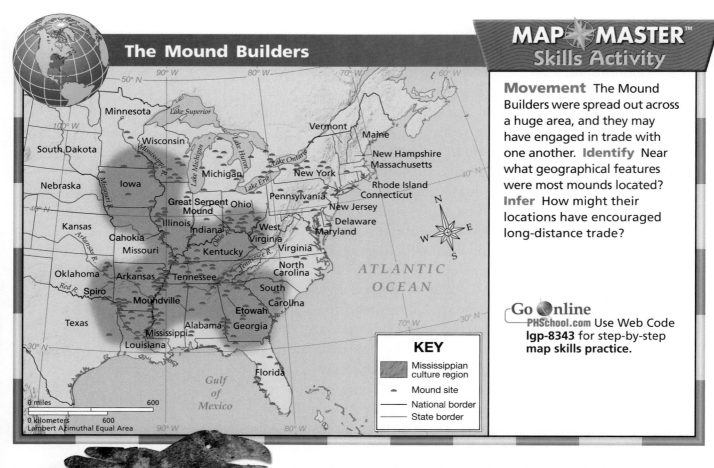

MAP★MASTER™
Skills Activity

Movement The Mound Builders were spread out across a huge area, and they may have engaged in trade with one another. **Identify** Near what geographical features were most mounds located? **Infer** How might their locations have encouraged long-distance trade?

Go Online
PHSchool.com Use Web Code **lgp-8343** for step-by-step map skills practice.

KEY
▧ Mississippian culture region
◣ Mound site
— National border
— State border

The Hopewell made figures like the copper raven (above) and the hand (bottom right), which is made of mica, a soft mineral.

The Hopewell Culture About 100 years before the Adena disappeared, another culture appeared along the Ohio and upper Mississippi rivers. Called the Hopewell, these peoples built larger mounds. The Hopewell did not have a highly organized society with a single ruler. Instead, they lived in many small communities with local leaders.

The Hopewell peoples grew a greater variety of crops than did the Adena. They also seem to have traded over a wider area. There is evidence that goods were traded from the Gulf of Mexico to present-day Canada and from the Rocky Mountains to the Atlantic Ocean. Hopewell sites have silver from the Great Lakes region and alligator teeth from present-day Florida.

About A.D. 400, the long-distance trade across eastern North America seems to have faded out. Also, the Hopewell stopped building new mounds. Historians are not sure why. The climate may have turned colder and hurt agriculture. The Hopewell may have suffered a severe drought or been invaded. Overpopulation is also a possible reason for their decline.

The Mississippians By about A.D. 700, a new and important culture called Mississippian (mis uh SIP ee un) began to flower in eastern North America. These peoples inhabited both small and large communities. Like the earlier Mound Builders, the Mississippians lived along rivers and built mounds. They, too, grew new kinds of crops. Maize and beans became important parts of their diet. Both foods are easily dried and stored in large amounts. This helped the Mississippians protect themselves against years of drought and bad harvests.

The Mississippian culture spread over a wide area in the present-day South and Midwest. During this period, long-distance trade revived. Populations increased over time, and major centers of government and religion developed. These include Moundville in present-day Alabama, and Etowah (ET uh wah) in present-day Georgia. The largest center was Cahokia (kuh HOH kee uh), located in what is now Illinois. One of Cahokia's mounds, around 100 feet tall, was the largest mound in North America.

Cahokia was a large city for its day. Historians estimate that it reached its peak about A.D. 1100. At that time, as many as 20,000 to 30,000 people may have lived there. But by 1250, the population dropped. The disappearance of the last of the Mound Builders is as mystifying as the many earthworks they left behind.

✓ **Reading Check** **How did the Mississippians live?**

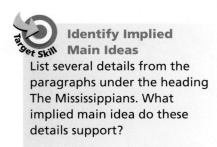

Identify Implied Main Ideas
List several details from the paragraphs under the heading The Mississippians. What implied main idea do these details support?

An archaeologist digs at Chaco Canyon, New Mexico.

Peoples of the Southwest and the Great Plains

The mounds of the Mound Builders are not the only amazing structures built by early Native American cultures. Other peoples in North America adapted to different landscapes and climates to create distinctive structures. One of these groups created remarkable multistory homes from the available materials of the Southwest.

The Ancient Ones The **Anasazi** (ah nuh SAH zee) were an ancient Native American peoples of the Southwest. Their name can be translated as "the ancient ones." Anasazi culture began about A.D. 100. Historians think that Chaco Canyon, in present-day New Mexico, was a trading center for the region. A network of roads connected distant Anasazi villages to Chaco Canyon. Archaeologists have found tens of thousands of turquoise pieces as well as baskets, pottery, shells, and feathers in Chaco Canyon.

Anasazi Cliff Village
Entire villages of Anasazi people lived under the shelter of massive stone cliffs like this one in Colorado. Anasazi craftspeople decorated pottery like the jar above with black and white patterns.
Analyze Images *What might be some advantages to living under cliffs like these?*

Southwestern North America has harsh winters in some areas and hot, dry summers. The soil is mostly poor, and there is little water. To capture rainwater for their fields, the Anasazi created a system of canals and dams. This system allowed them to grow maize, beans, and squash for food. They also grew cotton for cloth.

For their homes, the Anasazi constructed **pueblos** (PWEB lohz). These stone and adobe dwellings, built next to one another, helped to keep people warm in the winter and cool in the summer. Pueblos had thick walls, and many had high ceilings. Round rooms called **kivas** (KEE vuz) were used for special religious ceremonies. As the population grew, so did the pueblos. Some pueblos were five stories tall and had hundreds of rooms. Between 1275 and 1300, however, severe droughts hit the region. The Anasazi abandoned all their major pueblos, never to return.

Later Pueblo Peoples Anasazi customs survived among later groups who lived to the south of the Anasazi sites. They are called Pueblo peoples, or simply Pueblos. These groups also built apartment-style stone and adobe dwellings with kivas. Like the Anasazi, their crafts included weaving, basket-making, and pottery. They were also skilled farmers.

The region of New Mexico where the Pueblos lived receives only 8 to 13 inches of rain a year, but it does have rivers. The Pueblos planted corn, squash, beans, and other crops in the river bottoms near their dwellings. They relied on intensive irrigation to raise these crops. Hunting and gathering provided the Pueblos with the food they could not grow.

The Pueblos believed in many spirits, called kachinas (kuh CHEE nuz). They wanted to please these spirits, who they believed controlled the rain, wild animals, and harvests. Many times a year, the Pueblos gathered for ceremonies that involved prayer, dancing, and singing. They also appealed to their ancestors, another type of kachina. Today the modern descendants of the Pueblo peoples, including the Hopi and the Zuni, keep many of these traditions alive.

The Plains Indians West of the Mississippi River and east of the Rocky Mountains is a mostly flat and grassy region called the **Great Plains.** For centuries, this land was home to diverse groups of Native Americans called Plains Indians. Individual groups had their own languages and traditions. They used a form of sign language to trade with one another.

Some groups, such as the Mandan, were farmers. They lived in fenced villages along the Missouri River, in lodges made of earth and wood. Others, such as the Sioux (soo), followed herds of bison that roamed the plains. Dwellings such as tipis (TEE peaz)—easy to take apart, carry, and set up again—were ideal for such a lifestyle.

After the arrival of Europeans, the lives of Plains Indians changed rapidly. They had to share their land with eastern Native Americans, such as the Omaha, who had been forced west by white settlers. Newly introduced horses, guns, and railroads altered their traditions. Most groups suffered from diseases brought by Europeans and lost their land to European settlement. Many Native American cultures began to break down. Today, there is a strong effort to revive these traditional cultures.

√ Reading Check **How did the Sioux live?**

Links Across The World

The Arrival of the Horse
The arrival of the horse in the Americas brought major changes to the lives of many Plains Indians. Native Americans on horseback became expert buffalo hunters. They came to depend more and more on the buffalo for their existence, using the animal for food, clothing, and shelter. Many previously settled Indian groups became nomadic. They rode their horses across the plains, following the great herds of buffalo.

Peoples of the Woodlands

Native American groups lived in woodlands in different parts of present-day Canada and the United States. The peoples of the Northwest Coast hunted in the forests and fished in rivers full of salmon as well as in the Pacific Ocean. They lived in settlements of wooden homes. Like the Mound Builders and the Pueblos, early Native Americans of the Northwest Coast created remarkable structures. They were called totem poles.

Totem poles were carved and painted logs stood on end. They typically had images of real or mythical animals. Often the animals were identified with the owner's family line, much as a family crest is used in European cultures. Totem poles were a symbol of the owner's wealth, as were ceremonies called potlatches. At a potlatch, a person of high rank invited many guests and gave them generous gifts.

In the eastern woodlands, Native American groups such as the Iroquois (IHR uh kwoy) not only hunted in the forests but also cleared land for farms. Because the men were often at war, the women were the farmers. In the 1500s, five Iroquois nations—Mohawk, Onondaga, Cayuga, Seneca, and Oneida—formed a peace alliance. Nations of the Iroquois League governed their own villages, but they met to decide issues that affected the group as a whole. This was the best-organized political system in the Americas when Europeans arrived.

Totem pole in Vancouver, Canada

✓ **Reading Check** **What was the Iroquois League?**

Section 3 Assessment

Key Terms
Review the key terms at the beginning of this section. Use each term in a sentence that explains its meaning.

Target Reading Skill
State the main ideas in Section 3.

Comprehension and Critical Thinking
1. (a) Sequence List the three groups of Mound Builders, from earliest to latest.

(b) Compare In what ways were the three groups alike?

2. (a) Identify What is the climate of southwestern North America?

(b) Identify Cause and Effect Why did peoples of this region build pueblos rather than other types of structures?

3. (a) Define What are totem poles and potlatches?

(b) Infer Why were totem poles and potlatches symbols of a family's wealth?

Writing Activity
Study the photograph of the Anasazi cliff dwellings on pages 82–83. Write a paragraph describing the site. What are the buildings like? Where are they located? What might it be like there at night or during a storm?

> **Writing Tip** Use descriptive adjectives for colors, textures, and shapes. Also include any sounds and smells you might experience there at different times of the day or year.

Chapter 3

Review and Assessment

◆ Chapter Summary

Section 1: South America and the Incas

- The varied geography and climate of the Americas produced a diversity of Native American peoples and cultures.
- The Incas ruled a large, highly organized mountain empire in South America. Their accomplishments included long-lasting stone structures.

Section 2: Cultures of Middle America

- Mayan civilization was based on farming, which supported cities throughout the Yucatán Peninsula of Middle America.
- The Aztecs ruled a rich and powerful empire of diverse peoples in Middle America, from a magnificent capital called Tenochtitlán.

Aztec feather headdress

Section 3: Cultures of North America

- The Mound Builders lived along the rivers of eastern North America and built thousands of earthen mounds across the region.
- The Anasazi, and later the Pueblo peoples, adapted to the dry environment of the Southwest, while the Plains Indians farmed or followed herds of buffalo.
- Woodlands peoples of the Northwest Coast were hunters and fishers. In eastern forests, the Iroquois League was formed to bring peace to the region.

Anasazi clay vessel

◆ Key Terms

Match each term with its definition.

1. quipu
2. kivas
3. hieroglyphics
4. census
5. pueblos
6. maize
7. terraces

A corn
B an official count of people
C steplike ledges cut into mountains
D stone dwellings, built next to one another
E group of knotted strings used to record information
F round rooms used for religious ceremonies
G signs and symbols that made up the Mayan writing system

Review and Assessment (continued)

◆ Comprehension and Critical Thinking

8. (a) **Describe** What special farming methods were developed by the Incas and the Aztecs?
(b) **Compare** How were these methods similar?
(c) **Analyze Information** How did each method suit the geography of the region where it was used?

9. (a) **Recall** What type of government did Mayan cities have?
(b) **Analyze** Why is it not correct to call Mayan civilization an "empire"?
(c) **Make Generalizations** If a civilization like that of the Mayas came under attack, would it be easy or hard to defend? Explain your answer.

10. (a) **Identify** What city was the capital of the Aztec Empire?
(b) **Describe** What was this capital city like?
(c) **Generalize** In what ways are modern capital cities like the Aztec capital?

11. (a) **Locate** Where in North America are human-built mounds located?
(b) **Synthesize** What have archaeologists learned from studying these mounds?
(c) **Analyze** Why is it difficult to determine the exact use of some mounds?

12. (a) **Describe** Where are the Great Plains, and what are they like?
(b) **Identify Cause and Effect** What changes to their way of life did many Plains Indians experience, and why?
(c) **Infer** Why do you think some Plains Indians battled with European settlers?

◆ Skills Practice

Identifying Cause and Effect Review the steps to identify causes and effects that you learned in the Skills for Life activity in this chapter. Then reread the part of Section 3 titled The Plains Indians. Choose an event from this section, and decide if it is a cause or an effect. Look for earlier or later events that might be causes or effects. Then summarize the cause-and-effect relationships you have identified.

◆ Writing Activity: Science

Review this chapter to find out which crops were grown or collected for food by early Native Americans. Choose three crops. Do research to find out why each one might be important to a healthful diet. To which food group does it belong? What is its nutritional value? How is it different from or similar to other foods eaten by these people? Write a brief report on what you learn.

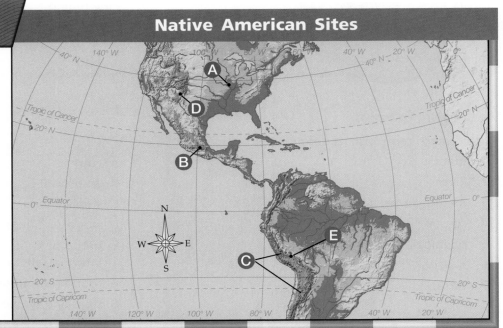

MAP MASTER™ Skills Activity

Native American Sites

Place Location For each place or feature listed below, write the letter from the map that shows its location.
1. Cuzco
2. Cahokia
3. Andes
4. Tenochtitlán
5. Chaco Canyon

Go Online
PHSchool.com Use Web Code lgp-8353 for an interactive map.

Standardized Test Prep

Test-Taking Tips

Some questions on standardized tests ask you to analyze a timeline. Study the timeline below. Then follow the tips to answer the sample question.

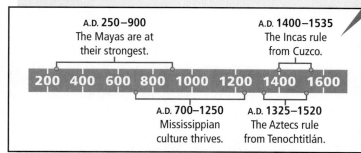

A.D. 250–900
The Mayas are at their strongest.

A.D. 1400–1535
The Incas rule from Cuzco.

200 400 600 800 1000 1200 1400 1600

A.D. 700–1250
Mississippian culture thrives.

A.D. 1325–1520
The Aztecs rule from Tenochtitlán.

> **TIP** Use the lines at the beginning and end of each civilization bracket to calculate how long each civilization lasted.

Think It Through You can see that the line marking the end of Mississippian culture falls after 1200. Therefore A is incorrect. "The Incas rule from Cuzco" starts at 1400 and ends before 1600, so you can rule out B, too. The brackets on the timeline show that the Incas and the Aztecs did live at the same time. And the dates for the Aztecs, 1325–1520, overlap with the dates for the Incas, 1400–1535. So C is incorrect. That leaves only D. You can see that the line marking the start of Mississippian culture does indeed fall halfway between 600 and 800. D is the correct answer.

> **TIP** Preview the question and skim over the answer choices before you look at the timeline. Keep the questions and possible answers in mind as you study the timeline.

Choose the letter of the best answer.

Based on the timeline, which statement is true?

A Mississippian culture ended at A.D. 1100.

B The Incas ruled from Cuzco for more than 400 years.

C The Aztecs and the Incas did not live at the same time.

D Mississippian culture began to thrive about A.D. 700.

Practice Questions

Use the timeline above to help you choose the letter of the best answer.

1. Based on the timeline, which statement is true?

   A The Incas began to rule from Cuzco about A.D. 1000.

   B The Aztecs and the Incas did not live at the same time.

   C The Mayas were at their strongest for more than 600 years.

   D Mississippian culture lasted for only 200 years.

Choose the letter of the best answer to complete each sentence.

2. The _____ built stone and adobe dwellings close together.

   A Incas

   B Hopewell peoples

   C Anasazi

   D Adena

3. The spectacular site of Machu Picchu is located in

   A the Great Plains.

   B South America.

   C North America.

   D Lake Texcoco.

4. The _____ lived along rivers in eastern North America.

   A Mound Builders

   B Aztecs

   C Mayas

   D Pueblo peoples

Use Web Code **lga-8303** for a **Chapter 3 self-test.**

Chapter Preview

This chapter will introduce you to the civilizations that thrived in China, Japan, and India during the medieval period.

Section 1
Golden Ages of China

Section 2
Medieval Japan

Section 3
The Great Mughal Empire in India

Target Reading Skill

Cause and Effect In this chapter you will focus on determining cause and effect in order to help you understand relationships among situations and events.

▶ A large stone statue of the Buddha in the Qian Qi Temple Cave, China, carved during the Tang dynasty

Civilizations of Asia

MAP MASTER™
Skills Activity

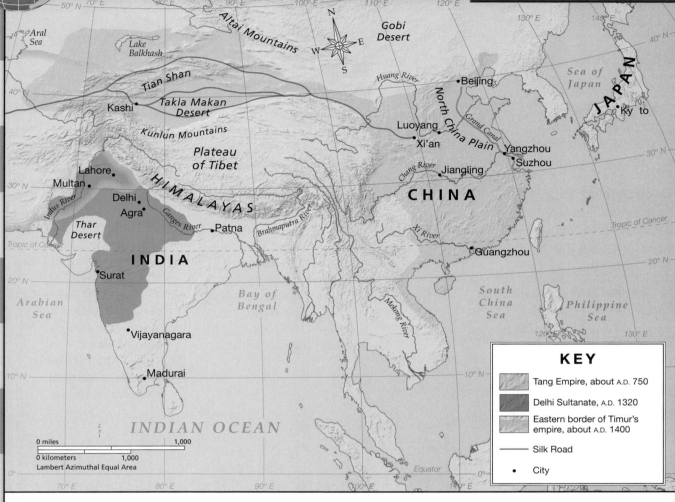

Aral
Sea

Lake
Balkhash

Altai Mountains

Gobi
Desert

N
W   E
S

50° N   70° E   80° E   90° E   100° E   110° E   120° E   130° E   140° E   40° N

Tian Shan

Kashi

Takla Makan
Desert

Kunlun Mountains

Huang River

Beijing

North China Plain

Sea of
Japan

JAPAN

Ky to

40° N

Luoyang

Xi'an

Grand Canal

30° N

Lahore

Multan

Delhi

Agra

HIMALAYAS

Plateau
of Tibet

Ganges River

Patna

Brahmaputra River

Chang River

Jiangling

CHINA

Yangzhou

Suzhou

Thar
Desert

Indus River

Tropic of Cancer

INDIA

Surat

Xi River

Guangzhou

Tropic of Cancer

20° N

Arabian
Sea

Bay of
Bengal

South
China
Sea

Philippine
Sea

20° N

Vijayanagara

Mekong River

10° N

10° N

Madurai

INDIAN OCEAN

0 miles   1,000

0 kilometers   1,000
Lambert Azimuthal Equal Area

Equator

0°

70° E   80° E   90° E   100° E   110° E   120° E   130° E

KEY

Tang Empire, about A.D. 750

Delhi Sultanate, A.D. 1320

Eastern border of Timur's
empire, about A.D. 1400

Silk Road

• City

Regions Between the A.D. 600s and 1400s, several great empires arose in Asia. **Locate** Find the Tang Empire and describe its shape. Find the trade routes called the Silk Road. **Infer** How do you think the Silk Road affected the Tang Empire?

Go Online
PHSchool.com Use Web Code
lgp-8411 for step-by-step
map skills practice.

Chapter 4 **89**

Section 1 — Golden Ages of China

Prepare to Read

Objectives

In this section you will
1. Learn about the Golden Age of the Tang dynasty.
2. Discover the achievements of the Song dynasty, which ruled China after the Tang.
3. Find out about Mongol rule of China.

Taking Notes

As you read this section, look for similarities and differences between the Tang and Song dynasties. Copy the diagram below and record your findings in it.

Two Dynasties of China

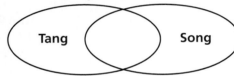

Tang — Song

Target Reading Skill

Identify Causes and Effects A cause makes something happen. An effect is what happens. Determining causes and effects helps you understand relationships among situations and events. As you read this section, think of the cultures of the Tang and Song dynasties as effects. Write their characteristics in your Taking Notes diagram. Then look for the causes of these effects.

Key Terms

- **Silk Road** (silk rohd) *n.* a chain of trade routes stretching from China to the Mediterranean Sea
- **dynasty** (DY nus tee) *n.* a series of rulers from the same family
- **Tang** (tahng) *n.* a dynasty that ruled China for almost 300 years
- **Song** (sawng) *n.* a dynasty that ruled China after the Tang
- **merit system** (MEHR it SIS tum) *n.* a system of hiring people based on their abilities
- **Kublai Khan** (KOO bly kahn) *n.* a Mongol emperor of China

Silk from the Tang dynasty

A Chinese traveler wrote, "You see nothing in any direction but the sky and the sands, without the slightest trace of a road; and travelers find nothing to guide them but the bones of men and beasts." He was describing crossing the Gobi Desert along the Silk Road. In spite of its name, the **Silk Road** was not a single road. It was a long chain of connecting trade routes across Central Asia. These routes stretched about 4,000 miles (6,400 kilometers), all the way from China to the eastern Mediterranean Sea.

For centuries, camels, horses, and donkeys carried traders and their precious goods along the Silk Road. Travelers braved blowing desert sands, cold and rocky mountain passes, and even robbers. Most of the goods they carried were small and very valuable. One—a beautiful, lightweight fabric called silk—was so important that it gave the route its name.

The Tang Dynasty

China covers much of East Asia. It is an immense land with a varied landscape. In the east are lowland and coastal regions. Fertile valleys lie along the Chang and the Huang (hwahng) rivers. To the north and west of these farmlands are great deserts and mountainous regions, including the Gobi Desert in the north and the Plateau of Tibet in the west.

Look at the map titled Tang and Song Empires on page 92. Notice that under the Tang, the land under Chinese control stretched westward into Central Asia. Peoples from these distant areas and traders traveling along the Silk Road introduced new ideas—as well as new goods—to China. In return, the Chinese traded their tea, jade, ivory, ceramics, and silk. Chinese ideas and inventions also spread to other nations. Such exchanges helped China become an important center of trade and culture.

Guarding the Silk Road
This beacon tower along the Silk Road is in western China. **Infer** *Why do you think towers like this were built along the Silk Road?*

Dynasties Rule China Throughout its long history, China has been ruled by many different dynasties. A **dynasty** is a series of rulers from the same family. For example, the Han dynasty ruled China from 206 B.C to A.D. 220. After the collapse of the Han dynasty, China broke up into several kingdoms, but Chinese culture survived. Buddhism spread throughout China, and the arts and learning continued to develop. In 581, the Sui (swee) dynasty came to power. The Sui ruled only until 618, but they united the north and south of China for the first time in centuries.

A Golden Age Begins In 618, the Sui dynasty was overthrown. The Tang came to power and ruled China for almost 300 years. The Tang dynasty was a golden age of political and cultural achievement. Under Tang rule, China grew in both area and population. Its capital, Chang'an (chahng ahn), was the world's largest city at that time. Historians estimate that it was home to about one million people. Chang'an was shaped like a rectangle and surrounded by tall walls for protection. A variety of foods, entertainment, and fine goods were available to those who lived there.

Tang Taizong

The Grand Canal Tang leaders continued projects that had been started under the Sui. One of the largest of these projects was the creation of a huge canal.

The Grand Canal was a waterway that linked the Huang River and the Chang River. Millions of workers took part in the construction of the canal. At more than 1,000 miles (1,600 kilometers) long, it is still the longest canal ever built. The Grand Canal helped join northern and southern China and made it possible to supply the capital with large amounts of grain grown in the south.

A Great Ruler The greatest ruler of the Tang dynasty was Tang Taizong (tahng ty ZAWNG). He began his military career at the age of 16, and helped his father establish the Tang dynasty. During his rule, from 626 to 649, he was not only a successful general, but also a scholar and historian. In addition, Tang Taizong was a master of calligraphy, the art of beautiful handwriting.

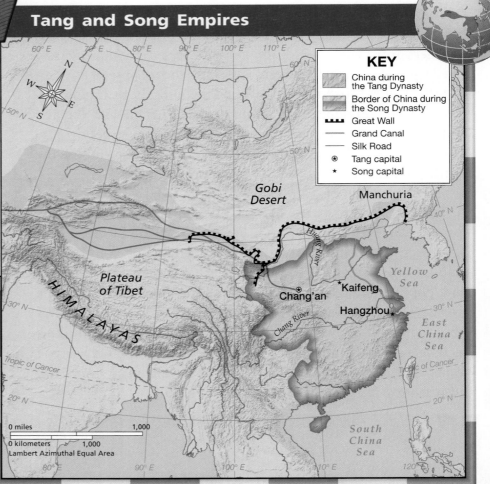

MAP☀MASTER™ Skills Activity

Regions Notice the difference in the areas controlled by the Tang and the Song dynasties. **Identify** Under which dynasty did China lose control of much of the Silk Road? **Infer** How might that have affected China's trade with lands to the west?

Go Online PHSchool.com Use Web Code lgp-8421 for step-by-step map skills practice.

Tang and Song Empires

KEY

- China during the Tang Dynasty
- Border of China during the Song Dynasty
- ▪▪▪▪ Great Wall
- ——— Grand Canal
- ——— Silk Road
- ⊛ Tang capital
- ★ Song capital

Gobi Desert

Manchuria

Plateau of Tibet

HIMALAYAS

Huang River

Yellow Sea

*Kaifeng
⊛Chang'an

Chang River

Hangzhou★

East China Sea

Tropic of Cancer

South China Sea

0 miles 1,000
0 kilometers 1,000
Lambert Azimuthal Equal Area

Late in his reign, Tang Taizong grew tired of war. He had been studying the teachings of Confucius (kun FYOO shus), an ancient Chinese teacher who had taught that all people had duties and responsibilities. Confucius had wanted to bring peace and stability to China. To create this kind of society, Confucius said, all people must treat one another with respect.

Tang Taizong began to reform the government according to Confucius's ideas. The Tang government hired officials trained in Confucian philosophy. It also began land reform, giving more land to the peasants who farmed it.

√ Reading Check **What are some achievements of Tang Taizong?**

The Song Dynasty

After 850, China's control of its westernmost lands weakened. Then fighting among different groups within China ended the Tang dynasty. Order was restored about 50 years later by the **Song** (sawng), the dynasty that ruled China from 960 to 1279.

Changes in Government At the beginning of the Song dynasty, the Chinese capital was located at Kaifeng (KY fung), along the Grand Canal. After the Song lost control of regions to the north, they moved the capital to Hangzhou (hahn JOH), near the coast.

The Song rulers made many advances in government. They expanded the **merit system** of hiring government officials. Under this system, officials had to pass tests and prove their ability to do the work. Before the Song, officials came from rich and powerful families. They were allowed to keep their positions for life even if they did not do a good job. Hiring people based on their abilities, rather than on their wealth or social position, greatly improved the Chinese government.

Improvements in Agriculture During the Song dynasty, new strains of rice and better irrigation methods helped peasants grow more rice. These two improvements allowed farmers to produce two crops a year instead of one. Food surpluses meant that more people could follow other trades or pursue the arts.

Links to
Language Arts

Poems and Legends Poetry was popular and respected during the Tang dynasty. Li Bo and Tu Fu were two of the greatest poets of the era. Li Bo was also famous for his adventurous life—once he was even accused of treason. His poems, however, dealt with quieter subjects, such as nature and friendship. After Li Bo died, this legend spread about his death: Li Bo was in a boat at night. The moon's reflection was so beautiful that he reached out to seize it, fell overboard, and drowned. This painting shows Li Bo at a waterfall.

The Arts and Trade Chinese rulers supported many different forms of art, including music and poetry. During the Song dynasty, artists created the earliest known Chinese landscape paintings. They were painted on silk and featured peaceful scenes of water, rocks, and plants. The Chinese believed that such scenes helped both the painter and the viewer think about important forces in the natural world.

Song rulers also prized graceful art objects, such as those made from porcelain (PAWR suh lin), a white and very hard type of ceramic. Because it was first made in China, porcelain is often called *china*. For hundreds of years, Chinese craftspeople produced the finest ceramics. Because the Chinese produced the best porcelain in the world, it became an important item for trade.

Another item of great beauty and value was silk. It was so beautiful that it was called the queen of fibers. Silk comes from the cocoons of caterpillars called silkworms. For a long time, only the Chinese knew how to make silk. Even after others learned the method, Chinese silk was still the highest quality in the world. People in southwest Asia and Europe were willing to pay high prices for Chinese silk.

Links to
Economics

From China to Boston Tea drinking has been a part of Chinese culture since at least A.D. 350. The custom of drinking tea spread from China to Japan and other Asian countries, and tea became a major Chinese export crop. European countries began importing tea around 1600. The English sent tea from England to their colonies in North America. Late in the 1700s, the colonists' desire for tea—and the British government's desire to tax tea—contributed to the colonies' movement toward independence.

Chinese Ceramics
Europeans paid dearly for Song dynasty wares, such as these beautiful ceramics.
Analyze Images *If you were a European trader, which of these objects would you buy? Explain your answer.*

◄ Gunpowder
The Chinese invented gunpowder in the 800s. At first, they used it to make fireworks. By about 1000, however, it was being used in weapons.

◄ Compass
In the 1000s, Chinese sailors were using the magnetic compass for navigation on long voyages. At the left is a replica of a compass from the Song dynasty.

▼ Movable Type
By 1045, Chinese printers used individual characters carved on small blocks to create a page of text. The blocks could be reused in a different order to produce various pieces of writing.

Smallpox Vaccine
As early as the 900s, the Chinese fought smallpox with a vaccine. They gave tiny doses of smallpox to healthy people so that they would develop an immunity to the deadly disease.

Printing, Books, and Learning One of the historic Song inventions was a new way to print books. For centuries, the Chinese had carved the characters of each page onto a wood block. They brushed ink over the carving and laid a piece of paper on it to print the page. Printers could make many copies of a book using these blocks, but carving the block for each page took a long time. Around 1045, Bi Sheng (bee sheng) developed a printing method that used movable type. He made many separate characters out of clay and rearranged them to make each page.

During the Song dynasty, books became less expensive. In earlier times, only the rich could buy them. With more people able to afford books, the number and kinds of books increased. More people, including women, also learned to read and write. By the 1200s, books about farming, medicine, religion, and poetry were in print. They helped to spread knowledge throughout China. This Song saying reflects the new importance of books:

> **❝To enrich your family, no need to buy good land: Books hold a thousand measures of grain. For an easy life, no need to build a mansion: In books are found houses of gold. ❞**
>
> — *A Song emperor*

Identify Causes and Effects
What made it easier for people to buy books? List that as a cause. What resulted from the increase in books? List those effects.

✓ Reading Check **What does the Song emperor's saying mean?**

The Mongols Conquer China

The Mongols were nomads from the plains of Central Asia, north of China. They were fierce warriors, said to "live in the saddle" because they spent so much time on horseback. By the 1200s, they were a tough military force. Under the leadership of Genghis Khan, they began forging an empire that eventually included China and Korea in the east, stretched into Russia and Eastern Europe in the west, and extended to the southwest as far as the Persian Gulf.

The Mongols Attack China
This illustration from the 1400s shows Kublai Khan's armies crossing a bridge to attack a Chinese fortress. **Conclude** *Use details in the illustration to draw conclusions about the dress, equipment, and methods of Kublai Khan's armies.*

Kublai Khan, Mongol Ruler of China Genghis Khan had conquered all of northern China by 1215. But the southern Song empire continued to resist. It was left to Genghis Khan's grandson **Kublai Khan** to complete the conquest of China and to rule it.

Kublai Khan came to power in 1259. Within 20 years, he had toppled the last Song emperor. From his capital at the present-day city of Beijing, Kublai Khan declared himself emperor of China. He named his new dynasty *Yuan,* which means "beginning," because he intended that Mongol rule of China would last for centuries.

China Under Mongol Rule
The Mongols centralized government in China. They did not allow the old Chinese ruling class to govern. High government positions were reserved for Mongols and were even given to foreigners rather than to Chinese. The Mongols also kept their own language and customs rather than adopting Chinese culture. They did, however, allow the practice of many religions.

Marco Polo at Kublai Khan's Court
The Italian Marco Polo, shown kneeling before Kublai Khan, worked for the khan for 17 years. **Analyze Images** *What detail in the painting indicates that Polo is reporting to Kublai Khan?*

Visitors from all lands were welcome at Kublai Khan's court. One of these was Ibn Battutah, an African Muslim. Another was a Christian from Europe, Marco Polo. He came from Venice in present-day Italy in 1271. After returning to Europe, Polo wrote about his travels. He described the riches of Kublai Khan's palace, China's efficient mail system, and its well-maintained roads.

Marco Polo's writings sparked increased trade between Europe and China. China prospered under Kublai Khan, but not under the khans, or emperors, who followed him. In 1368, a Chinese peasant led an uprising that overthrew the foreign rulers and ended Mongol rule of China.

Explore the history of kung fu.

✓ **Reading Check** **Describe Mongol rule of China.**

 Section 1 Assessment

Key Terms
Review the key terms at the beginning of this section. Use each term in a sentence that explains its meaning.

Target Reading Skill
What were two effects of the Mongol rule of China?

Comprehension and Critical Thinking
1. (a) Recall What is the Grand Canal?
(b) Synthesize Why was it important?
2. (a) Identify Describe one important change in government made by the Song.
(b) Identify Effects How did this change affect China?
3. (a) Summarize How did the Mongols conquer China?
(b) Identify Frame of Reference Why do you think the Mongols did not adopt Chinese customs?

Writing Activity
During the Song dynasty, printed materials became available to many more people. What would life be like today without books and other printed materials? Write a journal entry to express your thoughts.

For: An activity on Chinese inventions
Visit: PHSchool.com
Web Code: lgd-8401

Making an Outline

An outline is a way to organize information. It identifies the main ideas and supporting details. You can use an outline to take notes on what you read or to plan a report that you will write.

Learn the Skill

1 **Identify the most important points or main ideas, and list them with Roman numerals.** If you are outlining a text, look for headings stating these ideas.

2 **Decide on important subtopics for each main idea, and list them with capital letters.** Indent these entries under the main ideas, as shown in the sample outline below.

3 **Use Arabic numerals to list supporting ideas or details under each subtopic.** Indent these entries. Because an outline is a type of summary, you don't have to be as detailed or complete as your source. See the sample outline below.

4 **Check your outline for balance.** Make sure that the entries with Roman numerals are the most important ideas. Check that the ideas and information listed under the main ideas support those ideas. Make sure that main topics have at least two supporting subtopics or details.

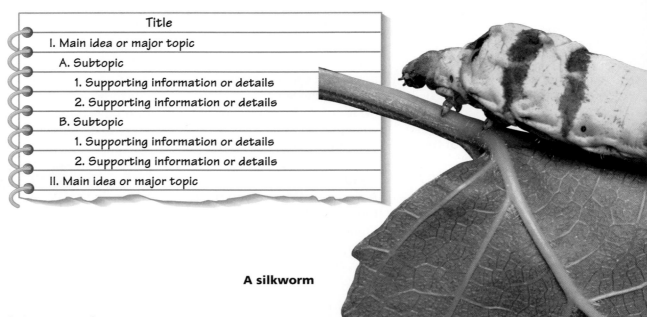

Title
I. Main idea or major topic
  A. Subtopic
    1. Supporting information or details
    2. Supporting information or details
  B. Subtopic
    1. Supporting information or details
    2. Supporting information or details
II. Main idea or major topic

A silkworm

Women preparing newly woven silk

Practice the Skill

Suppose you are outlining an article on silk making. You want to cover two main ideas: The Chinese were the first to make silk, and silk became an important trade product for China. Use the passage at the right as the source for the beginning of your outline. Then follow the steps below to outline it.

1 What is the main idea of the passage? Make it Roman numeral I of your outline.

2 Identify at least two important subtopics, and list them with capital letters.

3 Which details support the important topics or ideas? List those with Arabic numerals under the appropriate subtopics.

4 Reread your outline to be sure you have included all the important ideas and details. Make sure your outline correctly indicates which ideas are the most important and how other ideas and details support the main ideas.

Chinese Silk Making The fabric known as silk is made from the cocoons of caterpillars called silkworms. The cocoons are unwound very carefully, to avoid breaking the fibers. This process is long and difficult if done by hand—as it was in ancient China. The silk strands are then twisted together to form yarn, which is woven into fabric on a loom.

Silk making in China dates back more than 3,000 years. It is said that the empress Hsi Ling Shi, called the Goddess of Silk, invented the loom to weave this valuable fabric. She was a patron of the silk industry, which involved tending silkworms and cultivating the mulberry trees on which the caterpillars fed. This laborious work was done by women.

Silk was so beautiful and expensive that only royalty and nobles could afford to wear it. Because the fabric was so valuable and desirable, the Chinese kept the silk-making process a secret.

Apply the Skill

Reread the portion of text titled Achievements of the Song Dynasty on pages 93–95. Make an outline of that text.

Prepare to Read

Objectives

In this section you will
1. Learn about the geography of Japan.
2. Discover the changes that occurred during the Heian period of Japanese history.
3. Find out about feudalism and the rule of the shoguns in Japan.

Taking Notes

As you read this section, look for details about the major periods of Japan's history. Copy the table below and record your findings in it.

Japan, 794–1867	
Period	**Characteristics**
Heian period	
Rise of the samurai	
Kamakura shogunate	
Tokugawa shogunate	

Target Reading Skill

Understand Effects An effect is what happens as the result of a specific cause or factor. For example, you can see in the paragraphs on the next page that the geography of Japan has had several effects on that nation. This section also discusses how contact with the outside world affected Japan. As you read, note the effects on Japan of the contact with the Mongols and with Europeans.

Key Terms

- **archipelago** (ahr kuh PEL uh goh) *n.* a group or chain of many islands
- **Kyoto** (kee OH toh) *n.* the capital city of medieval Japan
- **feudalism** (FYOOD ul iz um) *n.* a system in which poor people are legally bound to work for wealthy landowners
- **samurai** (SAM uh ry) *n.* Japanese warriors
- **shogun** (SHOH gun) *n.* the supreme military commander of Japan

Japanese woodcut of Mount Fuji

In A.D. 882, a group of more than 100 officials sailed across the sea to Japan. They were from a kingdom in Manchuria, north of China. They carried greetings for the Japanese emperor, as well as gifts of tiger skins and honey. When the emperor heard the news, he was pleased. This visit would give the Japanese a chance to display their achievements. The emperor's name was Yozei (yoh zay ee). At the time, he was only 14 years old.

Yozei sent expensive gifts of food and clothing to the visitors. He also sent people to escort them to his capital. The officials from Manchuria had landed in the north, and the capital was far to the south. The journey over land would take five months. The Japanese quickly fixed roads and bridges along the way. When the visitors arrived, there was a celebration. Japan's nobles, government leaders, and best poets were invited. Horse races, archery, and a poetry contest took place. A great feast was held, too, with much music and dancing.

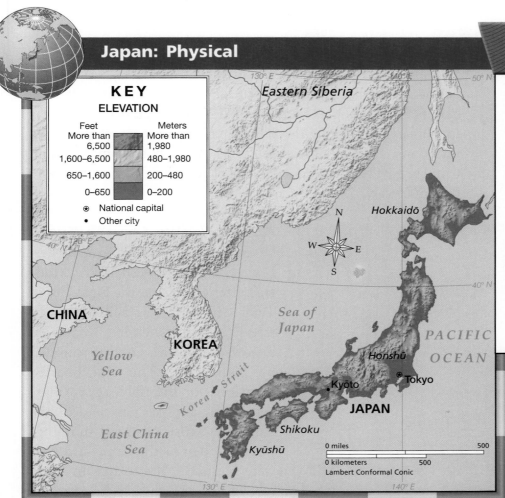

Japan: Physical

KEY
ELEVATION

Feet		Meters
More than 6,500		More than 1,980
1,600–6,500		480–1,980
650–1,600		200–480
0–650		0–200

⊛ National capital
• Other city

Eastern Siberia

Hokkaidō

N
W   E
S

CHINA

Sea of Japan

40° N

KOREA

PACIFIC OCEAN

Yellow Sea

Honshū

Kyōto ⊛ Tokyo

JAPAN

East China Sea

Shikoku

Kyūshū

0 miles   500
0 kilometers   500
Lambert Conformal Conic

Location The photo below shows Japan's highest mountain, Mount Fuji, on Honshū island. **Locate** Notice where Japan's mountains are located. **Apply Information** If you wanted to travel from Shikoku to Hokkaidō in medieval Japan, would you go by land or by sea? Would it be easier to go from Shikoku to Korea? Explain your answers.

Go Online
PHSchool.com Use Web Code **lgp-8432** for step-by-step map skills practice.

A Country of Islands

The visitors from Manchuria had a long trip over both land and sea to Japan. Japan is an **archipelago** (ahr kuh PEL uh goh), or chain of many islands, in the Pacific Ocean off the coast of the Asian mainland. It is about 500 miles (800 kilometers) from the coast of China but it is only 100 miles (160 kilometers) from Korea. The islands of Japan were formed by volcanoes, and earthquakes are common in the region.

Look at the map above. Notice that the islands of Japan are mountainous. The mountains make traveling by land difficult. As a result, the sea became an important highway for the Japanese— even for those traveling from place to place on the same island. On the other hand, for centuries, the sea helped to protect Japan from invaders. Over time, this isolation also led the Japanese to develop a distinctive way of life.

✓ **Reading Check** Describe Japan's geography.

The Heian Empire

The emperor Yozei ruled Japan during the Heian (HAY ahn) period, which lasted from 794 to 1185. Before this time, Japan's culture—including its literature, laws, and religion—was similar to China's. But during the 800s, Japan began to develop its own traditions. In fact, official relations between the Japanese and Chinese governments ended in 894. The split would last for more than 500 years.

Modern Kyoto
The traditional Japanese pagoda, or shrine, in the foreground is still an important part of the modern, bustling city. **Infer** *What does this blend of architecture suggest about modern Japanese culture?*

An Impressive Capital: Kyoto

Heian emperors ruled from a new capital, **Kyoto** (kee OH toh). Modeled after Chang'an, the great city of Tang China, it was a rectangle of tree-lined streets. Unlike Chang'an, however, Kyoto was not surrounded by high walls. The city boasted mansions for the nobles, two marketplaces, and a palace for the emperor. Most Japanese buildings were wooden at the time, and fires were common. Kyoto's main street was very wide—to keep fires on one side from spreading to the other. Canals running through the capital also provided water to help put out any fires.

The Japanese Nobility The Heian period was a mostly peaceful time, during which Japanese culture thrived. Fine architecture, literature, and beautiful gardens all became a part of life for the nobility. Life for most of the population, however, was very different. Farmers, fishers, traders, and builders were usually poor and spent their time doing hard work.

The nobles believed that the importance of their families and their positions within the government set them apart from others. But even among the nobles, people belonged to different ranks, or classes. In fact, noblemen wore specially colored robes related to their position in society. Noblewomen were not affected by such rules because they could not hold official positions in the government.

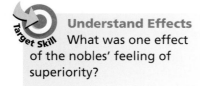

Target Skill
Understand Effects What was one effect of the nobles' feeling of superiority?

✓ Reading Check **How did nobles live during the Heian period?**

Feudalism in Japan

During the 1000s, the Japanese emperor began to lose power. He continued to rule the capital, but he had less control over the rest of Japan. At the same time, the nobles gained greater power and wealth. They owned estates, or large tracts of land, outside the capital. The work on these estates was done by peasants. This kind of economic system, in which poor people are legally bound to work for wealthy landowners, is called **feudalism.**

Samurai Warriors Rich estate owners became so independent that they often disobeyed the emperor. They even hired private armies. The nobles paid these armies to defend them, their estates, and the peasants who worked for them. The armies were made up of warriors called **samurai** (SAM uh ry).

Samurai warriors followed a strict set of rules for behavior, called *bushido* (BOO shee doh). They swore an oath to follow these rules without question. According to bushido, honor meant more than wealth or even life itself. This code said that a samurai must never show weakness or surrender to an enemy. The true samurai had no fear of death, and would rather die than shame himself. He was expected to commit ritual suicide rather than betray the code of bushido.

Prepared for War
Samurai armor was made of small scales tied with silk and leather. The painting below shows the charge of a samurai on horseback. **Analyze Images** *What do these two images suggest about samurai warriors?*

Citizen Heroes

A Peasant Warrior

Toyotomi Hideyoshi (toh yoh TOH mee hee duh YOH shee) started life as a peasant. Through hard work, he became a respected warrior. Because of his great military skills, he became a chief lieutenant in the army of a powerful daimyo. When the daimyo was assassinated in 1582, Hideyoshi took his place. A skillful leader, he went on to unite Japan. He then tried, but failed, to conquer Korea and China. Nevertheless, Hideyoshi, shown below, became one of the most admired heroes in Japan.

A New Class Gains Power Over time, the samurai warriors grew in number and formed their own clans. Each clan promised loyalty to a powerful warlord, or daimyo (DY myoh). The daimyo expected his samurai warriors to be willing to give their lives for him. As the different warlords grew in power, small wars broke out among them. Eventually the Minamoto clan became the most powerful.

In 1192, the emperor gave the title of **shogun** (SHOH gun), or supreme military commander, to the leader of the Minamoto clan. Minamoto Yoritomo (mee nah MOH toh yoh ree TOH moh) became the supreme ruler of all Japan. He set up the Kamakura (kah mah KUR ah) shogunate, a series of military dynasties.

✓ Reading Check **How did the samurai become powerful?**

Japan and the Outside World

Within a century after shogun rule began, Japan was threatened by outsiders. One group came from Mongolia, north of China. Under their fierce and brilliant leader Kublai Khan, the Mongols had already conquered China and Korea. Kublai Khan tried to invade Japan twice, and failed both times. For nearly 300 years after the Mongols were defeated in the 1200s, few foreigners came to Japan.

The Arrival of Europeans In 1543, several Portuguese ships were blown off course and landed on Japan's coast. The Japanese showed great interest in these foreigners—especially in their guns. In the years that followed, a lively trade developed between East and West. Many European traders and missionaries made the long voyage to these islands in the Pacific. And thousands of Japanese converted to Christianity. The European influence in Japan did not last long, however.

The Tokugawas Unify Japan In 1603, Tokugawa Ieyasu (toh koo GAH wah ee yay AH soo) became shogun. Ieyasu was determined to bring order to the country. To end the fighting among warring samurai bands, Ieyasu divided Japan into about 250 regions. The daimyo of each region promised to serve the shogun and swore loyalty to him. To control these local leaders, the Tokugawas required each daimyo to live in the shogun's capital, Edo (now called Tokyo), for several months every other year.

The Tokugawa shogunate ruled Japan until 1867. It was a period of peace. The economy thrived. Food was plentiful, the population increased, trade flourished inside Japan, and a merchant class developed. Cities grew, and the arts flourished. A type of Buddhism called Zen became popular in Japan. It emphasized meditation, the practice of good deeds, and reverence for nature.

Theater and poetry also thrived under the Tokugawas. Haiku—three-line poems that express a feeling or picture in only 17 syllables—were greatly admired. Plays featuring life-size puppets were popular. So was the Kabuki theater. Kabuki combines drama, dance, and music.

Kabuki Theater
Even today, men play women's roles in Kabuki theater, and many of the plays recount tales of feudal Japan. **Analyze Images** *What do the elaborate makeup, costumes, and gestures suggest about Kabuki performances?*

Japan Becomes Isolated Again At the same time, the Tokugawa shogunate was isolating Japan from foreign influences. Even Tokugawa Ieyasu had worried that Europeans might try to conquer Japan. He and the shoguns who ruled after him decided that Japan should remain isolated from Westerners. They outlawed Christianity and forced Europeans to leave. By 1638, they had closed Japan's ports, banning most foreign travel and trade. The shoguns also stopped the building of large ships that could travel long distances. For more than 200 years, the Japanese would remain cut off from the outside world.

 **Reading Check** **How did the Tokugawas change Japan?**

 Section 2 Assessment

Key Terms
Review the key terms at the beginning of this section. Use each term in a sentence that explains its meaning.

Target Reading Skill
What were two effects of the growing power of the daimyo?

Comprehension and Critical Thinking
1. (a) Describe What are the geographical features of Japan?
(b) Identify When did Japan start to develop its own traditions?
(c) Identify Causes What led to Japan's isolation?
2. (a) Recall What happened to the emperor and the nobles during the 1000s?
(b) Identify Causes What led to the establishment of shoguns?
3. (a) Recall How did trade develop between Japan and Europe in the 1500s?
(b) Synthesize How and why did the Tokugawas isolate Japan?

Writing Activity
Suppose you could interview a samurai. Write five questions that you would ask him. Then write a paragraph to introduce your interview.

For: An activity about the samurai
Visit: PHSchool.com
Web Code: lgd-8402

Focus On
A Japanese Home

In 1649, authorities of the Tokugawa government sent a decree to Japanese villages: "[Peasants] must not buy tea . . . to drink, nor must their wives. . . . The husband must work in the fields, [and] the wife must work at the loom. Both must do night work. However good-looking a wife may be, if she neglects her household duties . . . she must be divorced. Peasants must wear only cotton or hemp—no silk." This decree shows how the Tokugawa government tried to maintain a firm grip on Japanese society. Both outside and inside the home, the lives of the Japanese were guided by tradition and by law.

Tokugawa Fashions
This silk kimono, or robe, would have been worn by a wealthy person. Townspeople kept mud off their feet by wearing raised wooden clogs called geta (below). Peasants usually wore straw sandals.

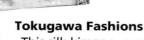

Inside a Japanese Farmhouse The illustration at the right shows a typical farmhouse during the Tokugawa shogunate. In Tokugawa, Japan, most houses had a main room with a sunken fire pit. The family gathered around the fire pit, and sat according to rank. At night, they slept on the floor on thin mattresses, which had been stored away in cupboards during the day.

Not shown are the two back rooms. One of these was the zashiki, a formal room used for receiving guests. Inside it was a butsudan, a Buddhist altar, and a tokonoma, a recessed space decorated with a flower vase, candlestick, and incense burner. The other back room was the nando, used for sleeping and for storage. In some farmhouses, women raised silkworms on a second floor.

The illustration shows raised wood floors covered with straw mats called tatami. It was customary to remove one's shoes before stepping onto the tatami. This custom is still practiced in Japan today.

Hiroma
This was the family's living and dining room.

Doma
This earthen-floored area was used for cooking and working, and sometimes, for sheltering farm animals.

Assessment

Describe Identify the features of a Japanese farmhouse during the Tokugawa shogunate.

Compare and Contrast Compare the Japanese farmhouse with the Bedouin tent on pages 24–25. How are they similar? How are they different?

The Great Mughal Empire in India

Prepare to Read

Objectives

In this section you will

1. Find out about the geography of the Indian subcontinent.
2. Learn about the Delhi Sultanate, a period of Muslim rule.
3. Learn about the founding and achievements of the Mughal Empire.

Taking Notes

As you read this section, look for important events in India's history, and note when they occurred. Copy the timeline below and record your findings on it.

India's History, 600–1707

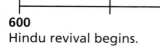

600
Hindu revival begins.

Target Reading Skill

Recognize Cause-and-Effect Signal Words
Sometimes certain words, such as *because, affect,* or *as a result,* signal a cause or an effect. In this section, you will learn about invasions of India and the rise and fall of two Indian empires. Look for signal words to help you understand the causes and effects of these events.

Key Terms

- **sultan** (SUL tun) *n.* a Muslim ruler
- **caste system** (kast SIS tum) *n.* a Hindu social class system that controlled every aspect of daily life
- **Mughal Empire** (MOO gul EM pyr) *n.* a period of Muslim rule of India from the 1500s to the 1700s
- **Akbar** (AK bahr) *n.* the greatest Mughal leader of India
- **Taj Mahal** (tahzh muh HAHL) *n.* a tomb built by Shah Jahan for his wife

Timur, from an Indian manuscript

Even before Timur (tee MOOR) invaded India, people there had heard of this Mongol conqueror. He had destroyed entire cities and their populations in other parts of Asia. In 1398, he and his troops marched into northern India, in search of fabled riches. They ruined fields of crops and quickly captured Delhi (DEL ee), the capital city. Timur and his troops killed many people and took hundreds of slaves. They also carried away great treasures—pearls, golden dishes, rubies, and diamonds.

For a brief time, Delhi became part of the huge empire that Timur controlled from his capital, Samarkand (sam ur KAND). But Timur was more interested in conquering new lands than in governing those he had defeated. Not long after the Mongols invaded Delhi, they departed. Once again, a **sultan,** or Muslim ruler, took control of the city. But Delhi did not regain its command over the region, as you will see.

India's Geography

The triangular Indian subcontinent forms the southernmost part of Central Asia. A mountain range called the Himalayas stretches across the north of India. Although these mountains have helped to isolate India from lands to the north, the passes through the Himalayas have allowed some conquerors from the north to enter the subcontinent. To the west of India is the Arabian Sea, and to the east is the Bay of Bengal.

A large plain lies to the south of the Himalayas. It is dominated by major river systems, including the Indus and Ganges rivers. These rivers are fed by melting mountain snows, and much of the land here is well suited to farming. Farther to the south are highlands and plains.

✓ Reading Check **Describe India's geography.**

The Delhi Sultanate

The Mongols led by Timur were not the first people to invade India. Long before they came, India's riches had tempted others. Muslim invaders began raiding the Indian subcontinent around A.D. 1000. From 1206 to 1526, a series of sultans controlled northern India as well as parts of present-day Bangladesh and Pakistan. This period of India's history is called the Delhi Sultanate—after the capital city, Delhi.

A Hindu Revival At the time of the Muslim invasion, the region was experiencing a revival of the ancient Hindu religion. This revival had begun about A.D. 600. Hindus accept many gods, but they believe that all of these gods are just different aspects of one supreme being. Hindus also believe that social classes are part of the natural order of the universe.

In India at this time, the Hindu **caste system**—a strict system of social classes—controlled everyday life. Caste determined a person's job and status. At the top of the caste system were priests, teachers, and judges. Warriors were second. Then came farmers and merchants. The fourth class included craftspeople and laborers. Finally, there was a group of poor and powerless people who were called untouchables.

A Himalayan Mountain Pass
Even today, it is difficult to cross the Himalayas. Infer *Why do you think modern travelers are still using pack animals rather than trucks or automobiles to cross these mountains?*

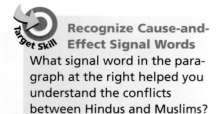
Recognize Cause-and-Effect Signal Words
What signal word in the paragraph at the right helped you understand the conflicts between Hindus and Muslims?

Akbar Holds Court
Akbar supported many kinds of artists, including those who made beautiful miniature paintings like this one. **Conclude** *What can you conclude about Akbar's court from this painting?*

The Muslims who controlled the Delhi Sultanate did not become part of Hindu society. As you read in Chapter 1, Muslim culture is based on beliefs that are very different from those of Hindu culture. These differences caused conflicts between the two groups. In fact, religious disagreements still divide the Hindus and Muslims who live in India today.

The Fall of the Delhi Sultanate In 1526, a Mongol prince named Babur (BAH bur) took advantage of the weakened Delhi Sultanate. Babur was a Muslim descendant of the Mongol conqueror Timur. Even though Babur and his troops were outnumbered almost ten to one, they attacked the sultan's army.

The sultan's forces had 100 elephants to help them fight. Babur's troops had none. But the Mongols had cannons—and they were better fighters. The prince defeated the sultan and went on to control the capital city, Delhi. A new period of India's history would now begin.

✓ **Reading Check** **How was the Delhi Sultanate defeated?**

The Mughal Empire

Babur founded the celebrated **Mughal Empire,** whose Muslim rulers controlled India until the 1700s. (*Mughal* is another word for "Mongol.") About 25 years after Babur's death, the empire came under the control of Babur's grandson. His name was **Akbar** (AK bahr), and he would become the greatest Mughal leader of India.

Akbar the Great When Akbar came to power, he was only 13 years old. He grew up to become a talented soldier. Through conquest, treaties, and marriage, he greatly expanded the Mughal Empire.

Akbar also encouraged the arts. He set up studios for painters at his court. He supported poets, although he himself never learned to read or write. Akbar also brought together scholars from different religions for discussions. He consulted with Muslims, Hindus, Buddhists, and Christians.

Although he was a Muslim, Akbar gained the support of his Hindu subjects through his policy of toleration. He allowed Hindus to practice their religion freely, and he ended unfair taxes that had been required of non-Muslims.

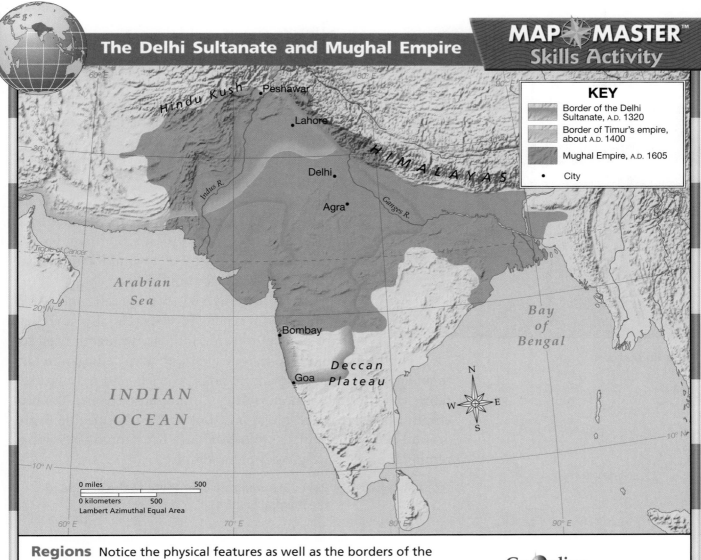

KEY

	Border of the Delhi Sultanate, A.D. 1320
	Border of Timur's empire, about A.D. 1400
	Mughal Empire, A.D. 1605
•	City

Regions Notice the physical features as well as the borders of the empires on the map. **Locate** Which empire was the oldest? Which one gained control of the mouths of India's two most important rivers? **Infer** Why do you think neither the sultans nor the Mughals extended their empires farther north?

Go Online
PHSchool.com Use Web Code **lgp-8443** for step-by-step map skills practice.

Akbar created a strong central government, and he gave government jobs to qualified people, whatever their religion or caste. Hindus served as generals, governors, administrators, and clerks. These policies helped Hindus and Muslims live together more peacefully. They also strengthened Mughal power in India.

In 1605, when Akbar died, most of northern India was under his control. Akbar had ruled the Mughal Empire for 49 years, earning himself the nickname "the Great." During this long reign, his system of government had become firmly established in India. This system allowed the empire to continue developing and expanding for the next 100 years—even under rulers who were less capable than Akbar the Great.

Royal emblem from the Gujari Palace, India

The Taj Mahal

The Reign of Shah Jahan More than 100 years after Akbar's death, the Mughal Empire began to fall apart. Akbar's grandson, Shah Jahan (shah juh HAHN), became emperor in 1628. Jahan spent a fortune on extravagant buildings. The most famous of these is the **Taj Mahal** (tahzh muh HAHL), a tomb for the emperor's wife, Mumtaz Mahal (mum TAHZ muh HAHL).

When his wife died, Jahan was overcome with grief. The two had been constant companions, and Jahan had asked his wife's opinion on many issues. After she died, Jahan set out to build a tomb "as beautiful as she was beautiful."

Jahan's son, Aurangzeb (AWR ung zeb), spent still more money on expensive wars. He also reversed Akbar's policies toward Hindus. Aurangzeb tried to force Hindus to convert to the Muslim faith, and he began to tax them again. As a result, many Hindus rebelled, and fighting the rebels cost still more money. After Aurangzeb died in 1707, the empire split into small kingdoms. But to this day, people from around the globe journey to see his mother's tomb—a lasting reminder of the once great Mughal Empire.

✓ **Reading Check** **How did Aurangzeb contribute to the decline of the Mughal Empire?**

Section 3 Assessment

Key Terms
Review the key terms at the beginning of this section. Use each term in a sentence that explains its meaning.

Target Reading Skill
What words in the last paragraph on this page signal cause and effect?

Comprehension and Critical Thinking
1. (a) Identify What are the major geographic features of the Indian subcontinent?

(b) Predict How might India's history have been different if there had been no mountain passes in the north?
2. (a) Define What was the Delhi Sultanate?
(b) Synthesize How did Hindus and Muslims live together in India during this time?
3. (a) Explain Why was Akbar called "the Great"?
(b) Identify Causes What caused the decline of the Mughal Empire?

Writing Activity
Suppose that Akbar is a leader under a system of government like the United States government. He is running for reelection, and you are his campaign manager. Write a short speech stating why voters should reelect him.

Writing Tip Remember to support your position with specific examples.

Review and Assessment

◆ Chapter Summary

Section 1: Golden Ages of China

Kublai Khan's court

- The Tang dynasty ruled China for almost 300 years. That period was the beginning of a golden age, during which China's territory increased, and Chinese culture and trade flourished.
- The Song dynasty, which ruled China after the Tang, expanded the merit system and promoted the spread of knowledge.
- The Mongols conquered China, and their leader, Kublai Khan, centralized China's government.

Section 2: Medieval Japan

- Japan is a mountainous island country of East Asia. The sea has provided both transportation and protection for the people of Japan.
- During the Heian period, the Japanese built a new capital and began to develop a distinctive culture.
- Warriors, called samurai, and powerful military leaders, called shoguns, took control away from the emperor. The shoguns eventually closed Japan to outsiders.

Section 3: The Great Mughal Empire in India

- The Indian subcontinent is shaped like a triangle, with mountains to the north and seas to the east and west.
- During the Delhi Sultanate, Muslim rulers called sultans ruled India.
- Mongols conquered India and established the Mughal Empire. Akbar the Great was the greatest Mughal leader.

Kabuki performer

◆ Key Terms

Define each of the following terms.

1. Silk Road
2. Tang
3. shogun
4. sultan
5. caste system
6. Kublai Khan
7. archipelago
8. samurai
9. Taj Mahal
10. dynasty

◆ Comprehension and Critical Thinking

11. (a) Identify Name two Chinese products that were important for trade.
(b) Explain Why were these products valued by other countries?
(c) Identify Effects How did trade in these products affect China?

12. (a) Recall How did the Song, and then the Mongols, change Chinese government?
(b) Evaluate Which changes benefited China? Which were harmful? Explain.

13. (a) Identify What are the major geographic features of Japan? Of India?
(b) Compare and Contrast How did the geography of these two places affect their history and culture?

14. (a) Define What is a shogunate?
(b) Summarize How did shoguns gain power in Japan?
(c) Identify Causes Why did shoguns ban most foreign travel and trade?

15. (a) Identify Who was the last ruler of India's Mughal Empire?
(b) Contrast How was his rule different from that of his great-grandfather, Akbar?
(c) Analyze What factors contributed to the downfall of the Mughal Empire?

◆ Skills Practice

Making an Outline In the Skills for Life activity in this chapter, you learned how to make an outline. Review the steps you followed to learn the skill. Then reread the text under the heading The Mughal Empire on pages 110–112. Make an outline of that text.

◆ Writing Activity: Science

Use encyclopedias, other reliable books, or reliable Internet sources to research one Chinese invention of the Tang or Song dynasty. Describe the invention, how it works, when and how it was invented, and why it was important. Write your findings as an essay or as an illustrated report that you can display in your classroom.

MAP MASTER™ Skills Activity

Civilizations of Asia

Place Location For each feature or place listed, write the letter from the map that shows its location.

1. Himalayas
2. Delhi
3. Silk Road
4. Japan
5. Delhi Sultanate
6. Ganges River
7. China during the Tang dynasty

Go Online
PHSchool.com Use Web Code **lpg-8453** for an **interactive map**.

Standardized Test Prep

Test-Taking Tips

Some questions on standardized tests may ask you to identify the main topic or the topic sentence of a passage. Read the paragraph below. Then use the tip to help you answer the sample question.

> Beginning in the 1600s, the powerful shoguns of Japan outlawed Christianity. The shoguns forced Europeans to leave the country. They also closed Japanese ports to foreigners and banned foreign trade. Through their efforts to isolate Japan, the shoguns hoped to protect it from foreign invasion.

Think It Through Read all four choices. Answers A and D tell about specific actions, not broad ideas or main topics. Even though C is the first sentence of the passage, it also describes one particular action. Therefore, it is not more important than A or D. Because B summarizes the information of the other sentences, it is the correct answer.

Pick the letter that best answers the question.

Which of these sentences states the <u>main topic</u> of the passage?

 A They also closed Japanese ports to foreigners and banned foreign trade.

 B Through their efforts to isolate Japan, the shoguns hoped to protect it from foreign invasion.

 C Beginning in the 1600s, the powerful shoguns of Japan outlawed Christianity.

 D The shoguns forced Europeans to leave the country.

TIP Many paragraphs have one sentence that states the main topic. The other sentences in the paragraph all support this topic sentence. The first and last sentences are the most likely to be the topic sentence.

Practice Questions

Pick the letter that best answers the question.

1. Read the passage below. Which of the sentences that follow states the main topic of the passage?

> Hideyoshi was born a poor peasant in Japan in the 1500s. Through hard work, he became a samurai warrior. Because of his military skills, Hideyoshi was promoted to an important position working for a powerful warlord. In 1582, the warlord was killed, and Hideyoshi took his place. A skillful leader from poor beginnings, Hideyoshi became ruler of Japan.

 A Through hard work, he became a samurai warrior.

 B Hideyoshi was born a poor peasant in Japan in the 1500s.

 C A skillful leader from poor beginnings, Hideyoshi became ruler of Japan.

 D In 1582, the warlord was killed, and Hideyoshi took his place.

Read each of the following statements. If the statement is true, write *true*. If it is false, write *false*.

2. The samurai warriors of Japan followed a set of strict rules for behavior.

3. Song rulers used the merit system in Chinese government.

4. The Indian subcontinent could not be invaded from the north.

5. Akbar was a great Mughal ruler of India.

6. Japan's islands are mostly flat, and traveling by land is easy.

Use Web Code **lga-8403** for a **Chapter 4 self-test.**

Chapter Preview

This chapter will introduce you to life in Europe during the Middle Ages.

**Target
Reading Skill**

Sequence In this chapter you will focus on using sequence to note the order in which events take place. This skill will help you understand and remember those events.

▶ The medieval castle at
Carcassonne, France

MAP MASTER™
Skills Activity

Europe in 1300

NORWAY
SWEDEN
SCOTLAND
IRELAND
(England)
North Sea
Copenhagen
TEUTONIC ORDER
NOVGOROD
WALES
(England)
ENGLAND
DENMARK
Baltic Sea
LITHUANIA
RUSSIAN STATES
ATLANTIC OCEAN
London
POLAND
Frankfurt
HOLY ROMAN EMPIRE
Kiev
Paris
FRANCE
GASCONY
(England)
Budapest
GOLDEN HORDE
NAVARRE
HUNGARY
Black Sea
EASTERN CHRISTIAN STATES
PORTUGAL
ARAGON
Venice
PAPAL STATES
VENICE
BULGARIA
CASTILE
Rome
SERBIA
Constantinople
Toledo
SARDINIA
(Aragon)
NAPLES
BYZANTINE EMPIRE
TURKISH AND MONGOL STATES
GRANADA
MALLORCA
SMALL GREEK STATES
SICILY
(Aragon)
CRETE
(Venice)
CYPRUS
Mediterranean Sea

KEY
— Border
• City

0 miles 500
0 kilometers 500
Lambert Azimuthal Equal Area

Regions In 1300, Europe was made up of many separate kingdoms and states. **Identify** Which names on the map are familiar to you? Which are not? **Apply Information** What route might merchants traveling from Constantinople to Venice take? Which states and bodies of water would they cross?

Go Online
PHSchool.com Use Web Code **lgp-8511** for step-by-step map skills practice.

Section 1

Feudalism and the Manor System

Prepare to Read

Objectives

In this section, you will
1. Learn when the Middle Ages were and what they were like.
2. Find out how land and power were divided under feudalism.
3. Learn how the manor system worked.
4. Discover what life was like for peasants and serfs.

Taking Notes

As you read this section, look for the major features of feudalism. Copy the web diagram below and record your findings in it.

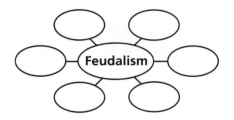

Target Reading Skill

Recognize Sequence Signal Words Noting the order in which important events take place can help you understand how the events relate to one another. Sequence signal words, such as *first, then, began,* and *in [date],* point out relationships in time. Look for such words in this section to help you understand the Middle Ages.

Key Terms

- **knight** (nyt) *n.* a man who received honor and land in exchange for serving a lord as a soldier
- **Middle Ages** (MID ul Ay juz) *n.* the years between ancient and modern times
- **medieval** (mee dee EE vul) *adj.* referring to the Middle Ages
- **feudalism** (FYOOD ul iz um) *n.* a system in which land was owned by kings or lords but held by vassals in return for their loyalty
- **manor** (MAN ur) *n.* a large estate, often including farms and a village, ruled by a lord
- **serf** (surf) *n.* a farm worker considered part of the manor on which he or she worked

A knighting ceremony

As darkness fell, a young man put on a white tunic and red and black cloaks. Then he walked to the church, where he spent the long night alone, praying. Soon he would no longer be a mere squire, or knight-in-training. He would become a real **knight,** who would receive honor and land in exchange for serving his lord as a soldier.

The next morning, the squire entered the castle courtyard, where knights and ladies had gathered. His lord presented him with his sword, spurs, and shield. The squire knelt. Then he felt the lord's sword lightly tap him on each shoulder. "In the name of God, Saint Michael, and Saint George, I call you a knight," declared the lord. "Be loyal, brave, and true."

A knight was expected to be loyal to the lord who knighted him. His lord was loyal to a more powerful lord or king. Knights and lords protected the less powerful people loyal to them. This system held society together.

The Middle Ages

A thousand years ago, scenes like the one you just read about took place throughout Western Europe. These were the times of knights in shining armor, lords and ladies, and castles and cathedrals. These were the **Middle Ages,** the years between ancient times and modern times.

Historians usually say that ancient times lasted until about A.D. 500 and that modern times started about 1500. The period in the middle, the Middle Ages, is also called the **medieval** period. *Medieval* comes from Latin words that mean "middle ages."

The Collapse of the Roman Empire The Middle Ages began with the collapse of the Roman Empire in Western Europe. For centuries, the Roman Empire had provided order and stability in the region. It had spread its culture, the Latin language, and Christianity across the continent. Over time, however, the Roman Empire grew weak. It suffered economic and social troubles. Worse, the Roman Empire also suffered from invasions by peoples from the north.

Bronze plaque of a Lombard warrior

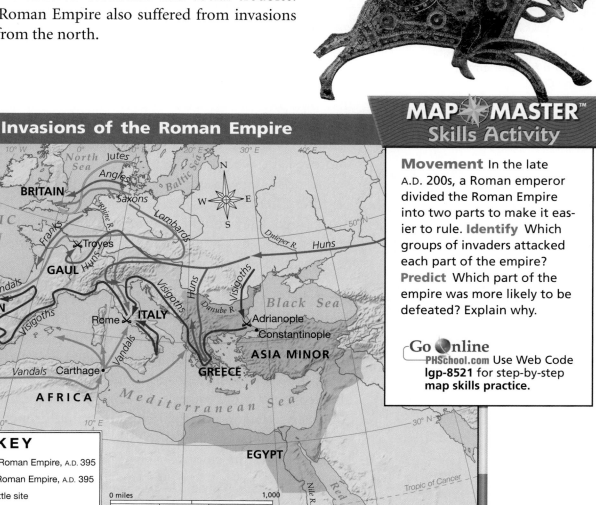

MAP MASTER™
Skills Activity

Invasions of the Roman Empire

KEY

Western Roman Empire, A.D. 395

Eastern Roman Empire, A.D. 395

⚔ Major battle site

• City

0 miles 1,000

0 kilometers 1,000

Lambert Azimuthal Equal Area

Movement In the late A.D. 200s, a Roman emperor divided the Roman Empire into two parts to make it easier to rule. **Identify** Which groups of invaders attacked each part of the empire? **Predict** Which part of the empire was more likely to be defeated? Explain why.

Go Online
PHSchool.com Use Web Code **lgp-8521** for step-by-step map skills practice.

The Emperor Charlemagne
In return for Charlemagne's support of the Church, Pope Leo III crowned him emperor in 800. **Analyze Images** *How does this statue show Charlemagne's greatness and power?*

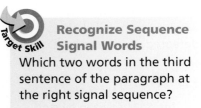

Recognize Sequence Signal Words
Which two words in the third sentence of the paragraph at the right signal sequence?

In wave after wave, the invaders destroyed Roman towns and cut off trade routes. They claimed parts of the empire for themselves. Because these peoples kept their own languages and laws, they broke the bonds that had held the Roman Empire together.

By about A.D. 500, the Roman Empire in Western Europe had completely collapsed. It was replaced by a patchwork of small kingdoms. Reading and writing were in danger of disappearing from Europe because many of the invading groups could not do either.

Charlemagne Reunites Western Europe One of the invading groups was the Franks. They claimed the area called Gaul, which is now France. In fact, the name *France* comes from the word "Franks." In 768, a skilled military leader named Charlemagne (SHAHR luh mayn) became king of the Franks.

At the time, the many small kingdoms of Western Europe were often at war with one another. Charlemagne expanded his kingdom by conquering these weaker kingdoms. Soon, he ruled an empire that stretched across most of Western Europe.

Charlemagne ruled his empire for nearly 50 years. During that time he worked hard to keep Western Europe united. He established schools throughout the land to promote learning and culture. He spread the Christian religion. He issued money and improved the economy. Western Europe had not been so prosperous or so united since the time of the Roman Empire.

After Charlemagne's death, his empire was divided among his three sons. They fought one another, weakening the empire. Other groups also attacked the weakened empire. Perhaps the fiercest attacks were made by the Vikings.

Attacks From the North The Vikings came from the far north of Europe—present-day Denmark, Sweden, and Norway. They were skilled sailors and tough warriors. Their attacks began around 800 and continued for about 300 years. Relying on surprise, the Vikings burned and looted European towns. But they also reopened trade routes to Mediterranean lands and beyond. And they settled in other parts of northern Europe, mixing with the local populations. Even so, the Vikings did not unite these lands into a lasting empire.

✓ Reading Check **Why did Charlemagne's empire fall apart?**

Feudalism: A Kind of Government

Charlemagne's empire was gone. Western Europe was again divided into many small kingdoms. Viking attacks were a constant threat. Life was dangerous. The people of Europe had to find a way to defend themselves and to organize their communities. Slowly they worked out a new system of government.

The Feudal System The system that developed was called feudalism. Under **feudalism**, land was owned by kings or lords but held by vassals in return for their loyalty. By about 1000, feudalism was the way of life throughout Western Europe. It would last for hundreds of years.

In medieval Europe, power belonged to those who controlled the land. These landowners were nobles, such as barons and princes. They gave a share of land, called a fief (feef) to each of their vassals, who promised to follow the landowner's laws and to fight for him. A vassal could also be a lord.

Feudal Duties Lords promised to treat their vassals with honor. In addition, the chief duty of lords was to protect their vassals and their lands. If a vassal with young children died, for example, the lord became the children's protector. The lord also asked his vassals' advice before making laws or going to war.

Vassals were expected to raise and lead armies that would fight for their lord. Many of these vassals were knights —professional horse soldiers who led other men into battle. Vassals also appeared at the lord's court when commanded to do so. And they paid taxes, often in the form of crops, to their lords.

✓ Reading Check **What did lords give vassals in exchange for the vassals' loyalty?**

The Manor System

Feudalism was the way medieval Europeans organized power and government. Manorialism was the way they organized their economy. This system was based on the **manor,** a large estate that included farm fields, pastures, and often an entire village. It also included a large house, called the manor house, where the lord, or ruler, of the manor lived.

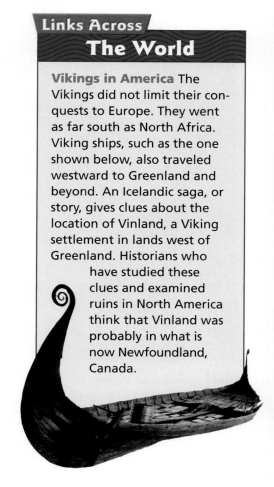

Links Across The World

Vikings in America The Vikings did not limit their conquests to Europe. They went as far south as North Africa. Viking ships, such as the one shown below, also traveled westward to Greenland and beyond. An Icelandic saga, or story, gives clues about the location of Vinland, a Viking settlement in lands west of Greenland. Historians who have studied these clues and examined ruins in North America think that Vinland was probably in what is now Newfoundland, Canada.

A medieval knight in armor

Noblewomen at Home
The larger illustration shows a lady in charge of a dinner where her guests are seated according to rank. A noblewoman sits at her desk in the smaller illustration. **Generalize** *What can you infer about the lives of noblewomen from these illustrations?*

Lords and Manors The lord of the manor was typically a vassal of a king or of a more powerful lord. The manor was part of his fief. Most manors were far from towns, villages, and other manors. Therefore, they had to be self-sufficient, or able to supply their own needs. Food, clothing, and other things needed by the people who lived on the manor were made there.

A lord depended on the wealth his manor provided. He ruled over his manor—and the poor people who lived there. He made the rules and acted as judge. He decided who would oversee the farming and other daily work. And he collected taxes from the peasants who lived on the manor.

The Role of Noblewomen Women of the noble classes also played an important part in feudal society. Like the men in her family, a noblewoman went to other noble families for training. Then, she took her place as lady of the household. She managed the household, performed necessary medical tasks, and supervised servants. When her husband or father was away fighting, she often served as "lord of the manor," making important decisions.

✓ **Reading Check** **Why did manors have to be self-sufficient?**

Peasants and Serfs

The majority of the people of medieval Europe were not lords, ladies, or knights. They were peasants, a group of people who made their living as farmers and laborers. Their lives were very different from the lives of the nobles.

Peasants were often very poor. They did all of the work on the manors of the Middle Ages. They farmed the lord's fields to raise food for his household. They were only allowed to farm a small strip of land for themselves. Even so, they had to give part of their own harvest to their lord.

DISCOVERY CHANNEL **SCHOOL** Video
Learn about the knights and castles of the Middle Ages.

Tied to the Manor Most peasants were also serfs. Serfs were peasants who were considered to be part of the manor. When a noble was given a manor as part of his fief, its serfs became his. They could not leave the manor, or even get married, without his permission.

Although serfs were property, they were not quite slaves. A serf who saved enough money to buy a plot of land could become a free peasant. A serf who escaped to a city and lived there for a year and a day without being caught also became free. Most serfs, however, remained serfs their whole lives.

A Hard Life Medieval peasants worked hard for most of their lives. They farmed their own fields and those of their lord. Men, women, and children were all required to work.

Peasants lived in one-room huts that often had only a single opening for a window. For heating and cooking, they built a fire on the dirt floor. Smoke filled the dark, cramped interior before drifting out of a hole in the roof. Peasants ate mostly simple foods such as black bread, cabbage, and turnips. They rarely ate meat, since the animals of the manor and surrounding land were reserved for their lord. Peasants even suffered when they slept: their mattresses were cloth sacks stuffed with straw.

Peasant Life
Peasant women worked in the fields along with the men. **Contrast** *Use this illustration and those on page 122 to contrast the lives of peasant women and noblewomen.*

 **Reading Check** **What was life like for medieval peasants?**

 Section 1 Assessment

Key Terms
Review the key terms at the beginning of this section. Use each term in a sentence that explains its meaning.

Target Reading Skill
Review the text under the heading The Collapse of the Roman Empire. List the words that signal the order of events.

Comprehension and Critical Thinking
1. (a) Recall When were the Middle Ages?

(b) Identify Cause and Effect Why did the collapse of the Roman Empire lead to a new age in Western Europe?
2. (a) Define What was feudalism?
(b) Explain How did the system of feudalism work?
3. (a) Describe How was a manor organized?
(b) Conclude Why did a manor produce a wide variety of goods?
4. (a) Explain What was the relationship of a serf to his or her manor?
(b) Infer How and why might a serf become free?

Writing Activity
During the Middle Ages, most poor peasants remained poor their entire lives. Why do you think this was so? Write a paragraph explaining what you think the reason or reasons were.

For: An activity on feudalism
Visit: PHSchool.com
Web Code: lgd-8501

Although peasants and nobles led very different lives, their reliance on the lands of the manor estate bound them together. Peasants worked the land to pay what they owed to their lords. Nobles depended on what the peasants produced so that they could pay taxes to higher nobles and to the king. In addition to cash, taxes were paid in grain, bread, fence posts, shingles and planks, linen cloth, shirts, honey, chickens, eggs, cheese, and butter. All of these goods were produced on the manor estate.

A peasant's house

The Manor Estate Medieval manors included the lord's home, the homes of the peasants and serfs, a mill for grinding grain, and often a chapel or a church. Attached to the manor house, or in a separate building, was a bakery that peasants and serfs would use for baking bread.

Most people in medieval Europe were agricultural workers. The lands and forests surrounding the manor and peasant houses provided grain, fruits, and vegetables. Peasants grazed cattle, sheep, and goats in the manor fields. Their pigs roamed the manor's woodlands in search of food. Woodlands also provided timber for building and fuel. Hunting in the forests was reserved for the nobles.

The illustration on the facing page shows a manor estate of the Middle Ages. At the top of this page is a shield painted with a noble's coat of arms.

A Manor Feast ▶
This illustration from the 1400s shows a duke feasting with his family and friends. In medieval times, guests brought their own knives to feasts, and many foods were eaten with the fingers. Diners often shared cups and dishes. Musicians, acrobats, and jugglers provided entertainment.

Manor House
A lord's house could be built of wood, stone, or clay bricks.

Village
These houses were usually made of wood and roofed with thatch—tightly bundled straw or reeds.

Mill
Peasants paid a fee to grind their grain.

Fields
Crops were planted in strips in two fields. A third field lay fallow, or unplanted.

Assessment

Describe What are the characteristics of a medieval manor?

Draw Conclusions Describe the relationship between the nobles and peasants. How did they depend upon one another and on the manor's lands?

The Church and the Rise of Cities

Prepare to Read

Objectives

In this section you will
1. Learn why the Roman Catholic Church was so important and powerful during the Middle Ages.
2. Discover the connection between an increase in trade and the growth of towns.
3. Find out what life was like in a medieval town.
4. Understand the role of culture and learning in the Middle Ages.

Taking Notes

As you read this section, think about what caused towns to grow in the Middle Ages and the effects of this growth. Copy the diagram below and record your findings in it.

CAUSES	EVENT	EFFECTS
• •	TOWNS GROW	• •

🎯 Target Reading Skill

Identify Sequence
Noting the order in which significant events occur can help you understand and remember them. You can track the order of events by making a list. Then use signal words and dates in the text to make sure your events are listed in the correct order.

Key Terms

- **clergy** (KLUR jee) *n.* persons with authority to perform religious services
- **excommunication** (eks kuh myoo nih KAY shun) *n.* expelling someone from the Church
- **guild** (gild) *n.* a medieval organization of crafts workers or tradespeople
- **apprentice** (uh PREN tis) *n.* an unpaid person training in a craft or trade
- **chivalry** (SHIV ul ree) *n.* the code of honorable conduct for knights
- **troubadour** (TROO buh dawr) *n.* a traveling poet and musician of the Middle Ages

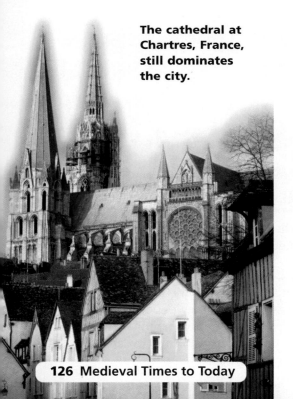

The cathedral at Chartres, France, still dominates the city.

Tall spires reach toward the heavens. Gorgeous stained-glass windows feature rich colors. Sculptures and carvings of people, plants, and animals seem to be everywhere. Amazing flying buttresses—masses of stonework or brickwork attached to the walls—help hold the building up. What is this building? It is a Gothic cathedral.

Even today, these huge medieval churches dominate towns in many parts of Europe. During the Middle Ages, cathedrals were built not only to glorify God but also to be a credit to their city. Entire communities worked for decades to build the biggest, tallest, most beautiful cathedral.

Once completed, a cathedral served as a house of worship, a gathering place, and even as a religious school. Its beautiful glass windows and sculptures told Bible stories and presented the lives of the saints to a population that could not read or write.

The Church in the Middle Ages

Most Gothic cathedrals were built in Western Europe between 1100 and 1400. *Gothic* refers to the style of architecture, as you can see in the Eyewitness Technology feature on page 128. A cathedral was the church of a bishop, an important leader of the Roman Catholic Church. During the Middle Ages, nearly all people in Western Europe were Roman Catholic. The Roman Catholic Church had so much influence that it was known simply as "the Church." Why was the Church so powerful? There were many reasons.

Religious and Economic Power During the Middle Ages, life was short and hard for most people. They were comforted by the Christian belief that they would enjoy the rewards of heaven after death if they lived according to Church teachings. The Church also held that if people *didn't* obey those rules, they would be punished after death. The promise of reward combined with the threat of punishment made most people follow the teachings of the Church.

The Church also had great economic power. It gained great wealth by collecting taxes. It also took fiefs from lords in exchange for services performed by **clergy,** or persons with authority to perform religious services. In fact, the Church was the single largest owner of land in Europe during the Middle Ages.

Teaching Tool
This stained glass window in Canterbury Cathedral, England, shows three kings following a star to the birth of Jesus. **Infer** *How might this window have helped medieval people understand Church teachings?*

Political Power of the Church The combination of religious and economic power enabled the Church to take on many of the roles that government performs today. It even made laws and set up courts to enforce them. People who did not obey the Church were threatened with being excommunicated. **Excommunication** means being expelled from membership in the Church and participation in Church life. This was a very serious threat. Few people would associate with someone who had been excommunicated.

High Church officials were advisors to kings and lords. The ever-present threat of excommunication gave Church officials great influence in political matters. The Church used its authority to limit feudal warfare. It declared periods of truce, or temporary peace. That was one reason warfare began to decline during the 1100s.

Gothic Cathedral

In the mid 1100s, Northern Europeans began to build large stone churches in a new style, called Gothic. This style allowed walls to be thinner and higher. The Gothic cathedral was an expression of medieval religion, and became a symbol of European medieval society.

Gargoyles
Carved stone figures called gargoyles sit high on the walls of Notre Dame Cathedral, Paris, France.

The spire soars to a height of 295 feet (90 meters).

Gargoyles

The building is cross-shaped.

South rose window 43 feet (13 meters) high

Flying buttresses

The altar

The nave

Main doors

Kings from the Bible gaze down.

Wooden roof frames

Guttering to gargoyle

Notre Dame
The cathedral above, named Notre Dame, was built on the site of an older Roman temple. Though the first stone was laid in 1163, it took medieval architects and craftsmen two centuries to finish the building.

Flying Buttresses
Stone arches called flying buttresses carry much of the roof's weight. They allow windows to take the place of solid stone walls.

ANALYZING IMAGES
What architectural features reflect medieval religious belief?

Church Organization The Church was highly organized. Almost every village had a priest. A bishop supervised several priests and an archbishop supervised several bishops. Finally, the archbishops were under the authority of the pope. The papacy, or government of the Church, was based in Rome. These areas of Church authority overlapped and crossed the boundaries of kingdoms. Thus, the Church had power in every kingdom, every fief, and every village.

The Church in Everyday Life The medieval Church touched nearly all aspects of life. Think of any major event—the birth of a child, a serious illness, a marriage, or a death. During the Middle Ages, the clergy were almost always in attendance to offer a blessing or to perform a service.

The clergy helped people follow Church rules about how to live. They also listened when people came to church to confess their sins. In the name of God, the clergy then forgave them for the wrongs to which they had confessed.

Medieval Wedding
In the Middle Ages, ceremonies such as weddings had to be performed by a priest. **Conclude** *How did this requirement increase Church power?*

Monasteries and Convents Some religious men felt that they should dedicate their lives to God by living together in religious communities called monasteries. Religious women, called nuns, lived in similar communities called convents. This form of religious life is called monasticism.

These religious communities developed better ways of growing crops and tending livestock. In this way, the Church helped improve the economy of the Middle Ages, which was based mostly on farming. Monks and nuns also looked after the sick and set up schools. Monks were more educated than most people. Because they copied books from ancient times, they preserved knowledge that otherwise would have been lost. Convents gave women a rare opportunity to become educated.

Scholasticism Some Christian scholars studied ancient Greek texts that said people should use reason to discover truth. However, the Church taught that many ideas must be accepted on faith. These medieval scholars worked out a system that tried to resolve the two philosophies. Called scholasticism, it used reason to support Christian beliefs.

√ Reading Check **What were monasteries and convents?**

This detail from a medieval manuscript shows a monk copying a manuscript.

This beautiful bottle from Syria, made in the 1300s, would have been a valued trade item.

Trade Revives and Towns Grow

By about A.D. 1000—the middle of the Middle Ages—feudalism was well established in Europe and the Church was a stabilizing force. Europe was becoming a safer place, and the population was growing.

The Revival of Trade As people felt safer, they began to travel more and learn more about distant places. As you will read in Section 3, the crusaders brought many desirable goods back from Asia. Europeans began to demand such things as spices and cloth that they could get only from Africa and Asia. Ancient trade routes came into use again. European merchants traveled abroad to buy and sell valued goods.

The Growth of Towns At first, local goods were traded in the markets of small villages. As trade grew, so did these markets. Some developed into major trade fairs. You can find these market towns on the map below.

MAP MASTER™ Skills Activity

Movement As trade increased, towns along major trade routes held trade fairs and became important business centers. **Identify** Name the major trade centers of Castile. Name French towns with trade fairs. **Infer** Why do you think places such as Valencia, Naples, and Rome became important trade centers?

Go Online
PHSchool.com Use Web Code **lpg-8532** for step-by-step **map skills practice**.

Trade Centers in Europe

SCOTLAND
North Sea
Baltic Sea
Danzig
IRELAND (England)
Hamburg   Lübeck
ENGLAND
WALES (England)
FLANDERS
London   Bruges
Winchester   Ghent
Lille
HOLY ROMAN EMPIRE
ATLANTIC OCEAN
Paris   Var-sur-Aube
Provins   Troyes
FRANCE
Lyon   Milan   Venice
Turin   Genoa   Verona
VENICE
NAVARRE   Bayonne
León   BÉARN
Florence   Siena
PAPAL STATES
Barcelona
Rome   KINGDOM OF NAPLES
Naples
CASTILE   ARAGON
SARDINIA (Aragon)
PORTUGAL
Toledo
Valencia
Mediterranean Sea
SICILY (Aragon)
Córdoba
Cádiz   GRANADA

0 miles   500
0 kilometers   500
Lambert Azimuthal Equal Area

KEY
• Major trade center
○ Towns with major trade fairs
— Border as of 1400

Traders also gathered at convenient places for travelers, such as river crossings and along highways. They chose important monasteries and fortified places built by nobles. Before long, towns developed in these locations, too.

Also during this time, many manors were becoming overcrowded. Providing food and clothing for everyone on the manor became difficult. Many lords gladly allowed peasants to buy their freedom and move to the new, growing towns.

✓ **Reading Check** **Why did towns begin to grow?**

Life in Towns and Cities

By about 1300, many towns in Western Europe were growing into cities. Paris, with a population approaching 300,000, was the largest city in the world.

The Rise of a Middle Class Town life was not at all like farm or manor life. Towns and cities were not self-sufficient. Instead, their economies were based on the exchange of money for goods and services. A new class of people developed, made up of merchants, traders, and crafts workers. In status, it was between nobles and peasants, and so it was called the *middle class.*

The Role of Guilds In many towns and cities, the merchants, traders, and crafts workers began to form associations called guilds. A **guild** included all the people who practiced a certain trade or craft. Thus there was a guild of weavers, a guild of grocers, a guild of shoemakers, and so on.

Guilds set prices and prevented outsiders from selling goods in town. They set standards for the quality of their goods. Guild members paid dues. This money was used to help needy members or to support the families of members who had died.

It took a long time to become a member of a guild. Between the ages of 8 and 14, a boy who wanted to learn a certain trade became an **apprentice, or unpaid worker being trained in a craft.** He lived and worked in the home of a master of that trade for as long as seven years. Then he could become a journeyman, or salaried worker. In time, if guild officials judged that the journeyman's work met their standards, he could join the guild.

◄ **A shield representing the Guild of Notaries, who prepared and verified documents**

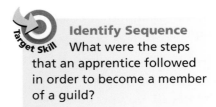
Identify Sequence What were the steps that an apprentice followed in order to become a member of a guild?

Overcrowding and Disease Medieval towns and cities were extremely crowded. Their lack of sanitation, or procedures for keeping the town clean, bred disease, and the overcrowded conditions meant that disease spread quickly. One disease, the bubonic plague, wiped out one third of Europe's population between 1347 and 1351. Called the Black Death, it was spread by fleas living on the rats that thrived in the unsanitary towns.

√ **Reading Check** What was the Black Death?

Troubadours provided entertainment and preserved traditional tales.

Medieval Culture

Despite its hardships, medieval life was not all a struggle for survival. The growing cities attracted traveling scholars, and young men flocked to cathedral schools. Many of these schools became great centers of learning. Much of the beautiful artwork of the Middle Ages was displayed in churches where many could enjoy it.

Stories, poems, and songs about chivalry were also very popular. **Chivalry** is the code of honorable conduct by which knights were supposed to live. Throughout Western Europe, traveling poets and musicians called **troubadours** went from place to place singing about the brave deeds performed by knights to win the love of a beautiful and worthy woman.

√ **Reading Check** Describe some advantages of living in a medieval city.

Section 2 Assessment

Key Terms
Review the key terms at the beginning of this section. Use each term in a sentence that explains its meaning.

Target Reading Skill
Identify and list in sequence three events or conditions that led to the growth of towns.

Comprehension and Critical Thinking
1. (a) **Recall** How was the Church important in everyday life?

(b) **Identify Effects** How did this importance contribute to the Church's power?
2. (a) **List** What factors led to the increase in trade in Western Europe?
(b) **Infer** How might the growth of trade have affected the life of an ordinary person?
3. (a) **Define** What were guilds?
(b) **Draw Conclusions** Why would someone join a guild?
4. (a) **Explain** What was chivalry?
(b) **Infer** Why was chivalry a popular topic for troubadours?

Writing Activity
During the Middle Ages, children began apprenticeships as early as the age of eight. Do you think that is too young an age to start such work? Write a paragraph that answers this question.

Writing Tip Begin your paragraph with a topic sentence that tells whether or not you think eight years old is too young. Use supporting sentences to give reasons for your position.

3 The Crusades

Prepare to Read

Objectives

In this section you will

1. Learn about the causes of the Crusades.
2. Find out about the different Crusades and what they accomplished.
3. Discover the effects the Crusades had on life in Europe.

Taking Notes

As you read this section, look for the ways various people or groups contributed to the Crusades. Copy the table below and record your findings in it.

Person or Group	Contribution

Target Reading Skill

Recognize Sequence Signal Words Signal words point out relationships between ideas or events. This section discusses the Crusades, which took place over many years. To help keep the order of events clear, look for words such as *first, then, finally,* and *in [date]* that signal the order in which the events took place.

Key Terms

- **Holy Land** (HOH lee land) *n.* Jerusalem and parts of the surrounding area where Jesus lived and taught
- **Crusades** (kroo SAYDZ) *n.* a series of military expeditions launched by Christian Europeans to win the Holy Land back from Muslim control
- **Jerusalem** (juh ROOZ uh lum) *n.* a city in the Holy Land, regarded as sacred by Christians, Muslims, and Jews
- **pilgrim** (PIL grum) *n.* a person who journeys to a sacred place

On November 18, 1095, a crowd gathered in the town of Clermont, located in present-day France. They came to hear an urgent message from the pope:

> **"You common people who have been miserable sinners, become soldiers of Christ! You nobles, do not [quarrel] with one another. Use your arms in a just war! Labor for everlasting reward."**
>
> —*Pope Urban II*

The crowd roared its approval. They shouted, "God wills it!"

Pope Urban II was calling the people of Europe to war. The purpose of this war was to capture the **Holy Land,** a region sacred to Christians because Jesus had lived and taught there. It was a small region on the eastern shore of the Mediterranean Sea, in present-day Israel, Jordan, and Palestine. Now, said the pope, the Holy Land has fallen to an enemy. Christians must win it back.

Pope Urban II calling for a crusade to the Holy Land

Chapter 5 Section 3 **133**

Embarking on a Crusade
Huge armies of crusader knights sailed to the Holy Land.
Conclude *What was involved in transporting these large armies?*

Causes of the Crusades

Over the next 200 years, the Church launched eight military expeditions, called the **Crusades**, to capture the Holy Land. The word comes from *crux,* the Latin word for "cross." People who carried the Christian cross into battle against the non-Christian enemy were called crusaders.

Pilgrims to the Holy Land Since about A.D. 200, European Christians had been traveling to **Jerusalem,** a city in the Holy Land regarded as sacred by Christians, Muslims, and Jews. These people were **pilgrims**—people who journey to a sacred place. Nobles and peasants alike made the long and difficult journey. They wanted to visit the places written about in the Bible.

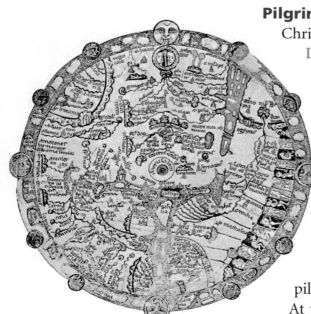

Many medieval Christians believed that Jerusalem was the center of the world, as this map from the 1200s shows.

The Rise of the Turks For centuries, Jerusalem had been controlled by Arab Muslims who generally welcomed Christian pilgrims. Then, in the 1000s, the Seljuk Turks (SEL jook turks) took control of the Holy Land. This Muslim group sometimes attacked the Christian pilgrims from Europe. Then they closed the pilgrimage routes to Jerusalem.

At the same time, the Turks were also conquering much of the Byzantine Empire. The Byzantine emperor in Constantinople asked Pope Urban II to send knights to defend his Christian empire. The pope agreed and called on the people of Europe to fight the Muslim Turks.

Why Go to War? Why did Pope Urban II agree to organize a war against the Muslim Turks? Mainly, he wanted the Holy Land to be under the control of Christians. He wanted Christian pilgrims to be able to visit Jerusalem and other religious sites.

But he also had other reasons. The pope thought a crusade would unite Europeans against a common enemy—the Muslim Turks—and they would stop fighting among themselves. He also hoped to gain power and prestige for himself and the Church.

Some Europeans had other reasons for encouraging the Crusades. They wanted to control not only the Holy Land but also key trade routes between Africa, Asia, and Europe.

✓ **Reading Check** **Why did the pope want to conquer the Holy Land?**

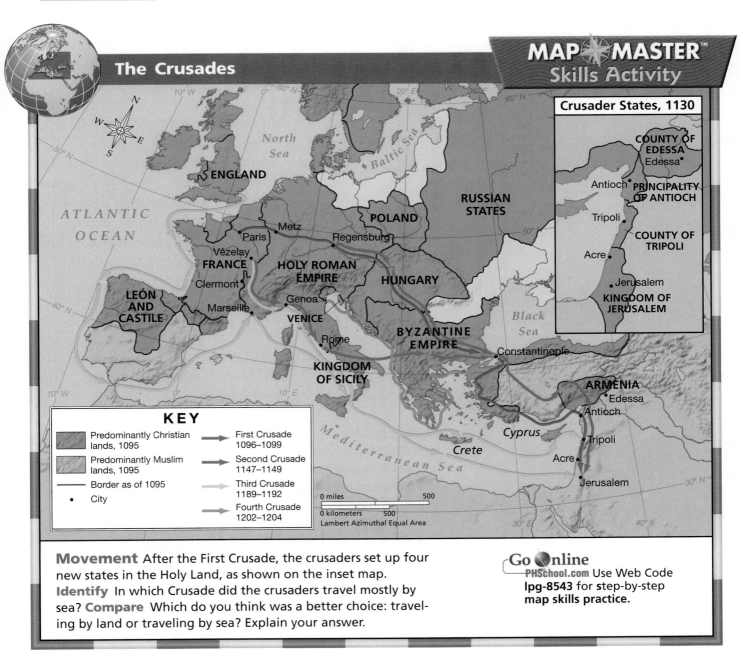

The Crusades

MAP MASTER™ Skills Activity

Crusader States, 1130

COUNTY OF EDESSA
Edessa
Antioch PRINCIPALITY OF ANTIOCH
Tripoli
COUNTY OF TRIPOLI
Acre
Jerusalem
KINGDOM OF JERUSALEM

ENGLAND
North Sea
Baltic Sea
RUSSIAN STATES
POLAND
ATLANTIC OCEAN
Metz
Paris
Regensburg
Vézelay
FRANCE
HOLY ROMAN EMPIRE
Clermont
HUNGARY
LEÓN AND CASTILE
Genoa
Marseille
VENICE
Rome
BYZANTINE EMPIRE
Black Sea
KINGDOM OF SICILY
Constantinople
ARMENIA
Edessa
Cyprus
Antioch
Crete
Tripoli
Acre
Mediterranean Sea
Jerusalem

KEY

Predominantly Christian lands, 1095

Predominantly Muslim lands, 1095

—— Border as of 1095

• City

→ First Crusade 1096–1099

→ Second Crusade 1147–1149

→ Third Crusade 1189–1192

→ Fourth Crusade 1202–1204

0 miles 500
0 kilometers 500
Lambert Azimuthal Equal Area

Movement After the First Crusade, the crusaders set up four new states in the Holy Land, as shown on the inset map. **Identify** In which Crusade did the crusaders travel mostly by sea? **Compare** Which do you think was a better choice: traveling by land or traveling by sea? Explain your answer.

Go Online
PHSchool.com Use Web Code **lpg-8543** for step-by-step map skills practice.

Target Skill

Recognize Sequence Signal Words

What word in the paragraph at the right signals sequence? How does this clue help you understand the next few paragraphs?

A Series of Crusades

The pope's best hope for capturing the Holy Land rested with European lords and their knights. But before these armies could assemble, a band of common people set out for Jerusalem.

Peter the Hermit and the People's Crusade Peter, a small man who wore monk's robes, gathered an "army" of common people. They set out in 1096. When they got to Constantinople, the Byzantine emperor advised them to wait for help from an army of knights from Europe. Peter agreed, but his followers rebelled. His soldiers attacked the Turks, who easily defeated them. Only a small part of his army survived.

The First Crusade At last, the European armies sent by Pope Urban II reached Constantinople. Joined by what remained of Peter's army, the knights fought their way to Jerusalem and captured it in 1099. While taking control of the city, the crusaders killed about 10,000 of its Muslim, Christian, and Jewish inhabitants.

After the capture of Jerusalem, most of the crusaders returned to Europe. Those who stayed in the Holy Land set up four Christian kingdoms. The Muslim Turks attacked these kingdoms repeatedly. European Christians then launched more Crusades to keep control of the region.

Later Crusades The Second Crusade had little success. Then a strong Arab Muslim leader rose to power. He was known to the Europeans as Saladin (SAL uh din). By 1187, Saladin had retaken Jerusalem. King Richard I of England tried to persuade Saladin to return the Holy City to the Christians. Saladin refused, saying,

Crusaders led by Louis IX of France retake the city of Damietta, near Jerusalem.

> **To us Jerusalem is as precious . . . as it is to you, because it is the place from where our Prophet [Muhammad] made his journey by night to heaven. . . . Do not dream that we will give it up to you.**
>
> —*Saladin*

Even so, Saladin negotiated a treaty with King Richard. He agreed to reopen Jerusalem to Christian pilgrims.

✓ **Reading Check** Why did Saladin refuse to give up Jerusalem?

The Results of the Crusades

Although crusaders did capture the Holy Land for a while, they were never able to gain firm control of it. Still, the Crusades brought important and lasting changes to Europe.

Increased Trade The European ships that carried crusaders and their supplies to the Holy Land returned with rugs, jewelry, glass, and spices. Soon, these goods were in great demand in Europe. Thus, the Crusades helped revive trade, which in turn led to the growth of towns and cities.

The Crusades also encouraged the use of money in Europe. For much of the Middle Ages, most people bartered, or traded goods for other goods or for land or protection. But the crusaders went far from home, where they needed to *buy* supplies. In that case, it was easier to use money than it was to barter.

New Ideas Returning crusaders also brought new ideas and technology back to Europe. You have read about the advances made by Arabs in medicine, mathematics, and technology. The crusaders helped increase European knowledge of these techniques. Europeans learned how to make better ships and maps—skills that would help them become worldwide explorers.

Medieval Banking
A man deposits gold in a bank.
Synthesize *Why did banking increase after the Crusades?*

✓ **Reading Check** **Describe two effects of the Crusades.**

Section 3 Assessment

Key Terms
Review the key terms at the beginning of this section. Use each term in a sentence that explains its meaning.

Target Reading Skill
Reread the text on page 134 under the heading The Rise of the Turks. What signal words helped you understand the sequence of these events?

Comprehension and Critical Thinking
1. (a) Find Main Ideas What was the chief goal of the crusaders?

(b) Infer Why do you think Pope Urban II called the First Crusade a "just," or honorable, war?

2. (a) Sequence List the events of the First Crusade in order.

(b) Identify Frame of Reference How do you think European Christians viewed the Muslim Turks? How do you think Muslims living in the Holy Land viewed the crusaders?

3. (a) Identify Effects What were the main effects of the Crusades on life in Europe?

(b) Predict What might have happened in Europe if the Crusades had never taken place?

Writing Activity
Suppose that there were European newspapers that published editorials at the time of the Crusades. Write an editorial either in support of or against the First Crusade.

Writing Tip Remember that editorials are persuasive writing. State your position. Then use reasons and facts to convince readers that your opinion is the right one.

Distinguishing Fact and Opinion

Richard I was born on September 8, 1157. He became king of England in 1189 but spent most of his reign fighting in the Crusades. He led his armies to free the Holy Land. Richard loved to be in the midst of battle and always fought bravely. He spent only six months of his reign in England, but his people loved him anyway. They admired his great courage and called him Richard the Lion-Hearted.

Richard won many battles, but he failed to free the Holy Land. He did make peace with the Muslim leader Saladin, who allowed Christians to visit the holy city of Jerusalem. That was a great accomplishment. Richard died in 1199. He was a good and kind king.

Facts are statements that can be proved true. Opinions are personal beliefs or value judgments. You will often need to make your own judgments or decisions based on facts, so you must be able to recognize them.

King Richard I of England

Learn the Skill

To distinguish fact from opinion, use the following steps:

1. **Look for facts by asking what can be proved true or false.** A fact usually tells who, what, when, where, or how much. A fact can be proved true.

2. **Ask how you could check whether each fact is true.** Could you do your own test by measuring or counting? Could you find information in an encyclopedia or in another reliable reference book?

3. **Look for opinions by identifying personal beliefs or value judgments.** Look for words that signal personal feelings, such as *I think* or *I believe*. Look for words that judge, such as *great* or *brave*, or *should* or *ought to*. An opinion cannot be proved true or false.

4. **Decide whether facts or good reasons support each opinion.** A well-supported opinion can help you make up your own mind—as long as you recognize it as an opinion and not a fact.

Practice the Skill

Read the passage about Richard the Lion-Hearted until you are sure that you understand it. Then reread it for facts and opinions.

1. Identify facts in the paragraph that tell who, what, when, where, and how much.

2. Explain how each fact could be proved true or false.

3. (a) Identify two examples of words that show personal feelings. Can these statements be proved true or false? (b) Now identify one word that signals judgment. Can the statement containing this word be proved true or false?

4. The last sentence in the passage expresses an opinion. Is the opinion well supported with facts and reasons? Explain your answer.

Richard I riding into battle

Burying victims of the Black Death, 1349

Apply the Skill

Read the passage at the right. List two facts and two opinions from the passage. If you found this passage in a book, how useful would it be as a source for a research paper? Explain your answer.

The Black Death was the worst thing that happened in medieval Europe. The disease struck quickly. It caused horrible spots and almost certain death. The Black Death eventually killed so many people—more than 25 million—that normal life broke down. There was a labor shortage, and those workers who survived the disease unfairly demanded higher wages. Farmers turned from growing crops to grazing sheep, which required fewer workers. Fear of the disease and economic disruption caused riots all over Europe. That kind of reaction would never happen today.

Prepare to Read

Objectives

In this section you will
1. Learn about the forces that led to nation building in Europe.
2. Find out about nation building in England.
3. Discover how the Hundred Years' War affected England and France.

Taking Notes

As you read this section, think about what factors led to nation building in England and France. Copy the table below and record your findings in it.

Nation Building	
England	**France**
•	•
•	•

Target Reading Skill

Identify Sequence Noting the order of events can help you understand and remember them. Make a sequence chart of events that led to nation building in England. Write the first event in the first box. Then write each additional event in a box. Use arrows to show how one event led to the next.

Key Terms

- **nation** (NAY shun) *n.* a community of people that shares territory and a government
- **Magna Carta** (MAG nuh KAHR tuh) *n.* the "Great Charter," in which the king's power over his nobles was limited, agreed to by King John of England in 1215
- **Model Parliament** (MAHD ul PAHR luh munt) *n.* a council of lords, clergy, and common people that advised the English king on government matters
- **Hundred Years' War** (HUN drud yeerz wawr) *n.* a series of conflicts between England and France, 1337–1453

Pope Gregory VII forgiving King Henry IV

For three days, the king waited outside the castle where Pope Gregory VII was staying. Barefoot in the winter cold, the king begged forgiveness. Would the pope forgive King Henry IV?

During the Middle Ages, kings and popes quarreled over who should select bishops. Because bishops were Church officials, popes claimed the right to choose them. Kings wanted this right because bishops often controlled large areas of their kingdoms. They also wanted to play a role in the Church.

In 1077, Henry IV of Germany ruled much of Europe. He had been choosing bishops even though Pope Gregory had ordered him not to. In response, the pope had excommunicated the king and declared that his people no longer had to obey him. However, after putting Henry off for three long, cold days, the pope gave in. He allowed Henry to rejoin the Church.

Pope Gregory had made a serious mistake. In 1081, King Henry invaded Italy, where the pope lived. By 1084, Henry had replaced Pope Gregory with a new pope, who crowned Henry emperor of the Holy Roman Empire. Gregory was sent into exile.

Nation Building

Henry's success in overthrowing the pope was a hint of things to come. As later kings gained power, they often dared to put their own wishes before those of the Church. They would soon increase their power in other ways as well.

Castle Stronghold
This English castle is protected by walls and water. **Infer** *What would be involved in defending this castle from attack?*

The Power of Nobles When the 1200s began, Europe was still a feudal society. While kings reigned over kingdoms, the wealthiest lords also had great power. Many saw themselves as nearly the king's equal. In fact, it was not unusual for a noble to have more land, vassals, and knights than his king. But the nobles' power was based on the feudal system. If the feudal system began to decline, so would the nobles' power.

The Decline of Feudalism One reason for the decline of the feudal system was the growth of trade and towns. Kings began to support the new towns in exchange for money. They agreed to protect towns and made laws to help towns grow rich. Then, with the money paid by townspeople, kings hired armies and used them to attack troublesome nobles.

The Crusades also weakened the nobles. Many gave up land to raise money so they could join the Crusades. Other nobles were killed in the Crusades, and kings claimed their land.

The Birth of Nations Over time, kings became more and more powerful. Instead of a patchwork of fiefs ruled by many nobles, large areas of Europe became united under a single king. The kings became strong enough to challenge the Church.

Gradually, these larger kingdoms began to turn into nations. A **nation** is a community of people that shares territory and a government. A common language and culture also often unite the people of a nation. The process of combining smaller communities into a single nation with a national identity and a national government is called nation building.

In the late Middle Ages, the idea of nationhood was taking hold in Europe. A royal marriage united the two largest kingdoms in Spain. In Russia, rulers called tsars were expanding their territory and their power over other nobles. In France, a long line of kings slowly but surely increased royal power. Louis IX, who ruled from 1226 to 1270, was a deeply religious king. He strengthened both Christianity and the central government in his kingdom.

✓ Reading Check **What is nation building?**

Identify Sequence
What events described in the paragraph at the right led to increased power of the king? Write these events in a sequence chart.

Changes in England

By the 1200s, England was already well on its way to becoming a unified nation. In 1066, William of Normandy, a duke from France, had conquered England in what came to be called the Norman Conquest. As king of England, William the Conqueror was a strong ruler who made sure to keep more power than his nobles. The kings who followed William—especially Henry I and Henry II—further increased the power of the king. Of course, the nobles began to resent this power. King John, a son of Henry II, would soon face their anger.

King John Angers the Nobles When John became king of England in 1199, he quickly moved to increase his wealth and power. He taxed people heavily. He jailed his enemies unjustly and without trial. Even the most powerful nobles were hurt by John's unfair actions.

John also clashed with the pope by objecting to the appointment of a bishop he did not like. The king seized Church property. The pope struck back by excommunicating John and declaring that he was no longer king.

King John at Runnymede
The Magna Carta marked the beginning of limitations on the power of the king. **Synthesize** *Which groups of English society are shown with King John in this engraving? How did they benefit from the Magna Carta?*

The Magna Carta John was now at the mercy of the nobles and clergy whom he had angered. With the backing of the bishops, English nobles demanded a meeting with the king. On June 15, 1215, about 2,000 English nobles gathered at Runnymede, a meadow along the Thames River. They presented John with a list of their demands. John was forced to place the royal seal on the document, and it became law. Called the **Magna Carta** (MAG nuh KAHR tuh), or the "Great Charter," it limited the king's power over the nobles. The king could no longer jail any freeman without just cause, and he could not raise taxes without consulting his Great Council of lords and clergy.

This council later became the **Model Parliament,** which included common people as well as lords and clergy. Eventually, Parliament evolved into a powerful legislature. As it gained power, Parliament also helped unify England. At the same time, however, the Magna Carta also strengthened the power of the king. Because nobles now had a say in government, they were more likely to support what the king did.

✓ Reading Check **How did the Magna Carta help unite England?**

The Hundred Years' War

Despite the growth of nations, Western Europe was not at peace. Now, instead of nobles fighting each other, the emerging nations went to war. One long series of clashes between England and France was called the **Hundred Years' War.** It lasted from 1337 to 1453.

Causes of the War In the 1300s, the borders of England and France were not the ones we know today. As a result of marriage and inheritance, the English king had come to be the lord of many counties in present-day France.

You have read that William the Conqueror, who became king of England in 1066, was also Duke of Normandy in France. The 1152 marriage of King Henry II of England and the French noblewoman Eleanor of Aquitaine brought more French land under English control.

Then, in 1328, the French king died. King Edward III of England, whose mother had been a French princess, claimed to be king of France under feudal law. The French nobles did not agree. Determined to get his way, Edward III invaded France—and began the Hundred Years' War.

There were other causes of the war. Both England and France wanted to control the English Channel, the waterway that separates their countries. Each nation also wanted to control trade in the region and the wealth it brought.

Joan of Arc's Victory The Hundred Years' War dragged on, fought by one king after another. England won most of the battles, but the French continued to fight. However, the tide turned in 1429 when a peasant girl called Joan of Arc took charge of the French forces at the battle of Orléans (awr lay AHN). French troops at Orléans greeted her with hope and curiosity.

Under Joan's command, the French defeated the English at Orléans. She then led her forces to victory in other battles. In 1430, Joan was taken prisoner by allies of the English. England tried Joan for witchcraft. She was convicted and burned at the stake.

The French saw Joan of Arc as a martyr, and her death inspired them to many victories. By 1453, the English had been driven from most of France. With the English troops in retreat, France was on its way to becoming a strong and united nation.

Citizen Heroes

Joan of Arc

The young girl who would become one of France's greatest heroes was the daughter of a tenant farmer. Joan was very religious and believed that she saw heavenly visions. In 1429, when she was only 17, she journeyed to the court of Charles, the heir to the French throne. She convinced him that God had called her to lead the French forces at the battle of Orléans. Charles finally agreed. He gave Joan armor, attendants, horses, and a special banner to carry into battle. You can see that banner in this statue of Joan, which stands in Paris.

King Henry VIII
The Tudor monarchs of England, 1485–1603, were very powerful. Yet Henry VIII consulted with Parliament on important issues. **Analyze Images** *How does this portrait show Henry's power and personality?*

The Growing Power of Kings The Hundred Years' War affected the balance of power in England and France. On the battlefield, new weapons such as the longbow and cannon increased the importance of footsoldiers. Armored knights, on the other hand, became less valuable in battle. Feudal castles could not stand up to the firepower of the new cannons. Kings now needed large armies, not small bands of knights, to fight for them.

The Hundred Years' War also led to national feeling. People began to think of themselves as citizens of England or of France, not simply as loyal to their local lords. Kings who had led their nations in battle became more powerful as the influence of nobles declined. On the other hand, the English king had been forced to ask Parliament for more and more money to fund the war. This helped Parliament win "the power of the purse" and increased its power in relation to the king. These two developments helped unify England.

The Hundred Years' War helped set the modern boundaries of England and France. Forced to give up their dream of an empire in Europe, the English began to look to more distant lands for trade and conquest. Leaving feudalism behind, Europe was becoming a continent of nations. And some of these nations, as you will read in Chapter 6, would soon rule much of the world.

✓ **Reading Check** **Explain two effects of the Hundred Years' War.**

Section 4 Assessment

Key Terms
Review the key terms at the beginning of this section. Use each term in a sentence that explains its meaning.

Target Reading Skill
Reread page 143. Write the events of Joan of Arc's life in a sequence chart.

Comprehension and Critical Thinking
1. (a) Recall How much power did kings have under feudalism?

(b) Identify Cause and Effect Why did feudalism decline, and how did this affect the power of kings?

2. (a) Identify What are two limits on the king's power established by the Magna Carta?

(b) Identify Effects How did the Magna Carta help unify England as a nation?

3. (a) Name Who fought the Hundred Years' War?

(b) Identify Effects How did this war help unify two nations?

Writing Activity
Suppose that you are a French soldier preparing for the battle of Orléans. Describe your reaction to the news that a young peasant girl is your new commander.

For: An activity on the Hundred Years' War
Visit: PHSchool.com
Web Code: lgd-8504

Chapter 5 — Review and Assessment

◆ Chapter Summary

Section 1: Feudalism and the Manor System

- The Middle Ages was the period from about A.D. 500 to 1500.
- Feudalism, in which land was owned by nobles but held by vassals in return for loyalty, was the medieval government system.
- The manor system, in which many people lived and worked on large estates owned by lords, was the medieval economic system.
- Most people of the Middle Ages were peasants. Serfs were peasants who were considered part of the manors on which they worked.

Section 2: The Church and the Rise of Cities

- During the Middle Ages, the Roman Catholic Church was a powerful force that touched nearly every aspect of people's lives.
- An increase in trade led to the growth of towns and cities.
- The new middle class organized craft and trade guilds. Medieval towns and cities were crowded and unsanitary.
- Culture and learning were limited to only a few people. Troubadours brought stories of chivalry from place to place.

Lombard warrior

Section 3: The Crusades

- The Crusades were a series of wars launched by European Christians to capture the Holy Land from Muslim Turks.
- The First Crusade succeeded in capturing the holy city of Jerusalem.
- Later Crusades were launched to defend the Christian kingdoms in the Holy Land from Muslim Turk attacks.
- The Crusades changed life in Europe: trade increased, towns grew, the use of money increased, and the learning of the Arab world came to Europe.

Section 4: The Power of Kings

- Nation building in Europe began as feudalism declined and kings increased their power.
- The Magna Carta limited the power of the English king but also helped unify England into a nation.
- The Hundred Years' War helped unify both England and France into nations.

◆ Key Terms

Write one or two paragraphs about life in the Middle Ages. Use all of the following terms correctly in your paragraphs.

1. Middle Ages
2. feudalism
3. vassals
4. fief
5. manor
6. serfs
7. clergy
8. apprentice
9. troubadour
10. Crusades

◆ Comprehension and Critical Thinking

11. (a) Recall In the feudal system, what was the role of a lord? Of a vassal?
(b) Synthesize How could one person be both a lord and a vassal at the same time?

12. (a) Describe What was a manor, and how did it meet people's needs?
(b) Explain What was the relationship of serfs to the manor?
(c) Draw Conclusions How did manorialism help support feudalism?

13. (a) Identify What was "the Church" in the Middle Ages?
(b) Draw Conclusions Why was the Church so powerful in the Middle Ages?

14. (a) Recall Where did towns spring up during the Middle Ages?
(b) Synthesize Information How was the growth of medieval towns related to the growth of guilds?

15. (a) Define What were the Crusades?
(b) Draw Conclusions Do you think the Crusades helped or hurt Europe? Explain.

16. (a) Define What is nation building?
(b) Identify Causes What factors led to nation building in Europe in the later Middle Ages?

17. (a) Recall Who was Joan of Arc?
(b) Identify Effects How did she influence the outcome of the Hundred Years' War?

◆ Skills Practice

Distinguishing Fact and Opinion In the Skills for Life activity in this chapter, you learned how to distinguish fact from opinion. Review the steps you followed to learn the skill. Then reread the opening paragraphs of Section 2 of this chapter on page 126. List the facts and opinions in this text. For each opinion, note whether or not you think the opinion is well supported and reliable.

◆ Writing Activity: Science

The bubonic plague—the Black Death that killed so many Europeans during the Middle Ages—still exists today. However, it is not nearly so common or deadly as it once was. Use an encyclopedia and other reliable sources to learn how modern medicine and sanitation prevent and control the disease. Write a brief report titled "The Bubonic Plague in Modern Times."

MAP✷MASTER™ Skills Activity

Europe and the Holy Land

Place Location For each place listed below, write the letter from the map that shows its location.
1. England
2. France
3. Jerusalem
4. Mediterranean Sea
5. Rome
6. Constantinople

Go Online
PHSchool.com Use Web Code
lgd-8554 for an **interactive map.**

Standardized Test Prep

Test-Taking Tips

Some questions on standardized tests ask you to identify cause and effect. Study the graphic organizer below. Then use the tip to help you answer the sample question.

```
┌─────────────────────────────────────┐
│              CAUSES                  │
│  • King John taxed people heavily.   │
│  • King John jailed enemies unfairly.│
│  • King John seized church property. │
└─────────────────────────────────────┘
                  ▽
┌─────────────────────────────────────┐
│        EVENT: MAGNA CARTA            │
└─────────────────────────────────────┘
                  ▽
┌─────────────────────────────────────┐
│              EFFECTS                 │
│  • King couldn't jail nobles.        │
│  • King couldn't tax without consent.│
│  •                                   │
└─────────────────────────────────────┘
```

TIP Remember that a *cause* is what makes something happen. An *effect* is what happens as a result of something else. Is the question asking for a cause or an effect?

Pick the letter that best answers the question.

What information belongs with the last bullet (•) in the graphic organizer?

  A King John clashed with the pope.
  B It became law with King John's seal.
  C It helped unite England.
  D King John seized Church property.

Think It Through The question is asking for an effect: What else happened as a result of the Magna Carta? You can eliminate A and D because both were causes, or events leading up to the Magna Carta. That leaves B and C. The Magna Carta did become law with King John's seal, but that was not an *effect* of the law. The answer is C: the Magna Carta had the effect of helping to unite England.

Practice Questions

Choose the letter of the best answer.

1. Which of the following was a major cause of the growth of towns during the Middle Ages?
   A a decrease in the power of the Church
   B an increase in trade
   C a decrease in Europe's population
   D an increase in the number of manors

2. Which of the following was NOT an effect of the Crusades?
   A The demand for foreign goods increased.
   B Europeans learned new shipbuilding techniques.
   C The use of money became more common.
   D The Holy Land came under permanent European control.

3. The decline of _____ helped the growth of _____.
   A trade, towns
   B feudalism, manorialism
   C Charlemagne's empire, feudalism
   D the Roman Empire, trade

Study the diagram. Then use it to answer the question that follows.

```
┌──────────┐    ┌──────────┐    ┌──────────┐
│    1     │    │    2     │    │    3     │
│ Factors  │──▶ │  Nation  │──▶ │Changes in│
│          │    │ Building │    │ England  │
└──────────┘    └──────────┘    └──────────┘
```

4. In the diagram,
   A **1** represents a single effect of nation building, and **2** and **3** represent several causes.
   B **1** represents a single cause of **2**, and **2** is a cause of **3**.
   C **2** is a cause of both **1** and **3**.
   D **1** represents several causes of **2**, and **3** represents how nation building affected England.

Go Online
PHSchool.com

Use Web Code **lga-8504**
for a **Chapter 5 self-test**.

Of Swords and Sorcerers:
The Adventures of King Arthur and His Knights
By Margaret Hodges and Margery Evernden

Prepare to Read

Background Information
How should a good and just ruler behave? What traits should a king or queen have? What do you admire in people who lead others?

People have read and enjoyed the stories of King Arthur for hundreds of years. To many, he symbolizes the virtue and justice of a good ruler. According to legend, he was loved and respected by all of his people.

Legends about King Arthur exist in many forms, and stories about him have been written and rewritten in several languages. The following selection is one tale of how Arthur met his friend Pellinore and found his sword, which was named Excalibur.

Objectives
As you read this selection, you will
1. Understand why King Arthur's subjects loved him.
2. Learn about some of the rules of honor in battle that were part of the code of chivalry.

petty (PET ee) *adj.* unimportant; of low rank

fealty (FEE ul tee) *n.* loyalty to a feudal lord

No king before Arthur had been able to unite the realm and rule it. This Arthur did. Lightnings and thunders surrounded him as he fought. In twelve great battles he defeated <u>petty</u> kings who had been constantly at war, laying waste all the land. The last to surrender was Arthur's own brother-in-law, King Lot of Orkney. When Lot laid down his arms and swore <u>fealty</u> to Arthur, he sent his sons to become knights at Camelot.

King Arthur standing with the crowns of 30 kingdoms, in an illustration from 1325

One son was Gawain, handsome and strong, whom Arthur called Gawain the Courteous. Another was Mordred, whose foxy smile and <u>gimlet eyes</u> concealed <u>malice</u> and a thirst for power. Gawain took the vows of knighthood in good faith, but Mordred's vows were insincere, and he soon began listening at the castle doors in hope of ferreting out secrets that might damage the court and someday play into his own hands. He saw that the time to strike had not yet come. The powers of heaven and earth all seemed to be on Arthur's side. The people loved him, and Camelot was in its glory.

Now there came a day when Arthur rode with Merlin seeking adventure, and in a forest they found a knight named Pellinore, seated in a chair, blocking their path.

"Sir, will you let us pass?" said Arthur.

"Not without a fight," replied Pellinore. "Such is my custom."

"I will change your custom," said Arthur.

"I will defend it," said Pellinore. He mounted his horse and took his shield on his arm. Then the two knights rode against each other, and each splintered his spear on the other's shield.

"I have no more spears," said Arthur. "Let us fight with swords."

"Not so," said Pellinore. "I have enough spears. I will lend you one."

Then a squire brought two good spears, and the two knights rode against each other again until those spears were broken.

"You are as good a fighter as ever I met," said Pellinore. "Let us try again."

Two great spears were brought, and this time Pellinore struck Arthur's shield so hard that the king and his horse fell to the earth.

Then Arthur pulled out his sword and said, "I have lost the battle on horseback. Let me try you on foot."

Pellinore thought it unfair to attack from his horse, so he dismounted and came toward Arthur with his sword drawn. Then began such a battle that both were covered with blood. After a while they sat down to rest and fought again until both fell to the ground. Again they fought, and the fight was even. But at last Pellinore struck such a blow that Arthur's sword broke into two pieces. Thereupon the king leaped at Pellinore. He threw him down and pulled off his helmet. But Pellinore was a very big man and strong enough to wrestle Arthur under him and pull off the

gimlet eyes (GIM lit eyez) *n.* eyes having a piercing quality
malice (MAL is) *n.* spite; a desire to damage or hurt someone

Knights in battle, in an illustration by N. C. Wyeth

✓ Reading Check

Why did Arthur and Pellinore fight?

king's helmet. All this time Merlin had watched, silent, but when he saw that Pellinore was about to cut off Arthur's head, he interfered.

"Do not kill this man," he said to Pellinore. "You do not know who he is."

"Why, who is he?" said the knight.

"It is King Arthur," said Merlin.

When he heard this, Pellinore trembled with fear of the royal <u>wrath</u>, for he would not knowingly have fought against the king. Then Merlin cast a spell of sleep on Pellinore so that he fell to the earth as if dead.

"Alas," said Arthur, "you have killed the best knight I ever fought."

"Have no fear," said Merlin. "He will awake in three hours as well as ever he was."

Then he mounted Pellinore's horse and led Arthur to a <u>hermit</u>, who bound up the king's wounds and healed them with good <u>salves</u>, so that he might ride again and go on his way.

But Arthur said, "I have no sword."

"Never fear," said Merlin. "Not far away is a sword that can be yours." So they rode on until they came to a broad lake of clear water. Far out in the middle of the lake Arthur saw an arm clothed in shining white and holding a noble sword, its golden hilt richly set with jewels.

"Lo," said Merlin, "yonder is the sword Excalibur."

wrath (rath) *n.* great anger or rage

hermit (HUR mit) *n.* a person who lives alone and away from others
salve (sahv) *n.* an oily substance used as medicine on the skin

King Arthur claiming Excalibur, in an illustration by N. C. Wyeth

Then they saw a lady floating toward them as if she walked on the water. Her garments were like a mist around her.

"That is the Lady of the Lake," said Merlin. "Within the lake is a rock, and within the rock is a palace, and within the palace lives this lady with many other ladies who serve her. She is called Vivien. Speak to her as a friend, and she will give you that sword."

So, when she had come close, Arthur said to her, "Lady, I wish that sword were mine, for I have no sword."

"It shall be yours," said the lady, and she showed Arthur a little boat lying at the edge of the lake. "Row out to the sword," she said. "Take it with its <u>scabbard</u>." Then she disappeared. Arthur and Merlin rowed out into the lake, and Arthur took the sword from the hand that held it. And the arm and the hand vanished under the water.

Arthur and Merlin rowed to shore and went on their way, and whenever Arthur looked on the sword, he liked it well.

"Which do you like better? asked Merlin. "The sword or the scabbard?"

"I like the sword better," said Arthur.

"The scabbard is worth ten such swords," said Merlin, "for while you wear the scabbard, you will never lose blood, no matter how sorely you are wounded."

So they rode back to Arthur's court, and all his knights marveled when they heard that the king risked his life in single combat as his poor knights did. They said it was merry to be under such a <u>chieftain</u>.

About the Selection

Of Swords and Sorcerers: The Adventures of King Arthur and His Knights was published in 1993. It includes nine episodes in the life of King Arthur.

scabbard (SKAB urd) *n.* a case or cover for a sword or dagger
chieftain (CHEEF tun) *n.* the head of a clan; leader of many people

✓ Reading Check

Which did Arthur like better, the sword or the scabbard?

Review and Assessment

Thinking About the Selection

1. **(a) Describe** How did Arthur and Pellinore fight?
(b) Predict How do you think the fight would have ended if Merlin had not interfered? Why do you think so?
2. **(a) Note** What did Arthur's knights think when they heard about his fight with Pellinore?
(b) Draw Conclusions What qualities does Arthur demonstrate in this episode that would make him a good ruler?

(c) Predict What kind of a ruler do you think Arthur would be in today's world? Explain your answer.

Writing Activity

Write a Poem or a Story Many characters in myths and legends have objects that protect them or give them special powers, as Arthur's sword and scabbard did for him. Write a poem or a story about a character who receives one such tool. What are its powers? How does it help the character?

About the Authors

Margaret Hodges (b.1911), above, was a children's librarian and a storyteller for a children's radio program. She believes that myths are still important in our modern world. **Margery Evernden** has written children's books, biographies, and plays.

A New Age in Europe

Chapter Preview

This chapter will introduce you to the ideas and events that changed Europe after the Middle Ages. These ideas and events led Europeans to new places and to new ways of looking at themselves and the world.

Section 1
The Renaissance and Reformation

Section 2
The Age of Exploration

Section 3
The Age of Powerful Monarchs

Section 4
Conquests in the Americas and Africa

Target Reading Skill

Context In this chapter you will focus on using context to help you understand unfamiliar words. Context includes the words, phrases, and sentences surrounding a word.

▶ The gardens at the Palace of Versailles, France

NORWAY

SWEDEN

MUSCOVY
(RUSSIA)

KHANATE
OF KAZAN

SCOTLAND

TEUTONIC ORDER

PSKOV

.Moscow

IRELAND
(England)

*North
Sea*

DENMARK
Copenhagen.

Baltic Sea

RYAZAN

KHANATE OF
THE GOLDEN
HORDE

ENGLAND

London.

Wittenberg.

POLAND-
LITHUANIA

KHANATE OF
ASTRAKHAN

*ATLANTIC
OCEAN*

HOLY

Paris.

ROMAN

FRANCE

EMPIRE

*Caspian
Sea*

NAVARRE

BÉARN

Venice.

VENICE

HUNGARY

Florence.

Black Sea

Lisbon.

SPAIN

PORTUGAL

PAPAL
STATES

Rome.

OTTOMAN EMPIRE

.Seville

NAPLES
(Spain)

Constantinople.

Mediterranean Sea

RHODES

KEY

— Border as of 1500

• City

CRETE
(Venice)

CYPRUS
(Venice)

0 miles   500

0 kilometers   500

Lambert Azimuthal Equal Area

Regions In 1500, many modern European countries did not exist
or their borders were different than they are today. **Identify** Which
countries on the map still exist today? **Compare** How do their borders in 1500 compare to their present borders?

Go Online
PHSchool.com Use Web Code
lgp-8611 for step-by-step
map skills practice.

The Renaissance and Reformation

Prepare to Read

Objectives

In this section, you will
1. Learn about the Renaissance and why it occurred when and where it did.
2. Find out about Renaissance art and artists.
3. Discover how the Reformation changed religious life in Europe.

Taking Notes

As you read this section, look for the main features of the Renaissance. Copy the diagram below and record your findings in it.

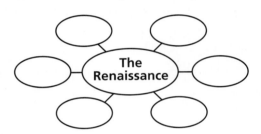

The Renaissance

Target Reading Skill

Use Context Clues You can often figure out the meaning of an unfamiliar word by using context clues in nearby words or sentences. One kind of context clue is a synonym, such as the one in italics in the following example: "The wealthy became great patrons, or *supporters*, of the arts."

Key Terms

- **Renaissance** (REN uh sahns) *n.* the period of the rebirth of learning in Europe between about 1300 and 1600
- **humanism** (HYOO muh niz um) *n.* a system of thought that focuses on the nature, ideals, and achievements of human beings, rather than on the divine
- **Reformation** (ref ur MAY shun) *n.* the effort to change or reform the Roman Catholic Church, which led to the establishment of Protestant churches
- **Protestant** (PRAHT us tunt) *adj.* referring to Christian religions that grew out of the Reformation

Have you ever wanted to fly like a bird? Leonardo da Vinci did. This brilliant artist and scientist, who lived about 500 years ago, thought that people could learn to fly. He studied birds and bats as well as winged seeds to learn about flying.

Leonardo never actually built a flying machine. But, as you can see from the drawing at the left, he drew plans for a machine that looks very much like a helicopter. His sketches also included designs for early examples of a parachute and an airplane.

Leonardo was just one of the many gifted Europeans who lived between about 1300 and 1600. This was the time of the **Renaissance,** a period of rebirth of learning in Europe. As you recall, learning was limited during the Middle Ages. The word *Renaissance* means "rebirth," and this period saw a reawakening of interest in art, literature, and science, as well as in the classical civilizations of Greece and Rome.

Leonardo da Vinci's sketch of a flying machine

The Renaissance

The Renaissance began in northern Italy. Why did it begin there?

During the Middle Ages, northern Italy, where Leonardo lived, was different from the rest of Western Europe. Most people in northern Europe lived under feudalism. They labored for their lords and depended on their lords for protection. Manors, rather than cities, were the centers of economic life.

The Italian City-States In northern Italy, however, people lived in city-states, or cities that were both cities and independent states. They had their own governments and were not as closely controlled by nobles or the Church. Instead, wealthy families or wealthy merchants held power. These merchants controlled European trade with Asia. Italian merchants bought precious goods such as silk and spices in Muslim trading centers around the Mediterranean Sea. Then they transported these goods throughout Europe, reselling them at high prices. The city of Venice, built on islands in the Adriatic Sea, was a leader in this trade.

Being at the center of this lively international trade exposed the Italian city-states to other cultures and ideas. And because trade brought them wealth, many northern Italians had more time to think, to read, and to create and enjoy art. The wealthy became great patrons, or financial supporters, of scholarship and the arts. By the 1430s, the city of Florence, ruled by the prosperous Medici family, had become a center for the arts. Lorenzo de Medici, called the Magnificent, was a generous and powerful patron of artists, poets, and philosophers.

Links to
Government

Machiavelli's *The Prince* Niccolò Machiavelli (nee koh LOH mahk ee uh VEL ee) was a Florentine diplomat. He drew on his experience of politics and his study of Roman history to write *The Prince,* which he dedicated to Lorenzo de Medici (photo). This book was a guide for gaining and keeping power. Machiavelli said rulers should use whatever methods were necessary to accomplish their goals. He advised rulers that getting results was more important than keeping promises. *The Prince* became famous—and controversial. Today, the term *Machiavellian* still refers to cynical dishonesty in politics.

Renaissance Florence
This 1490 view of Florence shows how the city-state spanned the banks of the Arno River. **Conclude** *How do you think its location on the Arno affected the growth of Florence and life within its borders?*

A New Realism
Both paintings above were done in Italy. Duccio painted the one on the left around 1311. The painting by Raphael on the right was done about 200 years later. **Compare and Contrast** *What elements make one painting more realistic than the other? Consider the treatment of people, buildings, scenery, and three-dimensional space.*

Old Ideas and New Ideas In the 1300s, the scholars and artists of Italy began to look at life in a new way. First, they looked back—not to the Middle Ages, but to the literature, science, and art of ancient Greece and Rome. Ruins of fine architecture and realistic statues were all around them, especially in the city of Rome. These works inspired study and curiosity as well as a new focus on the achievements of individual people.

Renaissance scholars and artists developed a new focus on the nature, ideals, and achievements of human beings, rather than on the divine. This philosophy is called **humanism.** The ideal of this new era was someone with talent and achievements in many fields, such as Leonardo. Such a person came to be called a Renaissance man.

The Northern Renaissance A rebirth of culture occurred somewhat later in northern Europe. In the early 1400s, artists such as Jan van Eyck developed a distinctive Flemish style of painting. By the 1450s, newly prosperous cities in the north were the center of a Northern Renaissance. Scholars and artists, such as the German artist Albrecht Dürer, traveled to Italy and helped spread the ideas of the Italian Renaissance in the north. By the late 1500s, the Renaissance had reached England, where the plays of William Shakespeare drew large audiences.

✓ Reading Check **What was the Northern Renaissance?**

The Renaissance Artist

Artists of the Middle Ages had not painted people or nature realistically. Their goal had been to celebrate God, the saints, and the Church. In contrast, the artists of the Renaissance studied and copied the more realistic art of ancient Greece and Rome. While they continued to do religious paintings, they often used the architecture and clothing of their own time for these biblical scenes.

In keeping with their interest in individual achievement, these artists also painted realistic portraits of important people of the day—including their patrons. One of the most famous Renaissance paintings, the *Mona Lisa* by Leonardo da Vinci, depicts a woman who was not famous. In fact, to this day, no one is sure who she was.

Art Meets Science To better understand how to portray people, Italian painters and sculptors studied the bones and muscles of the body. Some artists even dissected corpses to learn about anatomy. Renaissance painters also used a new technique called perspective to make objects and landscapes look more realistic. By making distant objects smaller, artists could create scenes that appeared three-dimensional. They also used light and shadow to make objects look solid.

Michelangelo Michelangelo was one of the greatest artists of the Renaissance. He could sculpt marble so that it looked like flowing cloth, rippling muscle, and twisting hair. However, his most famous work is not a sculpture but a series of paintings that cover the ceiling and walls of the Sistine Chapel in Vatican City in Rome. The Vatican is the headquarters of the Roman Catholic Church.

Painting and sculpture were not Michelangelo's only achievements. He was also a poet and an architect. Michelangelo designed the dome of St. Peter's Cathedral in Rome as well as military fortifications for the city of Florence. Like Leonardo, Michelangelo was a Renaissance man.

✓ **Reading Check** Why is Michelangelo called a Renaissance man?

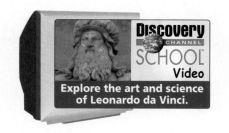
Explore the art and science of Leonardo da Vinci.

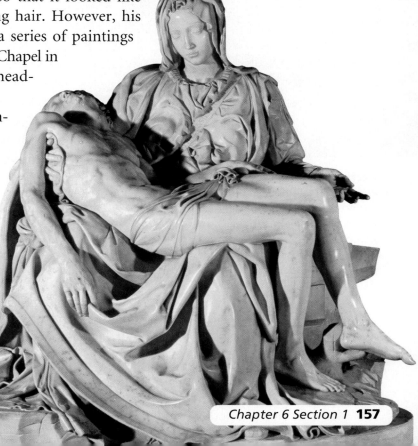

Mastery in Marble
In 1499, when he was in his early twenties, Michelangelo carved this statue of the Virgin Mary holding the body of Jesus. **Infer** *What can you infer about Michelangelo from this work of art?*

The Protestant Reformation

Michelangelo painted many religious works. His patrons included Lorenzo de Medici as well as two popes. Clearly, the Roman Catholic Church still held great power during the Renaissance. But that power was about to be challenged.

In 1517, only five years after Michelangelo finished the Sistine Chapel, a German monk named Martin Luther began to criticize the Church. Following the custom of the time, he posted a list of his complaints on the door of his church in Wittenberg, Germany. This act is regarded as the beginning of the **Reformation**, an effort to reform, or improve, the Catholic Church. At first, instead of reform, it led to the establishment of new forms of Christianity.

Luther's Beliefs Luther disagreed with many of the teachings and practices of the Roman Catholic Church of the early 1500s. He believed that people did not need popes or other Church officials to tell them what God wanted them to do. In Luther's view, faith in God coupled with common sense, and not obedience to the Church, was the key to a proper Christian life.

Luther also felt that ordinary people could understand the Bible for themselves. He translated the Bible into German so that ordinary people could read it. He was in favor of creating town schools that would teach everyone to read.

Luther especially despised the Church practice of selling indulgences, or pardons for sins. At that time, people were asked to pay money to the Church to be forgiven for their sins. Luther felt that the Church did not have the power to exchange God's forgiveness for money. What's more, the Church often sold indulgences more to raise money than for any truly religious reason.

Martin Luther
This modern stained-glass window illustrates the story of Martin Luther nailing his complaints to the church door. **Analyze Images** *What details suggest Luther's dual roles as professor and monk?*

Luther's Teachings Spread In Germany, priests, nobles, and ordinary people rallied behind Luther's ideas. Some priests agreed with Luther about corruption in the Church. Nobles were eager to limit the Church's overwhelming power. They wanted to collect their own taxes and make their own laws, like the leaders of Italy's city-states.

Meanwhile, a revolution in technology had begun in Germany. In the 1400s, the German printer Johann Gutenberg invented the first European printing press using movable type. He printed a Bible in 1455. The development of the European printing press helped spread Luther's writings across Europe. Bibles printed in German became available. By the time Luther died in 1546, most of the people in what is now northern Germany were Lutheran, or followers of Luther's teachings.

Protestant Churches Soon, people in much of northern Europe held views similar to Luther's. They created their own Christian churches, free of Roman Catholic control. These came to be called **Protestant** churches because they grew out of protests against the power and abuses of the Roman Catholic Church. Their members, even today, are called Protestants.

Use Context Clues If you do not know what *Lutheran* means, look for a definition in the nearby words and phrases. What is the definition of *Lutheran*, and where did you find it?

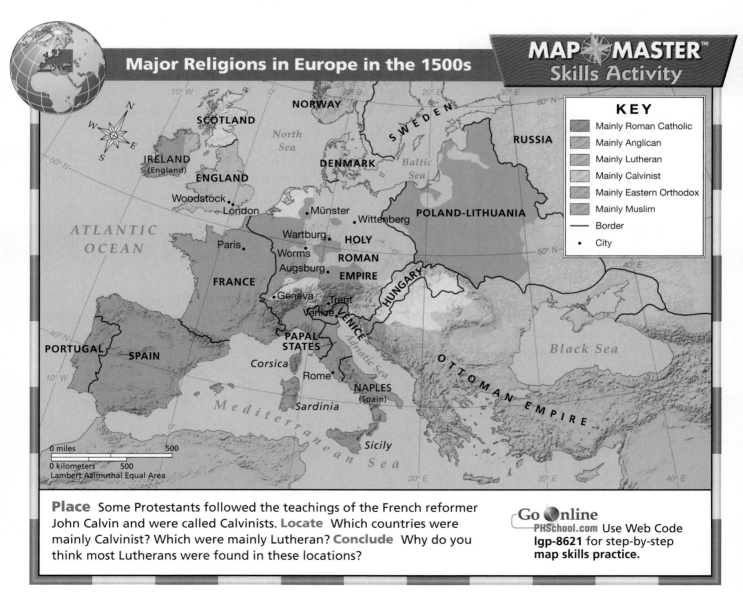

Major Religions in Europe in the 1500s

MAP MASTER™ Skills Activity

KEY
- Mainly Roman Catholic
- Mainly Anglican
- Mainly Lutheran
- Mainly Calvinist
- Mainly Eastern Orthodox
- Mainly Muslim
- Border
- City

Place Some Protestants followed the teachings of the French reformer John Calvin and were called Calvinists. **Locate** Which countries were mainly Calvinist? Which were mainly Lutheran? **Conclude** Why do you think most Lutherans were found in these locations?

Go Online
PHSchool.com Use Web Code **lgp-8621** for step-by-step **map skills practice.**

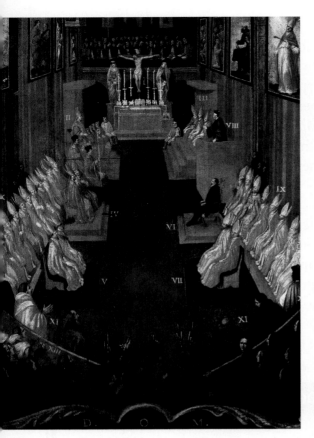

The opening session of the
Council of Trent, 1545

The Catholic Reformation Many Roman Catholics agreed with some criticisms made by Protestants. Instead of turning away from the Church, however, they worked to reform it. As part of this Catholic Reformation, Pope Paul III set up the Council of Trent in 1545. For almost 20 years, it worked to correct the worst abuses of the Church. But it also maintained the basic teachings of the Catholic Church.

The Catholic Reformation also strove to bring Protestants back to the Catholic Church and to make sure that Catholics held strictly to Church teachings. In an effort to wipe out heresy, or beliefs that did not conform to Church teachings, the Church strengthened the power of the Inquisition. The Inquisition was a system of church courts that used secret testimony and torture to root out heresy and force non-Catholics to convert to Catholicism.

At the same time, the effort to reform the Church led to a rebirth of sincere faith among many Catholics. St. Vincent de Paul worked to help the poor people of Paris. Teresa of Avila set up a new order of nuns in Spain. Ignatius of Loyola founded the Society of Jesus. Jesuits, as members of this society are called, were among the best-educated people of Europe at this time. They became well known as teachers and missionaries.

✓ **Reading Check** Who were the Jesuits?

Section 1 Assessment

Key Terms
Review the key terms at the beginning of this section. Use each term in a sentence that explains its meaning.

**Target Reading Skill**
Find the word *city-states* on page 155. What context clue helps you understand it? What does *city-states* mean?

Comprehension and Critical Thinking
1. (a) Identify Where in Europe did the Renaissance begin?

(b) Identify Causes Why did it begin there?
(c) Analyze How did the Renaissance combine old ideas with new ideas?
2. (a) Compare How was Renaissance art different from the art of the Middle Ages?
(b) Conclude How did Renaissance art represent the new ideas of the age?
3. (a) Define What was the Reformation?
(b) Compare How were the Protestant Reformation and the Catholic Reformation alike? How were they different?

Writing Activity
Write a paragraph explaining how the Renaissance represented a change in the way Europeans viewed the world and themselves. Be sure to include the reason this era is called the Renaissance.

For: An activity on the Renaissance
Visit: PHSchool.com
Web Code: lgd-8601

The Age of Exploration

Prepare to Read

Objectives

In this section, you will
1. Discover why Europeans set out to explore the world in the 1400s.
2. Learn how the Portuguese reached India by sailing east and how Columbus reached the Americas by sailing west.
3. Find out how Magellan's expedition sailed all the way around the world.

Taking Notes

As you read this section, look for the major causes and effects of the Age of Exploration. Copy the diagram below and record your findings in it.

CAUSES	EVENT	EFFECTS
• • •	The Age of Exploration	• • •

Target Reading Skill

Use Context Clues When you come across an unfamiliar word, you can sometimes figure out its meaning from clues in the context. Context refers to the surrounding words and sentences. One type of context clue is an explanation of the term. It may appear either before or after the term. In the following example, the clue is in italics: "The Portuguese developed *a new type of ship* called the caravel."

Key Terms

- **Age of Exploration** (ayj uv eks pluh RAY shun) *n.* the period of European exploration overseas from about 1400 to 1600
- **Cape of Good Hope** (kayp uv good hohp) *n.* the southern tip of Africa
- **Northwest Passage** (nawrth WEST PAS ij) *n.* a sea route through North America
- **Strait of Magellan** (strayt uv muh JEL un) *n.* a waterway near the southern tip of South America
- **circumnavigate** (sur kum NAV ih gayt) *v.* to sail or fly completely around something, such as Earth

Look at the map on this page. It was drawn in the 1470s by an Italian mapmaker. Europe, Asia, and Africa cover the whole map. North America and South America are nowhere to be seen. Why? Because the people in Europe didn't even know that these continents existed.

During the Middle Ages, Europeans had done little exploring beyond their own shores. Except for the Holy Land, they had very little knowledge of, or interest in, other lands. During the Renaissance, however, Europeans became curious about the world around them. This led to an interest in science and technology. It also led to exploration.

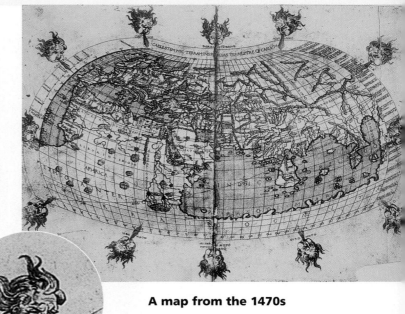

A map from the 1470s

Astrolabes, invented by the Greeks and improved by the Arabs, were used to measure the angles of the sun and stars in order to determine latitude. An Arabian astrolabe is shown at the right. ▶

▲ The magnetic compass was invented in the 1100s. By the1200s, the needle pivoted on a pin over a card that showed the directions. This Italian mariner's compass is from 1570.

Caravels adopted the triangular lateen sails found on Arab ships. Lateen sails allowed ships to sail into the wind. Some caravels also used traditional European square sails. The watercolor at the right depicts the ships of Columbus. ▶

Europeans Begin to Explore

Driven by curiosity, a desire for trade, and great advances in sailing technology, Europeans soon traveled far beyond their homelands—and all the way around the world. From about 1400 to 1600, Europeans sailed across the vast oceans to explore Asia, Africa, and the Americas. This period is called the **Age of Exploration.** Eventually, Europeans would control much of these lands and change the course of world history.

Technology Opens New Worlds   What prompted Europeans to make dozens of dangerous and dramatic voyages during the Age of Exploration? One reason is simply that they could. Before this time, European ships were not capable of such long ocean crossings. By the early 1400s, though, Portuguese shipbuilders had developed a new type of ship called the caravel. Strong, maneuverable, and able to sail against the wind, it was the best sailing vessel of its time.

The Europeans also had two improved navigation tools, the mariner's compass and the astrolabe. Further, they had learned how to make better, more accurate maps. Now they were able to set out on long voyages. But technology alone was not enough to explain why they made those long and hazardous expeditions.

Trade Inspires Travel By the early 1400s, many Europeans had grown tired of paying high prices to Italian merchants for Asian goods. These merchants, in turn, had paid high prices to the Muslim traders of the Ottoman Empire, which controlled the trade routes between Europe and Asia.

Europeans wanted to gain control of the rich trade with Asia themselves. To do this, they would have to find a new route to Asia—one that did not use the Mediterranean Sea and the land routes controlled by the Ottomans. Two European nations, Portugal and Spain, set out to find a sea route starting from their Atlantic coasts.

✓ **Reading Check** **Why did Europeans seek a new route to Asia?**

The Portuguese Head East

By the 1400s, the small nation of Portugal was already a strong and successful seafaring power. It had even conquered some territory on the coast of North Africa. The Portuguese wanted to continue exploring the African coast. And they thought that the best sea route to Asia might be one that went east, around the southern tip of Africa.

Prince Henry the Navigator The search for this eastern sea route was led by Prince Henry, the son of Portugal's king. In 1419, he opened a school to encourage exploration. He invited mapmakers, shipbuilders, and expert sailors called navigators from all over the country.

Henry oversaw more than 50 expeditions. Although he did not go exploring himself, his work won him the title of Henry the Navigator. As expeditions pushed farther south along the western coast of Africa, sailors set up trading posts there. They also gathered information on winds, currents, and coastlines.

Henry's Dream Is Fulfilled Henry the Navigator died in 1460, but his dream of an eastern sea route to Asia lived on. In 1488, the Portuguese sea captain Bartolomeu Dias sailed all the way around the southern tip of Africa, which we now call the Cape of Good Hope.

Ten years later, Vasco da Gama sailed around the Cape of Good Hope, up Africa's eastern coast, and then across the Indian Ocean to India. He returned with a cargo of spices and precious stones. Soon the Portuguese seized important ports around the Indian Ocean. They had their trade route to Asia.

✓ **Reading Check** **Why was Vasco da Gama's voyage important?**

Monument to the Explorers
This monument showing Prince Henry at the prow of a ship followed by explorers and other royal patrons is in Lisbon, Portugal. **Analyze Images** *How does the statue suggest Portugal's contributions to the Age of Exploration?*

Christopher Columbus

Columbus Heads West

While the Portuguese were exploring to the east, an Italian sea captain named Christopher Columbus became convinced that he could reach Asia by sailing west, across the Atlantic. At that time, educated Europeans knew that the world was round. It made sense to Columbus that a ship sailing west would eventually reach Asia.

Columbus convinced Queen Isabella and King Ferdinand of Spain to pay for an expedition that headed west across the Atlantic. They knew of the great riches to be gained if Spain had a sea route to Asia.

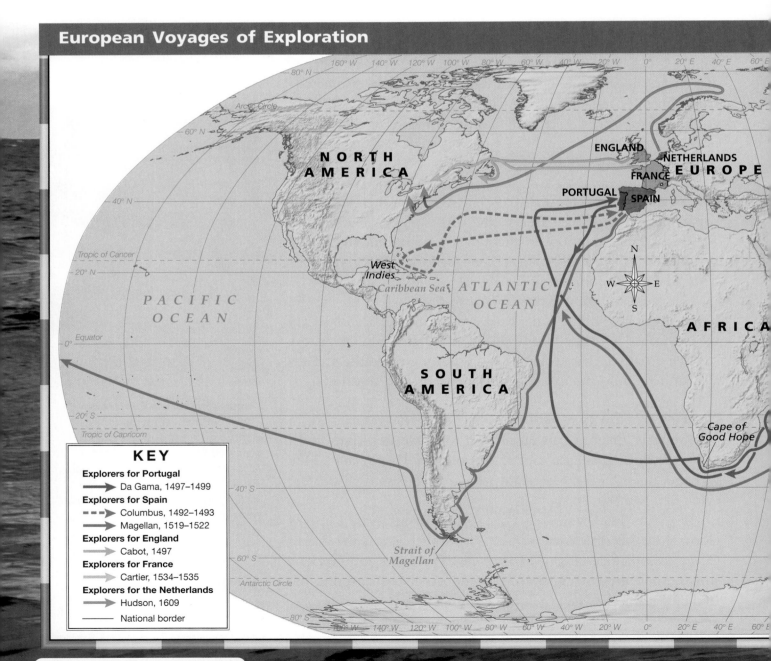

European Voyages of Exploration

KEY

Explorers for Portugal
→ Da Gama, 1497–1499

Explorers for Spain
---→ Columbus, 1492–1493
→ Magellan, 1519–1522

Explorers for England
→ Cabot, 1497

Explorers for France
→ Cartier, 1534–1535

Explorers for the Netherlands
→ Hudson, 1609

— National border

Columbus Lands in the Americas What neither Columbus nor the Spanish monarchs—nor anyone else—knew was that two huge continents lay between Europe and Asia. So in August 1492, Columbus set sail for Asia—westward across the Atlantic Ocean.

Columbus's expedition included three ships—the *Niña*, the *Pinta*, and the *Santa Maria*—and about 90 sailors. After two months, on October 12, 1492, they landed on a little island in the Caribbean Sea, off the coast of North America. Because he thought he had reached the Indies in Asia, Columbus called the people he found there *Indians*. He claimed the land for Spain.

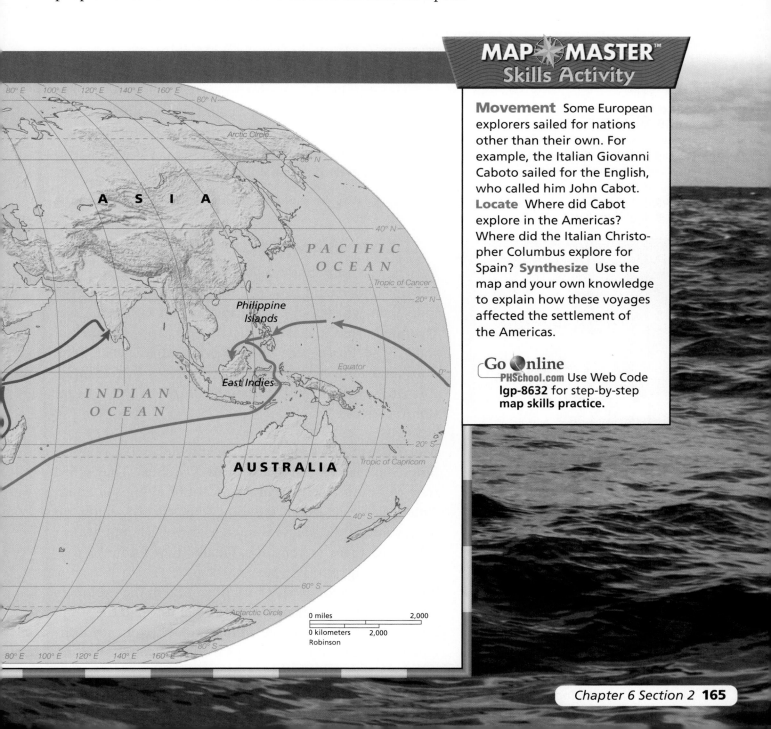

MAP MASTER™
Skills Activity

Movement Some European explorers sailed for nations other than their own. For example, the Italian Giovanni Caboto sailed for the English, who called him John Cabot. **Locate** Where did Cabot explore in the Americas? Where did the Italian Christopher Columbus explore for Spain? **Synthesize** Use the map and your own knowledge to explain how these voyages affected the settlement of the Americas.

Go Online
PHSchool.com Use Web Code **lgp-8632** for step-by-step **map skills practice.**

Target Skill

Use Context Clues
As you read the paragraph at the right, you may not immediately know what the term *Line of Demarcation* refers to. What clues are there in the paragraph? What is the Line of Demarcation?

Exploring the Americas News of Columbus's discovery electrified Europe. Spain and Portugal became rivals. They tried to stop each other from claiming lands in the Americas. In 1494, they signed a treaty that set a Line of Demarcation through the Americas at about 50° W longitude. Spain had the right to settle west of the line. Portugal could do the same east of the line.

England sent the Italian sailor John Cabot across the Atlantic just five years after Columbus's first voyage. He reached what is now Canada. A few years later, his son Sebastian followed. His goal was to find a **Northwest Passage,** a way to sail through North America and then on to Asia. Many other European explorers searched unsuccessfully for a way to continue the western sea route to Asia.

In 1513, a Spanish adventurer named Vasco Nuñez de Balboa led a land expedition across a narrow but hazardous strip of land in Central America. From a mountaintop, he saw a huge ocean to the south, which he claimed for Spain. The Spanish called it the South Sea. Balboa had become the first European to see the Pacific Ocean from the shores of the Americas. The Pacific was the sea that would eventually take Europeans all the way to Asia.

✓ Reading Check **Why did explorers search for a Northwest Passage?**

All the Way Around the World

Even after Columbus reached the Americas, Europeans did not understand how large Earth was. They believed that Japan, which they called Cipango (sih PANG goh), was separated from the Americas by a narrow channel of water. The Portuguese sailor Ferdinand Magellan (FUR duh nand muh JEL un) was eager to cross that channel. But one problem still remained: how to get around the Americas.

Magellan Sets Out With backing from the Spanish king, Magellan set sail in 1519 with five ships. They sailed west to South America and then south along the South American coast. After spending the stormy winter on land, some of the sailors wanted to turn back, but Magellan forced them to continue. Finally, they located a narrow, twisting passage near the tip of South America. Today, it is called the **Strait of Magellan,** in the explorer's honor. It took Magellan 38 days to sail through the strait. Strong currents and fierce winds made the journey difficult. Only three of the five ships made it through.

Ferdinand Magellan
Before 1519, Magellan had already sailed to India, Africa, and Southeast Asia. He had also studied other sailors' reports of winds and currents. **Analyze Images** *How does this painting suggest Magellan's knowledge and accomplishments?*

Sailing the Pacific The three ships emerged from the treacherous strait into the sea that Balboa had sighted. Magellan thought this ocean was much less stormy than the strait, so he called it *pacific,* which means "peaceful."

Magellan and his men had no idea how vast the Pacific Ocean was. Short of food and fresh water, they sailed for three months without sighting any land, except for a few tiny islands. Some men starved to death, while others died of disease. At last, they reached the Philippines. There, tragedy struck: Magellan was killed when he became involved in a local dispute. Thus, the leader of the expedition did not live to return to Spain.

The expedition continued, but only one ship finally made it back to Spain. Of the roughly 250 sailors who had set sail with Magellan, only 18 returned. On September 8, 1522, the survivors reached Seville, where the Spanish hailed them as the first people to **circumnavigate**, or sail around, the world.

An engraving of the *Vittoria,* the only one of Magellan's ships to reach Spain after circumnavigating the globe

✓ Reading Check **Explain why so few of Magellan's sailors returned to Spain.**

Section 2 Assessment

Key Terms

Review the key terms at the beginning of this section. Use each term in a sentence that explains its meaning.

Target Reading Skill

 Find the word *strait* on page 166. What clues in the paragraph help you understand what a strait is? Define *strait.*

Comprehension and Critical Thinking

1. (a) Recall When was the Age of Exploration?

(b) Identify Cause and Effect Why did Europeans set out on overseas voyages during this time?

2. (a) Identify Who was Prince Henry the Navigator?

(b) Conclude How was Prince Henry important to the Age of Exploration?

3. (a) Explain What was Columbus's "mistake"?

(b) Identify Effects Why did Columbus's voyages lead to more exploration?

Writing Activity

Explorers often had difficulty finding financial support for their expeditions. Take the role of either Columbus or Magellan and write a persuasive letter to a monarch asking for support for your voyage.

Writing Tip In your letter, explain why the voyage is important and how it will benefit the monarch. Be sure to use a respectful tone.

In the 1500s, a life at sea was a hard life. During lengthy voyages of exploration, sailors performed tiring physical labor, suffered from poor nutrition, and endured long stretches of boredom. They were often lonely, surrounded by vast and sometimes violent seas, far from home and family. They ate dried and salted food that was often infested with insects or gnawed by rats. They suffered injuries from their work or from fights with other sailors. Sailors' registries often identified men by their injuries, including crushed fingers and splinters embedded in the flesh.

Onboard a Ship Sailing was often the best job available for poor, uneducated men and orphaned boys who lived near busy ports. Boys as young as seven or eight served as ship's pages until they were about fifteen. A page's duties included scrubbing the ship and turning the sand clocks every half hour to mark the time. Unless they were assigned to specific officers, pages took orders from everyone on board. When they were old enough, pages became sailor's apprentices.

Apprentices were young men training to become sailors. They climbed the rigging in their bare feet to furl, or gather, the sails. They served as lookouts at the top of the masts, rowed smaller boats, and carried heavy cargo.

Sailors might work their way up to other positions, including that of ship's pilot, whose job it was to navigate. A very few men became the master of a ship. The master commanded the ship and was usually part owner of the vessel. The illustration at the right shows a vessel from the 1500s that sailed with about 45 crew members.

Sunken Treasures
This decorated plate and the pottery jug above were recovered from a Venetian shipwreck in the Adriatic Sea. The shipwreck probably occurred in the late 1500s.

Master's or Captain's Cabin
Common sailors slept on deck on straw-filled sacks.

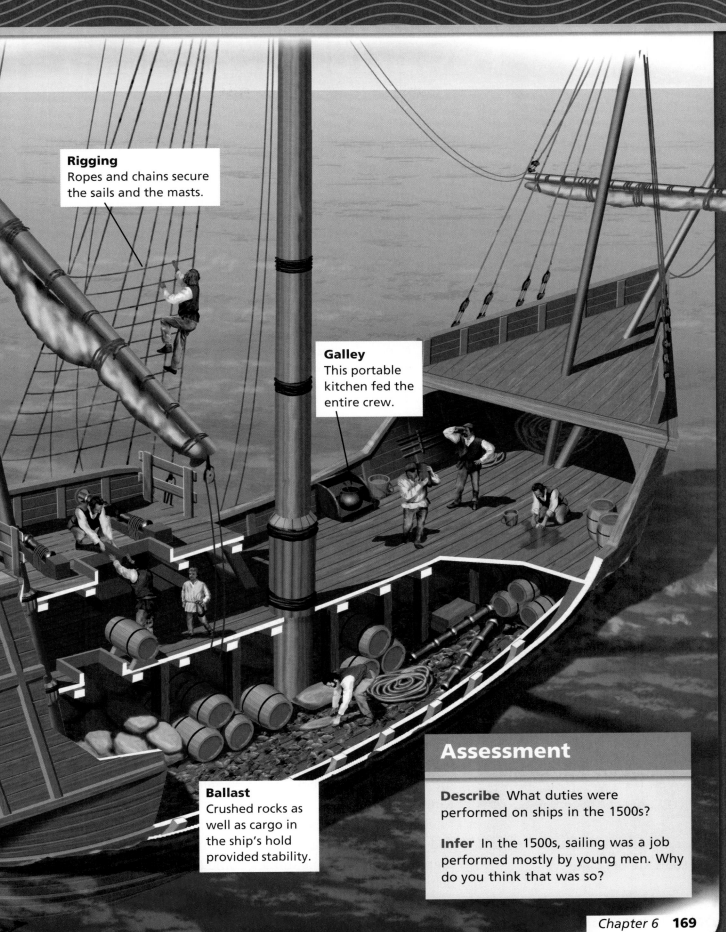

Rigging
Ropes and chains secure the sails and the masts.

Galley
This portable kitchen fed the entire crew.

Ballast
Crushed rocks as well as cargo in the ship's hold provided stability.

Assessment

Describe What duties were performed on ships in the 1500s?

Infer In the 1500s, sailing was a job performed mostly by young men. Why do you think that was so?

The Age of Powerful Monarchs

Prepare to Read

Objectives

In this section, you will
1. Learn about absolute rule in France.
2. Find out why the reign of Queen Elizabeth I was a golden age in England.
3. Discover the accomplishments of strong rulers in Spain and Russia.

Taking Notes

As you read this section, look for important ideas about absolute monarchs in Europe. Copy the diagram below and record your findings in it.

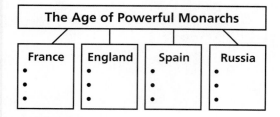

Target Reading Skill

Use Context Clues To understand an unfamiliar term, you can use your own knowledge along with context clues. For example, in the description of a meal below, the term *keeper of the king's china* is in a list of servants. You know that one meaning of *china* is "dishes." This servant is in charge of the king's dishes.

Key Terms

- **divine right of kings** (duh VYN ryt uv kingz) *n.* the belief that the authority of kings comes directly from God
- **absolute monarch** (AB suh loot MAHN urk) *n.* a king or queen with complete authority over the government and people in a kingdom
- **Versailles** (vur SY) *n.* the palace built for the French king Louis XIV
- **Elizabethan Age** (ee liz uh BEE thun ayj) *n.* a golden age of English history when Elizabeth I was queen, 1558–1603
- **tsar** (zahr) *n.* the Russian emperor

King Louis XIV of France

Louis XIV, king of France, was ready for his dinner. He would be dining alone this evening. That did not mean he would be by himself. It meant that he would be the only one who was eating.

Although the meal had just begun, a crowd of servants already surrounded him. It was time for his meat to be brought from the kitchen. Two guards entered first. They were followed by ushers, gentlemen-in-waiting, the keeper of the king's china, and more guards. Somewhere in the crowd were the officers of the food department who actually carried the meat. In all, it required 15 people to bring the meat to King Louis XIV.

Then, when Louis asked for a drink, the chief cupbearer and the gentleman cupbearer sprang into action. Before King Louis XIV finished his dinner, some 500 people would have helped to prepare and serve it.

Absolute Rule in France

Why did Louis XIV have so many people waiting on him? What right did he have to this type of service?

Louis XIV was king of France in the 1600s and early 1700s. In Europe at this time, the people did not choose their leaders. They believed that God chose the king. The king's authority came directly from God, and was therefore divine. This belief was called the **divine right of kings.** It seemed logical that a leader chosen by God would be entitled to the best of everything.

Absolute Rule Therefore, it also seemed logical that a leader chosen by God should have more power than anyone else. Louis XIV was an **absolute monarch,** or royal ruler with absolute, or complete, authority over the government and people in his or her kingdom. Absolute monarchs did not share power with nobles, with common people, or with anyone else. From the 1400s to the 1700s, much of Europe was governed by absolute monarchs.

Cardinal Richelieu French kings had not always been absolute monarchs. Over a period of about 150 years, starting in the late 1400s, French kings had gradually taken power away from the nobles. Much of this transfer of power was accomplished not by a king but by a cardinal. (A cardinal is a high official in the Roman Catholic Church.) Cardinal Richelieu served as chief minister to Louis XIV's father, King Louis XIII.

To limit the power of the French nobles, Richelieu allowed wealthy merchants to buy titles of nobility. Then he stripped the nobles of some of their rights. He also started businesses for the French government. These businesses earned a great deal of money for the crown. Altogether, as these changes made the nobles weaker, the king became wealthier and more powerful.

The Power Behind the Throne The action of the famous novel *The Three Musketeers* unfolds against the backdrop of the secret plots and schemes of Cardinal Richelieu (below). **Conclude** *Why do you think a king might have appointed a cardinal to such an important government post?*

Louis XIV Both Richelieu and Louis XIII died in 1643, and Louis XIV became king. He was the absolute monarch of France for 72 years. King Louis XIV was so powerful that he became known as the Sun King. Just as the sun was the center of the solar system, Louis XIV was the center of the French nation. He went so far as to declare, "I am the state."

The Sun King's Court One way in which Louis showed his power was through his lifestyle. He lived in incredible luxury at **Versailles,** his huge palace outside Paris.

It took 40 years to complete this magnificent estate. At times, as many as 30,000 laborers worked on its construction. Many nobles lived at the palace of Versailles with the king. Having the nobles at Versailles made it easier for Louis to keep them in check. At home on their estates, they might have become a threat to his power. To keep the nobles happy, Louis XIV gave huge parties with fabulous entertainment. For the most part, the king also excused the nobles from paying taxes.

All of this luxury and entertainment was very expensive. To raise the money, the king taxed the peasants. This meant that the poorest and least powerful people in France paid for the luxury of the Sun King's court.

France at War King Louis XIV had more power and wealth than any other person in France. And he wanted France to have more power and wealth than any other nation in Europe.

The Splendor of Versailles
These photos show the emblem of the Sun King (inset), the queen's bedroom (below), and the Gallery of Mirrors (bottom). **Infer** *How do you think the people of France felt about the luxury shown here? Explain your answer.*

To accomplish this goal, he encouraged the growth of industry and supported efforts to build an empire in Asia and in the Americas. Louis also went to war to gain new territories. From 1667 to 1713, France was almost constantly at war with other European countries.

These wars cost huge sums of money, yet they won France little in the way of land or power. By the time King Louis XIV died in 1715, France had huge debts. Even the silverware at Versailles had to be sold to help pay for France's wars.

✓ **Reading Check** **Why did King Louis XIV go to war?**

A Powerful Queen of England

Nearly a century before King Louis XIV took the throne of France, England already had a powerful monarch ruling over a golden age. This monarch, however, was a woman— Queen Elizabeth I. She became the most powerful and successful ruler England had ever known.

When Elizabeth I became queen in 1558, she found herself in a position of great power. Her grandfather, Henry VII, had ended fighting among local lords. He had made sure that England's monarch would be more powerful than any of the nobles. Her father, Henry VIII, had broken away from the Roman Catholic Church and started a new Protestant church, the Church of England. The English monarch became head of the Church of England and no longer had to share power with the Church based in Rome.

Regal Image
Queen Elizabeth was careful about how she appeared to her people during her travels and when she posed for portraits. **Classify** *What elements in the painting suggest Elizabeth's power and success?*

Queen Elizabeth Like her father, Elizabeth was determined and intelligent. She spoke French and Italian, and she could read the classical languages of Greek and Latin. Unlike her father, who had married six times, Elizabeth never married. She knew that if she married, she would lose some of her authority to her husband.

Elizabeth was also wise enough to gain the support of the English people. After she became queen, she often traveled through the English countryside so her people could see her. The English people came to love and admire their queen, whom they called "Good Queen Bess."

The Elizabethan Age Elizabeth's rule, from 1558 to 1603, is called the **Elizabethan Age.** During this time, England grew increasingly powerful and prosperous. Elizabeth strengthened England by using compromise to prevent religious wars between Protestants and the Catholics who were still numerous in England. She made sure that England remained a Protestant nation and that the monarch remained head of the Church of England. However, she also allowed much of Catholic tradition to be practiced in the English church.

At first, Elizabeth avoided war with other European powers. She used the possibility of her marriage with their kings as one way to prevent war. Meanwhile, Elizabeth supported English sea power and exploration in the Americas. The English sea captain Sir Francis Drake sailed around the world. He also delighted Elizabeth by leading attacks on Spanish ships carrying treasure from the Americas. By 1588, Spain had had enough. The Spanish king sent a huge armada, or fleet of ships, to invade England. With the help of a storm that destroyed much of the armada, the lighter English ships defeated the larger, awkward Spanish vessels. Now England had the most powerful navy in the world.

Elizabethan England was not only powerful, it also enjoyed a golden age of science, art, and literature. Elizabeth loved the theater. She often attended and helped promote the plays of William Shakespeare. Today, Shakespeare is regarded as perhaps the greatest writer in the English language. His plays include *Hamlet, King Lear,* and *Romeo and Juliet.*

✓ **Reading Check** **Why was the Elizabethan Age considered a golden age?**

Links to
Language Arts

Shakespeare's Globe Theatre
In Elizabethan times, the plays of William Shakespeare were performed in the Globe Theatre, in London. The theater was almost round. Much of it was open to the weather; a thatched roof protected the stage and some of the seats. The least expensive seats weren't seats at all—"groundlings" stood in front of the stage. In the 1990s, a replica of the Globe (photos below) was completed near the site of the original theater. Now modern audiences can see Shakespeare's plays the way they were performed during his lifetime.

Strong Rulers Unite Spain

Spain, too, came under the control of strong monarchs. When Ferdinand of Aragon and Isabella of Castile married in 1469, their separate kingdoms became one. Together, they ruled almost all of present-day Spain.

Like other European monarchs, King Ferdinand and Queen Isabella worked to limit the power of the nobles. They also used their power to strengthen the Roman Catholic Church throughout Spain. Under their rule, Jews were forced to convert to Catholicism or leave the country. The Moors, North African Muslims who had controlled part of southern Spain since the 700s, were driven out of Spain in 1492. Ferdinand and Isabella also established the Spanish Inquisition, a court that tried and executed people who did not obey the Roman Catholic Church.

The Spanish monarchs also supported voyages of exploration, including those of Christopher Columbus. These voyages eventually led to the creation of a huge Spanish empire in the Americas.

Two Monarchs
Ferdinand and Isabella, shown together on a Spanish coin, ruled Spain jointly. Their Alcazar castle is shown above. **Analyze Images** *What does the coin suggest about their roles as rulers?*

Absolute Rule in Russia

Russia shared many of the religious and political developments of Europe, including the rule of Christian absolute monarchs. But Russia was also different. First of all, not all of Russia is in Europe. Much of it is in Asia. Today, Russia extends all the way from the Pacific coast of Asia to the coasts of the Baltic and the Black seas in Europe.

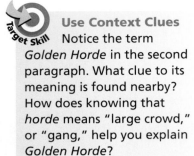

Use Context Clues
Notice the term *Golden Horde* in the second paragraph. What clue to its meaning is found nearby? How does knowing that *horde* means "large crowd," or "gang," help you explain *Golden Horde*?

The Rise of Kiev In the 700s and 800s, Kiev, a city in present-day Ukraine, became an important center of trade. It developed ties to the Byzantine Empire, which sent Christian missionaries to Kiev. In 957, Princess Olga converted to Christianity. Her grandson, Vladimir, expanded the territory ruled by Kiev and also made Orthodox Christianity its official religion. Byzantine arts and architecture influenced the culture of Kiev, which thrived in the 1000s. By the 1200s, however, Kiev had come under the control of invaders.

As you read in Chapter 4, during the early 1200s, the Mongols had conquered much of Asia. In the 1230s, Mongol armies known as the Golden Horde turned west. They took over much of Russia, including Kiev.

Mongol Rule of Russia The Mongols ruled Russia for 240 years. Although they required heavy tribute, the Muslim Mongols allowed Russians to practice Christianity and brought peace to their large empire. However, Mongol rule cut Russia off from Western Europe and many of the advances being made there.

During this period, the princes of Moscow gained power. Moscow was a center of trade, and its princes were the tax collectors for the Mongol rulers. The area they controlled was called Muscovy. Meanwhile, the Russian Orthodox Church made Moscow its headquarters.

Symbol of Moscow
The Cathedral of St. Basil the Blessed, built in the 1550s, shows influences of Byzantine style.
Contrast *How does this church differ from the Gothic cathedrals shown on pages 126 and 127?*

Russian Rulers Take Power In the 1300s, the leaders of Moscow led other Russian groups in a rebellion against Mongol rule. By 1505, Prince Ivan of Moscow had brought much of Russia under his own control. He then turned to strengthening his power by limiting the power of Russian nobles. Ivan the Great, as he came to be called, declared himself absolute ruler of Russia, "in authority like the highest God." His grandson, Ivan the Terrible, strengthened the monarch's power even more. He was crowned **tsar,** the Russian word for "caesar" or "emperor."

Peter the Great Peter the Great became tsar of Russia in 1682 and ruled for more than 40 years. Peter modernized the Russian army and navy and improved Russian farming and industry by adopting Western European technology. But he also strengthened serfdom, which had already died out in the rest of Europe. Peter expanded Russia's territory, but he could not achieve one of his major goals: a port that would not freeze over in the winter, so that Russia could trade by sea all year.

Like other absolute monarchs, Peter the Great limited the power of the nobles in order to strengthen his own position. Peter also wanted Russia to become more like Western Europe. He built St. Petersburg, a magnificent capital city near the Baltic coast, which he called "a window on the West." The city became a symbol of Peter's power and his desire to make Russia a modern nation.

Peter the Great

 **Reading Check** **What were Peter the Great's accomplishments?**

Section 3 Assessment

Key Terms
Review the key terms at the beginning of this section. Use each term in a sentence that explains its meaning.

Target Reading Skill
How do context clues and your own knowledge help you understand *Sun King,* on page 172?

Comprehension and Critical Thinking
1. (a) Summarize How did Cardinal Richelieu increase the power of the French king?

(b) Synthesize How did Louis XIV represent the idea of absolute rule?

2. (a) Describe What was Queen Elizabeth I like?

(b) Identify Causes What did Elizabeth I do to encourage the golden age that bears her name?

3. (a) Recall How did the princes of Moscow gain power in Russia?

(b) Compare How were Ivan the Great and Peter the Great similar? How were they different?

Writing Activity
Write a description of a day at Versailles from the point of view of a noble. Then write a description of how the day might have looked to a French peasant who had the chance to observe it.

For: An activity on Louis XIV
Visit: PHSchool.com
Web Code: lgd-8603

Like many explorers of his time, Henry Hudson hoped to find a short route from Europe to Asia. He made four voyages to look for this Northwest Passage. When his final expedition was stranded by the arctic winter, Hudson's crew mutinied. They put him, his son, and several others into a small boat and cast them adrift. Years later, in the 1630s, another explorer found ruins of a shelter that might have been built by the small group of castaways.

A route map is a type of special-purpose map. In addition to showing location, physical features, and distances, a route map shows movement: how people got from one place to another. Many journeys have played important roles in history, and historical route maps show the paths of such journeys.

Learn the Skill

Use these steps to analyze and interpret a route map.

1. **Read the map title and look at the map to get a general idea of what it shows.** Identify the regions that appear on the map—both physical features and political boundaries. Notice what route or routes the map shows.

2. **Read the key to understand how the map uses symbols, colors, and patterns.** On most route maps, lines show the paths of journeys. Often, each journey is shown in a different color or style (such as a dotted line). Notice how the key identifies the routes and the dates of journeys.

3. **Use the key to interpret the map.** Look for places where the symbols in the key appear on the map. Find the separate routes, their dates, and where each one begins and ends.

4. **Draw conclusions about what the map shows.** Information you discover when you analyze a route map can help you draw conclusions about why a route was chosen or why it was successful or unsuccessful.

◀ **A 1686 map of the Americas**

Practice the Skill

Use the steps below to analyze the route map on this page.

1. What is the topic of the map at the right? What routes does it show?

2. Look at the key. How many journeys does the map show? What colors are the voyages? How do you know when they took place?

3. Trace the routes that Hudson took in order. Where did each journey begin? How did the last journey end? What places on the map bear Hudson's name?

4. You know that Hudson was looking for a Northwest Passage across North America. Did he achieve this goal? What did he accomplish?

The Hudson River today

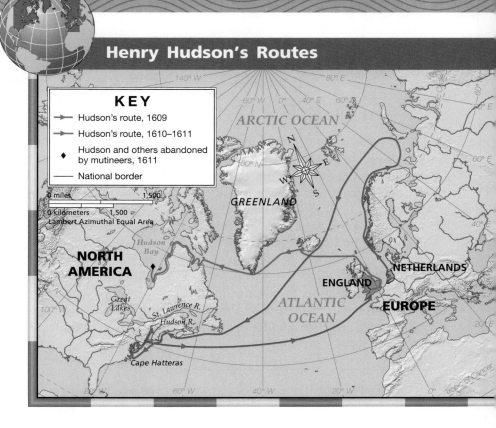

Henry Hudson's Routes

KEY
- Hudson's route, 1609
- Hudson's route, 1610–1611
- ◆ Hudson and others abandoned by mutineers, 1611
- National border

0 miles 1,500
0 kilometers 1,500
Lambert Azimuthal Equal Area

ARCTIC OCEAN

GREENLAND

NORTH AMERICA

Hudson Bay

Great Lakes

St. Lawrence R.

Hudson R.

Cape Hatteras

ATLANTIC OCEAN

NETHERLANDS

ENGLAND

EUROPE

Apply the Skill

Turn to the map named European Voyages of Exploration on pages 164–165. Use the steps in this lesson to draw conclusions about the voyages of the explorers sailing for Portugal and Spain.

Conquests in the Americas and Africa

Prepare to Read

Objectives

In this section, you will
1. Discover how Spanish conquistadors conquered great civilizations in the Americas.
2. Find out why the African slave trade developed and what its effects were.

Taking Notes

As you read this section, look for the important events in the Spanish conquest of the Americas. Copy the timeline below and record your findings on it.

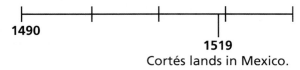

1490

1519
Cortés lands in Mexico.

Target Reading Skill

Use Context Clues When you come across an unfamiliar word, you may have to look for context clues to its meaning in the paragraphs preceding or following the word. For example, to understand the word *withstand* at the bottom of page 182, keep reading to see what happened to the Incan empire.

Key Terms

- **conquistador** (kahn KEES tuh dawr) *n.* a Spanish conqueror in the Americas

- **Hernán Cortés** (hur NAHN kohr TEZ) *n.* the Spanish conquistador who conquered the Aztecs
- **encomienda** (en koh mee EN dah) *n.* a system in which the Spanish king gave Spanish settlers the right to the labor of the Native Americans who lived in a particular area
- **Francisco Pizarro** (frahn SEES koh pea SAHR oh) *n.* the Spanish conquistador who conquered the Incas

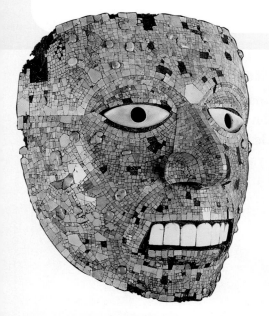

The Aztec god Quetzalcoatl

You read about the splendid dinner of King Louis XIV in Section 3. About a hundred years before Louis ruled France, another king had sat down to a splendid dinner. Moctezuma was the supreme ruler of the Aztec empire in the Valley of Mexico. Like Louis, Moctezuma was usually the only one who ate at his dinners, which took more than 400 people to serve. After his servants brought the food, Moctezuma looked over the huge selection and chose what he wanted. Then a screen was drawn around him for privacy while his food was served by his personal servants.

Moctezuma was powerful, but the Aztecs believed in gods that were even more powerful. An Aztec legend said that long ago the white-skinned god Quetzalcoatl (ket sahl koh AHT el) had sailed away to the east. The Aztecs believed that someday Quetzalcoatl would return to rule them. In 1519, that seemed to happen. Moctezuma heard about a group of pale-skinned men who had landed on the east coast. He wondered if these men could be Quetzalcoatl and his followers.

Spain's Empire in the Americas

The leader of the pale-skinned men was not an Aztec god but a Spanish conquistador. A **conquistador** was a Spanish soldier who conquered Native American peoples in the 1500s. Ever since Columbus had brought back reports of new lands, Europeans had dreamed about the riches that might be found there. The Spanish sent expeditions to look for gold and other treasures.

The Conquest of the Aztecs One of these expeditions was led by the conquistador **Hernán Cortés.** Soon after landing in present-day Mexico, Cortés heard about the wealth of the Aztecs. He also heard that many of the local peoples hated the Aztecs, because the Aztecs had conquered them and taxed them heavily. Cortés persuaded some of these groups to help him fight the Aztecs.

Cortés headed for the Aztec capital with 500 soldiers and 16 horses. Aztec spies saw them coming. They had never seen horses before. Moctezuma's spies described the Spanish as "supernatural creatures riding on hornless deer, armed in iron, fearless as gods." When Cortés and his men arrived in Tenoch-

A Fateful Meeting
This painting shows the first meeting of Moctezuma and Hernán Cortés. **Analyze Images** *What attitude do the two leaders seem to have toward each other? What details support your inference?*

titlán, the Aztec capital, they were amazed. The city was larger than any European city at the time. As you read in Chapter 3, the Aztecs had developed a very advanced civilization. The Aztec leader Moctezuma welcomed Cortés and his men. He and his advisers were afraid that Cortés might be the returning Quetzalcoatl, so they treated him and his men as honored guests.

In order to gain control of the Aztecs, Cortés kidnapped Moctezuma. The Aztec people soon rebelled. The battle was fierce and bloody. Moctezuma was killed, but the Aztecs drove Cortés and his army out of Tenochtitlán.

Outside the city, Cortés regrouped. The Spaniards and their Native American allies attacked Tenochtitlán. In 1521, the Aztecs finally surrendered. By then, about 240,000 Aztecs had died, and 30,000 of Cortés's allies had been killed. Tenochtitlán and the Aztec empire lay in ruins.

Use Context Clues
How does the description of events both before and after the word *regrouped* help you figure out its meaning? How does the prefix *re-* also help?

European Empires in the Americas

Regions These colonial empires affect the language and culture of the Americas to this day. **Locate** On which coast did Portugal claim land? Which empire extended into both North and South America? **Synthesize** How does this map reflect the Line of Demarcation you read about on page 166?

Go Online
PHSchool.com Use Web Code **lgp-8644** for step-by-step **map skills practice**.

KEY
- Spanish empire
- Portuguese empire
- - - - Viceroyalty border
- • City

0 miles   2,000
0 kilometers   2,000
Lambert Azimuthal Equal Area

New Spain Cortés took control of the region, which he called New Spain. He built his new capital, Mexico City, on the site of Tenochtitlán.

Cortés tried to make life in New Spain like that in his home country. He imported European plants and farm animals. He also introduced the **encomienda** system, in which the Spanish king gave Spanish settlers the right to the labor of the Native Americans who lived in a particular area. The settlers were expected to convert the Native Americans to Christianity and to treat them well. In reality, the settlers treated them as slaves. Many Native Americans were worked to death, and many others died of European diseases.

The Conquest of the Incas Like the Aztecs, the Incas had built an advanced civilization. Their vast empire covered most of the western coast of South America and was tied together by a well-constructed network of roads and bridges. For all its achievements and power, however, the Incan empire could not withstand the Spanish. In 1531, the conquistador **Francisco Pizarro** led his men into the northern Incan empire. He drove south, and within two years he and his 200 soldiers had conquered an empire of some 12 million people.

How did he do it? First, a war was already raging within the Incan empire. Some of the people rebelling against Incan rule sided with Pizarro. Further, as Cortés had done, Pizarro kidnapped the empire's ruler. Leaderless, the empire was easy prey. Finally, European diseases such as smallpox killed or weakened millions of people in the region.

Effects of Spanish Conquests The Spanish takeover of the Aztec and Incan empires eventually led to Spanish control of most of Central and South America. The riches of gold and silver that Spain brought back to Europe made Spain even more powerful. The large numbers of Spanish settlers changed the course of history in the Americas. And the Spaniards' cruel treatment of the Native Americans—along with the diseases they accidentally brought—devastated the peoples of the Americas.

✓ Reading Check **How did the Spanish conquest affect the Americas?**

The African Slave Trade

Europeans did not limit their conquests to the Americas. They were looking for riches in other lands as well.

You have read that Prince Henry the Navigator helped start trade between Portugal and the west coast of Africa. Soon, British, French, and Dutch ships also sailed to Africa to trade for gold, ivory, and pepper. Then they began to trade for enslaved people as well. One ship brought five enslaved Africans to England in the 1540s. No one would buy them, so they were taken back to Africa. Because it had plenty of cheap labor, Europe did not offer a big market for slavery.

Slavery Comes to the Americas There was a market for slaves in the Americas, however. Spanish and Portuguese settlers in the Americas wanted workers for their plantations and mines. At first they enslaved Native Americans. When many of these slaves died, the Europeans began importing enslaved Africans.

Some historians put the number of Africans taken to the Americas at about 11 million. As many as 2 million may have died on the overcrowded and unsanitary slave ships. Men, women, and children were packed and chained tightly together in the dark holds of the ships. The air was so foul that there was often not enough oxygen to keep a candle burning. "The shrieks of the women, and the groans of the dying, rendered the whole a scene of horror," one survivor recalled.

Links Across
The World

The Columbian Exchange
The movement of peoples from Africa and Europe to the Americas opened up a global exchange of goods and ideas. Europeans introduced cattle, horses, chickens, goats, and pigs to the Americas. From Africa and Asia, they brought such plants as bananas, coffee, and sugar cane. All became major foods in the Americas. The introduction of food crops such as corn, potatoes, and beans from the Americas made it easier to feed more people in Europe and Africa. Because Columbus's famous voyages made this exchange possible, it is called the Columbian Exchange.

This 1846 painting of a Spanish slave ship was done by the British captain who captured the ship and freed the slaves.

Effects of the Slave Trade The slave trade created a disaster, both in the Americas and in Africa. In addition to being deprived of their liberty and taken from their homeland, enslaved Africans suffered terrible brutality. In the Americas, slavery was damaging to both slaves and slaveholders because the society that developed was based on injustice and inequality.

In Africa, groups who were victorious in war had often enslaved the people they conquered. Some of these enslaved people were sold to foreigners. But in the 1500s, the slave trade became big business. As the demand for slaves increased in the Americas, European slave traders lured African groups into wars against their neighbors. These wars guaranteed the traders a steady supply of slaves. Other people were kidnapped in slave raids and sold by African rulers and traders to the Europeans. The captives were exchanged for textiles, metalwork, weapons, and luxury goods.

European settlers wanted Africans who were young, healthy, and strong to work on their plantations in the Americas. The loss of so many young people in their prime was a serious blow to many African societies. Wars also caused death and destruction. These harmful effects of the slave trade lasted for centuries.

The waiting rooms of the House of Slaves on Gorée Island, in present-day Senegal, Africa

✓ **Reading Check** **How did the slave trade affect African society?**

Section 4 Assessment

Key Terms
Review the key terms at the beginning of this section. Use each term in a sentence that explains its meaning.

Target Reading Skill
Find the word *prey* in the first paragraph on page 183. Use the text both before and after the word to explain how it is being used in this context.

Comprehension and Critical Thinking
1. (a) Recall Which conquistador conquered the Aztec empire?

(b) Recall Which conquistador conquered the Incan empire?
(c) Compare and Contrast How were these two events similar and different?
2. (a) Explain Why did the Europeans take enslaved Africans to the Americas?
(b) Describe What were conditions like on the ships that brought enslaved Africans to the Americas?
(c) Identify Effects What were two effects of the African slave trade?

Writing Activity
Write two paragraphs, one from the viewpoint of an Aztec soldier defending Tenochtitlán, and the other from the perspective of a Spanish soldier trying to conquer the city.

> **Writing Tip** Think about what the two people might agree on and what they would view differently. Jot down notes or make a chart to help you plan your paragraphs.

Review and Assessment

◆ Chapter Summary

Section 1: The Renaissance and Reformation

Painting by Raphael

- The Renaissance, a period marked by a rebirth of learning and advances in the arts and sciences, took place in Europe from about 1300 to 1600.
- Renaissance artists used scientific techniques to portray the world around them realistically.
- The Reformation began as an effort to correct abuses of the Roman Catholic Church and resulted in the creation of Protestant churches.

Section 2: The Age of Exploration

- Advances in technology, a desire for trade, and curiosity about the world led Europeans to undertake long sea voyages during the Age of Exploration.
- Encouraged by Prince Henry the Navigator, the Portuguese sailed around Africa to India.
- Christopher Columbus sailed west and landed in the Americas. Many European explorers followed him to these lands.
- Ferdinand Magellan led the first expedition to circumnavigate the world.

Section 3: The Age of Powerful Monarchs

- King Louis XIV, absolute monarch of France for 72 years, lived lavishly and taxed his people heavily.
- Queen Elizabeth I ruled over England during the late 1500s. Her long reign, called the Elizabethan Age, was a golden age for England.
- King Ferdinand and Queen Isabella united Spain and drove non-Christians from the country.
- After being ruled by the Mongols, Russia was governed by tsars, or Russian emperors.

Section 4: Conquests in the Americas and Africa

- Spanish conquistadors conquered the Aztec and Incan empires in the Americas.
- Europeans brought enslaved Africans to the Americas to work on plantations and in mines.

Aztec mask

◆ Key Terms

Each of the statements below contains a key term from the chapter. If the statement is true, write *true*. If it is false, rewrite the statement to make it true.

1. The Renaissance was the effort to reform the Catholic Church.

2. The period marked by a rebirth of learning in Europe was called humanism.

3. The Cape of Good Hope was a sea route through North America.

4. To circumnavigate the world means to sail all the way around it.

5. People who believed in the divine right of kings thought that a king's right to rule came directly from God.

6. A tsar was an absolute ruler of Spain.

7. Encomienda was the capital of the Aztecs.

8. Francisco Pizarro was the conquistador who conquered the Incas.

◆ Comprehension and Critical Thinking

9. (a) **Describe** What changes occurred during the Renaissance?
(b) **Identify Causes** What caused these changes?
(c) **Draw Conclusions** How did these changes lead to the Age of Exploration?

10. (a) **Define** What was humanism?
(b) **Explain** How did Renaissance artists exhibit humanism in their work?

11. (a) **Recall** What were Martin Luther's objections to the practices of the Roman Catholic Church?
(b) **Conclude** Why did the Reformation spread?

12. (a) **Identify** Who was Henry the Navigator?
(b) **Identify Causes** Why did Spain and Portugal start making voyages of exploration?
(c) **Synthesize** How did the Age of Exploration lead to the conquest of Native American peoples?

13. (a) **Name** What ruler said, "I am the state"?
(b) **Explain** How did that statement demonstrate the concept of absolute monarchy?

14. (a) **Recall** When was the Elizabethan Age?
(b) **Describe** What was the Elizabethan Age like?
(c) **Draw Conclusions** What qualities and actions made Elizabeth I a successful ruler?

15. (a) **Name** Which conquistador conquered the Aztecs? The Incas?
(b) **Describe** How did the Spanish set up an empire in the Americas?
(c) **Identify Causes** Why did Europeans bring enslaved Africans to the Americas?

◆ Skills Practice

Using Route Maps In the Skills for Life activity in this chapter, you learned how to analyze route maps. Review the steps you followed to learn the skill.

Turn to the map named Invasions of the Roman Empire on page 119. Follow the steps of the skill to analyze the map. Then use the map to draw at least three conclusions about the invasions of the ancient Roman Empire.

◆ Writing Activity: Art

Study some Renaissance paintings that use perspective, such as Raphael's painting on page 156. Then do research to find out how perspective helps artists make their paintings more realistic. Explore how the use of a vanishing point creates the illusion of three-dimensional space. Try drawing your own scene using perspective. Finally, write a brief report explaining how perspective allowed Renaissance artists to create more realistic artwork. Use illustrations if you wish.

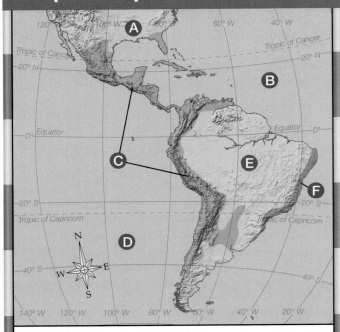

MAP MASTER™
Skills Activity

European Empires in the Americas

Place Location For each place listed below, write the letter from the map that shows its location.

1. Atlantic Ocean
2. North America
3. Pacific Ocean
4. Portuguese empire
5. South America
6. Spanish empire

Go Online
PHSchool.com Use Web Code **lgp-8654** for an **interactive map**.

Standardized Test Prep

Test-Taking Tips

Some questions on standardized tests ask you to analyze a passage. Read the passage below. Follow the tips to answer the sample question.

> In 1519, Ferdinand Magellan sailed from Spain for South America with five ships. From early in the voyage, he had problems with his crew. After the expedition reached the coast of South America, the crews of three ships refused to sail on. Magellan had to use both skill and force to keep the men from turning back. The ships continued south, searching for a passageway to the other side of South America.

TIP Notice the structure of the passage. Is it organized by cause and effect, by topics, or by chronological order? That will help you determine what may come next.

TIP Use what you already know to help you answer social studies questions.

Pick the letter that best answers the question.

What information would you expect to find in the *next* paragraph of this article?

A what Magellan's childhood was like

B what happened after Magellan reached the Pacific Ocean

C how Magellan's crew got through the Strait of Magellan

D how Magellan died in the Philippines

Think It Through The structure of this passage is chronological, so you can easily rule out A, which happened long before the voyage. You can also rule out D, which happened after Magellan entered the Pacific. That leaves B and C. You can use your knowledge of geography to determine that the passage through the Strait of Magellan would logically come before the crew reached the Pacific Ocean. The correct answer is C.

Practice Questions

Read the passage below. Choose the letter of the best answer to the questions that follow.

> Christopher Columbus led four voyages to the Americas. The first and most famous one began in 1492 and included just three ships. His second voyage, which included 17 ships, founded Nueva Isabela, the first European colony in the Americas. On his third voyage, which left Spain in 1498, Columbus became the first European to visit South America. Columbus's final voyage lasted from 1502 to 1504. He hoped to find a passage through the new lands he had discovered and sail on to Asia, but he never did.

1. During what time period can you infer that Columbus made his second voyage?

   A before 1492

   B between 1498 and 1502

   C between 1492 and 1498

   D after 1504

2. What was significant about Columbus's second voyage to the Americas?

   A He realized he had found a new land.

   B He found a passage through the continent.

   C He began a settlement.

   D He finally reached Asia.

3. What information would you expect to find in the *next* paragraph of this article about Christopher Columbus?

   A what his childhood was like

   B why he founded Nueva Isabela

   C where he landed in South America

   D how he spent his later years

Go Online
PHSchool.com

Use Web Code **lga-8604**
for a **Chapter 6 self-test.**

Changes in the Western World

Chapter Preview

This chapter will introduce you to important changes that took place primarily in the 1700s and 1800s. They include revolutions in thought, in the way goods were produced, and in the way nations governed themselves at home and conducted themselves around the world.

Target Reading Skill

Comparison and Contrast In this chapter you will focus on using comparison and contrast to help you sort out and analyze information.

► A Northern Pacific Railroad train, 1900

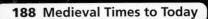

Europe in 1700

KEY
—— Border as of 1700
• City

NORWAY (Denmark)
SWEDEN
• Stockholm
SCOTLAND
North Sea
Baltic Sea
DENMARK
Moscow •
IRELAND (England)
Copenhagen
PRUSSIA (Brandenburg)
RUSSIA
ENGLAND
NETHERLANDS
BRANDENBURG
London •
• Warsaw
SPANISH NETHERLANDS (Spain)
SMALL GERMAN STATES
POLAND
ATLANTIC OCEAN
• Paris
FRANCE
SWITZERLAND
Vienna •
COSSACKS
MILAN (Spain)
VENICE
AUSTRIA-HUNGARY
• Venice
PORTUGAL
SMALL ITALIAN STATES
PAPAL STATES
Black Sea
• Lisbon
• Madrid
Rome •
OTTOMAN EMPIRE
SPAIN
NAPLES (Spain)
• Constantinople
Mediterranean Sea
MOREA (Venice)

N W E S

0 miles 500
0 kilometers 500
Lambert Azimuthal Equal Area

Regions In 1700, some European nations that are independent today were ruled by other European nations. **Locate** Find the nations with another name in parentheses under their names. The second name is that of the ruling nation. **Predict** How might this political situation affect European peace and stability?

Go Online
PHSchool.com Use Web Code
lgp-8711 for step-by-step
map skills practice.

Prepare to Read

Objectives

In this section, you will

1. Find out about the Age of Reason and how it grew out of the Renaissance and the Scientific Revolution.
2. Explore the Enlightenment idea of natural rights.
3. Learn how the French thinkers called philosophes contributed to the Enlightenment.

Taking Notes

As you read this section, look for the achievements of the Enlightenment. Copy the concept web below and record your findings in it.

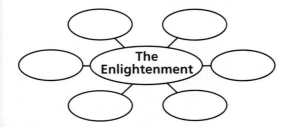

The Enlightenment

Target Reading Skill

Compare and Contrast Comparing is examining the similarities between things. Contrasting is looking at the differences. These skills can help you sort out and analyze information. As you read this section, compare and contrast Enlightenment ideas with the ideas of earlier time periods.

Key Terms

- **Enlightenment** (en LYT un munt) *n.* a philosophical movement, primarily of the 1700s, that was characterized by reliance on reason and experience

- **Age of Reason** (ayj uv REE zun) *n.* the period of the Enlightenment
- **Scientific Revolution** (sy un TIF ik rev uh LOO shun) *n.* a time when scientists began to rely on observation of the natural world
- **scientific method** (sy un TIF ik METH ud) *n.* a method involving careful observation of nature and, in some sciences, controlled experiments
- **natural rights** (NACH ur ul ryts) *n.* rights that belong to all human beings from birth
- **philosophe** (fee luh ZOHF) *n.* a French thinker of the Enlightenment

Galileo

The whole room was silent. Members of the court leaned forward, waiting for Galileo Galilei (gal uh LEE oh gal uh LAY) to respond to the question. Did the great Italian scientist really believe that Earth moved around the sun?

This was an important question in 1633. The Roman Catholic Church taught that God had made Earth the center of the universe. If that were true, everything—sun, planets, and stars—moved around Earth. But in the 1500s, the Polish astronomer Nicolaus Copernicus (nik uh LAY us koh PUR nih kus) had said that Earth moved around the sun.

Galileo had supported the ideas of Copernicus. Now the Church court was asking Galileo what he really believed. He knew that he could be tortured to death if he disagreed with the Church. So the old man told the court what it wanted to hear— that Earth did not move. Yet, as Galileo was being led away, he is said to have muttered, "Nevertheless, it does move."

The Age of Reason

As you have read, for hundreds of years the Roman Catholic Church had been the most powerful institution in Europe. The Church told people what to believe about the physical world and how they should behave, based on the Bible and on faith. To protect its power, the Church excommunicated people who questioned its authority or teachings. It also gave the Inquisition, or Church courts, the power to torture, imprison, or condemn to death those who did not strictly obey the Church in thought and deed.

Nevertheless, there were those who questioned Church teachings. Protestants broke away from the Church. The Renaissance encouraged the study of ancient texts and the development of new ideas. As scientists began to make careful observations of nature, they started a revolution in the way people looked at themselves and the world.

Learn about Galileo, the first scientist to use a telescope.

A Change in Perspective This revolution in thought was called the **Enlightenment.** It was characterized by reliance on reason and experience rather than on religious teachings and faith. The 1700s, when Enlightenment ideas were the leading ideas in Europe, is called the **Age of Reason.**

New World View
This diagram illustrates the view of the universe put forth by Copernicus, who is shown at the left below. *Infer Compare this diagram to the one on pages M2–M3. How "modern" was Copernicus's view?*

Enlightenment thinkers used reason, or logical thought, to shed a new "light" on traditional beliefs. In many cases, they challenged those beliefs. The Enlightenment affected politics, art, literature, science, and religion—almost every field of human thought.

Galileo and Gravity In addition to studying the heavens, Galileo also experimented with gravity. According to legend, he dropped a light object and a heavy object from a tower at the same time. They landed at the same instant. Even though it seemed logical that a heavier object would fall faster, Galileo concluded—based on his experiment—that the speed of a falling object does not depend on its weight.

The Scientific Revolution Many Enlightenment ideas were rooted in the Scientific Revolution of the 1500s and 1600s. The **Scientific Revolution** was a time when scientists began to rely on what they could observe for themselves. It was the birth of modern science.

One of these scientists was Nicolaus Copernicus, who put forth the idea that Earth moved around the sun. He published his findings in 1543. At that time, people believed that Earth was the center of the universe and that the sun revolved around it. Both ancient Greek science and the Church supported that view. Many experts rejected Copernicus's theory.

In the late 1500s, however, the Danish astronomer Tycho Brahe (TEE koh BRAH uh) provided evidence to support Copernicus. In the early 1600s, Johannes Kepler (yoh HAHN us KEP lur) used Brahe's data to accurately calculate the orbits of the planets around the sun. Galileo also studied the planets. Using a new scientific tool—the telescope—he was able to observe four moons orbiting around Jupiter.

Milestones in the Scientific Revolution

Scientific Thought
In the early 1600s, Francis Bacon stressed the importance of experiment and observation.

◀ René Descartes said that human reasoning leads to understanding the world.

Medicine
Andreas Vesalius published the first accurate, detailed study of human anatomy in 1543.

◀ In the early 1600s, William Harvey discovered how the blood circulates and how the heart acts as a pump.

Anton van Leeuwenhoek perfected the microscope and in 1684 was the first to accurately describe red blood cells.

Chemistry
In the mid-1600s, Robert Boyle, "the father of chemistry," based his work on experiment and observation. He said that everything is made up of very tiny particles of matter.

Astronomy
In 1543, Nicolaus Copernicus published his theory that Earth and the other planets move around the sun.

▼ In 1609, Galileo used a telescope of his own design to observe the planets.

In England, Isaac Newton developed a theory about why the planets move the way they do. You have probably heard how Newton observed an apple falling from a tree. This observation led him to wonder whether the force that made the apple fall might be the same force that kept the moon in its orbit around Earth. He called that force gravity. He found that gravity also holds Earth and the other planets in their orbits around the sun. In 1687, Newton published a book about the workings of the universe. He said that the natural world follows "natural laws," or rules that can be measured and described mathematically.

The Scientific Method Scientists were developing a new way of learning about the world. This **scientific method** involves careful observation of nature and, in some sciences, controlled experiments. To use the scientific method, scientists make predictions and develop theories based on their observations. Then they test their predictions by doing experiments and by careful observations. Logic and mathematics are used to analyze observations and compare them to the results expected from their theories. As scientists observe and learn more, they replace old theories with new ones that explain the facts better.

✓ Reading Check **What are natural laws?**

Newton's Rainbow
Isaac Newton studied optics, or the science of light. Here, he uses a prism to disperse light into a spectrum of colors. **Conclude** *Why do you think Newton conducted this experiment in a dark room?*

New Political Ideas

Scientists were finding out that nature worked according to certain natural laws. Other Enlightenment thinkers declared that there were also natural laws that applied to human society.

John Locke One of these thinkers was the English philosopher John Locke. He said that natural laws govern human behavior. Government, he said, should be based on these natural laws.

Locke believed that people were basically reasonable and good. He argued that people also had **natural rights,** or rights that belonged to all human beings from birth. They included the right to life, the right to liberty, and the right to own property.

According to Locke, people form governments to protect their natural rights. Governments draw the right to rule from the people they govern. Therefore, rulers should govern only as long as they have the support of the people. If a government breaks the agreement by taking away people's rights, the people have the right to change, or even replace, that government.

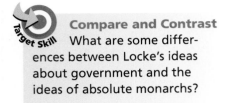

Compare and Contrast What are some differences between Locke's ideas about government and the ideas of absolute monarchs?

Locke's Impact Locke's ideas were startling. He was saying that monarchs like those of France, Spain, and Russia did not have a divine right to rule. They should not have absolute power. They could—even *should*—be replaced if they did not meet their responsibilities toward those they ruled. People in many countries read about these new ideas and began to wonder whether their rulers were governing properly. As you will see in Section 2, some people eventually translated Locke's ideas into action.

✓ **Reading Check** What natural rights did Locke describe?

The French Philosophes

Enlightenment ideas were also being explored in France. The **philosophes** (fee luh ZOHF) were a group of French thinkers and scientists who believed that the ideas of the Enlightenment could be used to reform and improve government and society. They spoke out against inequality and injustice. The philosophes distrusted institutions, like most governments and the Church, that did not support freedom of thought.

One of the most important philosophes was Jean Jacques Rousseau (zhahn zhahk roo SOH). Like Locke, Rousseau thought that people were naturally good. He added that imperfect institutions such as the Church and governments corrupted, or spoiled, this natural goodness. In his 1762 book *The Social Contract*, Rousseau argued that governments should express the will of the people and put few limits on people's behavior.

Discussing Enlightenment Ideas Voltaire (with arm raised) hosts a gathering of philosophes. **Infer** *What class of French society do these men probably belong to? Explain your answer.*

Perhaps the most famous philosophe was Voltaire (vohl TEHR). His essays, plays, and novels exposed many of the abuses of his day. He used his biting wit to attack inequality, injustice, and religious prejudice. Voltaire was a great champion of freedom of speech. He once stated, "I disapprove of what you say, but I will defend to the death your right to say it."

In the mid-1700s, articles by many of the philosophes were collected by Denis Diderot (duh nee DEE duh roh) in the *Encyclopedia*. One purpose of this huge work was to bring together information on all of the arts and sciences. Another purpose was to make this information available to the public. A third goal was to advance the ideas of the Enlightenment. Articles in the *Encyclopedia* attacked slavery, urged education for all, and promoted freedom of expression. They also challenged traditional religions and the divine right of kings. Both the French government and the Catholic Church tried to ban the *Encyclopedia*, but it still was an important influence on Enlightenment thinkers.

Pages from the *Encyclopedia*

✓ **Reading Check** **What was the *Encyclopedia*?**

Section 1 Assessment

Key Terms
Review the key terms at the beginning of this section. Use each term in a sentence that explains its meaning.

Target Reading Skill
Compare and contrast the view of the universe held by the Church with the view held by Copernicus and Galileo.

Comprehension and Critical Thinking
1. (a) Identify Name two scientists of the Scientific Revolution and describe their contributions.

(b) Contrast How was the scientific method different from the thinking of the Middle Ages?

2. (a) Recall According to John Locke, why do governments exist?
(b) Identify Effects How were Locke's ideas a threat to some governments of the 1700s?
3. (a) Identify Which philosophe wrote *The Social Contract*? Who edited the *Encyclopedia*?
(b) Synthesize Information How did the philosophes contribute to the Enlightenment?

Writing Activity
Suppose you could do a television interview with one of the important thinkers you read about in this section. Write a list of questions you would ask him. Then write a short introduction to your interview.

Writing Tip Capture your viewers' attention by telling how the person on your show changed the world.

Interpreting Diagrams

Diagrams present information in both words and pictures. To interpret a diagram, you need to discover what each picture or symbol represents. You must also understand the labels or captions that provide additional information. Finally, you must see how all parts of the diagram— the words, pictures, and symbols—work together to explain how a process works or how something is put together.

Learn the Skill

Use these steps to interpret a diagram.

1. **Look at the title and at the diagram to get a general idea of what it shows.** What is the subject of the diagram? What is its purpose? Does it show how something works or a process for doing something?

2. **Study each part of the diagram, and read the captions or labels that go with each part.** Interpret each picture or symbol. The words will help you understand what each picture or symbol represents.

3. **Notice how each part of the diagram relates to the other parts.** Does the diagram show steps in sequence? If so, notice what happens first, second, and so forth. Does it show details, such as close-ups or cutaways of the inside of something? How do the parts relate to the whole?

4. **Use your understanding of both the pictures and the words to draw a conclusion about the diagram.** Summarize the process or construction shown in the diagram. Think about how using words and pictures *together* helps make the meaning clear.

Practice the Skill

Use the steps on the previous page to interpret the diagram shown at the right.

Francis Bacon (1561–1626), who said that truth is discovered through observation and reason

1 What is the subject of this diagram? What is its purpose?

2 What does each small illustration mean? How do the numbers and arrows help you understand the diagram? Do the captions tell what something is or describe a step in a process?

3 How do the parts of the diagram relate to one another? What does the fact that it is a circle suggest? What does Step Seven mean?

4 Summarize the process shown in the diagram in your own words. Be sure to explain how Step Seven relates to Step One. How does this diagram add to your understanding of the Scientific Revolution?

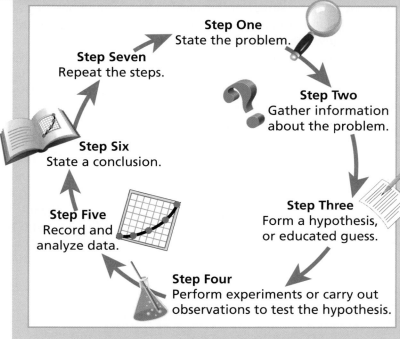

The Scientific Method

Step One
State the problem.

Step Two
Gather information about the problem.

Step Three
Form a hypothesis, or educated guess.

Step Four
Perform experiments or carry out observations to test the hypothesis.

Step Five
Record and analyze data.

Step Six
State a conclusion.

Step Seven
Repeat the steps.

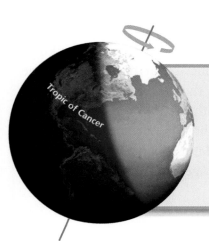

Apply the Skill

Turn to the diagram of the movements of Earth on pages M2–M3 of the MapMaster Skills Handbook. Use the steps of this skill to interpret the large diagram.

Prepare to Read

Objectives

In this section, you will
1. Learn how a power struggle between English kings and Parliament led to the creation of a limited, constitutional monarchy.
2. Find out how the American Revolution put Enlightenment ideas into practice.
3. Discover how the French Revolution ended the monarchy in France.

Taking Notes

As you read this section, identify the major changes that took place in England, America, and France in the 1600s and 1700s. Copy the flowchart below and record your findings in it.

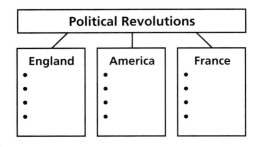

Political Revolutions		
England	**America**	**France**
•	•	•
•	•	•
•	•	•
•	•	•

Target Reading Skill

Make Comparisons
Comparing two or more situations enables you to see how they are alike. As you read this section, compare the revolutions it describes. Consider their causes and effects as well as the ways they were accomplished.

Key Terms

- **English Civil War** (ING glish SIV ul wawr) *n.* the military clash between forces loyal to King Charles I and the forces of Parliament that overthrew the monarchy
- **English Bill of Rights** (ING glish bil uv rytz) *n.* acts passed by Parliament in 1689 guaranteeing certain rights of English people and limiting the power of the monarch
- **colony** (KAHL uh nee) *n.* territory settled and ruled by a distant country
- **Declaration of Independence** (dek luh RAY shun uv in dee PEN duns) *n.* the document in which the United States announced its independence from Britain
- **Reign of Terror** (rayn uv TEHR ur) *n.* the period (1793–1794) of the French Revolution during which many people were executed for opposing the revolution

As you have read, England enjoyed a golden age under Queen Elizabeth I. Shortly before she died in 1603, Elizabeth told Parliament, "Though God hath raised me high, yet this I count the glory of my crown, that I have reigned with your loves."

Elizabeth I was a very powerful monarch, but she knew that her power was not absolute. As far back as 1215, the Magna Carta had put limits on the power of English rulers. Elizabeth knew that she ruled with the approval of Parliament and the people—and she knew how important that approval was to her success. What she did not know was that the peace and stability of the Elizabethan Age would soon be destroyed by her successors.

Queen Elizabeth I

Changes in England

Queen Elizabeth died without children. Her crown went to her cousin, the king of Scotland, James Stuart. Although he had agreed to rule according to English laws and custom, James I believed that he was king by divine right and that his power was absolute.

King Charles I

James, and his son Charles I who ruled after him, clashed with Parliament, the council that had been advising English monarchs since the 1200s. Over the centuries, Parliament had grown in size and power. Divided into the House of Lords and the House of Commons, it had become a true legislature, passing bills that became law with the monarch's approval. Nevertheless, when Parliament would not approve the taxes he wanted, James dissolved, or closed, Parliament.

A Power Struggle Over time, a power struggle developed between the king and Parliament. Both James and Charles often refused to allow Parliament to meet. But when Charles needed money, he summoned Parliament, which could levy taxes. Parliament responded by trying to limit the king's power.

The English Civil War Charles summoned Parliament in 1640, when he needed funds to put down a rebellion in Scotland. This Parliament refused to bow to the king. It tried and executed some of the king's ministers, and declared that it could not be dissolved without its own consent. In response, Charles led troops into the House of Commons. Parliament leaders who escaped raised their own army. Forces loyal to the king fought forces loyal to Parliament in the **English Civil War.**

England at War
In this painting, Oliver Cromwell leads the forces of Parliament during the English Civil War.
Analyze Images *What does the painting reveal about the weapons and tactics of this war?*

Led by Oliver Cromwell, a skilled general, the military forces of Parliament were victorious. In 1646, they captured Charles I. Parliament set up a court that tried and convicted the king as "a tyrant . . . and public enemy." Charles I was beheaded in 1649. It was the first time a European monarch had been tried and executed by his own people.

After the war, Parliament abolished, or did away with, the monarchy. Oliver Cromwell ruled England through a committee of Parliament. Cromwell was a Puritan, a member of a Protestant group that wanted to simplify the services of the Church of England and to enforce strictly moral behavior. When he faced challenges to his power, Cromwell took the title Lord Protector and set up military rule.

The Monarchy Is Restored In 1660, just two years after Cromwell's death, Parliament invited the son of King Charles I to return from exile and rule the country. This re-establishment of the monarchy under Charles II is called the Restoration. Charles II was a popular king, but his brother, James II, who became king in 1685, was not. Not only was James Catholic, he also behaved like an absolute monarch.

Ruler But Not King
After the English Civil War, Oliver Cromwell was offered the throne but refused to become king.
Predict *What do you think might have happened in England if Cromwell had become king?*

Parliament's leaders wanted a Protestant king who respected Parliament. In 1688, they invited James's Protestant daughter Mary and her husband, the Dutch prince William of Orange, "to rescue the nation and the religion." When William and Mary's armies landed in England, James fled to France. This bloodless overthrow of James II is called the Glorious Revolution.

Parliament officially offered the throne to William and Mary—with one condition. They had to accept the **English Bill of Rights,** which stated that all laws had to be approved by Parliament and gave the House of Commons the power of the purse—the power to raise and spend money. Parliament had to be summoned regularly. The Bill of Rights also restated the traditional rights of English citizens, such as trial by jury. In 1689, William and Mary agreed, and Britain became a constitutional monarchy, or a government in which the monarch's power is limited by a set of laws.

Make Comparisons
How was England's government before the English Civil War similar to the government established by the Glorious Revolution?

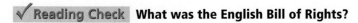

✓ Reading Check **What was the English Bill of Rights?**

The American Revolution

By the 1750s, about two million people lived in British colonies in North America. A **colony** is a territory settled and ruled by a distant nation. To help pay for the defense of their faraway colonies, the British wanted to collect taxes from the American colonists.

No Taxation Without Representation Under British law, people could not be taxed unless they had representatives in the Parliament that had voted for the tax. But the colonists had no representatives in Parliament. They complained that by taxing them, the British government was taking away their rights.

As American protests increased, British leaders feared that they were losing control of their colonies. They approved more taxes and stricter laws. Americans grew angrier. Leaders such as Thomas Jefferson and Benjamin Franklin, who admired the Enlightenment ideas of John Locke, started to think about rebelling against British rule. The colonists began to gather weapons and ammunition.

On April 19, 1775, British soldiers marched to Lexington and Concord, towns near Boston, Massachusetts. Their purpose was to take weapons and ammunition away from the Americans. The Americans, however, fought back. The American Revolution had begun.

The Colonies Become the United States In 1776, thirteen North American colonies officially declared their independence from Britain with a document called the **Declaration of Independence.** It was written by Thomas Jefferson. Echoing Locke's ideas, Jefferson stated that governments have power only because the people give it to them. If a government takes away people's rights, the people have a right to change the government or put an end to it.

With the aid of the French, the Americans won their independence in 1781. In 1789, the Constitution became the supreme law of the new nation. It was based largely on the ideas of the Enlightenment and on the traditional rights of English citizens. A written Bill of Rights protecting individual citizens became part of the Constitution.

✓ Reading Check **What is the Constitution?**

Links to
Government

The Declaration of Independence How do these famous words from the Declaration reflect the ideas of the Enlightenment?

"We hold these truths to be self-evident, that all men are created equal, that they are endowed by their Creator with certain unalienable Rights, that among these are Life, Liberty and the pursuit of Happiness. That to secure these rights, Governments are instituted among Men, deriving their just powers from the consent of the governed; That whenever any Form of Government becomes destructive of these ends it is the Right of the People to alter or to abolish it. . . ."

A committee worked with Thomas Jefferson (second from left) on the Declaration of Independence. This pen was used to sign it.

When news of the French Revolution reached the French island colony of Saint-Domingue (san du MAYNG) in the Caribbean Sea, enslaved Africans there were inspired. The ideas of the Enlightenment encouraged them to rebel against their white masters. Their revolt was led by a former slave, Toussaint L'Ouverture (too SAN loo vehr TOOR). He was determined to end slavery on his island. In that, he was successful. However, he was captured by the French in 1802, and died in exile before his goal of an independent nation of Haiti was achieved in 1804.

The French Revolution

King Louis XVI of France had helped the American colonists win their independence. Yet he was no great friend of liberty. He had helped because he wanted to reduce the power of the British. The Americans appreciated the help. The French people did not. They had to pay heavy taxes to support the French army.

France Faces Severe Problems Under the French political system, only the working people paid taxes. Nobles and clergy paid hardly anything. Thus the poorest people carried the heaviest tax burden. As France's debt increased, the French government increased taxes even more. The French people grew resentful and demanded that Louis share power. They used the arguments of Enlightenment thinkers to support their demands.

Adding to France's economic problems, poor harvests in the late 1780s sent food prices soaring. Millions of people were going hungry. Riots broke out as poor people demanded bread. Finally, the king called a meeting of representatives of the three estates, or divisions, of French society—the nobles, the clergy, and the middle class. When these representatives met in 1789, they declared themselves the National Assembly.

The Revolution Begins As food shortages worsened and rumors spread that royal troops were going to occupy the capital, the people of Paris reacted. On July 14, 1789, they attacked the Bastille (bas TEEL), a prison that held political prisoners. To this day, July 14 is celebrated as Bastille Day, the French national holiday.

Rioting continued all over France. Meanwhile, the National Assembly passed laws to make the people of France equal under the law. The Assembly's Declaration of the Rights of Man echoed the American Declaration of Independence. In 1791, the National Assembly produced a constitution setting up a limited monarchy.

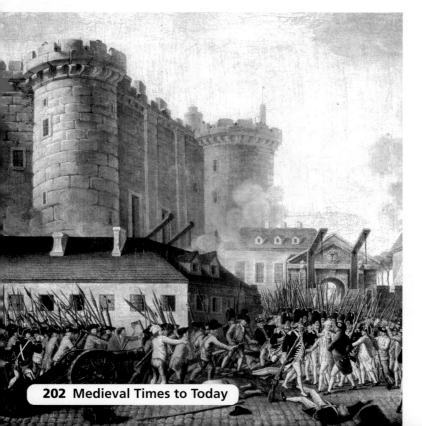

The Storming of the Bastille
This painting shows French citizens attacking the Bastille, the building in the left background. **Analyze Images** *Describe the Bastille. Which group is the citizens? Does it look as if they will be successful?*

European monarchs were horrified. Fearing that the "French plague" would spread and that they would lose their own power, they sent armies to France to help the king. The National Assembly declared war on these foreign powers. When the war began to go badly for France, rioting French citizens stormed the palace and captured the king. A few months later, Louis XVI was executed.

The Reign of Terror A group called the Committee of Public Safety took power to defend France and the revolution. The Committee declared that the constitution was no longer in effect. Maximilien Robespierre (mahk see mee LYAHN ROHBZ pyehr) led the Committee in carrying out what became known as the **Reign of Terror.** For nearly a year, people who were considered enemies of the revolution were executed—perhaps as many as 70 to 80 in a day. No one was safe. As political power shifted, those who had helped to create the constitution were killed as well as those who had fought against it. Finally, Robespierre himself was executed, and the Reign of Terror soon ended.

The French Revolution lasted ten years. It was a time of chaos and tyranny as well as of reform and idealism. The English novelist Charles Dickens called it "the best of times [and] the worst of times." The Revolution would finally end when one of the most powerful leaders in history took control of France in 1799. You will read about him in Section 4.

The guillotine (GIL uh teen), a device for beheading people, was used during the Reign of Terror.

✓ Reading Check   **What was the Reign of Terror?**

Section 2 Assessment

Key Terms
Review the key terms at the beginning of this section. Use each term in a sentence that explains its meaning.

Target Reading Skill
What did the three revolutions described in this section have in common?

Comprehension and Critical Thinking
1. (a) Describe How did James I and Charles I clash with Parliament?

(b) Analyze Information How did the Glorious Revolution show that Parliament had gained more power than the monarch?

2. (a) Identify Cause and Effect What role did taxes play in the American Revolution?

(b) Synthesize Information How did the ideas of John Locke affect the American Revolution?

3. (a) Identify What were two causes of the rioting that began the French Revolution?

(b) Identify Frame of Reference Why did European rulers fear the French Revolution?

Writing Activity
Write a paragraph that answers this question: How was the French Revolution both "the best of times" and "the worst of times"?

Writing Tip Begin by making two lists, one of the benefits of the French Revolution and another of the harm that it caused. You can use the quotation from Dickens as your topic sentence. Support it with details from your list.

The Industrial Revolution

Prepare to Read

Objectives

In this section, you will
1. Learn about the Industrial Revolution and how it changed the world forever.
2. Identify some serious problems of the Industrial Age.

Taking Notes

As you read this section, look for the major causes and effects of the Industrial Revolution. Copy the flowchart below and record your findings in it.

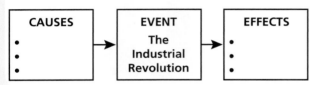

CAUSES	EVENT The Industrial Revolution	EFFECTS
• • •		• • •

Target Reading Skill

Identify Contrasts When you contrast two situations, you examine how they are different. In this section you will read about a major historical turning point. Keeping track of the various changes caused by the Industrial Revolution will help you understand its significance. As you read, list the differences between life before and during the Industrial Age.

Key Terms

- **Industrial Revolution** (in DUS tree ul rev uh LOO shun) *n.* the change in methods of producing goods—from hand tools at home to machines in factories, 1760s–1860s
- **textile industry** (TEKS tyl IN dus tree) *n.* the making of cloth
- **labor union** (LAY bur YOON yun) *n.* an organization of workers formed to bargain with employers for better pay and working conditions

British factory workers forging an anchor in the early 1800s

Here are the sights and sounds of a revolution. Look at the painting on this page, and then read the two quotations below.

> ❝The thunder of the blast deafens you. The ever-brightening flame, flashing up finally as high as fifty feet, blinds you; sparks fall everywhere. ❞

> ❝ . . . the rumbling growl of rollers, the howls of horrible saws . . . the crashing thunder of falling iron plate, the hoarse coughing of great engines, and the hissing of steam. ❞
>
> — *visitors to an American factory, around 1900*

What was it like to work in these places? Very different than work had been in previous centuries! The painter of *Forging an Anchor* and the visitors to the American factory were witnessing one of the greatest turning points in human history. This revolution in the way things were made would change the way people lived all around the world.

A New Kind of Revolution

Until the middle of the 1700s, most people lived on farms or in very small towns. Agriculture was the basis of their economies. Most goods that people needed were made by hand, either at home or in small shops.

Then, in only 100 years, this way of life changed in a large part of the world. From about 1760 to about 1860, the way manufactured goods were produced shifted from simple hand tools in homes and shops to complex machines in factories. This change is called the **Industrial Revolution.**

The Industrial Revolution Begins The Industrial Revolution began in Great Britain in the 1760s. At that time, trade from its growing overseas empire was fueling the rapid growth of Britain's economy. British colonies provided both the raw materials needed to manufacture goods and the people to buy the goods once they were produced. British businesspeople became wealthy and had money to invest in new ventures, such as factories.

Factory Production
The Cyclops Steel Works in Sheffield, England, 1853.
Analyze Images *Which details in the painting suggest advances in technology and production? Which details suggest possible problems of industrialization?*

Inventions Change the World

◀ James Watt is called the Father of the Industrial Revolution because of his improvements to the steam engine in the 1760s.

Samuel F. B. Morse invented the telegraph in the 1830s.

In 1876, Alexander Graham Bell patented the telephone. ▶

◀ Thomas Edison invented many useful devices, including the phonograph in 1877 and the first practical electric light bulb in 1879.

▼ Robert Fulton built the first practical steamboat in 1807 and revolutionized water transportation.

The Textile Industry In the 1760s, the leading industry in Britain was the **textile industry, or the making of cloth.** Spinning and weaving were done mostly by people working in their homes. It took a long time to make each piece of cloth, so textiles were expensive. Only the wealthy had more than one change of clothes.

Several inventions of the 1760s made it possible to produce more cloth more quickly and more cheaply. For example, the spinning jenny allowed one worker to do the work of eight people using spinning wheels. On the other hand, the new textile machines were so big and so fast that they needed more power than one person could supply.

Inventors came up with ways of using flowing water to supply power to these huge machines. They dammed rivers and built mills that used water wheels. Later, steam engines were used to supply power. Britain's large deposits of coal powered these engines. The new textile machines had to be housed in large buildings called factories. Now, in order to work, people had to leave their homes and families and go to the factories. The Industrial Revolution was underway.

The Industrial Revolution Grows Soon other industrial inventions took advantage of the new power supply. Mighty steam-driven hammers forged iron parts for the newly invented farm machines, railroad cars, and engines. Trains powered by steam locomotives, traveling on steel rails, moved people and goods more quickly, cheaply, and reliably. Even agriculture became more like industry, as farmers used new, steam-driven machines to plant, harvest, and process crops.

Effects of the Industrial Revolution The Industrial Revolution spread to other nations in Europe and to the United States, and it affected more than production. It changed people's lives and the structure of society. One change was a huge increase in the amount and variety of goods available to ordinary people. Cities grew as people left their farms and settled near the new factories. Instead of providing for themselves on farms, people bought the things they needed with the money they earned working in factories.

Assembly Line

The modern age owes much to the work of Henry Ford. He did not invent the automobile. That was done in Germany in 1885. He did not invent the idea of interchangeable parts for making identical products. Nor did he invent the assembly line. But he combined all of these ideas into a process for making affordable cars in huge numbers. This process changed the lives of millions of people throughout the world.

Making Cars
Like the men in this Ford automobile plant, each assembly-line worker has a single task to complete, over and over again. The product moves slowly along a track or conveyor belt.

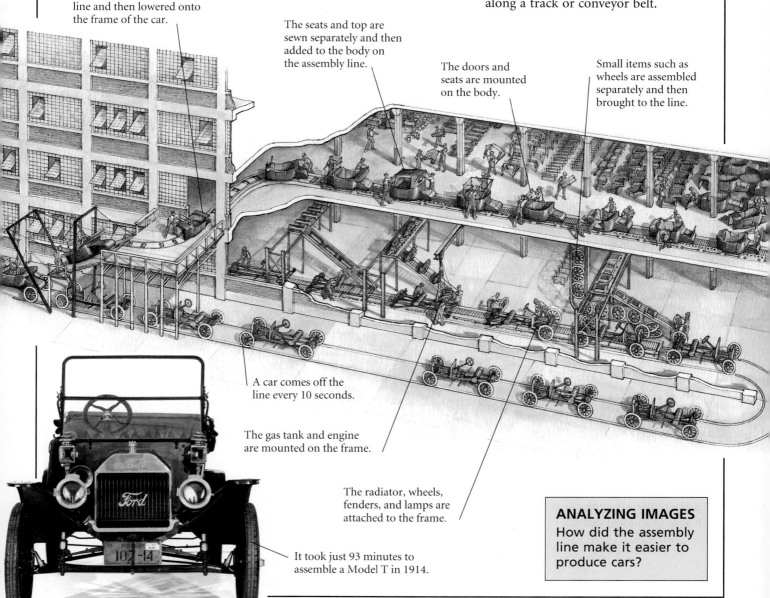

The wooden-framed body is made on another assembly line and then lowered onto the frame of the car.

The seats and top are sewn separately and then added to the body on the assembly line.

The doors and seats are mounted on the body.

Small items such as wheels are assembled separately and then brought to the line.

A car comes off the line every 10 seconds.

The gas tank and engine are mounted on the frame.

The radiator, wheels, fenders, and lamps are attached to the frame.

It took just 93 minutes to assemble a Model T in 1914.

ANALYZING IMAGES
How did the assembly line make it easier to produce cars?

Urban Growth, 1800–1900

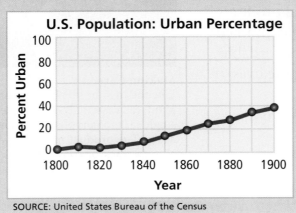

U.S. Population: Urban Percentage

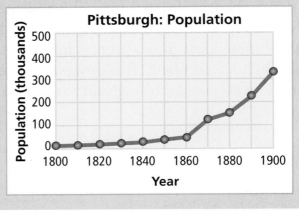

Pittsburgh: Population

SOURCE: United States Bureau of the Census

■ Graph Skills

The Industrial Revolution caused people to move from farms to cities. Pittsburgh (above) became an important center of steel production. **Identify** What percentage of the United States was urban in 1800? In 1900? When did Pittsburgh's population begin to grow rapidly? **Conclude** When did steel production become important in Pittsburgh?

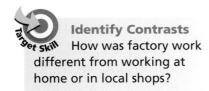

Identify Contrasts How was factory work different from working at home or in local shops?

The Industrial Revolution also changed society. It created jobs not only for factory workers but also for managers who ran the factories and for merchants who sold the many new goods. These new jobs presented opportunities for more people to move into the middle class. The middle class had the money to purchase many new products that could make people's lives easier.

✓ **Reading Check** **What changes did the Industrial Revolution bring?**

Problems of the Industrial Age

The Industrial Revolution gave more people than ever before the ability to have comfortable lives. But for many of those who worked in the new factories, life actually became harder.

Work in a Factory People who had produced goods in their homes or in local shops had been able to spend time with their families. Industrial workers, on the other hand, often spent 12 to 14 hours a day, every day, away from home at work in a factory.

Factories were noisy and dirty. The work was mind-numbing: A typical factory worker did the same simple action, over and over, hundreds of times a day. The work could also be dangerous. The large, powerful machines sometimes injured or even killed workers. And factory workers were paid very poorly. Often parents had to put their children to work in a factory just so the family could earn enough money to live.

Life in Industrial Towns By 1800, in many industrial areas, home offered little relief from the dirt and danger of the factory. Workers lived in small, cramped quarters. Soot from factory smokestacks and trains covered everything, even indoors. Often many families shared a single bathroom or had no indoor plumbing at all.

Garbage piling up in the streets attracted rats and packs of dogs. Dyes and dust from textile mills poisoned the air and water. Diseases swept easily through such cities. Many people died of cholera and typhus. Even minor diseases could be fatal under such conditions.

Workers Fight Back In response to the problems of industrialization, some workers formed **labor unions**. These were organizations that helped workers bargain with employers to improve their pay and working conditions. Factory owners fought against unionization, sometimes with violence. And at first, governments passed laws to keep the unions from becoming powerful. By the late 1800s, however, labor unions were well established. They won shorter hours, better pay, and safer working conditions for their members and for other workers. Eventually, unions became important political forces in many countries.

 Reading Check **What did labor unions fight for?**

The Rise of Unions
This illustration is from an 1880s British union membership card. **Conclude** *What types of workers belong to this union, and what issues are important to them?*

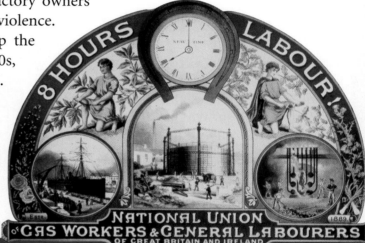

Section 3 Assessment

Key Terms
Review the key terms at the beginning of this section. Use each term in a sentence that explains its meaning.

Target Reading Skill
How was life before the Industrial Revolution different from life in the Industrial Age?

Comprehension and Critical Thinking
1. (a) Recall Where and when did the Industrial Revolution begin?

(b) Identify Causes Why did it begin in that time and place?
(c) Synthesize Information How did the Industrial Revolution change society?
2. (a) Describe What was life like for factory workers and their families in the 1700s?
(b) Identify Cause and Effect How did these conditions lead to the growth of labor unions?
(c) Draw Conclusions Do you think the Industrial Revolution helped or hurt society during the 1800s? Explain your answer.

Writing Activity
Suppose you are a worker in a textile factory in the late 1700s. Write a journal entry describing your workday. You may wish to compare it with your workday when you made cloth at home.

For: An activity on the Industrial Revolution
Visit: PHSchool.com
Web Code: lgd-8703

Focus On
The Mill Girls

In the mid-1800s, they left their family farms—many of them for the first time—to work in textile factories throughout New England. There they worked from dawn until past dark. These young women were known as the mill girls. Although the work was difficult, most mill girls gladly chose factory life over farm life. One mill girl wrote to her sister, "[A]nother pay day has come around. . . . I like [the work] as well as ever and Sarah don't I feel independent of everyone! The thought that I am living on no one is a happy one indeed to me."

Working in a Textile Factory In the mid-1800s, Lowell, Massachusetts, was an important leader in the textile industry. Child labor was used at textile mills during this time, but most laborers at Lowell and similar mill towns were single young women from rural areas. These women, about 15 to 25 years old, usually worked in the mills for about four years.

Workers' lives were strictly regulated. Factory bells woke them up in the morning, sent them to and from meals during the day, and rang them home again at night. The mill girls ate and slept at company-owned boarding-houses and agreed to strict rules, including regular church attendance and a 10 P.M. curfew. During their precious free time they might attend lectures, shop, or read books.

As the textile industry grew, working conditions declined. Factory owners cut wages and made employees work faster. By the 1860s, fewer and fewer native-born women worked at the mills. Instead, they stayed at home or searched for better opportunities.

Spinning Room ▶

The French Canadian girl at the right worked in the spinning room of a Massachusetts mill, where thread was spun onto bobbins. As fewer native-born women sought work in the mills, the jobs were filled by new immigrants, and increasingly, by immigrant children and men.

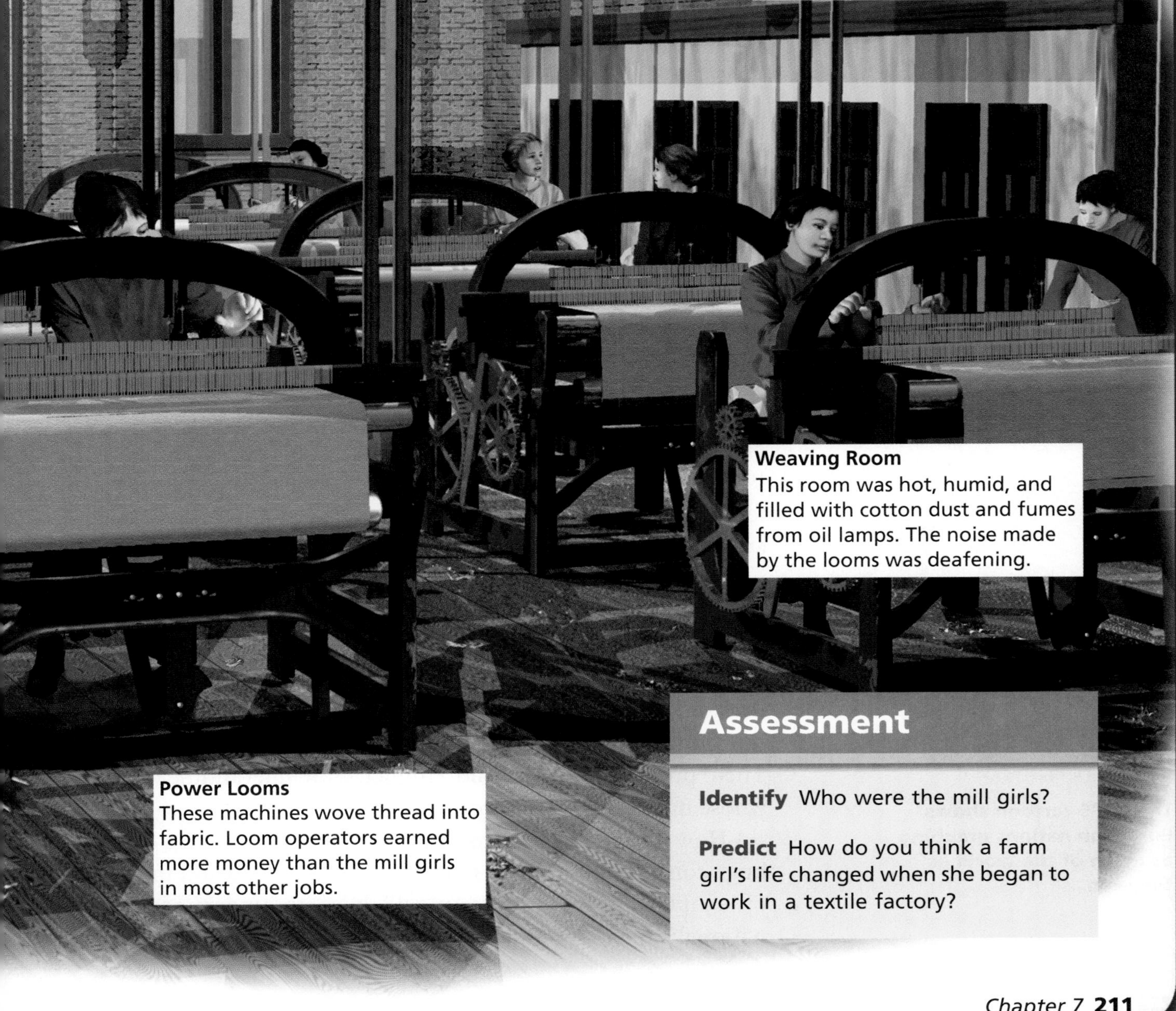

Weaving Room

This room was hot, humid, and filled with cotton dust and fumes from oil lamps. The noise made by the looms was deafening.

Power Looms

These machines wove thread into fabric. Loom operators earned more money than the mill girls in most other jobs.

Assessment

Identify Who were the mill girls?

Predict How do you think a farm girl's life changed when she began to work in a textile factory?

Nationalism and Imperialism

Prepare to Read

Objectives

In this section, you will
1. Learn how Napoleon rose to power in France and conquered much of Europe.
2. Understand the growth of nationalism in Europe.
3. Find out how imperialist European nations gained control over much of the world.

Taking Notes

As you read this section, look for the most important points about European imperialism. Copy the concept web below and record your findings in it.

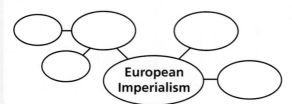

European Imperialism

Target Reading Skill

Compare and Contrast One way to understand different historical eras is to compare and contrast them, or to identify their similarities and differences. When you compare, you look at the similarities between things. When you contrast, you look at the differences. As you read this section, compare and contrast the Age of Napoleon with the era of European imperialism.

Key Terms

- **Napoleonic Code** (nuh poh lee AHN ik kohd) *n.* the French legal system based on Enlightenment ideas, set up during Napoleon's rule
- **nationalism** (NASH uh nul iz um) *n.* a feeling of pride in one's country and a desire for its independence
- **imperialism** (im PIHR ee ul iz um) *n.* the effort of a nation to create an empire of colonies

This 1885 cartoon shows European nations grabbing as much of the world as they can.

It was November 1884. The weather in Berlin was cold and gray. A group of men from Britain, Belgium, France, Germany, Portugal, Spain, and other countries had assembled for a conference. They were not thinking about the gloom of Europe in autumn. They were thinking about Africa. For months, they negotiated, drawing lines on maps of Africa. Finally, they reached an agreement: They had divided up Africa—an entire continent—among themselves.

No one from Africa participated in this conference. Those who did attend were not interested in the African people. The Europeans were interested only in the continent's resources. Their purpose was to avoid conflict with one another about whose nation would control these riches.

How could a few European countries simply take over a huge continent filled with many different cultures and millions of people? To find out, you will have to understand how nationalism and imperialism developed in the 1800s.

MAP★MASTER™
Skills Activity

ICELAND
(Denmark)

RUSSIA

SWEDEN

• Moscow

Borodino

KINGDOM OF
NORWAY
AND
DENMARK

Smolensk

Baltic Sea

PRUSSIA   Friedland

KEY

French territory

State under French influence

French ally, 1812

Independent European state

Battle site, 1800–1815

Route of Napoleon's invasion of Russia

Border

• City

North Sea

• Berlin

GRAND DUCHY
OF WARSAW

UNITED
KINGDOM

Leipzig

CONFEDERATION
OF THE
RHINE

Waterloo

Versailles • Paris

Vienna •   ★ Austerlitz

*ATLANTIC
OCEAN*

SWITZERLAND

AUSTRIA-
HUNGARY

Black Sea

FRANCE

OTTOMAN EMPIRE

Elba

Adriatic Sea

Corsica

• Rome

PORTUGAL   SPAIN

KINGDOM
OF
NAPLES

*Aegean
Sea*

SARDINIA

SICILY

0 miles   500

0 kilometers   500

Mediterranean Sea

Lambert Azimuthal Equal Area

Movement By 1812, Napoleon controlled much of Europe, but he wanted to rule Russia as well. **Identify** Where were Napoleon's armies turned back? **Compare** How were Napoleon's ambitions, as shown above, similar to the ambitions of the characters in the cartoon on page 212?

Go Online
PHSchool.com Use Web Code
lgd-8724 for step-by-step **map skills practice.**

The Age of Napoleon

You have read how other European nations invaded France during the French Revolution. At that time, one of the most capable officers in the French army was the young Napoleon Bonaparte. He won victory after victory against the foreign armies, rising quickly from captain to general. Then, in 1799, he took control of the French government. The beginning of Napoleon's rule marked the end of the French Revolution in France but the beginning of its influence on government and culture across Europe.

Napoleon

Napoleon's Accomplishments Claiming he was defending the ideals of the revolution, Napoleon brought many reforms to France. Perhaps the most important one was reforming French law. The new system of laws, called the **Napoleonic Code,** embodied such Enlightenment principles as equality of all citizens before the law. The Napoleonic Code had far-reaching effects. It became the basis for the legal systems of many European countries that came under French control in the 1800s.

Napoleon made another important change. He permitted the Catholic Church to operate freely again, but he also allowed freedom of worship to followers of other religions.

An Emperor's Resting Place
Although he died in exile, Napoleon's remains were brought back to France. His tomb is shown above. To the right is the crown Napoleon wore at his coronation. **Infer** *What does the setting of his tomb suggest about how the French people regard Napoleon?*

The Rise and Fall of Napoleon's Empire In 1804, Napoleon convinced the French parliament to name him emperor. He then set out to make Europe a French empire. As you can see on the map on page 213, he almost succeeded. In 1805, however, when Napoleon tried to invade Britain, the French fleet was destroyed at the Battle of Trafalgar. Soon, other nations began to rebel against French domination.

When Russia withdrew from its alliance with France, Napoleon invaded Russia and marched to Moscow. But his freezing, starving armies were forced into a disastrous retreat in 1812. That was the beginning of the end of his power. An alliance of European nations finally defeated Napoleon at Waterloo, Belgium, in 1815.

✔ **Reading Check** **What happened to Napoleon's armies in Russia?**

Nationalism

Napoleon's armies carried the ideas and the spirit of the French Revolution with them. One of these ideas was **nationalism,** which includes pride in one's own nation and a desire for independence. Pride in France spurred Napoleon's armies to win battles for their nation. However, this spirit of nationalism also led many countries that Napoleon conquered to rebel against French rule.

France, England, and Spain were already nations by the time Napoleon came to power. Much of the rest of Europe, however, was divided into small kingdoms. During the 1800s, many of these kingdoms were unified into nations. Both Germany and Italy became nations in the 1870s.

✔ **Reading Check** **Which two nations were formed in the 1870s?**

Compare and Contrast
Target Skill Notice the word *however* in the last paragraph. Does it signal similarities or differences? State the meaning of the first two sentences in your own words—without using *however*.

Imperialism in Africa and Asia

By the 1800s, some European countries had already claimed land in distant parts of the world. For example, the Spanish, French, English, and Portuguese had established colonies in the Americas. Now, confident of their economic and political strength, they wanted to expand their power even more.

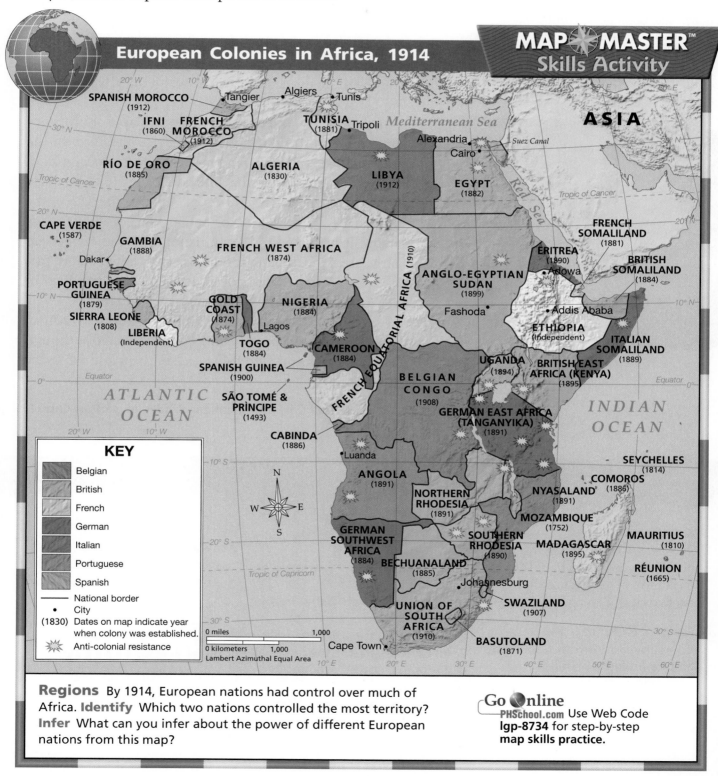

European Colonies in Africa, 1914

MAP MASTER™ Skills Activity

ASIA

Mediterranean Sea

SPANISH MOROCCO (1912)
Tangier
Algiers
Tunis
IFNI (1860)
FRENCH MOROCCO (1912)
TUNISIA (1881)
Tripoli
Alexandria
Suez Canal
Cairo
RÍO DE ORO (1885)
ALGERIA (1830)
LIBYA (1912)
EGYPT (1882)
Tropic of Cancer

CAPE VERDE (1587)
GAMBIA (1888)
FRENCH WEST AFRICA (1874)
FRENCH SOMALILAND (1881)
ERITREA (1890)
BRITISH SOMALILAND (1884)
Dakar
Adowa
PORTUGUESE GUINEA (1879)
GOLD COAST (1874)
NIGERIA (1884)
ANGLO-EGYPTIAN SUDAN (1899)
Addis Ababa
SIERRA LEONE (1808)
Lagos
Fashoda
ETHIOPIA (Independent)
ITALIAN SOMALILAND (1889)
LIBERIA (Independent)
TOGO (1884)
CAMEROON (1884)
UGANDA (1894)
BRITISH EAST AFRICA (KENYA) (1895)
SPANISH GUINEA (1900)
FRENCH EQUATORIAL AFRICA (1910)
BELGIAN CONGO (1908)
Equator
SÃO TOMÉ & PRÍNCIPE (1493)
CABINDA (1886)
ATLANTIC OCEAN
GERMAN EAST AFRICA (TANGANYIKA) (1891)
INDIAN OCEAN
Luanda
SEYCHELLES (1814)
ANGOLA (1891)
NORTHERN RHODESIA (1891)
NYASALAND (1891)
COMOROS (1886)
MOZAMBIQUE (1752)
GERMAN SOUTHWEST AFRICA (1884)
SOUTHERN RHODESIA (1890)
MADAGASCAR (1895)
MAURITIUS (1810)
BECHUANALAND (1885)
Tropic of Capricorn
RÉUNION (1665)
Johannesburg
SWAZILAND (1907)
UNION OF SOUTH AFRICA (1910)
BASUTOLAND (1871)
Cape Town

KEY

Belgian
British
French
German
Italian
Portuguese
Spanish
— National border
• City
(1830) Dates on map indicate year when colony was established.
Anti-colonial resistance

0 miles 1,000
0 kilometers 1,000
Lambert Azimuthal Equal Area

Regions By 1914, European nations had control over much of Africa. **Identify** Which two nations controlled the most territory? **Infer** What can you infer about the power of different European nations from this map?

Go Online PHSchool.com Use Web Code **lgp-8734** for step-by-step map skills practice.

Effects of Industrialization and Nationalism European factories needed more of the raw materials—cotton, metals, coal, and rubber—that were plentiful in other lands. These factories also needed people to buy their goods. To gain both raw materials and new markets, European countries established colonies in less-industrialized regions of Africa and Asia. Colonies also helped European nations to protect their trade routes. This effort to create an empire of colonies is called **imperialism.**

Nationalism also contributed to imperialism. Controlling vast territory fueled national pride. And pride led to rivalry. Each country wanted more power and greater wealth than its neighbors.

British Imperialism
By 1900, Great Britain controlled about one quarter of the land and people in the world. This flag shows Britain's Queen Victoria. **Analyze Images** *How does the flag represent British imperialism?*

Imperialism Reshapes the World Europeans had a long history of trade with Africa and Asia. In the 1800s, however, European nations colonized nearly all of Africa, as shown on the map on page 215. They also gained control of large areas of Asia. In the 1850s, the British began their rule of India. France, Russia, Germany, Britain, and the Asian nation of Japan divided up large areas of China in the 1890s. The United States, too, became an imperialist power. It claimed Puerto Rico in the Caribbean and the Philippines in the Pacific.

By 1900, the richest and most powerful countries were the imperial powers of Europe. It seemed as though Europe was destined to rule much of the world for a very long time.

✓ Reading Check **Which nations divided up parts of China?**

Section 4 Assessment

Key Terms
Review the key terms at the beginning of this section. Use each term in a sentence that explains its meaning.

Target Reading Skill
Compare and contrast Napoleon's empire-building with later European imperialism.

Comprehension and Critical Thinking
1. (a) Describe How did Napoleon come to power?
(b) Identify Effects What lasting effects did Napoleon have on France and on the rest of Europe?
2. (a) Identify Name the imperialist European powers, and locate their colonies.
(b) Identify Cause and Effect How did industrialization lead to imperialism?

Writing Activity
Write a paragraph answering this question: Was Napoleon a positive or a negative influence on Europe?

For: An activity on the British Empire
Visit: PHSchool.com
Web Code: lgd-8704

Review and Assessment

◆ Chapter Summary

Section 1: The Enlightenment

Galileo

- During the Enlightenment, or Age of Reason, people began to rely on reason and observation rather than on faith and tradition.
- John Locke and other Enlightenment thinkers said that people had natural rights and that governments should protect those rights.
- The French philosophes Rousseau, Voltaire, and Diderot attacked the abuses of their age and favored freedom of speech and limited government.

Section 2: Political Revolutions

- During the 1600s, the English Civil War resulted in the overthrow and execution of the king. Later, a limited constitutional monarchy was established in Britain.
- Britain's American colonies based their successful revolution and new government on Enlightenment ideas.
- The French Revolution, a period of great turmoil and terror, overthrew the monarchy and established the Rights of Man.

The guillotine

Section 3: The Industrial Revolution

- The Industrial Revolution was the dramatic change from making goods by hand in homes and small shops to producing goods by machine in factories.
- The Industrial Revolution led to poor pay and bad working conditions for factory workers. Labor unions were formed to improve these conditions.

Robert Fulton's steamboat *Clermont*

Section 4: Nationalism and Imperialism

- Napoleon became the leader of France in the early 1800s and conquered most of Europe.
- Feelings of nationalism caused European nations to rebel against French rule and led to the unification of small kingdoms into new nations.
- The desire for raw materials and new markets led the imperialist nations of Europe to take control of large areas of Asia and Africa.

◆ Key Terms

Write one or two paragraphs about important changes of the 1700s and 1800s. Use at least six of the terms below in your paragraphs.

1. Enlightenment
2. labor union
3. imperialism
4. Declaration of Independence
5. Industrial Revolution
6. scientific method
7. Napoleonic Code
8. nationalism

Review and Assessment (continued)

◆ Comprehension and Critical Thinking

9. **(a) Identify** Who were Nicolaus Copernicus and Isaac Newton?
(b) Synthesize How did they change the way people thought about the universe?

10. **(a) Recall** Explain John Locke's idea of natural rights.
(b) Identify Effects Describe two events of the 1700s in which Locke's ideas were put into practice.

11. **(a) Summarize** How did England become a constitutional monarchy?
(b) Conclude How did these events lead to protections for English citizens?

12. **(a) Recall** Who paid most of the taxes in France before the French Revolution?
(b) Explain Under British law, how could taxes be imposed on citizens?
(c) Compare and Contrast Explain how taxes contributed to both the French and the American revolutions.

13. **(a) Explain** Why did many people move away from the countryside during the Industrial Revolution?

(b) Identify Causes How did working conditions in factories lead to the formation of labor unions?

14. **(a) Recall** How did Napoleon reform the legal system of France?
(b) Compare and Contrast How did the efforts of Napoleon to conquer Europe compare with the desire of imperialist nations to establish colonies in Africa and Asia?

◆ Skills Practice

Interpreting Diagrams In the Skills for Life activity in this chapter, you learned how to interpret a diagram. Review the steps of this skill. Then write an interpretation of the diagram in the Eyewitness Technology feature on page 207.

◆ Writing Activity: Math

In this chapter you read that the spinning jenny allowed one worker to do the work of eight workers using spinning wheels. Use your math skills to find out how much more thread could be produced using this new technology or what percentage of time could be saved. Write a letter that manufacturers of the spinning jenny might send to textile companies to persuade them to buy this new machine.

MAP MASTER™ Skills Activity

The Western World

Place Location For each place listed below, write the letter from the map that shows its location.
1. Moscow
2. Africa
3. France
4. Waterloo
5. Paris
6. London
7. Great Britain

Go Online
PHSchool.com Use Web Code **lgp-8744** for an **interactive map.**

Standardized Test Prep

Test-Taking Tips

Some questions on standardized tests ask you to analyze a graphic organizer. Study the concept web below. Then follow the tips to answer the sample question at the right.

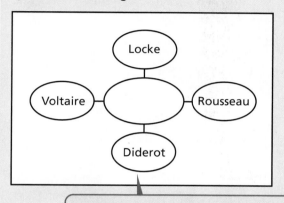

TIP As you review a concept web, notice the kind of information included in each part. Are the entries people, events, dates, or ideas?

Choose the letter that best answers the question.

Which title should go in the center of the concept web?

A Thinkers of the Enlightenment

B Revolution

C Declaration of Independence

D Thomas Jefferson

TIP Try to find the BEST answer, because sometimes more than one answer choice seems possible.

Think It Through A title for the center of a web should be a broad idea that covers the information in all of the outer ovals. You can rule out D because it is too specific: Jefferson is a person like the entries in the outer ovals. B is too general. That leaves A or C. None of these people were directly involved in the Declaration of Independence, but they all had similar ideas. Therefore the answer is A—they were all Enlightenment thinkers.

Practice Questions

Use the concept web below to answer the following questions.

1. Which title should go in the center of the web?

   A Results of the Scientific Revolution

   B Effects of the Industrial Revolution

   C Major Ideas of the Enlightenment

   D Reasons for the Growth of Imperialism

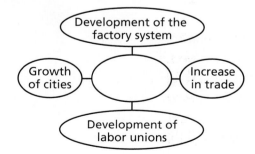

2. According to the web, which is most important?

   A development of labor unions

   B increase in trade

   C growth of cities

   D It is impossible to tell.

3. If you were to add another outer oval to the web, which of the following should it be?

   A increase in the amount of goods produced

   B better working conditions

   C reduction in transportation

   D shrinking of the middle class

Use Web Code **lga-8704** for a **Chapter 7 self-test.**

Chapter

8 Modern Times

Chapter Preview

This chapter will introduce you to the history of the world from the early 1900s to the present day.

 **Target Reading Skill**

Word Analysis In this chapter you will focus on looking at parts of unfamiliar words to understand their meaning. Suffixes, prefixes, and roots are parts of a word that can give clues to its meaning.

▶ Astronaut Jeff Wisoff on the Space Shuttle *Discovery* in 2000, with the planet Earth behind him

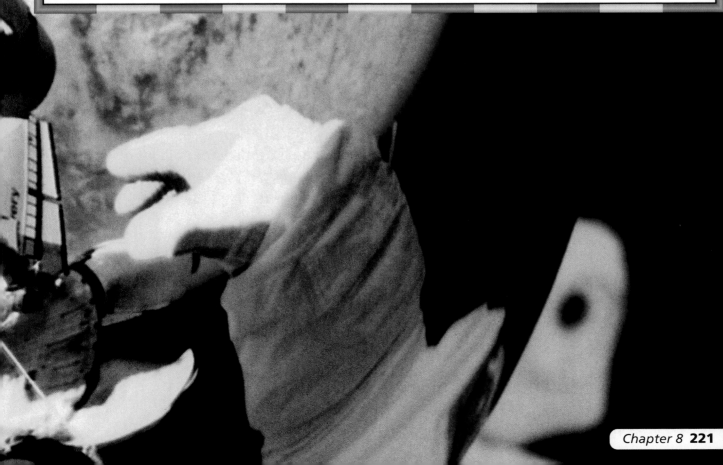

MAP★MASTER™
Skills Activity

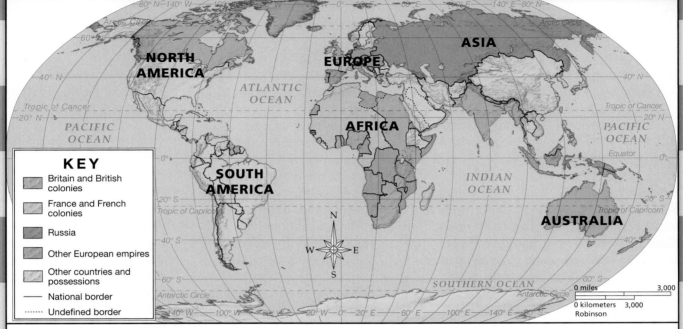

NORTH
AMERICA

EUROPE

ASIA

ATLANTIC
OCEAN

Tropic of Cancer

PACIFIC
OCEAN

AFRICA

Tropic of Cancer

PACIFIC
OCEAN

Equator

KEY

Britain and British colonies

France and French colonies

Russia

Other European empires

Other countries and possessions

— National border

⋯⋯ Undefined border

SOUTH
AMERICA

Tropic of Capricorn

INDIAN
OCEAN

AUSTRALIA

Tropic of Capricorn

N
W ✦ E
S

SOUTHERN OCEAN

Antarctic Circle

Antarctic Circle

0 miles   3,000

0 kilometers   3,000
Robinson

Place In the early 1900s, European powers controlled almost all of Africa and large areas on other continents. **Read a Map Key** Which European power controlled Australia? **Apply Information** On which other continents did this European power have colonies?

Go Online
PHSchool.com Use Web Code
lgp-8811 for step-by-step
map skills practice.

Section 1

War and Revolution

Prepare to Read

Objectives

In this section you will
1. Examine the causes and effects of World War I and the Russian Revolution.
2. Find out about the Great Depression.
3. Discover the ways in which World War II affected the world.

Taking Notes

As you read this section, look for the main ideas about this time of war and revolution. Copy the table below, and record your findings in it. Add boxes and rows as needed.

War and Revolution	
World War I	• Causes included nationalism, alliances, and militarism. •
The Russian Revolution	• •

Target Reading Skill

Use Word Parts Sometimes you can break an unfamiliar word into parts to help you recognize and pronounce it. A root is the base of the word and often has meaning by itself. A prefix comes before the root and changes its meaning. In the word surrender, -render is the root, meaning "to give." Sur- is the prefix, meaning "on" or "over."

Key Terms

- **World War I** (wurld wawr wun) *n.* the first global war of the 1900s (1914–1918)
- **dictator** (DIK tay tur) *n.* an absolute ruler of a country
- **Great Depression** (grayt dee PRESH un) *n.* the worldwide economic downturn of the 1930s
- **World War II** (wurld wawr too) *n.* the second global war of the 1900s (1939–1945)
- **Holocaust** (HAHL uh kawst) *n.* Nazi Germany's mass killing of Jewish people

I t was New Year's Eve. All over the world, people were about to celebrate the new year. But this was no ordinary New Year's Eve. It was a once-in-a-lifetime event. For the next day would bring not just a new year; it would bring a new century.

One writer summed up the feelings of millions of Americans when he wrote: "1900! The beginning of a new century! When I think of the strides our nation has made in its last century, what great inventions have been made . . . I wonder what will be done in the next hundred years."

This writer had good cause to wonder. Not he, nor anyone else, could possibly have foreseen how much the world would change over the next 100 years. The changes would be dramatic. In some ways, the world would change more in the 1900s than it had in all of recorded history. Sadly, much of this change would come at a terrible cost.

Cars were an exciting new invention in 1900.

1900 Oldsmobile

222 Medieval Times to Today

World War I

The 1900s were marred by wars fought around the world. The first global war of the 1900s was **World War I.**

Causes of World War I World War I began in Europe. There, many countries were rivals in a struggle for power. They built strong armies and navies. They also formed military alliances, or agreements among countries to help one another in case of attack.

Rivalries, the military build-up, and the growth of alliances kept tensions high. Europe in the early 1900s was like a gunpowder keg, and one spark could set it off.

The War Begins The spark that set off World War I was the murder in 1914 of Archduke Franz Ferdinand of Austria-Hungary by a Serb. Austria-Hungary declared war on Serbia.

Then the system of alliances caused the war to spread. Alliances linked Russia, France, and Britain with Serbia. These countries were known as the Allied Powers. Later, the United States joined the Allied Powers. They fought the Central Powers, including Germany and Austria-Hungary.

Trench Warfare Soldiers from each side dug lines of muddy trenches to avoid enemy fire. Regularly, soldiers were ordered "over the top" to charge the enemy's trenches. Often, they were cut down by enemy machine-gun fire. Machine guns and poison gas made this war deadlier than any earlier war. More than 8 million soldiers died. Millions of civilians also were killed.

The End of the War In 1918, the Central Powers surrendered. Germany and Austria-Hungary were forced to accept harsh punishments in the Treaty of Versailles (vur SY).

✓ Reading Check **How many soldiers died in World War I?**

World War I Trench Warfare and Recruitment Poster
Some French troops in the photo at the top stand in a trench, while others stand just outside it. The British poster below calls for new recruits. **Analyze Images** *Would the photo at the top be an effective recruitment poster? Explain why or why not.*

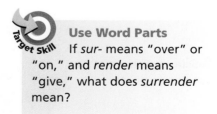

Use Word Parts
If *sur-* means "over" or "on," and *render* means "give," what does *surrender* mean?

The Russian Revolution

World War I made life hard for the Russian people. Much of the country's food, fuel, and supplies went for the war effort. This meant that the people at home could not meet basic needs.

Street Battle, St. Petersburg
People run for cover at the start of a gun battle during the Russian Revolution in 1917. **Identify Effects** *How might gun battles affect daily life in a city?*

A Russian communist propaganda poster

Overthrowing the Tsar Tsars, or emperors, had ruled Russia for hundreds of years. The tsars were absolute rulers. In the early 1900s, Russians grew more and more unhappy with their government. The hardships of the war increased opposition to the tsar.

In 1917, a revolution forced the tsar, Nicholas II, to give up the throne. Later in the year, rebels led by Vladimir Lenin took control of the government. In 1918, Lenin's government made peace with Germany but executed the tsar and his family. In 1922, the Russian Empire was renamed the Union of Soviet Socialist Republics (USSR), or the Soviet Union.

A Communist Dictatorship Lenin and his followers belonged to the Communist Party. They fought to establish communism, a system in which the government controls most businesses. Communists imposed this system after winning a civil war against anticommunists in 1920. Communists promised everyone an equal share of the country's wealth. Many Russians supported communism because they were tired of living in poverty under the tsars. In theory, communism seemed fair.

In reality, though, communism was brutally unfair. The Communist Party used the country's wealth to support its own power. Lenin became the **dictator,** or absolute ruler, of the Soviet Union. After Lenin's death in 1924, the dictator Joseph Stalin ruled the Soviet Union ruthlessly until 1953. Stalin curtailed people's freedoms. He set up brutal prison camps. He punished anyone who challenged his rule. In all, Stalin was probably responsible for the deaths of more than 10 million of his own people.

✓ Reading Check **Why did Russians oppose the tsar?**

The Great Depression

The end of World War I brought jubilation in the victorious countries. In the United States, people celebrated the growing strength of their country.

The Roaring Twenties The middle and late 1920s were a time of great prosperity in America and other countries. The economy grew rapidly. Some people enjoyed great wealth. During the 1920s, the United States was richer than any other country had ever been. Americans used their wealth to buy many new things. Many people bought cars, electric appliances, and radios for the first time. New art forms, such as jazz music, flourished. The economic boom and the fast-paced lifestyle of the decade earned it the nickname "the Roaring Twenties."

Economic Collapse This prosperity, however, did not last. In 1929, there was a stock market crash, or a sharp drop in the market value of companies owned by investors. The economy of the United States and other countries around the world went from boom to bust. The worldwide economic downturn of the 1930s is known as the **Great Depression**. The downturn lasted through the 1930s.

The economy during the Great Depression was so weak that about one fourth of the people in America couldn't find a job. Many took to the road, traveling around the country, desperately looking for work. More than a million people became homeless. Many people did not have enough to eat.

America was not alone in its hard times. Almost every country suffered from the economic downturn. The Great Depression continued until countries began to increase the production of goods. Unfortunately, these goods went to fight another world war, which began in 1939.

✓ Reading Check **During which decade did the Great Depression occur?**

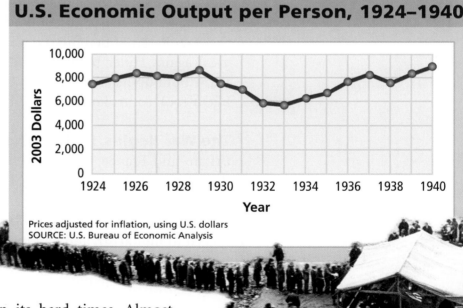

U.S. Economic Output per Person, 1924–1940

Prices adjusted for inflation, using U.S. dollars
SOURCE: U.S. Bureau of Economic Analysis

World War II Sea Battle
Sailors on the U.S.S. Enterprise ready planes to attack Japanese warships during the Battle of Midway in the Pacific Ocean.
Infer *How would airplanes be useful during a sea battle?*

World War II

The Great Depression hit Germany especially hard. The country was still suffering from the harsh peace treaty of Versailles. The German people felt that they had been unfairly punished for their part in World War I.

Nazi Germany A political leader named Adolf Hitler took advantage of German discontent. He led an organization called the Nazi Party. Hitler and the Nazis promised to make Germany great again. Hitler became the dictator of Germany. Nazi Germany built up its armed forces. Using threats and military force, Hitler took control of lands that bordered Germany.

The War Begins In 1939, Nazi Germany invaded Poland. Britain and France, who had pledged their support to Poland, then declared war on Germany. This was the beginning of **World War II,** the second global war of the 1900s.

Japan and Italy sided with Germany. Like Germany, they had turned to militarism and had invaded other countries. Germany, Japan, and Italy were known as the Axis Powers. Britain, France, and their allies were known as the Allied Powers, or the Allies.

In 1941, Japan attacked American forces at Pearl Harbor, Hawaii. The attack drew the United States into the war on the side of the Allies. Also in 1941, Hitler invaded the Soviet Union. The Soviet Union joined the Allies as well.

The Holocaust The Nazis committed some of the worst horrors of World War II. They tried to destroy entire groups of people, particularly Jews. The Nazis sent Jews and other minorities to concentration camps.

DISCOVERY
CHANNEL
SCHOOL Video
Find out about the Holocaust.

In the camps, prisoners were often worked to death, tortured, or simply killed. The Nazis killed about 6 million Jews. Nazi Germany's mass killing of Jewish people is known as the **Holocaust.**

Allied Victories In 1944, the Allies invaded France, which was occupied by Germany. They then attacked Germany from the west. Meanwhile, Soviet forces attacked Germany from the east. As the Allies advanced, they freed people in the brutal Nazi concentration camps. Soon, Allied forces surrounded Germany. The war ended in Europe when Germany surrendered on May 8, 1945.

Despite Germany's surrender, Japan fought on. Allied forces were slowly nearing Japan. U.S. President Harry S Truman believed that invading Japan itself would cost the lives of tens of thousands of Allied soldiers. To end the war quickly, President Truman ordered the first use of a new weapon called the atomic bomb.

The atomic bomb was the most powerful weapon ever used. One bomb could destroy an entire city. The United States dropped atomic bombs on the Japanese cities of Hiroshima and Nagasaki. Over 100,000 people were killed. Faced with this terrible weapon, the Japanese surrendered on September 2, 1945.

World War II was over. The Allied Powers had won the most destructive war in human history. An appalling 55 million people, soldiers and civilians alike, had died in the war.

✓ Reading Check **What caused the Japanese to surrender?**

Citizen Heroes

Audie Murphy

Audie Murphy was the most decorated American combat soldier of World War II. He received every medal for bravery that the United States awards. He also received medals from Belgium and France. Murphy fought in nine major campaigns in Europe, and he was wounded three times. He killed, captured, or wounded hundreds of enemy soldiers. After the war, he became a movie star. The movie *To Hell and Back* was based on his autobiography.

Section 1 Assessment

Key Terms
Review the key terms at the beginning of this section. Use each term in a sentence that explains its meaning.

Target Reading Skill
Apply your knowledge of the prefix *sur-*. In the fifth sentence under the heading "Allied Victories," on p. 227, what does the word *surrounded* mean?

Comprehension and Critical Thinking
1. (a) Sequence During what years was World War I fought?

(b) Identify Cause and Effect How did World War I help cause the Russian Revolution?

2. (a) Recall When did the Great Depression begin?

(b) Explain How did it affect people's lives?

3. (a) Identify In what year did Japan's surrender end World War II?

(b) Explain What weapon led to Japan's surrender?

(c) Contrast How did this weapon differ from weapons used in the past?

Writing Activity
Based on the events described in this section, write a brief essay describing the role of the United States in defeating Germany and Japan in World War II.

Writing Tip Write at least two versions of your essay. The first version is called a rough draft. Revise it to make your writing clearer. Correct spelling and punctuation errors. Turn in your second or third draft.

In May 1940, Great Britain's Prime Minister Winston Churchill entered one of the basement rooms beneath a government building in London and said, "This is the room from which I'll direct the war." The room Churchill spoke of was part of the Cabinet War Rooms, a secret complex of specially equipped and protected underground rooms. During World War II, London suffered heavy bombing by German aircraft and threats of invasion. At such times, Churchill and his advisors met in the Cabinet War Rooms to discuss the war and to plan for their country's defense. Concrete, steel beams, heavy timber, and a special ventilation system protected the rooms from attack.

Map Room Annex
Officers prepared military reports in this room.

Underground Headquarters The Map Room, shown at the right, was the most important room in the underground complex. Here, army, air force, and naval officers gathered up-to-date information about the war's progress. These officers, called mapkeepers, prepared regular reports for their superiors and marked ship positions, battle fronts, and supply-line information on maps hung around the room. Some rooms within the complex were used only occasionally, but the Map Room was manned 24 hours a day throughout the war.

The Cabinet War Rooms also included offices, telephone switchboards, staff dormitories, a mess room where snacks were served, and a transatlantic telephone room—disguised as a bathroom—where Churchill had a direct phone line to Franklin Roosevelt, the President of the United States.

Map Room
Mapkeepers used pushpins to record allied and enemy movements on wall maps.

Winston Churchill inspects a bomb crater in London, 1940.

Map Room Exhibit
This is how the Map Room looked while it was in use. Today, the Cabinet War Rooms are a museum.

Telephone switchboard operators in the Cabinet War Rooms, 1945

Prime Minister's Room
This was Winston Churchill's office, from which he made some of his wartime radio broadcasts. Occasionally, he slept here.

Assessment

Describe What were the Cabinet War Rooms?

Infer Why was it important for Churchill and his war advisors to remain safe from enemy attacks?

2 The Postwar World

Prepare to Read

Objectives
In this section you will
1. Learn how the Cold War pitted the United States against the Soviet Union.
2. Discover how dozens of former colonies gained independence.

Taking Notes
As you read this section, identify important events of the Cold War and the era of independence. Copy the timeline below, add dates as needed, and record events with the dates when they happened.

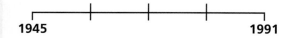

1945   1991

Target Reading Skill

Recognize Word Origins The word *decade*, on page 234, contains the root *dec-*, which means "ten" in Latin and Greek. The ending *-ad* or *-ade* refers to a group of elements. As you read, use your knowledge of these word parts to determine the meaning of this word.

Key Terms
- **postwar** (POHST wawr) *adj.* after war; after World War II

- **superpower** (SOO pur pow ur) *n.* a powerful country that has great influence over other countries
- **Cold War** (kohld wawr) *n.* a period of tension between the United States and the Soviet Union from 1945 to 1991
- **developing countries** (dih VEL up ing KUN treez) *n.* poor countries that have little industry
- **developed countries** (dih VEL upt KUN treez) *n.* rich countries that have much industry

Winston Churchill speaking in Fulton, Missouri, in 1946

I t was late winter, 1946. Former British Prime Minister Winston Churchill was in the college town of Fulton, Missouri. World War II had ended just a few months before. Churchill was touring a country still jubilant in its victory. The Soviet Union had been an ally of the United States and Britain during the war. But Churchill's words sent chills down people's spines:

> **[An] iron curtain has descended across the Continent [of Europe]. Behind that line lie all the capitals . . . of Central and Eastern Europe. . . . [A]ll these famous cities and the populations around them . . . are subject . . . to a very high . . . measure of control from Moscow. . . .**

Churchill meant that the Soviet Union controlled Eastern Europe from its capital in Moscow. He also meant that the Soviet system of government would deprive these people of freedom. It was as if an "iron curtain" now separated these people from the freedoms and democracies of Western Europe and the United States.

World War II was over. Would the **postwar** world, or the world after World War II, bring liberation, or something else?

The Cold War

Although they had cooperated during World War II, the United States and the Soviet Union had different economies and governments. The Soviet Union was a communist country. The government controlled property and businesses. In contrast, the United States was a capitalist country. Under capitalism, individuals, instead of the government, control property and businesses.

Beginning in 1945, the Soviet Union took control of Eastern European countries and forced them to adopt communism. The iron curtain separated those countries from the democratic countries of Western Europe. The Soviet Union wanted to expand its influence and its communist system throughout the world.

Growing Tensions In 1949, two crucial events increased U.S. concerns about the spread of communism. First, communists came to power in China. They were led by Mao Zedong. Second, the Soviets developed an atomic bomb. Before that time, only the United States had had this powerful weapon. The United States adopted a policy of containment, an effort to halt, or contain, the spread of communism.

By 1949, most of the countries of the world were on one of two sides. On one side were capitalist and democratic countries. They were led by the United States. On the other side were communist countries, which were led by the Soviet Union. Both the United States and the Soviet Union were superpowers. A **superpower** is a powerful country that has great influence over other countries.

Superpower Rivalry The period of tension between the United States and the Soviet Union from 1945 to 1991 is called the **Cold War.** It is called a "cold" war because the superpowers did not fight each other directly in a "hot" war. However, the Cold War was a frightening time because both countries built enough nuclear bombs to destroy the world's people.

A World Divided
At the top, planes flying above the U.S.S. Eisenhower reflect U.S. air and sea power during the Cold War. At the center, a Soviet soldier guards the Berlin Wall, along the "iron curtain." At the bottom, a parade in Moscow displays Soviet missiles.
Analyze Images *How do these images reflect Cold War tensions?*

MAP MASTER™ Skills Activity

Place Since 1945, many new nations have gained independence. **Read a Map Key** In which decade did many Eastern European nations gain independence? **Identify Effects** How was the spread of independence in that region connected with the end of the Cold War?

Go Online PHSchool.com Use Web Code **lgp-8821** for step-by-step **map skills practice.**

Independence Since 1945

ARCTIC OCEAN
Beaufort Sea
Arctic Circle
Hudson Bay
NORTH AMERICA
ATLANTIC OCEAN
Tropic of Cancer
BAHAMAS (1973)
BELIZE (1981)
JAMAICA (1962)
ANTIGUA & BARBUDA (1981)
ST. KITTS & NEVIS (1983)
DOMINICA (1978)
ST. LUCIA (1979)
BARBADOS (1966)
ST. VINCENT & THE GRENADINES (1979)
GRENADA (1974)
TRINIDAD AND TOBAGO (1962)
PACIFIC OCEAN
GUYANA (1966)
SURINAME (1975)
Equator
SAMOA (1962)
TONGA (1970)
SOUTH AMERICA
Tropic of Capricorn
Antarctic Circle
KEY
Decade country gained independence*
Before 1945
1940s
1950s
1960s
1970s
1980s
1990s
2000s
National border
Disputed border
*Specific year shown in parentheses on map

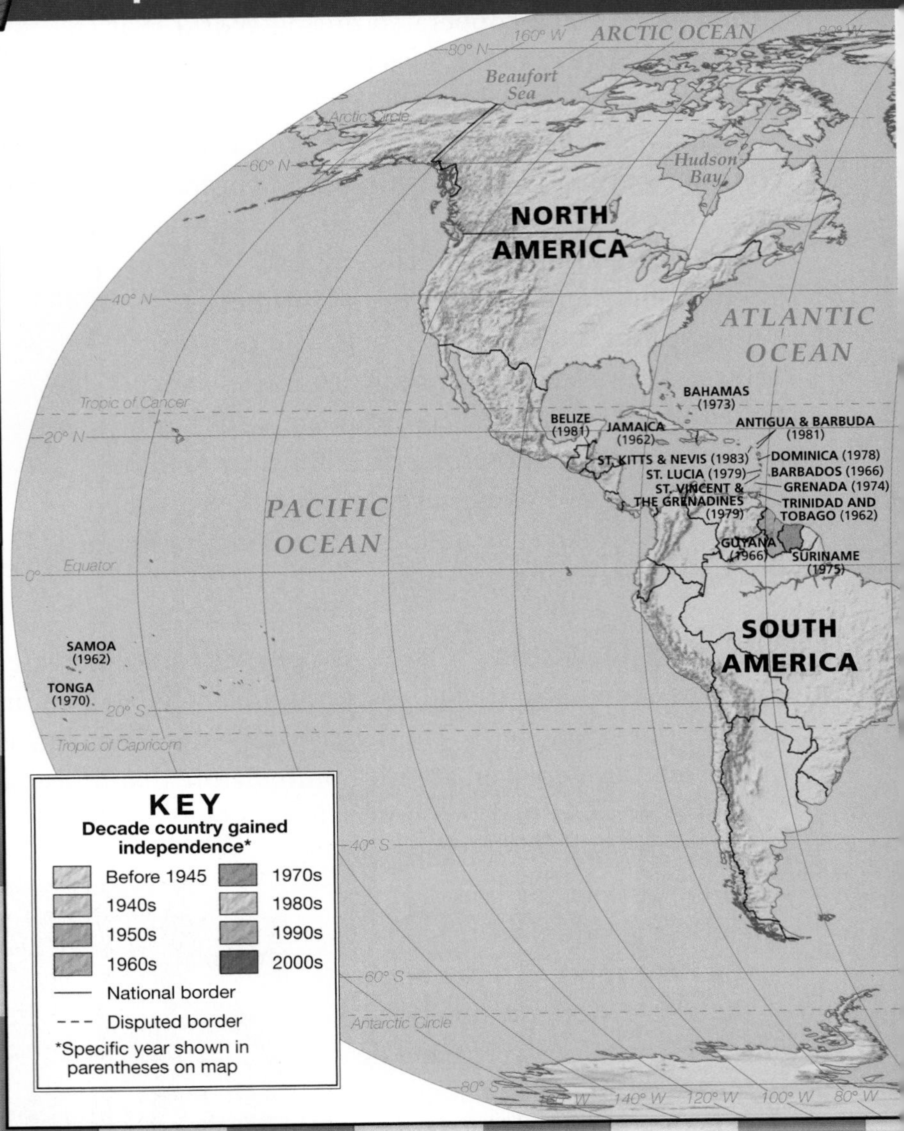

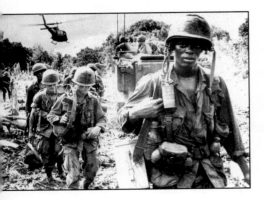

American soldiers in Vietnam, 1966

Hot Spots in the Cold War The Cold War also resulted in some hot wars. In 1950, communist North Korea invaded non-communist South Korea. During the Korean War, the United States and other democratic countries sent troops to support South Korea. Communist China supported North Korea. The war ended in 1953 in a stalemate.

In Southeast Asia, Vietnam had split into communist North Vietnam and noncommunist South Vietnam. In the 1960s, the United States sent troops to support South Vietnam and to fight communism in the Vietnam War. Thousands of Americans and millions of Vietnamese died. In 1975, North Vietnam defeated South Vietnam. The whole country became communist.

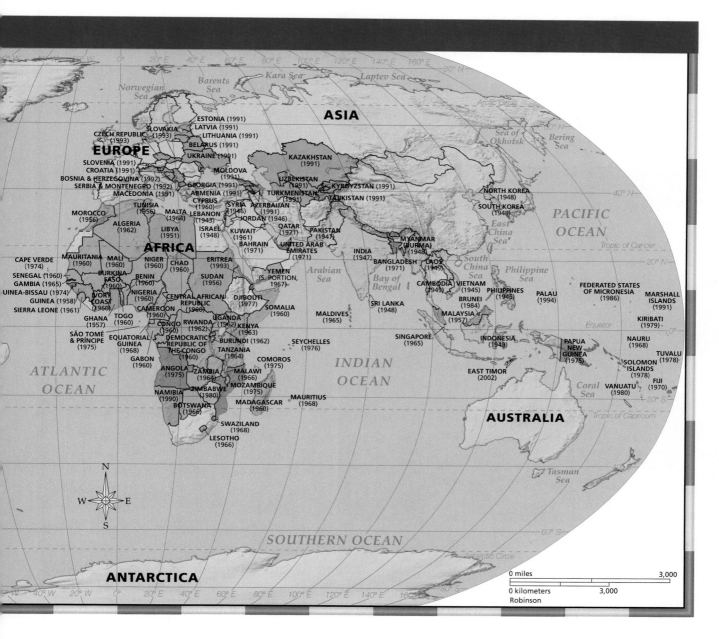

The Cold War Ends The Cold War ended in 1991, when communist rule collapsed in the Soviet Union. Most of Eastern Europe had rejected communism in 1989. Communism ended because Eastern Europeans and Soviet citizens demanded reforms. It also ended because capitalism produced more wealth than communism, and communism could no longer compete.

When the communist government fell in 1991, the Soviet Union broke up into several independent nations. The largest and most powerful of these nations, Russia, adopted capitalism. Russia also developed friendlier relations with the United States.

U.S. President George H. W. Bush with Russian President Boris Yeltsin, 1993, after the Cold War

✓ Reading Check   **Why did the United States send troops to Vietnam?**

A New Era of Independence

The Cold War shaped world events for more than 40 years. However, another major development affected the postwar world. Many new countries, especially in Africa and Asia, gained independence, or freedom from outside control, in the decades following World War II. These countries had been colonies of European nations.

Celebrating Independence
These children in Swaziland are celebrating the second anniversary, in 1970, of their country's independence. **Compare** *How is this celebration like American celebrations on the Fourth of July?*

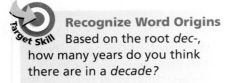

Recognize Word Origins
Based on the root *dec-*, how many years do you think there are in a *decade*?

The Colonial World In the centuries before World War II, Europeans had colonized much of the world. By 1914, European colonies covered much of Asia and almost all of Africa. There were also European colonies still left in the Americas, particularly in the Caribbean Islands.

When Europeans colonized an area, they did so for their own benefit and not for the people who lived there. Europeans ruled over the colonies, and local people had little or no part in their government. Europeans often damaged local economies. For example, native peoples were forced to grow crops that would benefit the colonizing country instead of crops they could use to feed themselves.

Desire for Independence Colonized peoples resented this treatment. They wanted to end European rule. During World War II, many colonies had helped their colonial rulers, and they wanted to be rewarded. Meanwhile, the United States and other countries had promised that the peoples of the world would be able to choose their own governments after the war. As a result, demands for independence increased after World War II.

New Countries World War II had weakened the European powers. They found it hard to deny these demands for independence. At first, they tried to keep their colonies by letting local people take part in colonial governments. But the colonies demanded full independence.

In the decades after World War II, more than 50 countries gained independence. Most of these countries were in Africa, and many became independent between 1957 and 1965. Some countries won independence peacefully. Others had to fight wars for their independence.

A Global Movement Great movements and great leaders appeared in many colonized countries. India is a good example. Mohandas Gandhi (moh HAHN dus GAHN dee) led this British colony to independence. Gandhi called for civil disobedience—the breaking of a law on purpose in order to protest it. He urged people to protest without using force—to be nonviolent. He helped Indians find ways to reduce their dependence on Britain. India won its independence in 1947.

Challenges for the New Countries Even after the former colonies won independence, they faced serious challenges. Often, their leaders lacked experience in government. Most of the new countries had had their borders drawn by Europeans. They often included people of different ethnic groups who did not get along. Civil wars sometimes resulted.

Poverty was another challenge that the new nations faced. Most of the world's former colonies are **developing countries,** or poor countries with few industries. The United States and the former colonial powers are **developed countries,** which have more wealth and many industries. Developing countries are sometimes also called third-world countries. Some developing countries have managed to improve their economies.

Indian independence leader Mohandas Gandhi, on the right, at a conference in Simla, India

 Reading Check **What is the difference between developing and developed countries?**

Section 2 Assessment

Key Terms

Review the key terms at the beginning of this section. Use each term in a sentence that explains its meaning.

 Target Reading Skill

Apply your knowledge of the word part *dec-*. What do words such as *decimal* and *decathlon* have in common?

Comprehension and Critical Thinking

1. (a) Identify What was the Cold War?

(b) Explain Which countries did it involve?
(c) Contrast How did it differ from other wars?
2. (a) Recall Which countries gained independence in the decades after World War II?
(b) Describe What problems have they faced?
(c) Draw Conclusions How might they solve those problems?

Writing Activity

Prepare a list of questions about life during the Cold War. Interview a parent or another adult about his or her memories of life during the Cold War. Write down their answers to your questions.

For: An activity on the end of colonialism
Visit: PHSchool.com
Web Code: lgd-8802

Interpreting Line Graphs

Makiko was almost finished with her report on Dallas, Texas. But whenever she tried to write about the number of people living in Dallas at different times in the city's history, it sounded too confusing. Maybe a graph or a diagram would be better. "I could show a population map of the city for each decade, but that's too many different maps," she thought. "Or I could make a table showing the population every 10 years, but that wouldn't show the changes at a glance. I need a graph that will show growth over time."

Downtown Dallas about 1910 (top) and today (directly above)

Makiko needed a line graph, which shows statistics as connected points. The line that connects the points shows a pattern over time.

Learn the Skill

Follow these steps to interpret a line graph:

1 **Read the title.** The title identifies the basic information shown on the graph.

2 **Read the graph labels.** An axis is a line at the side or bottom of a graph. Both the horizontal axis, or *x*-axis, and the vertical axis, or *y*-axis, have labels that give more specific information about the data. Also notice the intervals between the dates or other numbers.

3 **Read the numbers on the graph.** Use the lines on the grid to help you find the *x*- and *y*- values of the points on the graph.

4 **Interpret the numbers and draw conclusions.** Compare data to find similarities, differences, increases, or decreases. Draw a conclusion about what trends, or general changes, are shown by the graph.

Practice the Skill

Use the steps you just learned to read the line graph at the right.

1. Read the title. What is the subject of this graph?

2. Read the labels. What does the x-axis show? What does the y-axis show? How is each axis divided?

3. In what year was the population of Dallas just over 400,000? Interpret several other points on the graph.

4. What general trend does the line on the graph show? Look more closely to find more specific increases or decreases. For example, when did Dallas's population change the fastest? Write a conclusion of two or three sentences telling what you learned from the graph.

Population of Dallas, Texas, 1910–2000

SOURCE: U.S. Bureau of Labor Statistics

United States Employment, 1900–2000

SOURCE: U.S. Bureau of Labor Statistics

Apply the Skill

The line graph at the left has two lines instead of one. But it works the same way, and you can apply the same steps to interpret it. Write a conclusion of two or three sentences telling what you learned from this graph.

3 The World Today

Prepare to Read

Objectives

In this section you will
1. Learn how modern technology has transformed the world.
2. Explore how migration, trade, and closer economic ties have linked different parts of the world.
3. Consider the new challenges that the world will face during your lifetime.

Taking Notes

As you read this section, look for facts about the effects of technology, economic links, and new challenges. Copy the diagram below, and record your findings in it.

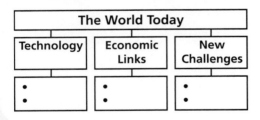

The World Today		
Technology	Economic Links	New Challenges
• •	• •	• •

🎯 Target Reading Skill

Use Word Parts When you come across an unfamiliar word, break the word into parts to help you recognize and pronounce it. You may find roots, prefixes, or suffixes. A root is the base of the word that often has meaning by itself. A suffix attaches to the end of a root and changes the root's function or meaning. For example, the word *transportation* combines the root *transport* and the suffix *-ation,* meaning "action" or "process."

Key Terms

- **millennium** (mih LEN ee um) *n.* a period of one thousand years
- **trading bloc** (TRAYD ing blahk) *n.* a group of countries that have agreed to reduce barriers to trade
- **terrorism** (TEHR ur iz um) *n.* the threat or use of violence to cause fear

New Year's fireworks in Paris, France, 2000

It was December 31, 1999. Around the globe people were celebrating the start of a new year, a new decade, and a new century. Above all, they were celebrating a new **millennium,** or a period of one thousand years. Huge parties, parades, and spectacular fireworks displays were held in cities around the world—in fact, most of the world seemed to join in one gigantic festival.

There was only one problem: The new millennium didn't technically begin until the year 2001! But it didn't seem to matter. It was a time for celebrating human accomplishments.

It was a time for reflecting on all the many historical events of the past millennium, events that fill up much of this book. It was a time to think about where those events had led us and to take stock of the state of the world. It was also a time to think about the world's future prospects. For the world of today and the world of the future are the worlds in which you will live. The world of the future is the world that you will help shape.

The Advance of Technology

One key process shaping the world to come is the steady development of technology. Until the mid-1800s, there were only two ways to deliver a message from North America to Europe or Asia: in person or on paper. In either case, the message would have taken weeks to reach its destination by sailing ship. Today, information can travel almost instantly via satellite and radio transmission. People can cross oceans in a few hours by plane.

Transportation In 1900, automobiles were a rarity. Today, automobiles are common throughout the world. Huge networks of roads link places that were once isolated. The airplane was developed in the early 1900s. Later in the 1900s, people walked on the moon. Satellites orbiting Earth helped people communicate and study the stars. By the end of the 1900s, space probes had traveled to distant planets.

Communication The first telephones were invented in the late 1800s. Few people could afford telephones, which had to be connected to wires. As the 1900s progressed, radio and then television brought new possibilities for communication. They allowed people to hear and see events thousands of miles away.

The most recent advance in communication has been the development of the Internet. The Internet is a worldwide network of computers. Using electronic mail, or e-mail, people can send and receive information across long distances in a fraction of a second. New handheld devices are making communication much more convenient.

Health and Comfort Since 1900, better ways of understanding and treating diseases have saved millions of lives. Clean water supplies, vaccines to prevent illness, and other medical advances have allowed people to live longer, healthier lives.

✓ Reading Check **How does information travel between continents today?**

Links to
Science

Science Versus Technology Science and technology are not the same thing. Science is using the scientific method to gain knowledge about the world. Technology is the way people make practical use of knowledge. The NASA technician in the top photo is using technology to monitor the Mars rover shown in the center photo. The rover uses a variety of technologies to conduct science. Its cameras provide images of the surface of Mars (background photo). It also analyzes the composition of Martian rocks and soil.

MAP MASTER™
Skills Activity

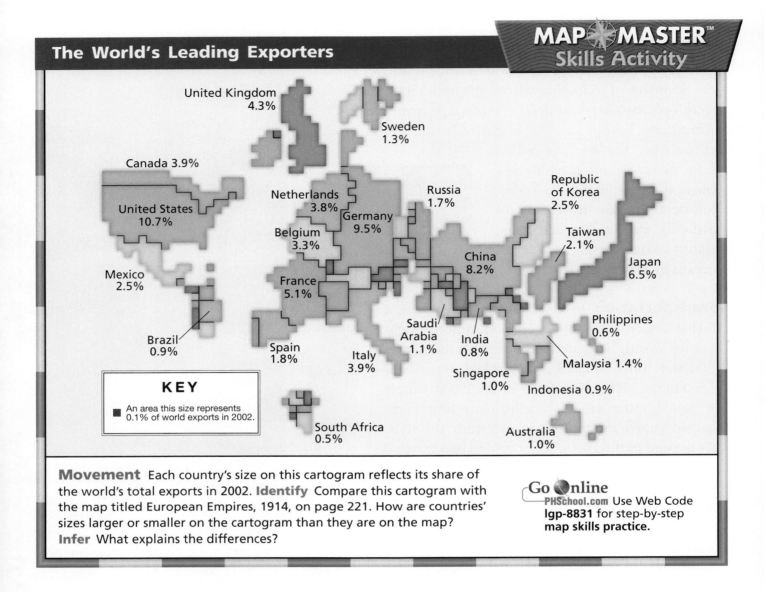

United Kingdom
4.3%

Sweden
1.3%

Canada 3.9%

Netherlands
3.8%

Russia
1.7%

Republic
of Korea
2.5%

United States
10.7%

Germany
9.5%

Belgium
3.3%

Taiwan
2.1%

Japan
6.5%

China
8.2%

Mexico
2.5%

France
5.1%

Saudi
Arabia
1.1%

India
0.8%

Philippines
0.6%

Brazil
0.9%

Spain
1.8%

Italy
3.9%

Malaysia 1.4%

Singapore
1.0%

Indonesia 0.9%

KEY

■ An area this size represents
0.1% of world exports in 2002.

South Africa
0.5%

Australia
1.0%

Movement Each country's size on this cartogram reflects its share of the world's total exports in 2002. **Identify** Compare this cartogram with the map titled European Empires, 1914, on page 221. How are countries' sizes larger or smaller on the cartogram than they are on the map? **Infer** What explains the differences?

Compare this cartogram with the map titled European Empires, 1914, on page 221.

Go Online
PHSchool.com Use Web Code
lgp-8831 for step-by-step
map skills practice.

A Smaller World

Two hundred years ago, when traveling across oceans took weeks or months, people seldom traveled far from home. Their food and clothes came mainly from local sources. Modern technologies have changed all of that.

An immigrant from Turkey working in Germany

Migration and Trade Better transportation technologies have helped more people relocate. People tend to go where the jobs are, even when those jobs are in different countries. Millions of people from developing countries have moved to find work in developed countries such as the United States, Canada, and Germany.

Transportation and communication technologies have also increased trade among nations. Someone can now order a product from another country almost instantly via the Internet. That same product can arrive overnight by plane.

A Global Economy New transportation and communication technologies have made it easier to do business across borders. A company based in the United States may employ engineers in India. It may have a factory in Honduras where its products are actually made. And it may have an office selling those products in Italy. This kind of worldwide business is possible with the help of technologies such as e-mail and air travel.

In some regions, countries have formed **trading blocs,** or groups of countries that have agreed to work together to reduce barriers to trade. Examples include the European Union in Europe and the North American Free Trade Agreement, or NAFTA, linking Canada, the United States, and Mexico.

✓ **Reading Check** **What is a trading bloc?**

Target Skill If *-ation* or *-tion* means "action" or "process," what does *transportation* mean? What does *communication* mean?

New Challenges

The world today is filled with challenges. The more you know about them, the better you will be prepared to deal with them.

Poverty and Population Poverty is a serious problem in many parts of the world. Almost half of the world's population lives on less than $2.15 a day per person. Hunger and poverty are widespread in parts of Latin America, Africa, and Asia.

In developing countries, populations are growing rapidly. For poor parents, having many children often makes sense. By the time these children reach their teens, they are expected to help support the family. More teenage children can provide more food for the family. As parents get older, having many children helps ensure their security in old age.

However, growing populations burden developing countries. Often there is not enough farmland or enough food for everyone to eat.

The Environment Growing populations in the developing world put stress on the environment. When forests are cut to create more farmland, valuable soil may be washed away and flooding may occur downstream.

In the developed world, the consumption of goods and the use of cars and trucks pollute the air, water, and soil. Heavy use of pesticides and fertilizers on farmland may also cause water pollution. However, using resources more carefully and efficiently can help solve these problems.

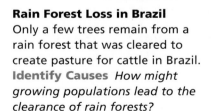

Rain Forest Loss in Brazil
Only a few trees remain from a rain forest that was cleared to create pasture for cattle in Brazil. **Identify Causes** *How might growing populations lead to the clearance of rain forests?*

Terrorism and War On September 11, 2001, 19 men from a group called al-Qaeda (ahl KY duh) purposely crashed two airliners into the World Trade Center in New York City and another into the Pentagon, near Washington, D.C. A fourth airliner crashed in a field in Pennsylvania. More than 3,000 people in all were killed.

Al-Qaeda is led by Osama bin Laden. Al-Qaeda hopes to achieve political goals by means of **terrorism,** an effort to cause fear through the threat or use of violence. People who practice terrorism are known as terrorists. Al-Qaeda seeks to force the United States to withdraw its troops from the Middle East and end its support for Israel.

In 2001 Osama bin Laden was hiding in Afghanistan under the protection of the brutal Taliban government. With the aid of Afghan rebels, American forces invaded Afghanistan and toppled the Taliban in December 2001. American and Afghan forces captured or killed many members of al-Qaeda.

In 2003, the United States invaded and occupied Iraq, a country in the Middle East. Iraq had been ruled by a cruel dictator, Saddam Hussein. The United States overthrew Hussein and later captured him. Despite the capture of the dictator, Iraq remained unstable in 2004.

The worldwide threat of terrorism continues. However, people around the world share a commitment to make the world safer.

 **Reading Check** What problem can result when forests are cut down?

A candlelight vigil in Brooklyn, New York, one year after the September 11 terrorist attacks

 Section 3 Assessment

Key Terms
Review the key terms at the beginning of this section. Use each term in a sentence that explains its meaning.

Target Reading Skill
Using your knowledge of the suffix -tion, give the meaning of the word *pollution,* in the second sentence from the bottom of page 241.

Comprehension and Critical Thinking
1. (a) Identify What are some modern advances in technology?

(b) Identify Effects What is one effect of these advances?
2. (a) Recall Over the past 200 years, have economic ties between countries increased or decreased?
(b) Identify Causes What accounts for this change?
3. (a) Describe How is the population of many developing countries changing?
(b) Explain How is the change in population affecting the environment?
(c) Infer What steps might help to slow the rate of population change in these countries?

Writing Activity
Write a journal entry that describes something you can do—now or when you are an adult—to help meet one of the challenges the world faces.

For: An activity on using the Internet
Visit: PHSchool.com
Web Code: lgd-8803

Review and Assessment

◆ Chapter Summary

Section 1: War and Revolution

- Nationalism, a military buildup, and a rigid system of alliances caused World War I, which led in turn to the Russian Revolution.

Recruiting poster

- The Great Depression was a worldwide economic downturn of the 1930s.
- World War II, fought from 1939 to 1945, left millions dead.

Section 2: The Postwar World

- The United States confronted the Soviet Union in the Cold War from 1945 to 1991.
- Many European colonies became independent countries after World War II.

Soviet missiles

Section 3: The World Today

- New technologies allow quicker communication and transportation as well as better health.
- Migration, trade, and economic alliances have linked different parts of the world.
- Challenges in today's world include poverty, population growth, environmental issues, terrorism, and war.

The Mars rover

◆ Key Terms

Write a paragraph titled The World Since 1900, using all of the following terms correctly in complete sentences.

1. World War I
2. communism
3. Great Depression
4. World War II
5. postwar

6. capitalism
7. Cold War
8. developing countries
9. trading bloc
10. terrorism

Review and Assessment (continued)

◆ Comprehension and Critical Thinking

11. (a) Recall What were three major causes of World War I?
(b) Explain What event led to the actual outbreak of war?
(c) Synthesize Information How did this event pull so many different countries into war?

12. (a) Identify Which major countries fought on each side in World War II?
(b) Explain How did these countries become involved in the war?
(c) Identify Causes and Effects What factors help explain the high death toll in the war?

13. (a) Recall When did the Cold War take place?
(b) Analyze Why did the Soviet Union lose the Cold War?

14. (a) Sequence When did many European colonies gain independence?
(b) Identify Causes Why did those countries gain independence at that time?

15. (a) Identify Which new communication technologies have developed since the mid-1900s?

(b) Describe What are some effects of those new technologies?
(c) Analyze How have those technologies affected economic ties between different parts of the world?

◆ Skills Practice

Interpreting Line Graphs In the Skills for Life activity in this chapter, you learned how to interpret line graphs. Review the steps of this skill.

Now look again at the line graph on page 225, titled U.S. Economic Output per Person, 1924–1940. What does the vertical axis show? What does the horizontal axis show? How does the line change over time? When is it high? When is it low? How does the graph show changes in the economy of the United States?

◆ Writing Activity: Science

There are many challenges facing the world today—poverty, population growth, pollution, and terrorism are some of them. Choose one of these challenges or another one that interests you. Then write a brief essay explaining how science or technology might help solve this problem in the future.

MAP MASTER™ Skills Activity

Eastern Hemisphere

Place Location For each place listed below, write the letter from the map that shows its location.
1. Western Europe
2. Algeria
3. Eastern Europe
4. India
5. Russia

Go Online
PHSchool.com Use Web Code lgp-8804 for an **interactive map.**

Standardized Test Prep

Test-Taking Tips

Some questions on standardized tests ask you to analyze point of view. Read the passage below. Then follow the tips to answer the sample question.

> In 1917, Vladimir Lenin took control of Russia. Hearing about the overthrow of Russia's government, someone said, "It is very good news indeed! Soon, the Russians will leave the world war. That will hurt the Allied Powers and help us."

Choose the letter that best answers the question.

Who might have made this statement?

A a French soldier fighting in the trenches

B a Russian nobleman opposed to the Communists

C a German general fighting in France

D an American soldier in Pearl Harbor after it was bombed

Think It Through You can eliminate D right away: Pearl Harbor was not bombed until 1941. Next, recall what happened when Lenin came to power: Communists gained power. So you can rule out B. Then think about which side would benefit from Lenin's taking Russia out of the war. Russia was an ally of France and Britain, so you can rule out A. French soldiers would not consider this good news. The correct answer is C.

TIP Make sure you understand what the question is asking: Who made the comment that begins with the words "It is very good news indeed"?

TIP Use logic, or good reasoning, to be sure you choose an answer that makes sense.

Practice Questions

Use the tips above and other tips in this book to help you answer the following questions.

1. Which group fought against European colonial rule?

    A American soldiers during World War II

    B African independence leaders during the 1950s

    C members of the Nazi Party in the 1930s

    D American presidents during the 1960s

2. What did the leaders of the Russian Revolution seek to achieve?

    A independence

    B capitalism

    C communism

    D democracy

3. Which of the following has strengthened global economic ties?

    A pollution

    B poverty

    C terrorism

    D e-mail

Read the statement below, and answer the question that follows.

"We must not allow communism to spread."

4. Who would have been most likely to make this statement?

    A an American senator

    B a dictator of the Soviet Union

    C a poor Russian during World War I

    D an Indian protesting British rule

Use Web Code **lga-8801** for a **Chapter 8 self-test.**

Projects

Create your own projects to learn more about medieval times to today. At the beginning of this book, you were introduced to the **Guiding Questions** for studying the chapters and special features. But you can also find answers to these questions by doing projects on your own or with a group. Use the questions to find topics you want to explore further. Then try the projects described on this page or create your own.

1. **Geography** How did physical geography affect the development of societies around the world?

2. **History** How have societies around the world been shaped by their history?

3. **Culture** What were the belief systems and patterns of daily life in these societies?

4. **Government** What types of government were formed in these societies?

5. **Economics** How did each society organize its economic activities?

Medieval bakers

Project

CREATE AN EXPANDED TIMELINE

One Job Through the Ages There were no airplane pilots 500 years ago, but there were doctors, carpenters, bakers, and teachers. Learn about one job that has been done at least since the Middle Ages. Find out how different cultures have practiced and changed this job over the course of history. Put major changes, inventions, and individual contributions in a timeline. Then add descriptive paragraphs and illustrations to some of your entries to highlight how the job affected or reflected life at that time.

Project

RESEARCH THE BIRTH OF A NATION

A Nation Celebration Today there are more than 250 nations in the world. Some are very ancient and others are quite new. Choose one, and research how it became an independent nation. Was it once part of another nation or empire? How did it achieve independence? How did it achieve its modern borders and government? What factors influenced its culture? Write a short history of the nation, including what it is like today. Present your work as part of a class Nation Celebration.

This Republic Day 2004 parade in New Delhi celebrates the unification of India into a democratic republic on January 26, 1950.

Table of Contents

Atlas

The World: Political

ARCTIC OCEAN

GREENLAND
(Denmark)

RUSSIA

ALASKA
(U.S.)

Reykjavík

C A N A D A

NORTH
AMERICA

Ottawa

AZORES
(Portugal)

UNITED STATES

Washington, D.C.

A T L A N T I C
O C E A N

MEXICO

HAWAII (U.S)

CAPE
VERDE

Mexico City

CENTRAL AMERICA
AND THE CARIBBEAN
For detail, see map
North and South
America: Political.

Praia

MARSHALL
ISLANDS
Majuro

Caracas

VENEZUELA Georgetown
Bogotá   Paramaribo
GUYANA   FRENCH GUIANA
COLOMBIA   SURINAME   (France)

K I R I B A T I

NAURU
Bairiki

Equator

PALMYRA ATOLL (U.S.)

GALÁPAGOS ISLANDS
(Ecuador)

Quito

ECUADOR

SOUTH
AMERICA

SOLOMON
ISLANDS
Honiara

TUVALU
Fongafale

COOK
ISLANDS
(New Zealand)

PACIFIC
OCEAN

Lima

PERU

B R A Z I L

Brasília

VANUATU
Port-Vila   FIJI
SAMOA
Apia AMERICAN
SAMOA
(U.S.)

FRENCH POLYNESIA
(France)

La Paz
BOLIVIA
Sucre

Suva

NIUE (New Zealand)

Nuku'alofa TONGA

PITCAIRN
ISLANDS
(U.K.)

Tropic of Capricorn

PARAGUAY
Asunción

NEW
CALEDONIA
(France)

CHILE

URUGUAY
Montevideo
Buenos Aires

Santiago

NEW
ZEALAND
Wellington

ARGENTINA

FALKLAND ISLANDS
(U.K.)

SOUTH GEORGIA &
SOUTH SANDWICH ISLANDS
(U.K.)

S O U T H E R N   O C E A N

Antarctic Circle

ANTARCTICA

Tropic of Cancer

0 miles   2,000

0 kilometers   2,000
Robinson

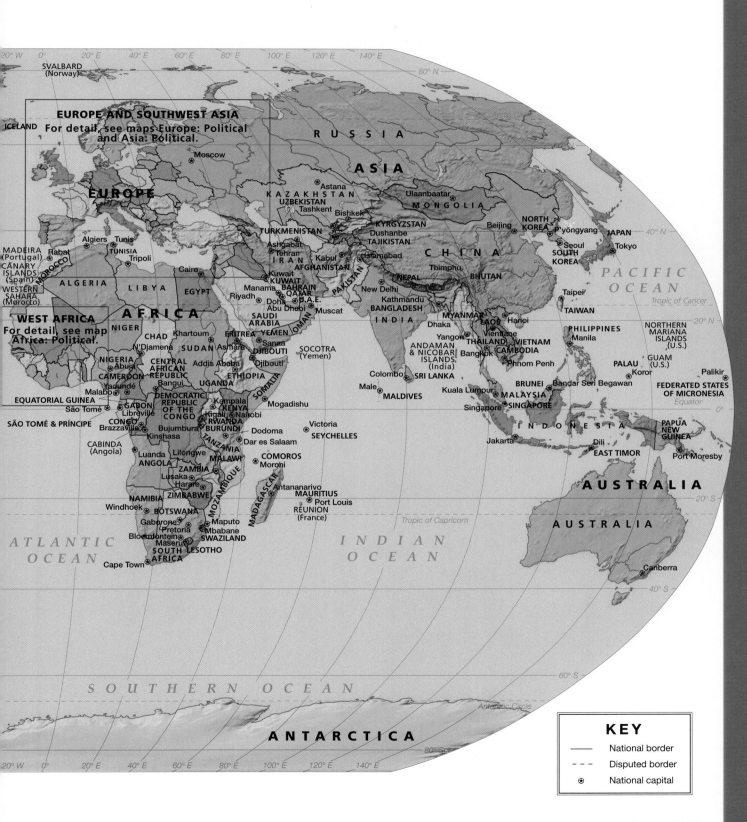

EUROPE AND SOUTHWEST ASIA
For detail, see maps Europe: Political
and Asia: Political.

WEST AFRICA
For detail, see map
Africa: Political.

20° W   0°   20° E   40° E   60° E   80° E   100° E   120° E   140° E

80° N

SVALBARD
(Norway)

ICELAND

RUSSIA

ASIA

Moscow

EUROPE

Astana
UZBEKISTAN
Tashkent   Bishkek
Ulaanbaatar

KAZAKHSTAN

MONGOLIA

Beijing
NORTH
KOREA

40° N

P'yŏngyang

JAPAN

Algiers   Tunis
MADEIRA
(Portugal)   Rabat
TUNISIA
Tripoli
CANARY
ISLANDS
(Spain)
WESTERN
SAHARA
(Morocco)

TURKMENISTAN
Ashgabat
Tehran
IRAN
Kabul
Cairo
AFGHANISTAN
Islamabad
Kuwait
KUWAIT
BAHRAIN
Manama
QATAR
Riyadh   Doha
Abu Dhabi   U.A.E.

KYRGYZSTAN
Dushanbe
TAJIKISTAN

CHINA
New Delhi
NEPAL
Kathmandu
PAKISTAN
BANGLADESH

Thimphu
BHUTAN

Seoul
SOUTH
KOREA
Tokyo

PACIFIC
OCEAN

Taipei
TAIWAN

Tropic of Cancer

ALGERIA   LIBYA
EGYPT

AFRICA
NIGER
CHAD
N'Djamena
Khartoum
SUDAN
NIGERIA
Abuja
CENTRAL
AFRICAN
REPUBLIC

SAUDI
ARABIA
OMAN
YEMEN
ERITREA
Sanaa
Asmara
DJIBOUTI
Djibouti
Addis Ababa

Muscat

SOCOTRA
(Yemen)

INDIA

ANDAMAN
& NICOBAR
ISLANDS
(India)

Dhaka
Yangon
MYANMAR   Hanoi
LAOS
THAILAND   VIETNAM
Bangkok
Phnom Penh
CAMBODIA

PHILIPPINES
Manila

NORTHERN
MARIANA
ISLANDS
(U.S.)

20° N

CAMEROON
Yaoundé
Malabo
EQUATORIAL GUINEA
São Tomé
SÃO TOMÉ & PRÍNCIPE
GABON   CONGO
Libreville
Brazzaville
Kinshasa
CABINDA
(Angola)
Luanda
ANGOLA

Bangui
ETHIOPIA
UGANDA
DEMOCRATIC
REPUBLIC
OF THE
CONGO
Kampala   KENYA
Kigali   Nairobi
RWANDA
Bujumbura
BURUNDI
TANZANIA
Dodoma
Dar es Salaam

SOMALIA
Mogadishu

Colombo
SRI LANKA
Male
MALDIVES

Kuala Lumpur
MALAYSIA
Singapore   SINGAPORE

BRUNEI
Bandar Seri Begawan

PALAU
Koror

GUAM
(U.S.)

Palikir
FEDERATED STATES
OF MICRONESIA

Jakarta
INDONESIA

PAPUA
NEW
GUINEA
Dili
EAST TIMOR
Port Moresby

Equator   0°

Victoria
SEYCHELLES

COMOROS
Moroni

Lilongwe
MALAWI
ZAMBIA
Lusaka   Harare

NAMIBIA
ZIMBABWE
Windhoek
BOTSWANA

MADAGASCAR
Antananarivo
MAURITIUS
Port Louis
RÉUNION
(France)

AUSTRALIA

20° S

MOZAMBIQUE

Gaborone
Maputo
Pretoria
Bloemfontein   Mbabane
Maseru   SWAZILAND
SOUTH   LESOTHO
AFRICA
Cape Town

ATLANTIC
OCEAN

INDIAN
OCEAN

Tropic of Capricorn

AUSTRALIA

Canberra

40° S

SOUTHERN   OCEAN

Antarctic Circle

ANTARCTICA

80° S

20° W   0°   20° E   40° E   60° E   80° E   100° E   120° E   140° E

60° S

KEY	
——	National border
- - -	Disputed border
⊛	National capital

The World: Physical

0 miles 2,000
0 kilometers 2,000
Robinson

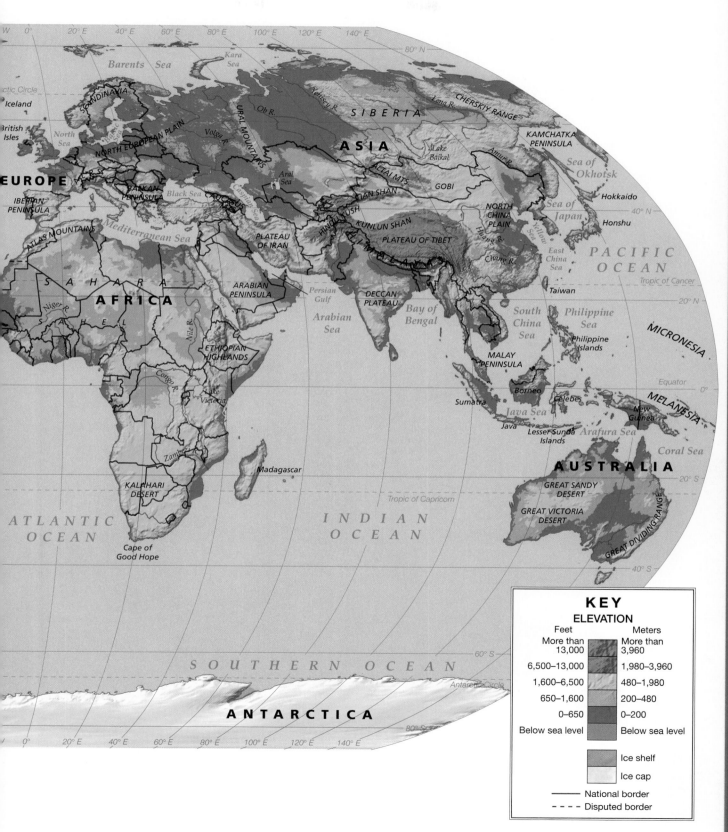

20° E 40° E 60° E 80° E 100° E 120° E 140° E

Barents Sea
Kara Sea
Iceland
Arctic Circle
SCANDINAVIA
British Isles
North Sea
URAL MOUNTAINS
SIBERIA
CHERSKIY RANGE
Yenisey R.
Ob R.
Lena R.
KAMCHATKA PENINSULA
ASIA
Lake Baikal
Amur R.
Sea of Okhotsk
EUROPE
NORTH EUROPEAN PLAIN
Volga R.
Aral Sea
ALTAI MTS.
GOBI
Hokkaido
Sea of Japan
IBERIAN PENINSULA
BALKAN PENINSULA
Black Sea
CAUCASUS MTS.
Caspian Sea
TIAN SHAN
NORTH CHINA PLAIN
Honshu
ATLAS MOUNTAINS
Mediterranean Sea
HINDU KUSH
KUNLUN SHAN
Yellow Sea
PLATEAU OF IRAN
PLATEAU OF TIBET
Huang R.
East China Sea
PACIFIC OCEAN
SAHARA
AFRICA
Niger R.
Red Sea
ARABIAN PENINSULA
Persian Gulf
DECCAN PLATEAU
Chang R.
Tropic of Cancer
Taiwan
SAHEL
Arabian Sea
Bay of Bengal
South China Sea
Philippine Sea
MICRONESIA
Nile R.
ETHIOPIAN HIGHLANDS
MALAY PENINSULA
Philippine Islands
Congo R.
Lake Victoria
Sumatra
Borneo
Celebes
Equator
MELANESIA
New Guinea
Java Sea
Java
Lesser Sunda Islands
Arafura Sea
Coral Sea
Zambezi
Madagascar
AUSTRALIA
KALAHARI DESERT
GREAT SANDY DESERT
Tropic of Capricorn
GREAT VICTORIA DESERT
GREAT DIVIDING RANGE
ATLANTIC OCEAN
INDIAN OCEAN
Cape of Good Hope
SOUTHERN OCEAN
Antarctic Circle
ANTARCTICA
0° 20° E 40° E 60° E 80° E 100° E 120° E 140° E

KEY
ELEVATION

Feet		Meters
More than 13,000		More than 3,960
6,500–13,000		1,980–3,960
1,600–6,500		480–1,980
650–1,600		200–480
0–650		0–200
Below sea level		Below sea level

Ice shelf
Ice cap
National border
- - - Disputed border

North and South America: Political

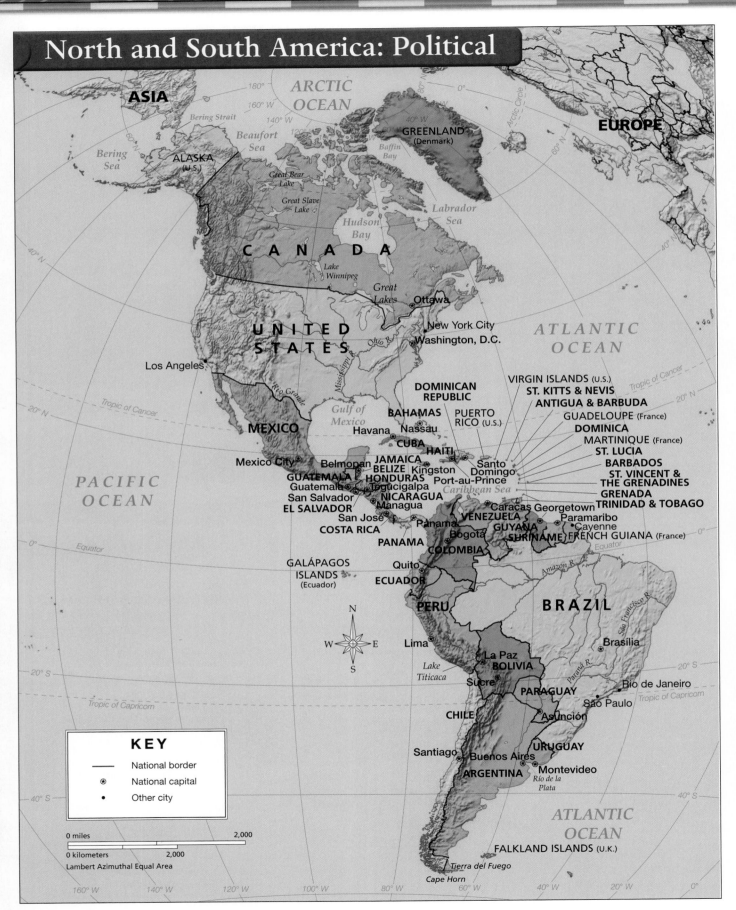

ASIA

ARCTIC OCEAN

Bering Strait

Beaufort Sea

Bering Sea

ALASKA (U.S.)

GREENLAND (Denmark)

EUROPE

Baffin Bay

Great Bear Lake

Great Slave Lake

Labrador Sea

Hudson Bay

C A N A D A

Lake Winnipeg

Great Lakes

Ottawa

New York City

ATLANTIC OCEAN

U N I T E D S T A T E S

Ohio R.

Washington, D.C.

Los Angeles

Mississippi R.

Rio Grande

Tropic of Cancer

DOMINICAN REPUBLIC

VIRGIN ISLANDS (U.S.)

ST. KITTS & NEVIS

ANTIGUA & BARBUDA

GUADELOUPE (France)

DOMINICA

MARTINIQUE (France)

ST. LUCIA

BARBADOS

ST. VINCENT & THE GRENADINES

GRENADA

TRINIDAD & TOBAGO

BAHAMAS

PUERTO RICO (U.S.)

MEXICO

Havana

Nassau

CUBA

HAITI

Santo Domingo

JAMAICA

Mexico City

Belmopan

BELIZE

Kingston

Port-au-Prince

GUATEMALA

HONDURAS

Guatemala

Tegucigalpa

Caribbean Sea

San Salvador

NICARAGUA

EL SALVADOR

Managua

Caracas

Georgetown

VENEZUELA

Paramaribo

San José

Panama

GUYANA

Cayenne

PACIFIC OCEAN

COSTA RICA

Bogotá

SURINAME

FRENCH GUIANA (France)

PANAMA

COLOMBIA

Equator

GALÁPAGOS ISLANDS (Ecuador)

Quito

Amazon R.

ECUADOR

B R A Z I L

São Francisco R.

PERU

Brasília

N

W   E

Lima

S

Río de Janeiro

Lake Titicaca

La Paz

BOLIVIA

Paraná R.

Sucre

PARAGUAY

São Paulo

Tropic of Capricorn

CHILE

Asunción

KEY

National border

National capital

Other city

URUGUAY

Santiago

Buenos Aires

Montevideo

ARGENTINA

Río de la Plata

ATLANTIC OCEAN

0 miles   2,000

0 kilometers   2,000

Lambert Azimuthal Equal Area

FALKLAND ISLANDS (U.K.)

Tierra del Fuego

Cape Horn

North and South America: Physical

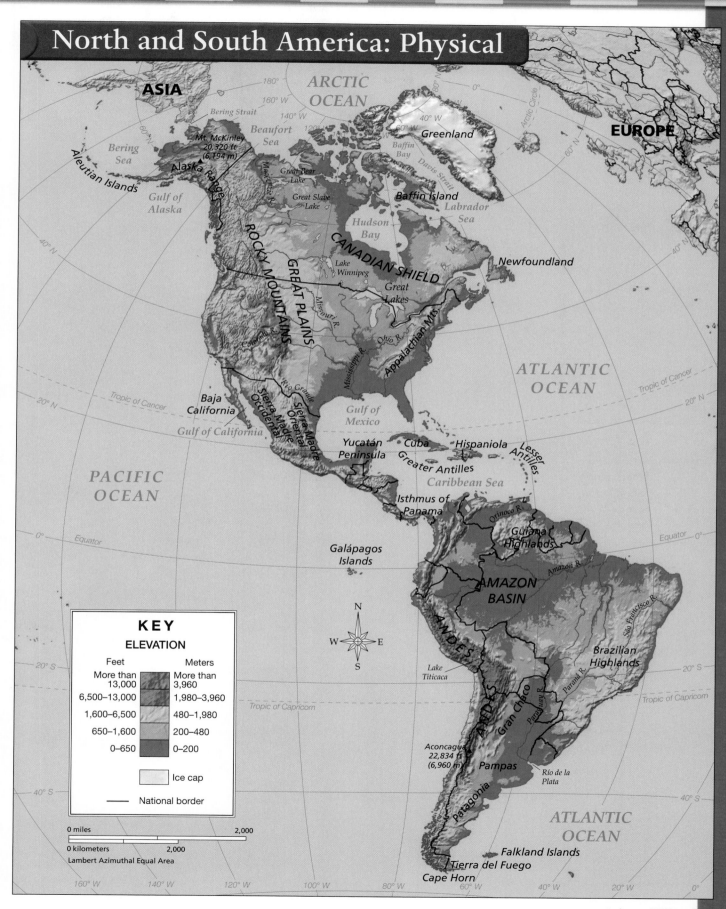

ASIA

ARCTIC OCEAN

EUROPE

Greenland

Bering Strait

Beaufort Sea

Mt. McKinley 20,320 ft (6,194 m)

Baffin Bay

Bering Sea

Alaska Range

Great Bear Lake

Davis Strait

Aleutian Islands

Gulf of Alaska

Mackenzie R.

Great Slave Lake

Baffin Island

Labrador Sea

Hudson Bay

CANADIAN SHIELD

Newfoundland

Lake Winnipeg

Great Lakes

ROCKY MOUNTAINS

GREAT PLAINS

Missouri R.

Colorado R.

Mississippi R.

Ohio R.

Appalachian Mts.

ATLANTIC OCEAN

Tropic of Cancer

Tropic of Cancer

Baja California

Río Grande

Sierra Madre Occidental

Sierra Madre Oriental

Gulf of Mexico

Gulf of California

Yucatán Peninsula

Cuba

Hispaniola

Lesser Antilles

Greater Antilles

PACIFIC OCEAN

Caribbean Sea

Isthmus of Panama

Orinoco R.

Galápagos Islands

Guiana Highlands

Equator

Equator

Amazon R.

AMAZON BASIN

ANDES

São Francisco R.

Brazilian Highlands

Lake Titicaca

20° S

20° S

KEY

ELEVATION

Feet	Meters
More than 13,000	More than 3,960
6,500–13,000	1,980–3,960
1,600–6,500	480–1,980
650–1,600	200–480
0–650	0–200

Ice cap

National border

ANDES

Gran Chaco

Paraguay R.

Paraná R.

Tropic of Capricorn

Tropic of Capricorn

Aconcagua 22,834 ft (6,960 m)

Pampas

Río de la Plata

Patagonia

ATLANTIC OCEAN

0 miles 2,000

0 kilometers 2,000

Lambert Azimuthal Equal Area

Falkland Islands

Tierra del Fuego

Cape Horn

N
W E
S

160° W   140° W   120° W   100° W   80° W   60° W   40° W   20° W   0°

United States: Political

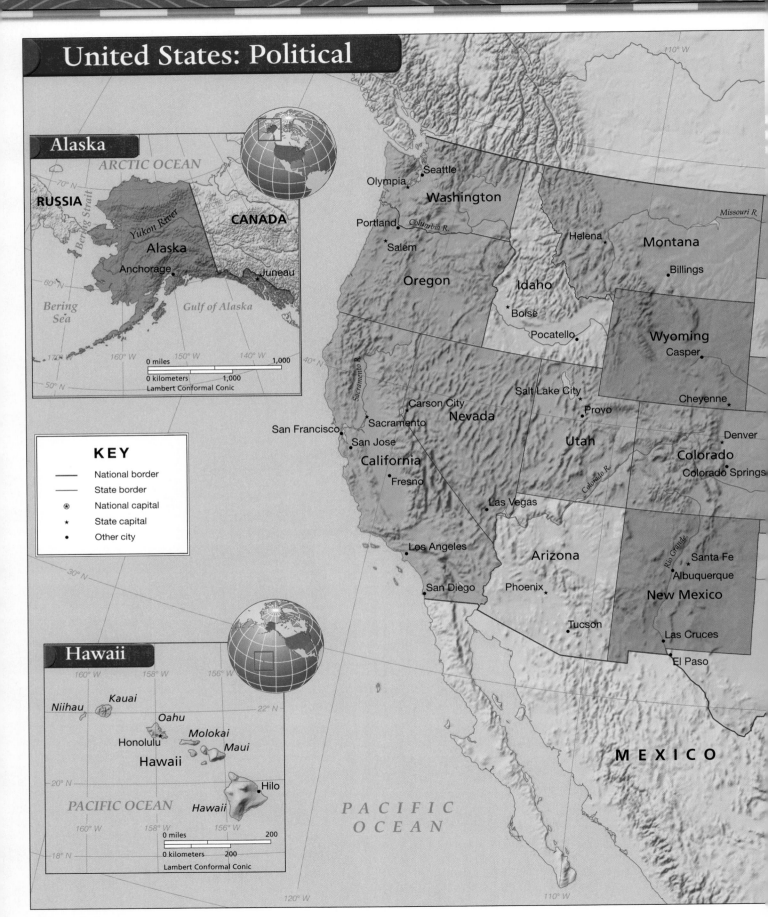

Alaska

ARCTIC OCEAN

RUSSIA

CANADA

Bering Strait

Yukon River

Arctic Circle

Alaska

Anchorage

Juneau

Bering Sea

Gulf of Alaska

70° N

60° N

50° N

170°

160° W   150° W   140° W

0 miles   1,000
0 kilometers   1,000
Lambert Conformal Conic

KEY

— National border
— State border
⊛ National capital
★ State capital
• Other city

Hawaii

160° W   158° W   156° W

Niihau   Kauai

Oahu   Molokai

Honolulu   Maui

Hawaii

Hilo

Hawaii

22° N

20° N

18° N

PACIFIC OCEAN

160° W   158° W   156° W

0 miles   200
0 kilometers   200
Lambert Conformal Conic

Seattle
Olympia
Washington

Portland   Columbia R.
Salem

Oregon

Helena
Montana

Billings

Idaho

Boise

Pocatello

Wyoming

Casper

Cheyenne

Missouri R.

110° W

Sacramento R.

San Francisco
San Jose

California

Fresno

Carson City
Sacramento

Nevada

Salt Lake City

Provo

Utah

Colorado R.

Denver

Colorado

Colorado Springs

40° N

Las Vegas

Los Angeles

San Diego

Arizona

Phoenix

Tucson

Rio Grande

Santa Fe
Albuquerque

New Mexico

Las Cruces

El Paso

30° N

M E X I C O

PACIFIC OCEAN

120° W   110° W

CANADA

North Dakota
Bismarck
Fargo

Minnesota

South Dakota
Pierre
Sioux Falls

St. Paul
Minneapolis

Mississippi R.

Wisconsin

Milwaukee
Madison

Lake Superior

Michigan

Lake Huron

Grand Rapids
Lansing
Detroit

Lake Erie

Lake Ontario

Buffalo

Albany

Maine
Augusta
Portland

Vermont
Montpelier
New Hampshire
Concord

New York

Boston
Massachusetts
Providence
Hartford
Rhode Island
Connecticut
New York City

Iowa
Des Moines

Nebraska
Omaha
Lincoln

Missouri R.

Cedar Rapids

Chicago

Illinois

Springfield

Fort Wayne

Indiana

Indianapolis

Ohio
Columbus

Cincinnati
Ohio R.

Cleveland
Pittsburgh

Pennsylvania
Harrisburg

Baltimore
Washington, D.C.

West
Virginia
Charleston

Richmond

New Jersey
Trenton
Philadelphia
Delaware
Dover
Annapolis
Maryland
District of Columbia

Virginia

Norfolk

Topeka

Kansas

Wichita

Kansas City
Jefferson City

Arkansas R.

St. Louis

Louisville

Missouri

Frankfort

Kentucky

Nashville
Knoxville

Raleigh

North Carolina

Charlotte

Oklahoma

Oklahoma City

Tulsa

Arkansas
Fort Smith
Little Rock

Red R.

Memphis

Mississippi R.

Tennessee R.

Tennessee

South Carolina
Columbia
Charleston

ATLANTIC
OCEAN

Texas

Fort Worth
Dallas

Austin
San Antonio
Houston

Shreveport
Louisiana

Mississippi

Jackson

Baton Rouge
Gulfport
New Orleans

Birmingham

Alabama
Montgomery

Mobile

Atlanta

Georgia
Columbus

Savannah

Jacksonville

Tallahassee

Florida

Orlando

Tampa

Miami

Gulf of Mexico

N
W E
S

0 miles 250
0 kilometers 250
Lambert Azimuthal Equal Area

100° W
90° W
80° W
70° W
50° N
40° N
30° N
90° W
80° W

Europe: Political

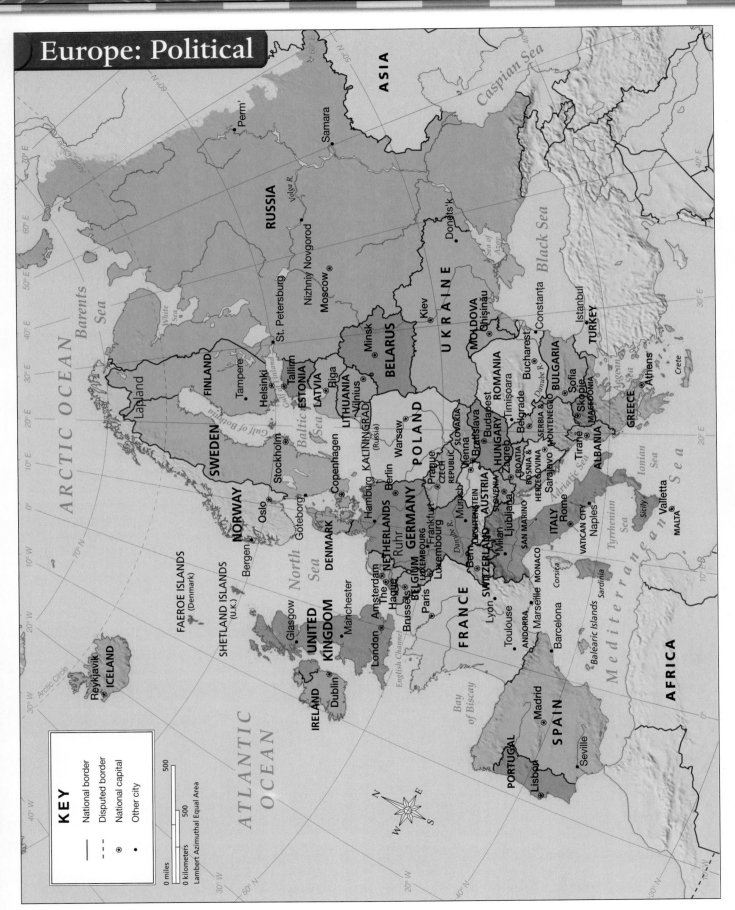

KEY

— National border
-- Disputed border
⊛ National capital
• Other city

0 miles   500
0 kilometers   500
Lambert Azimuthal Equal Area

ASIA

Caspian Sea

RUSSIA

Perm'

Samara

Volga R.

Nizhniy Novgorod

Donets'k

Sea of Azov

Moscow ⊛

UKRAINE

Kiev ⊛

Black Sea

St. Petersburg

White Sea

Constanţa

Istanbul

FINLAND

Tampere

Helsinki ⊛

Tallinn

Gulf of Finland

ESTONIA

LATVIA

Riga ⊛

LITHUANIA

Vilnius ⊛

Minsk ⊛

BELARUS

MOLDOVA

Chişinău ⊛

Bucharest ⊛

Danube R.

ROMANIA

Timişoara

TURKEY

Sofia ⊛

BULGARIA

Skopje ⊛

MACEDONIA

Athens ⊛

GREECE

Aegean Sea

Crete

SWEDEN

Stockholm ⊛

Göteborg

Lapland

NORWAY

Oslo ⊛

Bergen

Gulf of Bothnia

Baltic Sea

KALININGRAD (Russia)

Warsaw ⊛

POLAND

SLOVAKIA

Bratislava ⊛

Budapest ⊛

HUNGARY

Belgrade ⊛

SERBIA & MONTENEGRO

Sarajevo ⊛

BOSNIA & HERZEGOVINA

Tiranë ⊛

ALBANIA

Adriatic Sea

Ionian Sea

Copenhagen ⊛

DENMARK

Hamburg

Berlin ⊛

GERMANY

Prague ⊛

CZECH REPUBLIC

Vienna ⊛

AUSTRIA

SLOVENIA

Ljubljana ⊛

Zagreb ⊛

CROATIA

Munich

Frankfurt

Ruhr

ARCTIC OCEAN

Barents Sea

ICELAND

Reykjavik ⊛

Arctic Circle

FAEROE ISLANDS (Denmark)

SHETLAND ISLANDS (U.K.)

North Sea

UNITED KINGDOM

Glasgow

Manchester

London ⊛

IRELAND

Dublin ⊛

English Channel

NETHERLANDS

Amsterdam ⊛

The Hague

Brussels ⊛

BELGIUM

LUXEMBOURG

Luxembourg ⊛

Paris ⊛

Danube R.

Bern ⊛

LIECHTENSTEIN

SWITZERLAND

Milan

MONACO

SAN MARINO

Rome ⊛

VATICAN CITY

Naples

ITALY

Tyrrhenian Sea

Sardinia

Sicily

Valletta ⊛

MALTA

FRANCE

Lyon

Toulouse

Marseille

Corsica

ANDORRA

Barcelona

Balearic Islands

Mediterranean Sea

SPAIN

Madrid ⊛

Seville

PORTUGAL

Lisbon ⊛

ATLANTIC OCEAN

Bay of Biscay

AFRICA

N
E
S
W

Europe: Physical

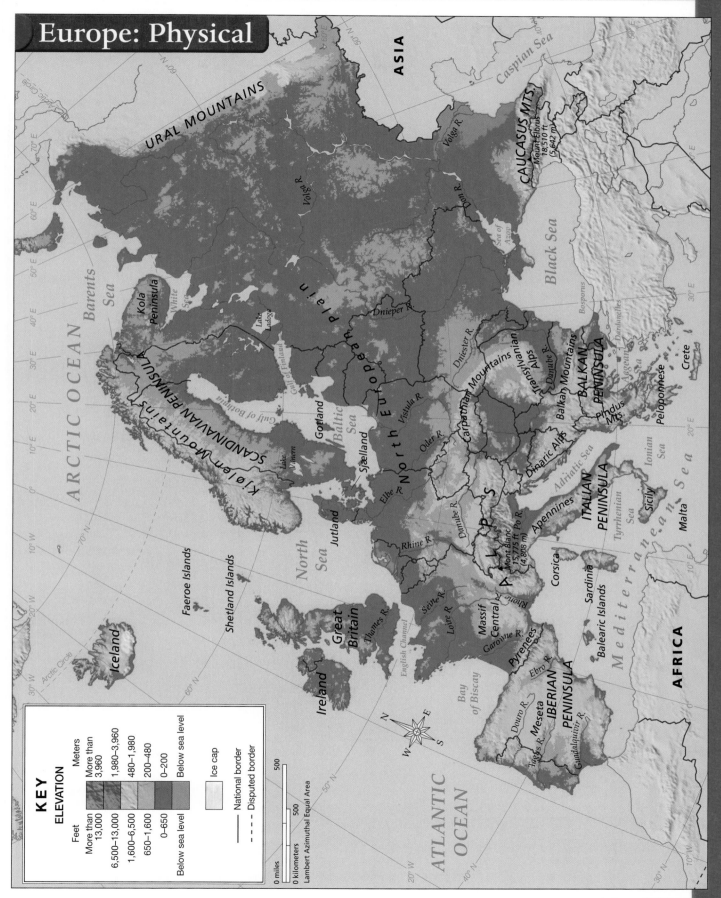

ASIA

Caspian Sea

URAL MOUNTAINS

CAUCASUS MTS.
Mount Elbrus
18,510 ft
(5,642 m)

Volga R.

Volga R.

Don R.

Black Sea

Sea of Azov

ARCTIC OCEAN

Barents Sea

Kola Peninsula

White Sea

Lake Ladoga

Dnieper R.

Bosporus

Dniestr R.

Carpathian Mountains

Transylvanian Alps

Danube R.

Balkan Mountains

BALKAN PENINSULA

Dardanelles

Aegean Sea

Crete

SCANDINAVIAN PENINSULA

Kjølen Mountains

Gulf of Bothnia

Gulf of Finland

Baltic Sea

Gotland

Sjælland

North European Plain

Vistula R.

Oder R.

Dinaric Alps

Pindus Mts.

Peloponnese

Ionian Sea

Sicily

Malta

Lake Vänern

Elbe R.

Danube R.

A L P S

Adriatic Sea

ITALIAN PENINSULA

Apennines

Tyrrhenian Sea

Sardinia

Mediterranean Sea

North Sea

Jutland

Rhine R.

Mont Blanc
15,775 ft
(4,808 m)

Rhône R.

Po R.

Corsica

Balearic Islands

Faeroe Islands

Shetland Islands

Great Britain

Thames R.

Seine R.

Loire R.

Massif Central

Garonne R.

Pyrenees

Ebro R.

IBERIAN PENINSULA

Meseta

Douro R.

Tagus R.

Guadalquivir R.

Ireland

Iceland

Arctic Circle

English Channel

Bay of Biscay

AFRICA

ATLANTIC OCEAN

N E S W

KEY
ELEVATION

Feet	Meters
More than 13,000	More than 3,960
6,500–13,000	1,980–3,960
1,600–6,500	480–1,980
650–1,600	200–480
0–650	0–200
Below sea level	Below sea level

Ice cap

National border
Disputed border

0 miles   500
0 kilometers   500
Lambert Azimuthal Equal Area

Africa: Political

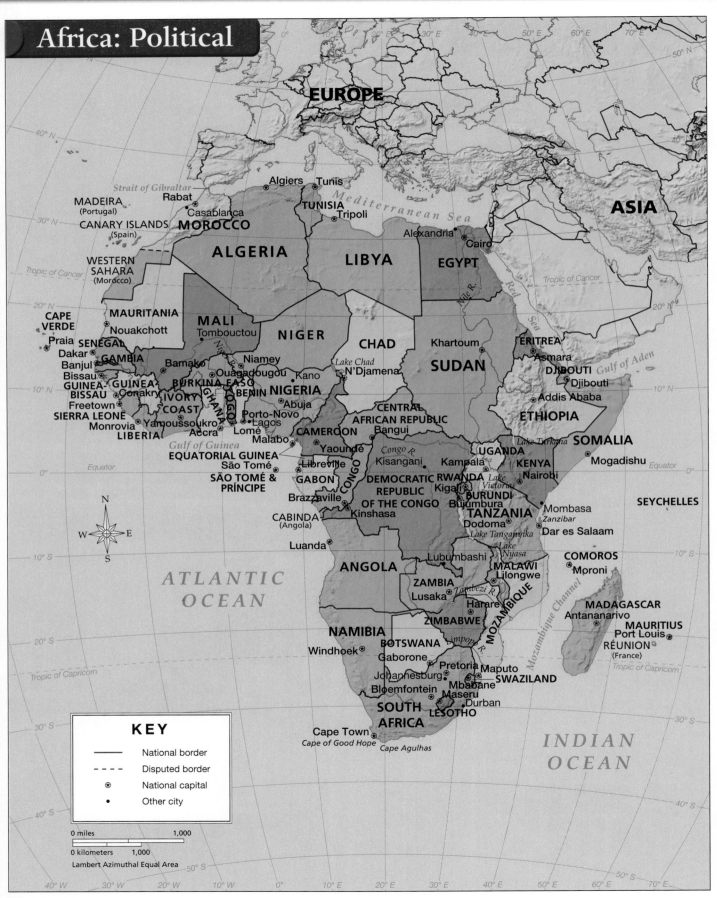

EUROPE

ASIA

Strait of Gibraltar

MADEIRA (Portugal)

CANARY ISLANDS (Spain)

Rabat
• Algiers   • Tunis
Casablanca   TUNISIA
MOROCCO   Tripoli

Mediterranean Sea

Alexandria   • Cairo

WESTERN SAHARA (Morocco)

ALGERIA   LIBYA   EGYPT

Tropic of Cancer   *Tropic of Cancer*

CAPE VERDE
Praia   • Nouakchott
MAURITANIA   MALI   NIGER   CHAD
Tombouctou   Niamey   N'Djamena
Dakar   SENEGAL   Bamako   Ouagadougou   Kano
GAMBIA   BURKINA FASO
Banjul   Niamey
Bissau   GUINEA   GUINEA-BISSAU   Conakry   IVORY   GHANA   BENIN   NIGERIA   Abuja
Freetown   COAST   TOGO
SIERRA LEONE   Yamoussoukro   Porto-Novo   Lagos
Monrovia   Accra   Lomé   Malabo
LIBERIA

Lake Chad
Khartoum
SUDAN

ERITREA
Asmara
DJIBOUTI   *Gulf of Aden*
Djibouti
Addis Ababa
ETHIOPIA

Gulf of Guinea
EQUATORIAL GUINEA
São Tomé
SÃO TOMÉ & PRÍNCIPE
GABON
Libreville
Yaoundé
CAMEROON
CENTRAL AFRICAN REPUBLIC
Bangui

Congo R.
Kisangani   Kampala   UGANDA   KENYA   Nairobi   • Mogadishu   SOMALIA
Lake Turkana
RWANDA
Kigali   *Lake Victoria*
DEMOCRATIC REPUBLIC OF THE CONGO   BURUNDI   Bujumbura
Brazzaville   Kinshasa   TANZANIA   Dodoma   Mombasa   *Zanzibar*   Dar es Salaam

Equator   *Equator*

CABINDA (Angola)
Luanda

SEYCHELLES

Lake Tanganyika
Lake Nyasa
Lubumbashi
COMOROS   Moroni

ANGOLA
ZAMBIA
Lusaka   MALAWI   Lilongwe
Zambezi R.
Harare
ZIMBABWE   MOZAMBIQUE   MADAGASCAR   Antananarivo   MAURITIUS   Port Louis
RÉUNION (France)

Mozambique Channel

ATLANTIC OCEAN

NAMIBIA
BOTSWANA
Windhoek   Gaborone
Limpopo R.
Pretoria   Maputo   SWAZILAND   Mbabane
Johannesburg
Bloemfontein   Maseru   Durban
SOUTH AFRICA   LESOTHO

INDIAN OCEAN

Tropic of Capricorn   *Tropic of Capricorn*

Cape Town
Cape of Good Hope   Cape Agulhas

KEY

— National border
- - - Disputed border
⊗ National capital
• Other city

0 miles   1,000
0 kilometers   1,000
Lambert Azimuthal Equal Area

Africa: Physical

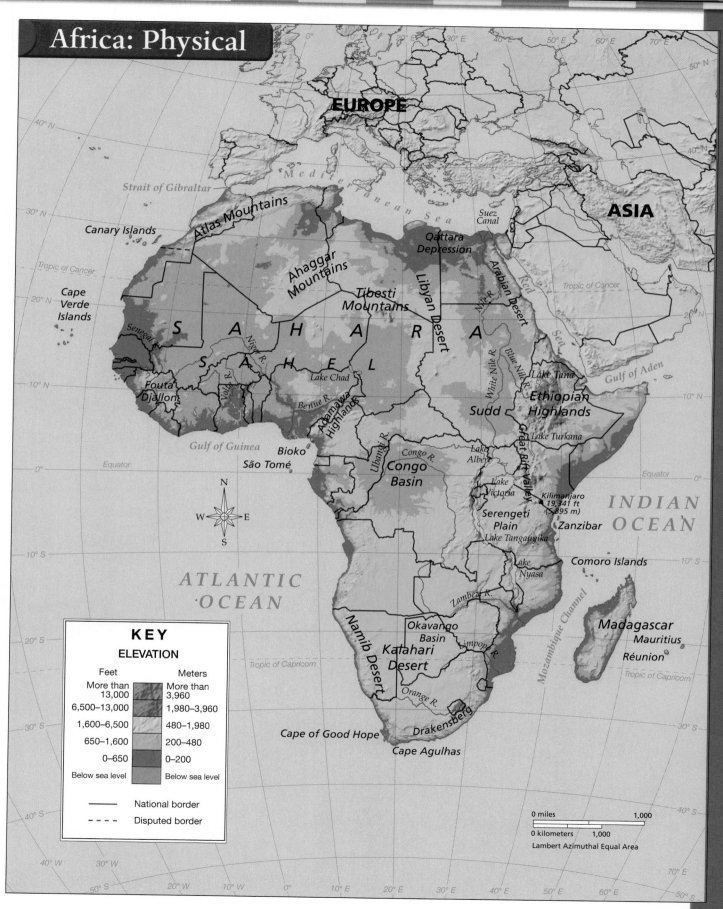

EUROPE

ASIA

Strait of Gibraltar

Mediterranean Sea

Canary Islands

Atlas Mountains

Cape Verde Islands

Tropic of Cancer

SAHARA

Ahaggar Mountains

Tibesti Mountains

Libyan Desert

Qattara Depression

Suez Canal

Arabian Desert

Red Sea

Tropic of Cancer

Senegal R.

SAHEL

Niger R.

Lake Chad

Nile R.

White Nile R.

Blue Nile R.

Lake Tana

Gulf of Aden

Fouta Djallon

Volta R.

Benue R.

Adamawa Highlands

Sudd

Ethiopian Highlands

Lake Turkana

Gulf of Guinea

Bioko

São Tomé

Ubangi R.

Congo R.

Congo Basin

Lake Albert

Lake Victoria

Great Rift Valley

Equator

Equator

Lake Tanganyika

Serengeti Plain

Kilimanjaro 19,341 ft (5,895 m)

Zanzibar

INDIAN OCEAN

ATLANTIC OCEAN

Lake Nyasa

Comoro Islands

Zambezi R.

Namib Desert

Okavango Basin

Kalahari Desert

Limpopo R.

Madagascar

Mauritius

Réunion

Tropic of Capricorn

Mozambique Channel

Tropic of Capricorn

Orange R.

Cape of Good Hope

Drakensberg

Cape Agulhas

KEY
ELEVATION

Feet		Meters
More than 13,000		More than 3,960
6,500–13,000		1,980–3,960
1,600–6,500		480–1,980
650–1,600		200–480
0–650		0–200
Below sea level		Below sea level

National border

Disputed border

0 miles 1,000

0 kilometers 1,000

Lambert Azimuthal Equal Area

Asia: Political

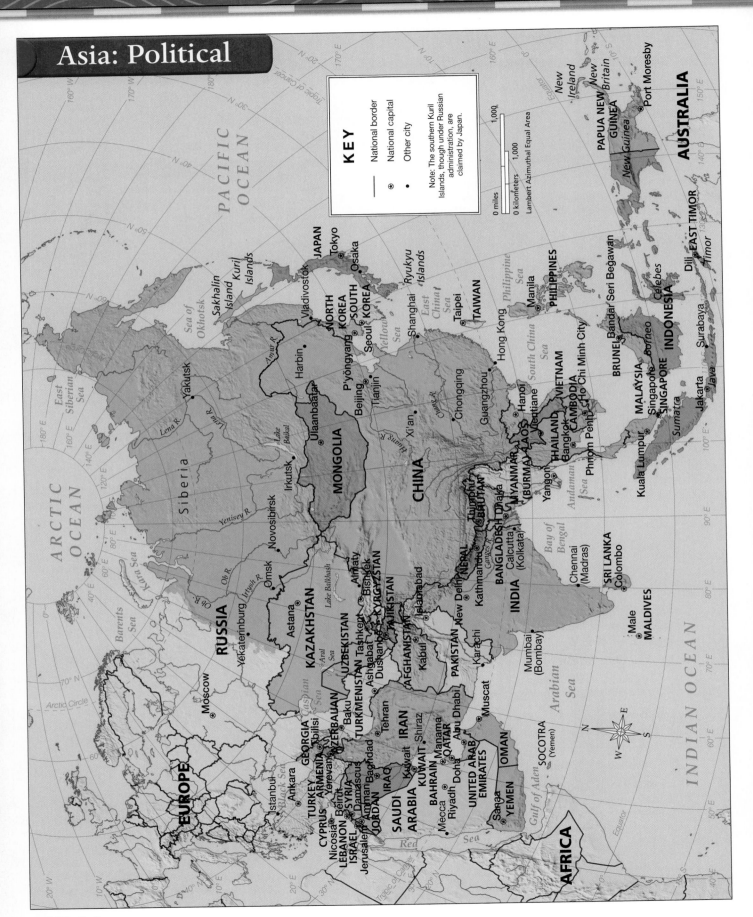

KEY

National border
National capital
Other city

Note: The southern Kuril Islands, though under Russian administration, are claimed by Japan.

1,000

0 miles   1,000
0 kilometers   1,000
Lambert Azimuthal Equal Area

PACIFIC OCEAN

ARCTIC OCEAN

East Siberian Sea

Sea of Okhotsk

Barents Sea

Kara Sea

Siberia

JAPAN
Tokyo
Osaka
Sakhalin Island
Kuril Islands
Ryukyu Islands

Yakutsk

Vladivostok

NORTH KOREA
P'yŏngyang
SOUTH KOREA
Seoul
Harbin
Amur R.
Lena R.

Shanghai
East China Sea
TAIWAN
Taipei

Irkutsk
Lake Baikal

Ulaanbaatar
MONGOLIA

Beijing
Tianjin
Yellow Sea

Hong Kong

PHILIPPINES
Manila
Philippine Sea

Novosibirsk
Yenisey R.
Ob R.

Xi'an
Chang R.
CHINA
Huang R.
Chongqing
Guangzhou
South China Sea

BRUNEI
Bandar Seri Begawan

Omsk
Irtysh R.

Yekaterinburg
Astana
KAZAKHSTAN
Lake Balkhash

Almaty
Bishkek
KYRGYZSTAN
Tashkent
UZBEKISTAN
TAJIKISTAN
Dushanbe

Hanoi
VIETNAM
LAOS
Vientiane
THAILAND
Bangkok
MYANMAR (BURMA)
Yangon
CAMBODIA
Phnom Penh
Ho Chi Minh City
Andaman Sea

MALAYSIA
Kuala Lumpur
SINGAPORE
Singapore
Borneo
Celebes
INDONESIA
Sumatra
Jakarta
Java
Surabaya

PAPUA NEW GUINEA
New Guinea
Port Moresby
AUSTRALIA

New Ireland
New Britain

EAST TIMOR
Dili
Timor

RUSSIA
Moscow

Aral Sea
TURKMENISTAN
Ashgabat
AFGHANISTAN
Kabul
Islamabad
PAKISTAN
NEPAL
Kathmandu
Thimphu
BHUTAN
BANGLADESH
Dhaka

New Delhi
Ganges R.
INDIA
Calcutta (Kolkata)
Bay of Bengal

SRI LANKA
Colombo
Chennai (Madras)

MALDIVES
Male

EUROPE

Black Sea
GEORGIA
Tbilisi
ARMENIA
Yerevan
AZERBAIJAN
Baku
Caspian Sea
Tehran
IRAN
Shiraz
Karachi
Mumbai (Bombay)
Arabian Sea

INDIAN OCEAN

Istanbul
Ankara
TURKEY
CYPRUS
Nicosia
LEBANON
Beirut
ISRAEL
Jerusalem
SYRIA
Damascus
JORDAN
Amman
Baghdad
IRAQ
Kuwait
KUWAIT
BAHRAIN
Manama
QATAR
Doha
Abu Dhabi
UNITED ARAB EMIRATES
OMAN
Muscat

SAUDI ARABIA
Mecca
Riyadh
YEMEN
Sanaa
Red Sea
Gulf of Aden
SOCOTRA (Yemen)

AFRICA

Arctic Circle

Equator

Tropic of Cancer

N
E
S
W

Asia: Physical

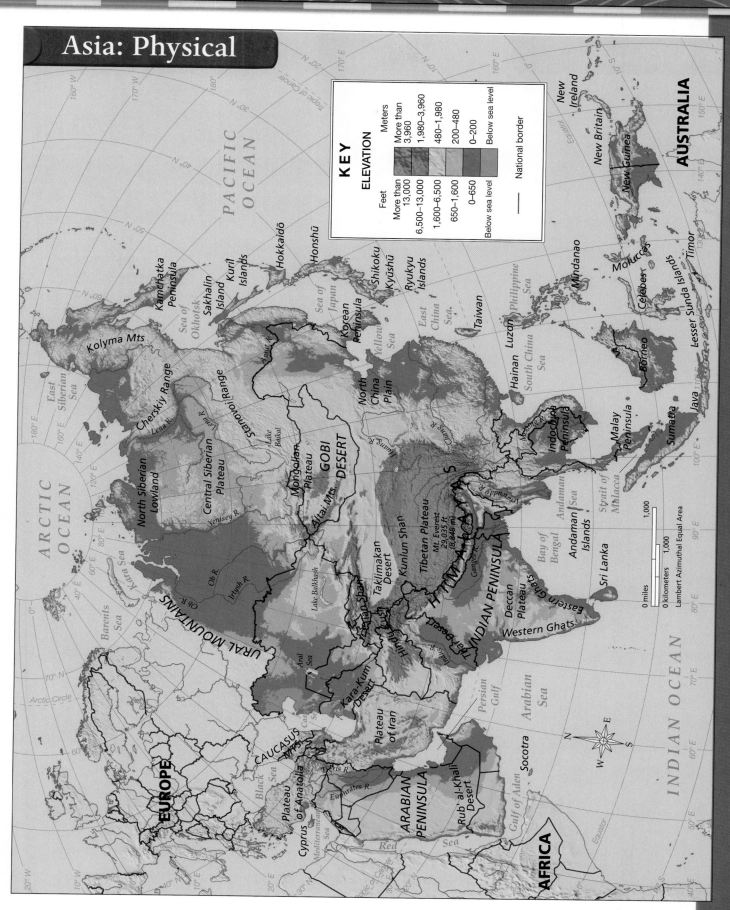

KEY

ELEVATION

Feet	Meters
More than 13,000	More than 3,960
6,500–13,000	1,980–3,960
1,600–6,500	480–1,980
650–1,600	200–480
0–650	0–200
Below sea level	Below sea level

— National border

PACIFIC OCEAN

ARCTIC OCEAN

Barents Sea

Kara Sea

East Siberian Sea

Kamchatka Peninsula

Sea of Okhotsk

Sakhalin Island

Kuril Islands

Hokkaidō

Honshū

Kolyma Mts

Cherskiy Range

Stanovoy Range

Lena R.

Lake Baikal

Sea of Japan

Korean Peninsula

Shikoku

Kyūshū

Ryukyu Islands

Amur R.

North Siberian Lowland

Central Siberian Plateau

Yenisey R.

Mongolian Plateau

Altai Mts

GOBI DESERT

Yellow Sea

North China Plain

East China Sea

Taiwan

Hainan

Luzon

Philippine Sea

Mindanao

New Ireland

New Britain

New Guinea

AUSTRALIA

Molucces

Celebes

Lesser Sunda Islands

Timor

Borneo

Java

Sumatra

Malay Peninsula

Indochina Peninsula

Mekong R.

Chang R.

Huang R.

South China Sea

Ob R.

Irtysh R.

URAL MOUNTAINS

Ob R.

Lake Balkhash

Tian Shan

Taklimakan Desert

Kunlun Shan

Tibetan Plateau

Mt. Everest 29,035 ft (8,848 m)

HIMALAYAS

Ganges R.

INDIAN PENINSULA

Deccan Plateau

Eastern Ghats

Western Ghats

Bay of Bengal

Andaman Sea

Andaman Islands

Sri Lanka

Strait of Malacca

Brahmaputra R.

Aral Sea

Kara-Kum Desert

Hindu Kush

Thar Desert

Indus R.

Caspian Sea

Plateau of Iran

Persian Gulf

Arabian Sea

Socotra

Gulf of Aden

CAUCASUS MTS.

Black Sea

Plateau of Anatolia

Cyprus

Mediterranean Sea

Tigris R.

Euphrates R.

ARABIAN PENINSULA

Rub' al-Khali Desert

Red Sea

EUROPE

AFRICA

INDIAN OCEAN

Arctic Circle

N
W   E
S

1,000

0 miles

0 kilometers   1,000

Lambert Azimuthal Equal Area

Oceania

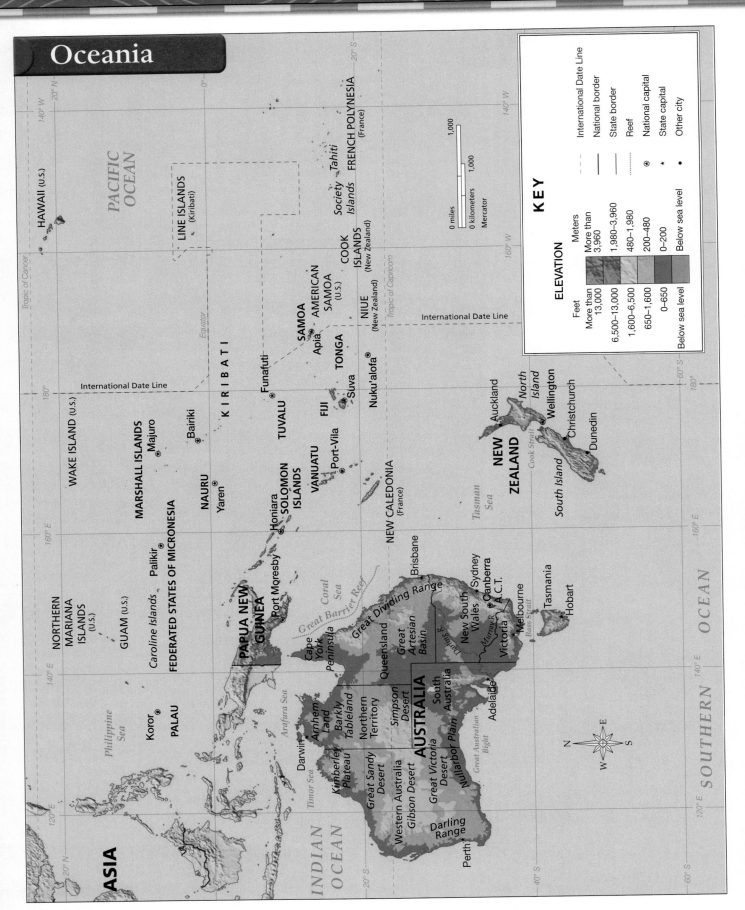

PACIFIC OCEAN

HAWAII (U.S.)

LINE ISLANDS
(Kiribati)

Tropic of Cancer

Society
Islands

Tahiti

FRENCH POLYNESIA
(France)

SAMOA
Apia

AMERICAN
SAMOA
(U.S.)

COOK
ISLANDS
(New Zealand)

NIUE
(New Zealand)

TONGA

Nuku'alofa

Tropic of Capricorn

International Date Line

KIRIBATI

Funafuti

TUVALU

FIJI

Suva

VANUATU

Port-Vila

Auckland

North
Island

Wellington

Christchurch

Dunedin

NEW
ZEALAND

Cook Strait

South Island

International Date Line

WAKE ISLAND (U.S.)

MARSHALL ISLANDS

Majuro

Bairiki

NAURU

Yaren

Honiara

SOLOMON
ISLANDS

NEW CALEDONIA
(France)

Tasman
Sea

Equator

NORTHERN
MARIANA
ISLANDS
(U.S.)

GUAM (U.S.)

Caroline Islands

Palikir

FEDERATED STATES OF MICRONESIA

Port Moresby

PAPUA NEW
GUINEA

Cape
York
Peninsula

Great Coral
Sea

Great Barrier Reef

Brisbane

Great Dividing Range

Sydney

Canberra

A.C.T.

New South
Wales

Melbourne

Victoria

Tasmania

Hobart

Bass Strait

Koror

PALAU

Philippine
Sea

ASIA

Darwin

Arafura Sea

Timor Sea

Arnhem
Land

Kimberley
Plateau

Barkly
Tableland

Northern
Territory

Simpson
Desert

Great
Artesian
Basin

Queensland

Darling R.

Murray R.

South
Australia

AUSTRALIA

Adelaide

Great Sandy
Desert

Western Australia

Gibson Desert

Great Victoria
Desert

Nullarbor Plain

Great Australian
Bight

Darling
Range

Perth

INDIAN
OCEAN

SOUTHERN OCEAN

N
E
S
W

KEY

ELEVATION

Feet	Meters
More than 13,000	More than 3,960
6,500–13,000	1,980–3,960
1,600–6,500	480–1,980
650–1,600	200–480
0–650	0–200
Below sea level	Below sea level

- - - - International Date Line
——— National border
——— State border
········· Reef
⊛ National capital
★ State capital
• Other city

1,000

0 miles   1,000
0 kilometers
Mercator

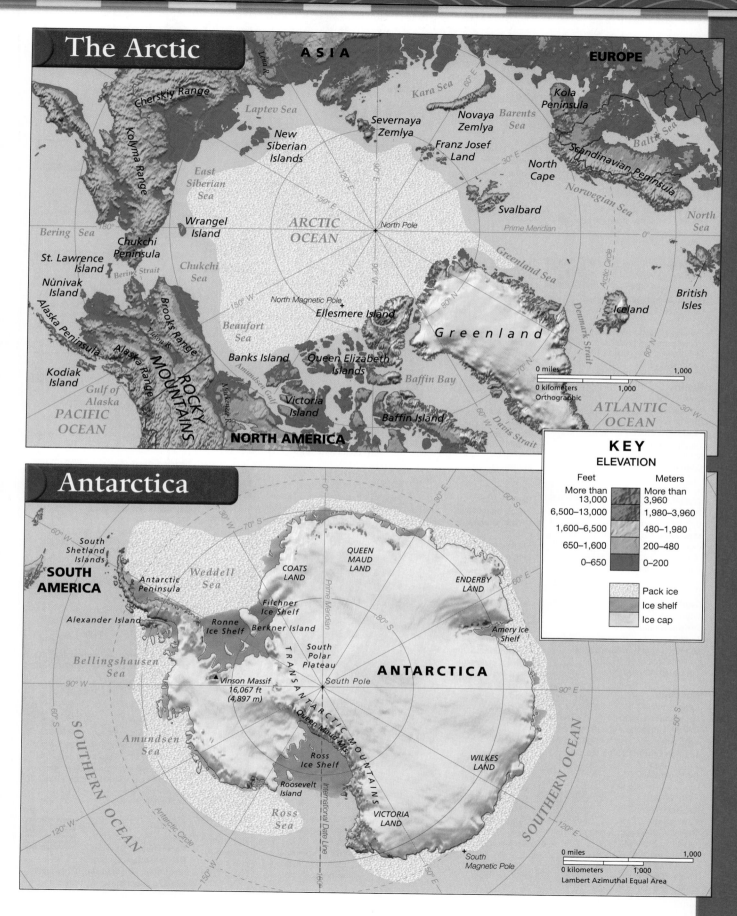

The Arctic

ASIA   EUROPE

Cherskiy Range
Lena R.
Kara Sea
60° E
Kola Peninsula
Laptev Sea
Severnaya Zemlya
Novaya Zemlya
Barents Sea
Baltic Sea
Kolyma Range
New Siberian Islands
Franz Josef Land
30° E
Scandinavian Peninsula
East Siberian Sea
North Cape
120° E
Svalbard
Norwegian Sea
North Sea
Wrangel Island
150° E
ARCTIC OCEAN
90° E
North Pole
Prime Meridian
0°
Bering Sea
180°
Greenland Sea
Arctic Circle
Chukchi Peninsula
Chukchi Sea
120° W
Iceland
British Isles
St. Lawrence Island
Bering Strait
90° W
80° N
Nunivak Island
150° W
North Magnetic Pole
Denmark Strait
60° N
Alaska Peninsula
Brooks Range
Yukon R.
Ellesmere Island
Greenland
Kodiak Island
Alaska Range
ROCKY MOUNTAINS
Beaufort Sea
70° N
Gulf of Alaska
Amundsen Gulf
Banks Island
Queen Elizabeth Islands
Baffin Bay
ATLANTIC OCEAN
30° W
PACIFIC OCEAN
Mackenzie R.
Victoria Island
Baffin Island
Davis Strait
60° N
NORTH AMERICA

0 miles   1,000
0 kilometers   1,000
Orthographic

Antarctica

60° W
South Shetland Islands
SOUTH AMERICA
Antarctic Peninsula
Weddell Sea
30° W
70° S
COATS LAND
QUEEN MAUD LAND
30° E
60° E
ENDERBY LAND
60° E
Alexander Island
Filchner Ice Shelf
Ronne Ice Shelf
Berkner Island
Prime Meridian
80° S
Amery Ice Shelf
Bellingshausen Sea
South Polar Plateau
ANTARCTICA
90° E
90° W
Vinson Massif 16,067 ft (4,897 m)
South Pole
TRANSANTARCTIC MOUNTAINS
Queen Maud Mts.
Amundsen Sea
Ross Ice Shelf
WILKES LAND
120° E
SOUTHERN OCEAN
Roosevelt Island
International Date Line
VICTORIA LAND
60° S
120° W
Ross Sea
50° S
SOUTHERN OCEAN
Antarctic Circle
150° W
South Magnetic Pole
120° E
Lambert Azimuthal Equal Area

0 miles   1,000
0 kilometers   1,000

KEY
ELEVATION

Feet	Meters
More than 13,000	More than 3,960
6,500–13,000	1,980–3,960
1,600–6,500	480–1,980
650–1,600	200–480
0–650	0–200

Pack ice
Ice shelf
Ice cap

Country Databank

Africa

Algeria
Capital: Algiers
Population: 32.3 million
Official Languages: Arabic and Tamazight
Land Area: 2,381,740 sq km; 919,590 sq mi
Leading Exports: petroleum, natural gas, petroleum products
Continent: Africa

Angola
Capital: Luanda
Population: 10.6 million
Official Language: Portuguese
Land Area: 1,246,700 sq km; 481,551 sq mi
Leading Exports: crude oil, diamonds, refined petroleum products, gas, coffee, sisal, fish and fish products, timber, cotton
Continent: Africa

Benin
Capital: Porto-Novo
Population: 6.9 million
Official Language: French
Land Area: 110,620 sq km; 42,710 sq mi
Leading Exports: cotton, crude oil, palm products, cocoa
Continent: Africa

Botswana
Capital: Gaborone
Population: 1.6 million
Official Language: English
Land Area: 585,370 sq km; 226,011 sq mi
Leading Exports: diamonds, copper, nickel, soda ash, meat, textiles
Continent: Africa

Burkina Faso
Capital: Ouagadougou
Population: 12.6 million
Official Language: French
Land Area: 273,800 sq km; 105,714 sq mi
Leading Exports: cotton, animal products, gold
Continent: Africa

Burundi
Capital: Bujumbura
Population: 6.4 million
Official Languages: Kirundi and French
Land Area: 25,650 sq km; 9,903 sq mi
Leading Exports: coffee, tea, sugar, cotton, hides
Continent: Africa

Cameroon
Capital: Yaoundé
Population: 16.1 million
Official Languages: English and French
Land Area: 469,440 sq km; 181,251 sqmi
Leading Exports: crude oil and petroleum products, lumber, cocoa, aluminum, coffee, cotton
Continent: Africa

Cape Verde
Capital: Praia
Population: 408,760
Official Language: Portuguese
Land Area: 4,033 sq km; 1,557 sq mi
Leading Exports: fuel, shoes, garments, fish, hides
Location: Atlantic Ocean

Central African Republic
Capital: Bangui
Population: 3.6 million
Official Language: French
Land Area: 622,984 sq km; 240,534 sq mi
Leading Exports: diamonds, timber, cotton, coffee, tobacco
Continent: Africa

Chad
Capital: N'Djamena
Population: 9 million
Official Languages: Arabic and French
Land Area: 1,259,200 sq km; 486,177 sq mi
Leading Exports: cotton, cattle, gum arabic
Continent: Africa

Comoros
Capital: Moroni
Population: 614,382
Official Languages: Arabic, Comoran, and French
Land Area: 2,170 sq km; 838 sq mi
Leading Exports: vanilla, ylang-ylang, cloves, perfume oil, copra
Location: Indian Ocean

Congo, Democratic Republic of the
Capital: Kinshasa
Population: 55.2 million
Official Language: French
Land Area: 2,267,600 sq km; 875,520 sq mi
Leading Exports: diamonds, copper, coffee, cobalt, crude oil
Continent: Africa

Congo, Republic of the
Capital: Brazzaville
Population: 3.3 million
Official Language: French
Land Area: 341,500 sq km; 131,853 sq mi
Leading Exports: petroleum, lumber, sugar, cocoa, coffee, diamonds
Continent: Africa

Djibouti
Capital: Djibouti
Population: 472,810
Official Languages: Arabic and French
Land Area: 22,980 sq km; 8,873 sq mi
Leading Exports: reexports, hides and skins, coffee (in transit)
Continent: Africa

Egypt
Capital: Cairo
Population: 70.7 million
Official Language: Arabic
Land Area: 995,450 sq km; 384,343 sq mi
Leading Exports: crude oil and petroleum products, cotton, textiles, metal products, chemicals
Continent: Africa

Equatorial Guinea
Capital: Malabo
Population: 498,144
Official Languages: Spanish and French
Land Area: 28,050 sq km; 10,830 sq mi
Leading Exports: petroleum, timber, cocoa
Continent: Africa

Eritrea
Capital: Asmara
Population: 4.5 million
Official Language: Tigrinya
Land Area: 121,320 sq km; 46,842 sq mi
Leading Exports: livestock, sorghum, textiles, food, small manufactured goods
Continent: Africa

Ethiopia
Capital: Addis Ababa
Population: 67.7 million
Official Language: Amharic
Land Area: 1,119,683 sq km; 432,310 sq mi
Leading Exports: coffee, qat, gold, leather products, oilseeds
Continent: Africa

Gabon
Capital: Libreville
Population: 1.2 million
Official Language: French
Land Area: 257,667 sq km; 99,489 sq mi
Leading Exports: crude oil, timber, manganese, uranium
Continent: Africa

Gambia
Capital: Banjul
Population: 1.5 million
Official Language: English
Land Area: 10,000 sq km; 3,861 sq mi
Leading Exports: peanuts and peanut products, fish, cotton lint, palm kernels
Continent: Africa

Ghana
Capital: Accra
Population: 20.2 million
Official Language: English
Land Area: 230,940 sq km; 89,166 sq mi
Leading Exports: gold, cocoa, timber, tuna, bauxite, aluminum, manganese ore, diamonds
Continent: Africa

Guinea
Capital: Conakry
Population: 7.8 million
Official Language: French
Land Area: 245,857 sq km; 94,925 sq mi
Leading Exports: bauxite, alumina, gold, diamonds, coffee, fish, agricultural products
Continent: Africa

Guinea-Bissau
Capital: Bissau
Population: 1.4 million
Official Language: Portuguese
Land Area: 28,000 sq km; 10,811 sq mi
Leading Exports: cashew nuts, shrimp, peanuts, palm kernels, lumber
Continent: Africa

Ivory Coast
Capital: Yamoussoukro
Population: 16.8 million
Official Language: French
Land Area: 318,000 sq km; 122,780 sq mi
Leading Exports: cocoa, coffee, timber, petroleum, cotton, bananas, pineapples, palm oil, cotton, fish
Continent: Africa

Kenya
Capital: Nairobi
Population: 31.3 million
Official Languages: Swahili and English
Land Area: 569,250 sq km; 219,787 sq mi
Leading Exports: tea, horticultural products, coffee, petroleum products, fish, cement
Continent: Africa

Lesotho
Capital: Maseru
Population: 2.2 million
Official Languages: Sesotho and English
Land Area: 30,355 sq km; 11,720 sq mi
Leading Exports: manufactured goods (clothing, footwear, road vehicles), wool and mohair, food and live animals
Continent: Africa

Liberia
Capital: Monrovia
Population: 3.3 million
Official Language: English
Land Area: 96,320 sq km; 37,189 sq mi
Leading Exports: rubber, timber, iron, diamonds, cocoa, coffee
Continent: Africa

Libya
Capital: Tripoli
Population: 5.4 million
Official Language: Arabic
Land Area: 1,759,540 sq km; 679,358 sq mi
Leading Exports: crude oil, refined petroleum products
Continent: Africa

Madagascar
Capital: Antananarivo
Population: 16.5 million
Official Languages: French and Malagasy
Land Area: 581,540 sq km; 224,533 sq mi
Leading Exports: coffee, vanilla, shellfish, sugar, cotton cloth, chromite, petroleum products
Location: Indian Ocean

Malawi
Capital: Lilongwe
Population: 10.7 million
Official Languages: English and Chichewa
Land Area: 94,080 sq km; 36,324 sq mi
Leading Exports: tobacco, tea, sugar, cotton, coffee, peanuts, wood products, apparel
Continent: Africa

Mali
Capital: Bamako
Population: 11.3 million
Official Language: French
Land Area: 1,220,000 sq km; 471,042 sq mi
Leading Exports: cotton, gold, livestock
Continent: Africa

Mauritania
Capital: Nouakchott
Population: 2.8 million
Official Language: Arabic
Land Area: 1,030,400 sq km; 397,837 sq mi
Leading Exports: iron ore, fish and fish products, gold
Continent: Africa

Mauritius
Capital: Port Louis
Population: 1.2 million
Official Language: English
Land Area: 2,030 sq km; 784 sq mi
Leading Exports: clothing and textiles, sugar, cut flowers, molasses
Location: Indian Ocean

Morocco
Capital: Rabat
Population: 31.2 million
Official Language: Arabic
Land Area: 446,300 sq km; 172,316 sq mi
Leading Exports: phosphates and fertilizers, food and beverages, minerals
Continent: Africa

Mozambique
Capital: Maputo
Population: 19.6 million
Official Language: Portuguese
Land Area: 784,090 sq km; 302,737 sq mi
Leading Exports: prawns, cashews, cotton, sugar, citrus, timber, bulk electricity
Continent: Africa

Namibia
Capital: Windhoek
Population: 1.8 million
Official Language: English
Land Area: 825,418 sq km; 318,694 sq mi
Leading Exports: diamonds, copper, gold, zinc, lead, uranium, cattle, processed fish, karakul skins
Continent: Africa

Niger
Capital: Niamey
Population: 11.3 million
Official Language: French
Land Area: 1,226,700 sq km; 489,073 sq mi
Leading Exports: uranium ore, livestock products, cowpeas, onions
Continent: Africa

Nigeria
Capital: Abuja
Population: 129.9 million
Official Language: English
Land Area: 910,768 sq km; 351,648 sq mi
Leading Exports: petroleum and petroleum products, cocoa, rubber
Continent: Africa

Rwanda
Capital: Kigali
Population: 7.4 million
Official Languages: Kinyarwanda, French, and English
Land Area: 24,948 sq km; 9,632 sq mi
Leading Exports: coffee, tea, hides, tin ore
Continent: Africa

São Tomé and Príncipe
Capital: São Tomé
Population: 170,372
Official Language: Portuguese
Land Area: 1,001 sq km; 386 sq mi
Leading Exports: cocoa, copra, coffee, palm oil
Location: Atlantic Ocean

Senegal
Capital: Dakar
Population: 10.6 million
Official Language: French
Land Area: 192,000 sq km; 74,131 sq mi
Leading Exports: fish, groundnuts (peanuts), petroleum products, phosphates, cotton
Continent: Africa

Seychelles
Capital: Victoria
Population: 80,098
Official Languages: English and French
Land Area: 455 sq km; 176 sq mi
Leading Exports: canned tuna, cinnamon bark, copra, petroleum products (reexports)
Location: Indian Ocean

Sierra Leone
Capital: Freetown
Population: 5.6 million
Official Language: English
Land Area: 71,620 sq km; 27,652 sq mi
Leading Exports: diamonds, rutile, cocoa, coffee, fish
Continent: Africa

Somalia
Capital: Mogadishu
Population: 7.8 million
Official Languages: Somali and Arabic
Land Area: 627,337 sq km; 242,215 sq mi
Leading Exports: livestock, bananas, hides, fish, charcoal, scrap metal
Continent: Africa

South Africa
Capital: Cape Town, Pretoria, and Bloemfontein
Population: 43.6 million
Official Languages: Eleven official languages: Afrikaans, English, Ndebele, Pedi, Sotho, Swazi, Tsonga, Tswana, Venda, Xhosa, and Zulu
Land Area: 1,219,912 sq km; 471,008 sq mi
Leading Exports: gold, diamonds, platinum, other metals and minerals, machinery and equipment
Continent: Africa

Sudan
Capital: Khartoum
Population: 37.1 million
Official Language: Arabic
Land Area: 2,376,000 sq km; 917,374 sq mi
Leading Exports: oil and petroleum products, cotton, sesame, livestock, groundnuts, gum arabic, sugar
Continent: Africa

Swaziland
Capital: Mbabane
Population: 1.1 million
Official Languages: English and siSwati
Land Area: 17,20 sq km; 6,642 sq mi
Leading Exports: soft drink concentrates, sugar, wood pulp, cotton yarn, refrigerators, citrus and canned fruit
Continent: Africa

Tanzania
Capital: Dar es Salaam and Dodoma
Population: 37.2 million
Official Languages: Swahili and English
Land Area: 886,037 sq km; 342,099 sq mi
Leading Exports: gold, coffee, cashew nuts, manufactured goods, cotton
Continent: Africa

Togo
Capital: Lomé
Population: 5.2 million
Official Language: French
Land Area: 54,385 sq km; 20,998 sq mi
Leading Exports: cotton, phosphates, coffee, cocoa
Continent: Africa

Tunisia
Capital: Tunis
Population: 9.8 million
Official Language: Arabic
Land Area: 155,360 sq km; 59,984 sq mi
Leading Exports: textiles, mechanical goods, phosphates and chemicals, agricultural products, hydrocarbons
Continent: Africa

Uganda
Capital: Kampala
Population: 24.7 million
Official Language: English
Land Area: 199,710 sq km; 77,108 sq mi
Leading Exports: coffee, fish and fish products, tea, gold, cotton, flowers, horticultural products
Continent: Africa

Zambia
Capital: Lusaka
Population: 10.1 million
Official Language: English
Land Area: 740,724 sq km; 285,994 sq mi
Leading Exports: copper, cobalt, electricity, tobacco, flowers, cotton
Continent: Africa

Zimbabwe
Capital: Harare
Population: 11.3 million
Official Language: English
Land Area: 386,670 sq km; 149,293 sq mi
Leading Exports: tobacco, gold, iron alloys, textiles and clothing
Continent: Africa

Asia and the Pacific

Afghanistan
Capital: Kabul
Population: 27.8 million
Official Languages: Pashtu and Dari
Land Area: 647,500 sq km; 250,000 sq mi
Leading Exports: agricultural products, hand-woven carpets, wool, cotton, hides and pelts, precious and semiprecious gems
Continent: Asia

Armenia
Capital: Yerevan
Population: 3.3 million
Official Language: Armenian
Land Area: 29,400 sq km; 10,965 sq mi
Leading Exports: diamonds, scrap metal, machinery and equipment, brandy, copper ore
Continent: Asia

Australia
Capital: Canberra
Population: 19.6 million
Official Language: English
Land Area: 7,617,930 sq km; 2,941,283 sq mi
Leading Exports: coal, gold, meat, wool, alumina, iron ore, wheat, machinery and transport equipment
Continent: Australia

Azerbaijan
Capital: Baku
Population: 7.8 million
Official Language: Azerbaijani
Land Area: 86,100 sq km; 33,243 sq mi
Leading Exports: oil and gas, machinery, cotton, foodstuffs
Continent: Asia

Bahrain
Capital: Manama
Population: 656,397
Official Language: Arabic
Land Area: 665 sq km; 257 sq mi
Leading Exports: petroleum and petroleum products, aluminum, textiles
Continent: Asia

Bangladesh
Capital: Dhaka
Population: 133.4 million
Official Language: Bengali
Land Area: 133,910 sq km; 51,705 sq mi
Leading Exports: garments, jute and jute goods, leather, frozen fish and seafood
Continent: Asia

Bhutan
Capital: Thimphu
Population: 2.1 million
Official Language: Dzongkha
Land Area: 47,000 sq km; 18,147 sq mi
Leading Exports: electricity, cardamom, gypsum, timber, handicrafts, cement, fruit, precious stones, spices
Continent: Asia

Brunei
Capital: Bandar Seri Begawan
Population: 350,898
Official Language: Malay
Land Area: 5,270 sq km; 2,035 sq mi
Leading Exports: crude oil, natural gas, refined products
Continent: Asia

Cambodia
Capital: Phnom Penh
Population: 12.8 million
Official Language: Khmer
Land Area: 176,520 sq km; 68,154 sq mi
Leading Exports: timber, garments, rubber, rice, fish
Continent: Asia

China
Capital: Beijing
Population: 1.29 billion
Official Languages: Mandarin and Chinese
Land Area: 9,326,410 sq km; 3,600,927 sq mi
Leading Exports: machinery and equipment, textiles and clothing, footwear, toys and sports goods, mineral fuels
Continent: Asia

Cyprus
Capital: Nicosia
Population: 767,314
Official Languages: Greek and Turkish
Land Area: 9,240 sq km; 3,568 sq mi
Leading Exports: citrus, potatoes, grapes, wine, cement, clothing and shoes
Location: Mediterranean Sea

East Timor
Capital: Dili
Population: 952,618
Official Languages: Tetum and Portuguese
Land Area: 15,007 sq km; 5,794 sq mi
Leading Exports: coffee, sandalwood, marble
Continent: Asia

Fiji
Capital: Suva
Population: 856,346
Official Language: English
Land Area: 18,270 sq km; 7,054 sq mi
Leading Exports: sugar, garments, gold, timber, fish, molasses, coconut oil
Location: Pacific Ocean

Georgia
Capital: Tbilisi
Population: 5 million
Official Languages: Georgian and Abkhazian
Land Area: 69,700 sq km; 26,911 sq mi
Leading Exports: scrap metal, machinery, chemicals, fuel reexports, citrus fruits, tea, wine, other agricultural products
Continent: Asia

India
Capital: New Delhi
Population: 1.05 billion
Official Languages: Hindi and English
Land Area: 2,973,190 sq km; 1,147,949 sq mi
Leading Exports: textile goods, gems and jewelry, engineering goods, chemicals, leather manufactured goods
Continent: Asia

Indonesia
Capital: Jakarta
Population: 231.3 million
Official Language: Bahasa Indonesia
Land Area: 1,826,440 sq km; 705,188 sq mi
Leading Exports: oil and gas, electrical appliances, plywood, textiles, rubber
Continent: Asia

Iran
Capital: Tehran
Population: 66.6 million
Official Language: Farsi
Land Area: 1,636,000 sq km; 631,660 sq mi
Leading Exports: petroleum, carpets, fruits and nuts, iron and steel, chemicals
Continent: Asia

Iraq
Capital: Baghdad
Population: 24.7 million
Official Language: Arabic
Land Area: 432,162 sq km; 166,858 sq mi
Leading Exports: crude oil
Continent: Asia

Israel
Capital: Jerusalem
Population: 6.0 million
Official Language: Hebrew, Arabic
Land Area: 20,330 sq km; 7,849 sq mi
Leading Exports: machinery and equipment, software, cut diamonds, agricultural products, chemicals, textiles and apparel
Continent: Asia

Japan
Capital: Tokyo
Population: 127 million
Official Language: Japanese
Land Area: 374,744 sq km; 144,689 sq mi
Leading Exports: motor vehicles, semiconductors, office machinery, chemicals
Continent: Asia

Jordan
Capital: Amman
Population: 5.3 million
Official Language: Arabic
Land Area: 91,971 sq km; 35,510 sq mi
Leading Exports: phosphates, fertilizers, potash, agricultural products, manufactured goods, pharmaceuticals
Continent: Asia

Kazakhstan
Capital: Astana
Population: 16.7 million
Official Language: Kazakh
Land Area: 2,669,800 sq km; 1,030,810 sq mi
Leading Exports: oil and oil products, ferrous metals, machinery, chemicals, grain, wool, meat, coal
Continent: Asia

Kiribati
Capital: Bairiki (Tarawa Atoll)
Population: 96,335
Official Language: English
Land Area: 811 sq km; 313 sq mi
Leading Exports: copra, coconuts, seaweed, fish
Location: Pacific Ocean

Korea, North
Capital: Pyongyang
Population: 22.3 million
Official Language: Korean
Land Area: 120,410 sq km; 46,490 sq mi
Leading Exports: minerals, metallurgical products, manufactured goods (including armaments), agricultural and fishery products
Continent: Asia

Korea, South
Capital: Seoul
Population: 48.3 million
Official Language: Korean
Land Area: 98,190 sq km; 37,911 sq mi
Leading Exports: electronic products, machinery and equipment, motor vehicles, steel, ships, textiles, clothing, footwear, fish
Continent: Asia

Kuwait
Capital: Kuwait City
Population: 2.1 million
Official Language: Arabic
Land Area: 17,820 sq km; 6,880 sq mi
Leading Exports: oil and refined products, fertilizers
Continent: Asia

Kyrgyzstan
Capital: Bishkek
Population: 4.8 million
Official Languages: Kyrgyz and Russian
Land Area: 191,300 sq km; 73,861sq mi
Leading Exports: cotton, wool, meat, tobacco, gold, mercury, uranium, hydropower, machinery, shoes
Continent: Asia

Laos
Capital: Vientiane
Population: 5.8 million
Official Language: Lao
Land Area: 230,800 sq km; 89,112 sq mi
Leading Exports: wood products, garments, electricity, coffee, tin
Continent: Asia

Lebanon
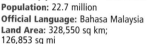
Capital: Beirut
Population: 3.7 million
Official Language: Arabic
Land Area: 10,230 sq km; 3,950 sq mi
Leading Exports: foodstuffs and tobacco, textile, chemicals, precious stones, metal and metal products, electrical equipment and products, jewelry, paper and paper products
Continent: Asia

Malaysia
Capital: Kuala Lumpur and Putrajaya
Population: 22.7 million
Official Language: Bahasa Malaysia
Land Area: 328,550 sq km; 126,853 sq mi
Leading Exports: electronic equipment, petroleum and liquefied natural gas, wood and wood products, palm oil, rubber, textiles, chemicals
Continent: Asia

Maldives
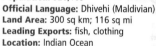
Capital: Malé
Population: 320,165
Official Language: Dhivehi (Maldivian)
Land Area: 300 sq km; 116 sq mi
Leading Exports: fish, clothing
Location: Indian Ocean

Marshall Islands
Capital: Majuro
Population: 73,360
Official Languages: Marshallese and English
Land Area: 181.3 sq km; 70 sq mi
Leading Exports: copra cake, coconut oil, handicrafts
Location: Pacific Ocean

Micronesia, Federated States of
Capital: Palikir (Pohnpei Island)
Population: 135,869
Official Language: English
Land Area: 702 sq km; 271 sq mi
Leading Exports: fish, garments, bananas, black pepper
Location: Pacific Ocean

Mongolia
Capital: Ulaanbaatar
Population: 2.6 million
Official Language: Khalkha Mongolian
Land Area: 1,555,400 sq km; 600,540 sq mi
Leading Exports: copper, livestock, animal products, cashmere, wool, hides, fluorspar, other nonferrous metals
Continent: Asia

Myanmar (Burma)
Capital: Rangoon (Yangon)
Population: 42.2 million
Official Language: Burmese (Myanmar)
Land Area: 657,740 sq km; 253,953 sq mi
Leading Exports: apparel, foodstuffs, wood products, precious stones
Continent: Asia

Nauru
Capital: Yaren District
Population: 12,329
Official Language: Nauruan
Land Area: 21 sq km; 8 sq mi
Leading Exports: phosphates
Location: Pacific Ocean

Nepal

Capital: Kathmandu
Population: 25.9 million
Official Language: Nepali
Land Area: 136,800 sq km; 52,818 sq mi
Leading Exports: carpets, clothing, leather goods, jute goods, grain
Continent: Asia

New Zealand

Capital: Wellington
Population: 3.8 million
Official Languages: English and Maori
Land Area: 268,680 sq km; 103,737 sq mi
Leading Exports: dairy products, meat, wood and wood products, fish, machinery
Location: Pacific Ocean

Oman

Capital: Muscat
Population: 2.7 million
Official Language: Arabic
Land Area: 212,460 sq km; 82,030 sq mi
Leading Exports: petroleum, reexports, fish, metals, textiles
Continent: Asia

Pakistan
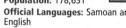
Capital: Islamabad
Population: 147.7 million
Official Languages: Urdu and English
Land Area: 778,720 sq km; 300,664 sq mi
Leading Exports: textiles (garments, cotton cloth, and yarn), rice, other agricultural products
Continent: Asia

Palau
Capital: Koror
Population: 19,409
Official Languages: English and Palauan
Land Area: 458 sq km; 177 sq mi
Leading Exports: shellfish, tuna, copra, garments
Location: Pacific Ocean

Papua New Guinea

Capital: Port Moresby
Population: 5.2 million
Official Language: English
Land Area: 452,860 sq km; 174,849 sq mi
Leading Exports: oil, gold, copper ore, logs, palm oil, coffee, cocoa, crayfish, prawns
Location: Pacific Ocean

Philippines

Capital: Manila
Population: 84.5 million
Official Languages: Filipino and English
Land Area: 298,170 sq km; 115,123 sq mi
Leading Exports: electronic equipment, machinery and transport equipment, garments, coconut products
Continent: Asia

Qatar
Capital: Doha
Population: 793,341
Official Language: Arabic
Land Area: 11,437 sq km; 4,416 sq mi
Leading Exports: petroleum products, fertilizers, steel
Continent: Asia

Samoa

Capital: Apia
Population: 178,631
Official Languages: Samoan and English
Land Area: 2,934 sq km; 1,133 sq mi
Leading Exports: fish, coconut oil cream, copra, taro, garments, beer
Location: Pacific Ocean

Saudi Arabia

Capital: Riyadh and Jiddah
Population: 23.5 million
Official Language: Arabic
Land Area: 1,960,582 sq km; 756,981 sq mi
Leading Exports: petroleum and petroleum products
Continent: Asia

Singapore

Capital: Singapore
Population: 4.5 million
Official Languages: Malay, English, Mandarin, Chinese, and Tamil
Land Area: 683 sq km; 264 sq mi
Leading Exports: machinery and equipment (including electronics), consumer goods, chemicals, mineral fuels
Continent: Asia

Solomon Islands

Capital: Honiara
Population: 494,786
Official Language: English
Land Area: 27,540 sq km; 10,633 sq mi
Leading Exports: timber, fish, copra, palm oil, cocoa
Location: Pacific Ocean

Sri Lanka

Capital: Colombo
Population: 19.6 million
Official Language: Sinhala, Tamil, and English
Land Area: 64,740 sq km; 24,996 sq mi
Leading Exports: textiles and apparel, tea, diamonds, coconut products, petroleum products
Continent: Asia

Syria
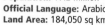
Capital: Damascus
Population: 17.2 million
Official Language: Arabic
Land Area: 184,050 sq km; 71,062 sq mi
Leading Exports: crude oil, textiles, fruits and vegetables, raw cotton
Continent: Asia

Taiwan

Capital: Taipei
Population: 22.5 million
Official Language: Mandarin Chinese
Land Area: 32,260 sq km; 12,456 sq mi
Leading Exports: machinery and electrical equipment, metals, textiles, plastics, chemicals
Continent: Asia

Tajikistan

Capital: Dushanbe
Population: 6.7 million
Official Language: Tajik
Land Area: 142,700 sq km; 55,096 sq mi
Leading Exports: aluminum, electricity, cotton, fruits, vegetables, oil, textiles
Continent: Asia

Thailand

Capital: Bangkok
Population: 62.5 million
Official Language: Thai
Land Area: 511,770 sq km; 197,564 sq mi
Leading Exports: computers, transistors, seafood, clothing, rice
Continent: Asia

Tonga

Capital: Nuku'alofa
Population: 106,137
Official Languages: Tongan and English
Land Area: 718 sq km; 277 sq mi
Leading Exports: squash, fish, vanilla beans, root crops
Location: Pacific Ocean

Turkey

Capital: Ankara
Population: 67.3 million
Official Language: Turkish
Land Area: 770,760 sq km; 297,590 sq mi
Leading Exports: apparel, foodstuffs, textiles, metal manufactured goods, transport equipment
Continent: Asia

Turkmenistan

Capital: Ashgabat
Population: 4.7 million
Official Language: Turkmen
Land Area: 488,100 sq km; 188,455 sq mi
Leading Exports: gas, oil, cotton fiber, textiles
Continent: Asia

Asia and the Pacific (continued)

Tuvalu

Capital: Fongafale
Population: 10,800
Official Language: English
Land Area: 26 sq km; 10 sq mi
Leading Exports: copra, fish
Location: Pacific Ocean

United Arab Emirates
Capital: Abu Dhabi
Population: 2.4 million
Official Language: Arabic
Land Area: 82,880 sq km; 32,000 sq mi
Leading Exports: crude oil, natural gas, reexports, dried fish, dates
Continent: Asia

Uzbekistan
Capital: Tashkent
Population: 25.5 million
Official Language: Uzbek
Land Area: 425,400 sq km; 164,247 sq mi
Leading Exports: cotton, gold, energy products, mineral fertilizers, ferrous metals, textiles, food products, automobiles
Continent: Asia

Vanuatu
Capital: Port-Vila
Population: 196,178
Official Languages: English, French, and Bislama
Land Area: 12,200 sq km; 4,710 sq mi
Leading Exports: copra, kava, beef, cocoa, timber, coffee
Location: Pacific Ocean

Vietnam
Capital: Hanoi
Population: 81.1 million
Official Language: Vietnamese
Land Area: 325,320 sq km; 125,621 sq mi
Leading Exports: crude oil, marine products, rice, coffee, rubber, tea, garments, shoes
Continent: Asia

Yemen
Capital: Sanaa
Population: 18.7 million
Official Language: Arabic
Land Area: 527,970 sq km; 203,849 sq mi
Leading Exports: crude oil, coffee, dried and salted fish
Continent: Asia

Europe and Russia

Albania
Capital: Tiranë
Population: 3.5 million
Official Language: Albanian
Land Area: 27,398 sq km; 10,578 sq mi
Leading Exports: textiles and footwear, asphalt, metals and metallic ores, crude oil, vegetables, fruits, tobacco
Continent: Europe

Andorra
Capital: Andorra la Vella
Population: 68,403
Official Language: Catalan
Land Area: 468 sq km; 181 sq mi
Leading Exports: tobacco products, furniture
Continent: Europe

Austria
Capital: Vienna
Population: 8.2 million
Official Language: German
Land Area: 82,738 sq km; 31,945 sq mi
Leading Exports: machinery and equipment, motor vehicles and parts, paper and paperboard, metal goods, chemicals, iron and steel, textiles, foodstuffs
Continent: Europe

Belarus

Capital: Minsk
Population: 10.3 million
Official Languages: Belarussian and Russian
Land Area: 207,600 sq km; 80,154 sq mi
Leading Exports: machinery and equipment, mineral products, chemicals, textiles, food stuffs, metals
Continent: Europe

Belgium
Capital: Brussels
Population: 10.3 million
Official Languages: Dutch and French
Land Area: 30,230 sq km; 11,172 sq mi
Leading Exports: machinery and equipment, chemicals, metals and metal products
Continent: Europe

Bosnia and Herzegovina
Capital: Sarajevo
Population: 4.0 million
Official Language: Serbo-Croat
Land Area: 51,129 sq km; 19,741 sq mi
Leading Exports: miscellaneous manufactured goods, crude materials
Continent: Europe

Bulgaria
Capital: Sofía
Population: 7.6 million
Official Language: Bulgarian
Land Area: 110,550 sq km; 42,683 sq mi
Leading Exports: clothing, footwear, iron and steel, machinery and equipment, fuels
Continent: Europe

Croatia
Capital: Zagreb
Population: 4.4 million
Official Language: Croatian
Land Area: 56,414 sq km; 21,781 sq mi
Leading Exports: transport equipment, textiles, chemicals, foodstuffs, fuels
Continent: Europe

Czech Republic
Capital: Prague
Population: 10.3 million
Official Language: Czech
Land Area: 78,276 sq km; 29,836 sq mi
Leading Exports: machinery and transport equipment, intermediate manufactured goods, chemicals, raw materials and fuel
Continent: Europe

Denmark
Capital: Copenhagen
Population: 5.4 million
Official Language: Danish
Land Area: 42,394 sq km; 16,368 sq mi
Leading Exports: machinery and instruments, meat and meat products, dairy products, fish, chemicals, furniture, ships, windmills
Continent: Europe

Estonia

Capital: Tallinn
Population: 1.4 million
Official Language: Estonian
Land Area: 43,211 sq km; 16,684 sq mi
Leading Exports: machinery and equipment, wood products, textiles, food products, metals, chemical products
Continent: Europe

Finland

Capital: Helsinki
Population: 5.2 million
Official Languages: Finnish and Swedish
Land Area: 305,470 sq km; 117,942 sq mi
Leading Exports: machinery and equipment, chemicals, metals, timber, paper, pulp
Continent: Europe

France

Capital: Paris
Population: 59.8 million
Official Language: French
Land Area: 545,630 sq km; 310,668 sq mi
Leading Exports: machinery and transportation equipment, aircraft, plastics, chemicals, pharmaceutical products, iron and steel, beverages
Continent: Europe

Germany

Capital: Berlin
Population: 83 million
Official Language: German
Land Area: 349,223 sq km; 134,835 sq mi
Leading Exports: machinery, vehicles, chemicals, metals and manufactured goods, foodstuffs, textiles
Continent: Europe

Greece

Capital: Athens
Population: 10.6 million
Official Language: Greek
Land Area: 130,800 sq km; 50,502 sq mi
Leading Exports: food and beverages, manufactured goods, petroleum products, chemicals, textiles
Continent: Europe

Hungary

Capital: Budapest
Population: 10.1 million
Official Language: Hungarian
Land Area: 92,340 sq km; 35,652 sq mi
Leading Exports: machinery and equipment, other manufactured goods, food products, raw materials, fuels and electricity
Continent: Europe

Iceland
Capital: Reykjavík
Population: 279,384
Official Language: Icelandic
Land Area: 100,250 sq km; 38,707 sq mi
Leading Exports: fish and fish products, animal products, aluminum, diatomite, ferrosilicon
Location: Atlantic Ocean

Ireland
Capital: Dublin
Population: 3.9 million
Official Languages: Irish Gaelic and English
Land Area: 68,890 sq km; 26,598 sq mi
Leading Exports: machinery and equipment, computers, chemicals, pharmaceuticals, live animals, animal products
Continent: Europe

Italy
Capital: Rome
Population: 57.7 million
Official Language: Italian
Land Area: 294,020 sq km; 113,521 sq mi
Leading Exports: fruits, vegetables, grapes, potatoes, sugar beets, soybeans, grain, olives, beef, diary products, fish
Continent: Europe

Latvia
Capital: Riga
Population: 2.4 million
Official Language: Latvian
Land Area: 63,589 sq km; 24,552 sq mi
Leading Exports: wood and wood products, machinery and equipment, metals, textiles, foodstuffs
Continent: Europe

Liechtenstein
Capital: Vaduz
Population: 32,842
Official Language: German
Land Area: 160 sq km; 62 sq mi
Leading Exports: small specialty machinery, dental products, stamps, hardware, pottery
Continent: Europe

Lithuania
Capital: Vilnius
Population: 3.6 million
Official Language: Lithuanian
Land Area: 65,200 sq km; 25,174 sq mi
Leading Exports: mineral products, textiles and clothing, machinery and equipment, chemicals, wood and wood products, foodstuffs
Continent: Europe

Luxembourg
Capital: Luxembourg
Population: 448,569
Official Languages: Luxembourgish, French, and German
Land Area: 2,586 sq km; 998 sq mi
Leading Exports: machinery and equipment, steel products, chemicals, rubber products, glass
Continent: Europe

Macedonia, The Former Yugoslav Republic of
Capital: Skopje
Population: 2.1 million
Official Languages: Macedonian and Albanian
Land Area: 24,856 sq km; 9,597 sq mi
Leading Exports: food, beverages, tobacco, miscellaneous manufactured goods, iron and steel
Continent: Europe

Malta
Capital: Valletta
Population: 397,499
Official Languages: Maltese and English
Land Area: 316 sq km; 122 sq mi
Leading Exports: machinery and transport equipment, manufactured goods
Location: Mediterranean Sea

Moldova
Capital:
Population: 4.4 million
Official Language: Moldovan
Land Area: 33,371 sq km; 12,885 sq mi
Leading Exports: foodstuffs, textiles and footwear, machinery
Continent: Europe

Monaco
Capital: Monaco
Population: 31,987
Official Language: French
Land Area: 1.95 sq km; 0.75 sq mi
Leading Exports: no information available
Continent: Europe

Netherlands
Capitals: Amsterdam and The Hague
Population: 16.1 million
Official Language: Dutch
Land Area: 33,883 sq km; 13,082 sq mi
Leading Exports: machinery and equipment, chemicals, fuels, foodstuffs
Continent: Europe

Norway
Capital: Oslo
Population: 4.5 million
Official Language: Norwegian
Land Area: 307,860 sq km; 118,865 sq mi
Leading Exports: petroleum and petroleum products, machinery and equipment, metals, chemicals, ships, fish
Continent: Europe

Poland
Capital: Warsaw
Population: 38.6 million
Official Language: Polish
Land Area: 304,465 sq km; 117,554 sq mi
Leading Exports: machinery and transport equipment, intermediate manufactured goods, miscellaneous manufactured goods, food and live animals
Continent: Europe

Portugal
Capital: Lisbon
Population: 10.1 million
Official Language: Portuguese
Land Area: 91,951 sq km; 35,502 sq mi
Leading Exports: clothing and footwear, machinery, chemicals, cork and paper products, hides
Continent: Europe

Romania
Capital: Bucharest
Population: 22.3 million
Official Language: Romanian
Land Area: 230,340 sq km; 88,934 sq mi
Leading Exports: textiles and footwear, metals and metal products, machinery and equipment, minerals and fuels
Continent: Europe

Russia
Capital: Moscow
Population: 145 million
Official Language: Russian
Land Area: 16,995,800 sq km; 6,592,100 sq mi
Leading Exports: petroleum and petroleum products, natural gas, wood and wood products, metals, chemicals, and a wide variety of civilian and military manufactured goods
Continents: Europe and Asia

San Marino
Capital: San Marino
Population: 27,730
Official Language: Italian
Land Area: 61 sq km; 24 sq mi
Leading Exports: building stone, lime, wood, chestnuts, wheat, wine, baked goods, hides, ceramics
Continent: Europe

Serbia and Montenegro
Capital: Belgrade
Population: 10.7 million
Official Language: Serbo-Croat
Land Area: 102,136 sq km; 39,435 sq mi
Leading Exports: manufactured goods, food and live animals, raw materials
Continent: Europe

Slovakia
Capital: Bratislava
Population: 5.4 million
Official Language: Slovak
Land Area: 48,800 sq km; 18,842 sq mi
Leading Exports: machinery and transport equipment, intermediate manufactured goods, miscellaneous manufactured goods, chemicals
Continent: Europe

Slovenia
Capital: Ljubljana
Population: 1.9 million
Official Language: Slovene
Land Area: 20,151 sq km; 7,780 sq mi
Leading Exports: manufactured goods, machinery and transport equipment, chemicals, food
Continent: Europe

Spain
Capital: Madrid
Population: 40.1 million
Official Languages: Spanish, Galician, Basque, and Catalan
Land Area: 499,542 sq km; 192,873 sq mi
Leading Exports: machinery, motor vehicles, foodstuffs, other consumer goods
Continent: Europe

Sweden
Capital: Stockholm
Population: 8.9 million
Official Language: Swedish
Land Area: 410,934 sq km; 158,662 sq mi
Leading Exports: machinery, motor vehicles, paper products, pulp and wood, iron and steel products, chemicals
Continent: Europe

Switzerland
Capital: Bern
Population: 7.3 million
Official Languages: German, French, and Italian
Land Area: 39,770 sq km; 15,355 sq mi
Leading Exports: machinery, chemicals, metals, watches, agricultural products
Continent: Europe

Ukraine
Capital: Kiev
Population: 48.4 million
Official Language: Ukrainian
Land Area: 603,700 sq km; 233,090 sq mi
Leading Exports: ferrous and nonferrous metals, fuel and petroleum products, machinery and transport equipment, food products
Continent: Europe

United Kingdom

Capital: London
Population: 59.8 million
Official Languages: English and Welsh
Land Area: 241,590 sq km; 93,278 sq mi
Leading Exports: manufactured goods, fuels, chemicals, food, beverages, tobacco
Continent: Europe

Holy See (Vatican City)
Capital: Vatican City
Population: 900
Official Languages: Latin and Italian
Land Area: 0.44 sq km; 0.17 sq mi
Leading Exports: no information available
Continent: Europe

Latin America

Antigua and Barbuda

Capital: Saint John's
Population: 67,448
Official Language: English
Land Area: 442 sq km; 171 sq mi
Leading Exports: petroleum products, manufactured goods, machinery and transport equipment, food and live animals
Location: Caribbean Sea

Argentina
Capital: Buenos Aires
Population: 37.8 million
Official Language: Spanish
Land Area: 2,736,690 sq km; 1,056,636 sq mi
Leading Exports: edible oils, fuels and energy, cereals, feed, motor vehicles
Continent: South America

Bahamas
Capital: Nassau
Population: 300,529
Official Language: English
Land Area: 10,070 sq km; 3,888 sq mi
Leading Exports: fish and crawfish, rum, salt, chemicals, fruit and vegetables
Location: Caribbean Sea

Barbados
Capital: Bridgetown
Population: 276,607
Official Language: English
Land Area: 431 sq km; 166 sq mi
Leading Exports: sugar and molasses, rum, other foods and beverages, chemicals, electrical components, clothing
Location: Caribbean Sea

Belize
Capital: Belmopan
Population: 262,999
Official Language: English
Land Area: 22,806 sq km; 8,805 sq mi
Leading Exports: sugar, bananas, citrus, clothing, fish products, molasses, wood
Continent: North America

Bolivia
Capital: La Paz and Sucre
Population: 8.5 million
Official Language: Spanish, Quechua, and Aymara
Land Area: 1,084,390 sq km; 418,683 sq mi
Leading Exports: soybeans, natural gas, zinc, gold, wood
Continent: South America

Brazil
Capital: Brasília
Population: 176 million
Official Language: Portuguese
Land Area: 8,456,510 sq km; 3,265,059 sq mi
Leading Exports: manufactured goods, iron ore, soybeans, footwear, coffee, autos
Continent: South America

Chile
Capital: Santiago
Population: 15.5 million
Official Language: Spanish
Land Area: 748,800 sq km; 289,112 sq mi
Leading Exports: copper, fish, fruits, paper and pulp, chemicals
Continent: South America

Colombia
Capital: Bogotá
Population: 41 million
Official Language: Spanish
Land Area: 1,038,700 sq km; 401,042 sq mi
Leading Exports: petroleum, coffee, coal, apparel, bananas, cut flowers
Continent: South America

Costa Rica
Capital: San José
Population: 3.8 million
Official Language: Spanish
Land Area: 51,660 sq km; 19,560 sq mi
Leading Exports: coffee, bananas, sugar, pineapples, textiles, electronic components, medical equipment
Continent: North America

Cuba
Capital: Havana
Population: 11.2 million
Official Language: Spanish
Land Area: 110,860 sq km; 42,803 sq mi
Leading Exports: sugar, nickel, tobacco, fish, medical products, citrus, coffee
Location: Caribbean Sea

Dominica
Capital: Roseau
Population: 73,000
Official Language: English
Land Area: 754 sq km; 291 sq mi
Leading Exports: bananas, soap, bay oil, vegetables, grapefruit, oranges
Location: Caribbean Sea

Dominican Republic
Capital: Santo Domingo
Population: 8.7 million
Official Language: Spanish
Land Area: 48,380 sq km; 18,679 sq mi
Leading Exports: ferronickel, sugar, gold, silver, coffee, cocoa, tobacco, meats, consumer goods
Location: Caribbean Sea

Ecuador

Capital: Quito
Population: 13.5 million
Official Language: Spanish
Land Area: 276,840 sq km; 106,888 sq mi
Leading Exports: petroleum, bananas, shrimp, coffee, cocoa, cut flowers, fish
Continent: South America

El Salvador

Capital: San Salvador
Population: 6.4 million
Official Language: Spanish
Land Area: 20,720 sq km; 8,000 sq mi
Leading Exports: offshore assembly exports, coffee, sugar, shrimp, textiles, chemicals, electricity
Continent: North America

Grenada
Capital: Saint George's
Population: 89,211
Official Language: English
Land Area: 344 sq km; 133 sq mi
Leading Exports: bananas, cocoa, nutmeg, fruit and vegetables, clothing, mace
Location: Caribbean Sea

Guatemala
Capital: Guatemala City
Population: 13.3 million
Official Language: Spanish
Land Area: 108,430 sq km; 41,865 sq mi
Leading Exports: coffee, sugar, bananas, fruits and vegetables, cardamom, meat, apparel, petroleum, electricity
Continent: North America

Guyana
Capital: Georgetown
Population: 698,209
Official Language: English
Land Area: 196,850 sq km; 76,004 sq mi
Leading Exports: sugar, gold, bauxite/alumina, rice, shrimp, molasses, rum, timber
Continent: South America

Haiti

Capital: Port-au-Prince
Population: 7.1 million
Official Language: French and French Creole
Land Area: 27,560 sq km; 10,641 sq mi
Leading Exports: manufactured goods, coffee, oils, cocoa
Location: Caribbean Sea

Honduras

Capital: Tegucigalpa
Population: 6.6 million
Official Language: Spanish
Land Area: 111,890 sq km; 43,201 sq mi
Leading Exports: coffee, bananas, shrimp, lobster, meat, zinc, lumber
Continent: North America

Jamaica

Capital: Kingston
Population: 2.7 million
Official Language: English
Land Area: 10,831 sq km; 4,182 sq mi
Leading Exports: alumina, bauxite, sugar, bananas, rum
Location: Caribbean Sea

Mexico

Capital: Mexico City
Population: 103.4 million
Official Language: Spanish
Land Area: 1,923,040 sq km; 742,486 sq mi
Leading Exports: manufactured goods, oil and oil products, silver, fruits, vegetables, coffee, cotton
Continent: North America

Nicaragua

Capital: Managua
Population: 5 million
Official Language: Spanish
Land Area: 120,254 sq km; 46,430 sq mi
Leading Exports: coffee, shrimp and lobster, cotton, tobacco, beef, sugar, bananas, gold
Continent: North America

Panama

Capital: Panama City
Population: 2.9 million
Official Language: Spanish
Land Area: 75,990 sq km; 29,340 sq mi
Leading Exports: bananas, shrimp, sugar, coffee, clothing
Continent: North America

Paraguay

Capital: Asunción
Population: 5.9 million
Official Language: Spanish
Land Area: 397,300 sq km; 153,398 sq mi
Leading Exports: electricity, soybeans, feed, cotton, meat, edible oils
Continent: South America

Peru

Capital: Lima
Population: 28 million
Official Languages: Spanish and Quechua
Land Area: 1,280,000 sq km; 494,208 sq mi
Leading Exports: fish and fish products, gold, copper, zinc, crude petroleum and byproducts, lead, coffee, sugar, cotton
Continent: South America

Saint Kitts and Nevis

Capital: Basseterre
Population: 38,736
Official Language: English
Land Area: 261 sq km; 101 sq mi
Leading Exports: machinery, food, electronics, beverages, tobacco
Location: Caribbean Sea

Saint Lucia

Capital: Castries
Population: 160,145
Official Language: English
Land Area: 606 sq km; 234 sq mi
Leading Exports: bananas, clothing, cocoa, vegetables, fruits, coconut oil
Location: Caribbean Sea

Saint Vincent and the Grenadines

Capital: Kingstown
Population: 116,394
Official Language: English
Land Area: 389 sq km; 150 sq mi
Leading Exports: bananas, eddoes and dasheen, arrowroot starch, tennis racquets
Location: Caribbean Sea

Suriname

Capital: Paramaribo
Population: 436,494
Official Language: Dutch
Land Area: 161,470 sq km; 62,344 sq mi
Leading Exports: alumina, crude oil, lumber, shrimp and fish, rice, bananas
Continent: South America

Trinidad and Tobago

Capital: Port-of-Spain
Population: 1.2 million
Official Language: English
Land Area: 5,128 sq km; 1,980 sq mi
Leading Exports: petroleum and petroleum products, chemicals, steel products, fertilizer, sugar, cocoa, coffee, citrus, flowers
Location: Caribbean Sea

Uruguay

Capital: Montevideo
Population: 3.4 million
Official Language: Spanish
Land Area: 173,620 sq km; 67,100 sq mi
Leading Exports: meat, rice, leather products, wool, vehicles, dairy products
Continent: South America

Venezuela

Capital: Caracas
Population: 24.3 million
Official Language: Spanish
Land Area: 882,050 sq km; 340,560 sq mi
Leading Exports: petroleum, bauxite and aluminum, steel, chemicals, agricultural products, basic manufactured goods
Continent: South America

United States and Canada

Canada

Capital: Ottawa
Population: 31.9 million
Official Languages: English and French
Land Area: 9,220,970 sq km; 3,560,217 sq mi
Leading Exports: motor vehicles and parts, industrial machinery, aircraft, telecommunications equipment, chemicals, plastics, fertilizers, wood pulp, timber, crude petroleum, natural gas, electricity, aluminum
Continent: North America

United States

Capital: Washington, D.C.
Population: 281.4 million
Official Language: English
Land Area: 9,158,960 sq km; 3,536,274 sq mi
Leading Exports: capital goods, automobiles, industrial supplies and raw materials, consumer goods, agricultural products
Continent: North America

SOURCE: CIA World Factbook Online, 2002

Glossary of Geographic Terms

basin
an area that is lower than surrounding land areas; some basins are filled with water

bay
a body of water that is partly surrounded by land and that is connected to a larger body of water

butte
a small, high, flat-topped landform with cliff-like sides

▲ **butte**

canyon
a deep, narrow valley with steep sides; often with a stream flowing through it

cataract
a large waterfall or steep rapids

◄ **cataract**

delta
a plain at the mouth of a river, often triangular in shape, formed where sediment is deposited by flowing water

flood plain
a broad plain on either side of a river, formed where sediment settles during floods

glacier
a huge, slow-moving mass of snow and ice

hill
an area that rises above surrounding land and has a rounded top; lower and usually less steep than a mountain

island
an area of land completely surrounded by water

isthmus
a narrow strip of land that connects two larger areas of land

mesa
a high, flat-topped landform with cliff-like sides; larger than a butte

mountain
a landform that rises steeply at least 2,000 feet (610 meters) above surrounding land; usually wide at the bottom and rising to a narrow peak or ridge

▶ **glacier**

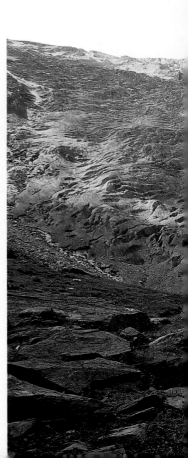

◄ delta

mountain pass
a gap between mountains

peninsula
an area of land almost completely surrounded by water but connected to the mainland

plain
a large area of flat or gently rolling land

plateau
a large, flat area that rises above the surrounding land; at least one side has a steep slope

river mouth
the point where a river enters a lake or sea

strait
a narrow stretch of water that connects two larger bodies of water

tributary
a river or stream that flows into a larger river

valley
a low stretch of land between mountains or hills; land that is drained by a river

volcano
an opening in Earth's surface through which molten rock, ashes, and gases escape from the interior

▶ volcano

Gazetteer

A

Afghanistan (33° N, 65° E) a country in Central Asia where Osama bin Laden's al-Qaeda network was based, p. 242

Africa (10° N, 22° E) the world's second-largest continent, surrounded by the Mediterranean Sea, the Atlantic Ocean, the Indian Ocean, and the Red Sea, pp. 37, 215

Aksum (14°8′ N, 38°43′ E) an ancient town in northern Ethiopia; a powerful kingdom and trade center about A.D. 200–600, p. 53

Andes (20° S, 67° W) a mountain system extending along the western coast of South America, p. 66

Arabian Peninsula (25° N, 45° E) a peninsula in Southwest Asia on which the present-day nations of Saudi Arabia, Yemen, Oman, the United Arab Emirates, Qatar, Bahrain, and Kuwait are located, p. 19

Asia (50° N, 100° E) the world's largest continent, surrounded by the Arctic Ocean, the Pacific Ocean, the Indian Ocean, and Europe, p. 91

Atlantic Ocean (5° S, 25° W) the second-largest ocean, extending from western Europe and Africa to eastern North and South America, p. 164

Austria-Hungary (47° N, 13° E) a former empire in central Europe; the assassination of its archduke in 1914 sparked World War I. p. 223

B

Baghdad (33°30′ N, 44°30′ E) capital city of present-day Iraq; capital of the Muslim empire during Islam's golden age, p. 28

Beijing (40° N, 116° E) capital of present-day China; capital of China under Kublai Khan in the 1200s, p. 96

Benin (6°19′ N, 5°41′ E) a kingdom in the West African rain forest, about 1200 to late 1600s, that was a major cultural and trading center; located in present-day Nigeria, p. 49

Berlin (52°33′ N, 13°30′ E) capital of Germany, p. 212

Bosporus (41°6′ N, 29°4′ E) a narrow strait that separates Europe and Asia and connects the Black Sea with the Sea of Marmara, p. 12

Britain (54° N, 4° W) historically, the island of Great Britain; currently, a term used informally to describe Great Britain or the United Kingdom, p. 205

Byzantium (41°1′ N, 28°58′ E) a city of ancient Greece, later called Constantinople; the site of present-day Istanbul, Turkey, p. 11

C

Cahokia (38°34′ N, 90°11′ W) center of the Mississippian culture which reached its peak about 1100; located in present-day Illinois, p. 81

Canada (60° N, 95° W) a country in North America that joined with Mexico and the United States in the NAFTA agreement, p. 240

Cape of Good Hope (34°24′ S, 18°30′ E) the southern tip of Africa, p. 163

Chaco Canyon (36° N, 108° W) center of the Anasazi culture, located in present-day New Mexico, p. 81

Chang River (32° N, 121° E) the longest river in China and Asia, p. 91

Chang'an (34°15′ N, 108°52′ E) the capital city of China during the Tang dynasty, p. 91

China (35° N, 105° E) a country occupying most of the mainland of East Asia; site of Tang and Song dynasties, p. 91

Constantinople (41°1′ N, 28°58′ E) formerly the ancient city of Byzantium; renamed in A.D. 330 after the Roman emperor Constantine, who made it the new capital of the Eastern Roman, or Byzantine, Empire; now Istanbul, Turkey, p. 10

Cuzco (13°31′ S, 71°59′ W) a city in Peru; the capital city of the Incan empire, p. 64

D

Delhi (28°40′ N, 77°13′ E) the third-largest city in India; capital of medieval India, p. 108

Djenné (13°54′ N, 4°33′ W) a city in Mali, Africa; an important center of Muslim learning in the kingdoms of Mali and Songhai in the 1300s, p. 46

E

East Africa the eastern region of the continent of Africa, p. 53

England (53° N, 2° W) a country in northwestern Europe; the country where the approval of the Magna Carta in 1215 limited the power of the monarchy, p. 173

Ethiopia (9° N, 39° E) a country in East Africa, officially the People's Republic of Ethiopia; site of an empire ruled by Aksum from about A.D. 100s to 600s, p. 53

Europe (50° N, 28° E) the world's second-smallest continent, a peninsula of the Eurasian landmass bounded by the Arctic Ocean, the Atlantic Ocean, the Mediterranean Sea, and Asia, pp. 12, 119

F

Florence (43°46′ N, 11°15′ E) a city in central Italy; an important city-state during the Renaissance, p. 155

France (46° N, 2° E) a country in Western Europe; its monarchy was overthrown during the French Revolution. pp. 171, 202

G

Gaul (46° N, 2° E) a region inhabited by the ancient Gauls, including present-day France and parts of Belgium, Germany, and Italy, p. 120

Ghana (8° N, 1° W) a country in West Africa officially known as the Republic of Ghana; a powerful West African kingdom, A.D. 400s–1200s, p. 45

Gobi Desert (43° N, 105° E) a desert in Mongolia and northern China, p. 90

Grand Canal the 1,085-mile (1,747-kilometer) humanmade waterway linking the Chang and Huang rivers in China, p. 92

Great Plains (42° N, 100° W) a mostly flat and grassy region of western North America; home to the Plains Indians, p. 83

Great Serpent Mound (39° N, 83° W) an enormous earthwork built by the Mound Builders; located in present-day Ohio, p. 78

Great Zimbabwe (20°17′ S, 30°57′ E) a powerful southeast African city, 1100s–1400s, p. 55

Gulf of Mexico (25° N, 90° W) an arm of the Atlantic Ocean in southeastern North America, bordering on eastern Mexico, the southeastern United States, and Cuba, p. 80

H

Himalayas (the) (28° N, 84° E) a mountain system in south central Asia that extends along the border between India and Tibet and through Pakistan, Nepal, and Bhutan, p. 109

Hiroshima (34°30′ N, 133° E) a city on the island of Honshu, Japan; the first city on which an atomic bomb was used in warfare, p. 227

Holy Land (32° N, 35° E) a small region on the Mediterranean Sea, which includes parts of modern Israel and Jordan; considered holy by Jews, Christians, and Muslims, p. 133

Huang River (38° N, 118° E) the second-longest river in China, beginning in Tibet and emptying into the Yellow Sea, p. 91

I

Ile-Ife (7°30′ N, 4°30′ E) the capital of a kingdom in the West African rain forest and a major cultural and trading center, p. 48

Incan empire an empire ruled by the Incas during the 1400s to the 1500s: it stretched along the Andes in South America, p. 64

India (20° N, 77° E) a large country occupying most of the Indian subcontinent in South Asia; site of the Mughal empire, p. 109

Iraq (33° N, 44° E) a country in Southwest Asia; invaded and occupied by the United States in 2003, p. 242

Italy (43° N, 13° E) a boot-shaped country in southern Europe, including the islands of Sicily and Sardinia; birthplace of the Renaissance, p. 155

J

Japan (36° N, 138° E) an island country in the Pacific Ocean off the east coast of Asia; achieved a golden age under the medieval shoguns, p. 101

Jerusalem (31°46′ N, 35°14′ E) the capital of modern Israel; a holy city for Jews, Christians, and Muslims; a battleground during the Crusades, p. 134

K

Kilwa (9°18′ S, 28°25′ E) a medieval Islamic city-state on the East African coast; located in present-day Tanzania, pp. 52, 55

Kyoto (35°5′ N, 135°45′ E) a city in west central Japan; Japan's capital until the late 1800s, p. 102

L

Lowell (42°38′ N, 71°19′ W) a city in Massachusetts that was an important textile manufacturing center in the 1800s, p. 210

M

Machu Picchu (13°7′ S, 72°34′ W) a city in the Andes built by the Incas; located near the present-day city of Cuzco in Peru, p. 62

Mali (17° N, 4° W) a country in West Africa, officially the Republic of Mali; a powerful West African trading kingdom from about 1240 to 1500, p. 45

Mecca (21°27′ N, 39°49′ E) a city in western Saudi Arabia; birthplace of the prophet Muhammad; the holiest Muslim city, p. 20

Medina (41°8′ N, 81°52′ W) a city in western Saudi Arabia; a city where Muhammad preached, p. 21

Mediterranean Sea (35° N, 20° E) the large sea that separates Europe and Africa, p. 12

Mexico (23° N, 102° W) a country in North America that joined with Canada and the United States in the NAFTA agreement, p. 240

Moscow (55°45′ N, 37°35′ E) the capital city of modern Russia; capital of Muscovy and of the early Russian tsars, p. 176

Muscovy (55° N, 37° E) an area of present-day Russia that was controlled by the princes of Moscow from the 1300s to the 1500s, p. 176

N

Nagasaki (32°48′ N, 129°55′ E) a city on the island of Kyushu, Japan; the city on which the second atomic bomb used in warfare was used, p. 227

O

Orléans (47°55′ N, 1°54′ E) a city in north central France; the site of battles in which Joan of Arc led French forces during the Hundred Years' War, p. 143

P

Pacific Ocean (10° S, 150° W) the largest of the world's oceans; extends from the western Americas to eastern Asia and Australia, pp. 84, 166

Paris (48°52′ N, 2°20′ E) the capital of France, p. 131

Persia (32° N, 53° E) part of the Muslim empire of medieval times; the region including present-day Iran, p. 26

Peru (10° S, 76° W) a country in northwestern South America; site of the Incan empire, p. 62

Poland (52° N, 19° E) a country in Europe, invaded by Nazi Germany in 1939 to start World War II, p. 226

Portugal (40° N, 8° W) a country in Western Europe; with Spain, occupies the Iberian Peninsula; important sponsor of expeditions during the Age of Exploration, p. 163

R

Rome (41°54′ N, 12°29′ E) the capital city of Italy; the capital of the ancient Roman Empire; the seat of the Roman Catholic Church, p. 12

Russia (40° N, 84° W) a country in northern Eurasia; ruled by the tsars from the 1500s until 1917, p. 175

S

Sahara (26° N, 13° E) the largest tropical desert in the world, covering almost all of North Africa, p. 37

Silk Road an ancient trade route between China and Europe, p. 90

Songhai (16° N, 0°) a leading kingdom of the West African savanna during the 1400s, p. 47

Soviet Union (40° N, 84° W) officially the Union of Soviet Socialist Republics; the communist nation formed after the Russian Revolution, which included Russia and 14 other republics; adversary of the United States during the Cold War, p. 230

Spain (40° N, 4° W) a country in Western Europe; with Portugal, occupies the Iberian Peninsula; sponsor of Columbus's voyages, pp. 164, 175

St. Petersburg (59°55′ N, 30°15′ E) large city in Russia; capital city of Peter the Great, p. 177

Strait of Magellan (54° S, 71° W) the channel linking the Atlantic and Pacific oceans near the tip of South America; discovered by Ferdinand Magellan, p. 166

T

Tenochtitlán (19°29′ N, 99°9′ W) the capital city of the Aztec empire, located on islands in Lake Texcoco, now the site of Mexico City, pp. 70, 181

Tombouctou (16°46′ N, 3°1′ W) a city in Mali near the Niger River; an important center of trade from the 1400s to the 1600s, p. 50

Turkey (39° N, 35° E) a country located in Southwest Asia, p. 16

U

United States of America (38° N, 97° W) a country in North America; achieved independence from Britain and established a federal republic, p. 201

V

Valley of Mexico (19° N, 99° W) area of present-day Mexico where the Aztec empire flourished from the 1400s to 1521, p. 70

Venice (45° 27′ N, 12° 21′ E) a major seaport in northern Italy; important Renaissance city-state, p. 155

Versailles (48°48′ N, 2°8′ E) a city in France; site of the Palace of Versailles built by Louis XIV, p. 172

Vietnam (16° N, 108° E) a country located in Southeast Asia; site of Vietnam War during the Cold War period, p. 232

W

Waterloo (50°43′ N, 4°23′ E) a village south of Brussels, Belgium, where Napoleon was defeated, p. 214

West Africa the countries in the western region of Africa, p. 44

Wittenberg (51°52′ N, 12°39′ E) the city in Germany where Martin Luther posted his complaints against the Catholic Church, p. 158

Biographical Dictionary

A

Akbar (AK bahr) (1542–1605) called "the Great;" Mughal emperor of India who expanded the empire, strengthened the government, and granted religious freedom to Hindus, p. 110

B

Babur (BAH bur) (1483–1530) founder of the Mughal dynasty in India and emperor from 1526 to 1530, p. 110

Balboa, Vasco Núñez de (bal BOH uh, VAHS koh NOO nyeth theh) (1475–1519) Spanish explorer who led an expedition across the Isthmus of Panama and became the first European to see the Pacific Ocean from the Americas, p. 166

bin Laden, Osama (bin LAH dun, oh SAH muh) (born 1957) leader of the al-Qaeda terrorist organization that attacked the United States on September 11, 2001, p. 242

Bonaparte, Napoleon (BOH nuh pahrt, nuh POH lee un) (1769–1821) general, consul, and emperor of France; brought reforms to France and extended French rule over much of Europe, p. 213

C

Cabot, John (KAB ut, jahn) (about 1450–1498) Italian sailor sponsored by England, who explored the coast of North America in the 1490s, p. 166

Charlemagne (SHAHR luh mayn) (742–814) king of the Franks who conquered and ruled much of Western Europe; patron of literature and learning, p. 120

Charles I (chahrlz thuh furst) (1600–1649) king during the English Civil War; captured by the Parliamentary forces, tried as a tyrant, and executed, p.199

Churchill, Winston (CHUR chil, WIN stun) (1874–1965) prime minister of Great Britain during World War II, pp. 228, 230

Columbus, Christopher (kuh LUM bus, KRIS tuh fur) (1451–1506) Italian navigator sailing for Spain, who landed in the Americas while looking for a westward sea route from Europe to Asia, p. 164

Constantine (KAHN stun teen) (about A.D. 278–337) emperor of Rome (A.D. 306 to 312) who made Constantinople the imperial capital and encouraged the spread of Christianity, p. 11

Copernicus, Nicolaus (koh PUR nih kus, nik uh LAY us) (1473–1543) Polish astronomer who developed the theory that Earth revolves around the sun, p. 192

Cortés, Hernán (kohr TEZ, hur NAHN) (1485–1547) Spanish conquistador who reached Mexico in 1519, conquered the Aztecs, and won Mexico for Spain, p. 181

Cromwell, Oliver (KRAHM wel, AHL uh vur) (1599–1658) military leader of the forces of Parliament during the English Civil War; ruled England as Lord Protector from 1653 to 1658, p. 200

D

da Gama, Vasco (duh GAM uh, VAHS koh) (about 1469–1524) Portuguese explorer who was the first European to sail around Africa to India, p. 163

da Vinci, Leonardo (duh VIN chee, lee uh NAHR doh) (1452–1519) Italian Renaissance artist, scientist, and inventor; his works include the *Mona Lisa* and *The Last Supper.* p. 154

Dias, Bartolomeu (DEE us, bahr too loo MEE oo) (about 1450–1500) Portuguese explorer; first European to sail around the southern tip of Africa, p. 163

Diderot, Denis (DEE duh roh, duh nee) (1713–1784) French Enlightenment thinker, or philosophe, who edited the *Encyclopedia*, p. 195

E

Elizabeth I (ee LIZ uh buth thuh furst) (1533–1603) queen of England from 1558 to 1603; her reign, called the Elizabethan Age, was a golden age for England. pp. 173, 198

F

Ferdinand II (FUR duh nand thuh SEK und) (1452–1516) Spanish king (1474–1516) who, with his wife Isabella, ruled the first united Spanish kingdom, drove the Muslims from Spain, and sponsored Columbus's voyages, p. 175.

G

Galilei, Galileo (gal uh LAY, gal uh LEE oh) (1564–1642) Italian mathematician, astronomer, and physicist; arrested and tried by the Inquisition for claiming that Earth revolved around the sun, p. 190

Gandhi, Mohandas (GAHN dee, moh HAHN dus) (1869–1948) known as Mahatma (great-souled); led the nonviolent movement that freed India from British rule, p. 235

Gregory VII (GREG uh ree thuh SEV unth) (about 1020–1085) pope from 1073 to 1085; excommunicated Henry IV and then forgave him, and later was deposed by Henry, p. 140

Gutenberg, Johann (GOOT un burg, YOH hahn) (died 1468) German printer who invented movable type and used this technology to print a Bible in 1455, p. 159

H

Harun ar-Rashid (hah ROON ahr rah SHEED) (A.D. 786–809) caliph of Baghdad who ruled during the golden age of the Muslim empire, p. 29

Henry (HEN ree) (1394–1460) prince of Portugal, called Henry the Navigator for sponsoring exploration and trade, p. 163

Henry IV (HEN ree thuh fawrth) (A.D. 1050–1106) king of Germany and emperor of the Holy Roman Empire; excommunicated and then forgiven by Pope Gregory VII, p. 140

Henry VIII (HEN ree thuh ayth) (1491–1547) king of England from 1509 to 1547; separated the English Church from Rome to begin the English Reformation; father of Elizabeth I, pp. 144, 173

Hitler, Adolf (HIT lur, AD awlf) (1889–1945) dictator of Nazi Germany; led military invasions that began World War II; led a campaign of genocide against European Jews, p. 226

Hudson, Henry (HUD sun, HEN ree) (died about 1611) English sailor sponsored by England and the Netherlands; explored parts of the North American coast, p. 178

I

Isabella I (iz uh BEL uh thuh furst) (1451–1504) Spanish queen (1474–1504) who, with her husband Ferdinand, ruled the first united Spanish kingdom, drove the Muslims from Spain, and sponsored Columbus's voyages, p. 175

Ivan the Great (Y vun thuh grayt) (1440–1505) Russian prince who led the rebellion against Mongol rule and became absolute monarch of Russia, p. 177

J

Jefferson, Thomas (JEF ur sun, TAHM us) (1743–1826) statesman, Enlightenment thinker, author of the Declaration of Independence, and third president of the United States (1801–1809), p. 201

Joan of Arc (john uv ahrk) (about 1412–1431) religious peasant girl who led French forces to victory over the English in several battles of the Hundred Years' War; captured by England's allies and executed for witchcraft by the English, p. 143

John (jahn) (1167–1216) king of England (1199–1216); in 1215 was forced to approve the Magna Carta, which limited the power of the king and established the rights of English freemen, p. 142

Justinian (jus TIN ee un) (A.D. 483–565) the greatest Byzantine emperor (527–565), responsible for codifying Roman laws into Justinian's Code, p. 12

K

Kublai Khan (KOO bly kahn) (1215–1294) Mongol emperor who founded the Yuan dynasty in China; encouraged the arts, trade, and religious tolerance, pp. 96, 104

L

Lalibela (lah lee BAY lah) (late 1100s–early 1200s) Christian king of Ethiopia who ordered the construction of churches carved into rock, p. 54

Lenin, Vladimir (LEN in, vlad uh MIHR) (1870–1924) founder of the Russian Communist Party, leader of the Russian Revolution of 1917, and dictator of the Soviet Union (1917–1924), p. 224

Locke, John (lahk, jahn) (1632–1704) English philosopher of the Enlightenment who put forth the idea of natural rights, p. 193

Louis XIV (LOO ee thuh FAWR teenth) (1638–1715) king of France (1643–1715); absolute monarch, called the Sun King, who built Versailles, p. 170

Louis XVI (LOO ee thuh SIKS teenth) (1754–1793) king of France (1774–1792), overthrown and then executed during the French Revolution, p. 202

L'Ouverture, Toussaint (loo vehr TOOR, too SAN) (about 1743–1803) former slave who led the Haitian fight for independence, p. 202

Luther, Martin (LOO thur, MAHRT un) (1483–1546) German monk whose protests against certain abuses of the Roman Catholic Church led to the Protestant Reformation, p. 158

M

Magellan, Ferdinand (muh JEL un, FUR duh nand)) (about 1480–1521) Portuguese explorer who sailed around the tip of South America; his crew was the first to sail all the way around the world. p. 166

Maimonides (my MAHN uh deez) (1135–1204) Spanish-born medieval Jewish philosopher and teacher, p. 30

Mansa Musa (MAHN sah MOO sah) (died about 1332) Muslim king of Mali known for his pilgrimage to Mecca in 1324; encouraged the arts and learning, p. 44

Medici, Lorenzo de (MED uh chee, law REN zoh duh) (1449–1492) ruler of the Renaissance city-state of Florence (1469–1492) and patron of the arts; called "the Magnificent," p. 155

Michelangelo (my kul AN juhl loh) (1475–1564) Italian Renaissance artist, architect, and poet; famous for his sculptures and his painting of the ceiling of the Sistine Chapel, p. 157

Minamoto Yoritomo (mee nah MOH toh yoh ree TOH moh) (1147–1199) founder of the shogunate, a Japanese feudal system that lasted for 700 years, p. 104

Moctezuma (mahk tih ZOO muh) (1466–1520) last emperor of the Aztec empire, conquered and killed by the Spanish, pp. 75, 180

Muhammad (muh HAM ud) (about A.D. 570–632) prophet and founder of Islam; Muslims believe he proclaimed the message of God. p. 18.

N

Newton, Isaac (NOOT un, Y zuk) (1642–1727) English mathematician and scientist who said that the universe obeys certain "laws," such as the law of gravity, p. 193

O

Omar Khayyam (OH mahr ky AHM) (1048–1131) Persian poet, mathematician, and astronomer, p. 26

P

Peter the Great (PEET ur thuh grayt) (1672–1725) tsar, or emperor, of Russia (1682–1725); modernized and westernized Russia; built Saint Petersburg, p. 177

Pizarro, Francisco (pea SAHR oh, frahn SEES koh) (about 1475–1541) Spanish conquistador who conquered the Incan empire and claimed Peru for Spain, pp. 67, 182

Polo, Marco (POH loh, MAHR koh) (1254–1324) Italian traveler who journeyed to China in 1271 and was employed by Kublai Khan for 17 years; his writings sparked European interest in China and increased European-Chinese trade. p. 97

R

Richelieu, Cardinal Armand (RISH loo, KAHRD un ul AHR mund) (1585–1642) cardinal of the Roman Catholic Church and chief minister to King Louis XIII of France; helped establish the absolute power of French monarchs, p. 171

Rousseau, Jean-Jacques (roo SOH, zhahn zhahk) (1712–1778) French Enlightenment thinker, or philosophe, who argued that governments should reflect the will of the people, p. 194

S

Saladin (SAL uh din) (c. 1137–1193) Arab Muslim leader who reconquered Jerusalem during the Crusades but allowed Christian pilgrimages, p. 136

Shah Jahan (shah juh HAHN) (1592–1666) Mughal emperor of India and builder of the Taj Mahal, p. 112

Shakespeare, William (SHAYK spihr, WIL yum) (1564–1616) poet, actor, and playwright of the English Renaissance, who is generally considered the greatest writer in the English language, p. 174

Stalin, Joseph (STAH lin, JOH zuf) (1879–1953) dictator of the Soviet Union (1929–1953) who "purged," or killed, more than 10 million people, p. 224

Sundiata (sun JAH tah) (died 1255) West African king who united the kingdom of Mali, p. 46

T

Tang Taizong (tahng ty ZAWNG) (A.D. 600–649) helped his father establish the Tang dynasty and was emperor from 626 to 649; brought Confucian principles to government, p. 92

Timur (tee MOOR) (1336–1405) Mongol conqueror of northern India, whose empire was based in Samarkand, p. 108

Tokugawa Ieyasu (toh koo GAH wah ee yay AH soo) (1543–1616) founder of the last shogunate in Japan; closed his country off from the rest of the world, p. 104

Toyotomi Hideyoshi (toh yoh TOH mee hee duh YOH shee) (1536–1598) Japanese warrior who united Japan and became its ruler in 1590, p. 104

U

Urban II (UR bun thuh SEK und) (about 1035–1099) pope who began the Crusades, p. 133

V

Voltaire (vohl TEHR) (1694–1778) French Enlightenment thinker, or philosophe, who criticized intolerance and governments that abused their power, p. 195

Glossary

A

absolute monarch (AB suh loot MAHN urk) *n.* a king or queen with complete authority over the government and people in a kingdom, p. 171

Age of Exploration (ayj uv eks pluh RAY shun) *n.* the period of European exploration overseas from about 1400 to 1600, p. 162

Age of Reason (ayj uv REE zun) *n.* the period of the Enlightenment, p. 191

Akbar (AK bahr) *n.* Mughal ruler of India from 1156 to 1605, who encouraged the arts, strengthened the central government, and practiced religious toleration; known as "the Great," p. 110

Aksum (AHK soom) *n.* an important East African center of trade, p. 53

Anasazi (ah nuh SAH zee) *n.* one of the early Native American peoples of the Southwest, p. 81

Andes (AN deez) *n.* a mountain chain of western South America, p. 62

apprentice (uh PREN tis) *n.* an unpaid person training in a craft or trade, p. 131

archipelago (ahr kuh PEL uh goh) *n.* a group or chain of many islands, p. 101

Aztecs (AZ teks) *n.* a people who lived in the Valley of Mexico, p. 70

B

Bantu (BAN too) *n.* a large group of central and southern Africans who speak related languages, p. 36

Benin (beh NEEN) *n.* a kingdom of the West African rain forest, p. 48

C

caliph (KAY lif) *n.* a Muslim ruler, p. 28

Cape of Good Hope (kayp uv good hohp) *n.* the southern tip of Africa, p. 163

capitalism (KAP ut ul iz um) *n.* a system in which individuals control property and business, p. 231

caravan (KA ruh van) *n.* a group of traders traveling together for safety, p. 19

caste system (kast SIS tum) *n.* a Hindu social class system that controlled every aspect of daily life, p. 109

census (SEN sus) *n.* an official count of people in a certain place at a certain time, p. 65

chivalry (SHIV ul ree) *n.* the code of honorable conduct for knights, p. 132

circumnavigate (sur kum NAV ih gayt) *v.* to sail or fly completely around something, such as Earth, p. 167

city-state (SIH tee stayt) *n.* a city that is also a separate, independent state, pp. 55, 155

clan (klan) *n.* a group of families who trace their roots to the same ancestor, p. 40

clergy (KLUR jee) *n.* persons with authority to perform religious services, p. 127

Cold War (kohld wawr) *n.* a period of tension between the United States and the Soviet Union from about 1946 to 1991, p. 231

colony (KAHL uh nee) *n.* territory settled and ruled by a distant country, p. 201

communism (KAHM yoo niz um) *n.* a system in which the government owns most businesses, p. 224

conquistador (kahn KEES tuh dawr) *n.* a Spanish conqueror in the Americas, p. 181

Constantine (KAHN stun teen) *n.* an emperor of the Roman Empire and the founder of Constantinople, p. 11

Constantinople (kahn stan tuh NOH pul) *n.* the capital of the Eastern Roman Empire and later of the Byzantine Empire, p. 10

containment (kun TAYN munt) *n.* the United States policy of trying to halt, or contain, the spread of communism, p. 231

Cortés, Hernán (kohr TEZ, hur NAHN) *n.* Spanish conquistador who conquered the Aztecs, p. 181

Crusades (kroo SAYDZ) *n.* a series of military expeditions launched by Christian Europeans to win the Holy Land back from Muslim control, p. 134

Cuzco (KOOS koh) *n.* the capital city of the Incan empire, located in present-day Peru, p. 64

D

Declaration of Independence (dek luh RAY shun uv in dee PEN duns) *n.* the document in which the United States announced its independence from Britain, p. 201

developed countries (dih VEL upt KUN treez) *n.* industrialized countries, p. 235

developing countries (dih VEL up ing KUN treez) *n.* poorer countries that have little industry, p. 235

dictator (DIK tay tur) *n.* the absolute ruler of a country, p. 224

divine right of kings (duh VYN ryt uv kingz) *n.* the belief that the authority of kings comes directly from God, p. 171

dynasty (DY nus tee) *n.* a series of rulers from the same family, p. 91

E

Elizabethan Age (ee liz uh BEE thun ayj) *n.* a golden age of English history when Elizabeth I was queen, p. 174

encomienda (en koh mee EN dah) *n.* a system in which the Spanish king gave Spanish settlers the right to the labor of the Native Americans who lived in a particular area, p. 182

English Bill of Rights (ING glish bil uv ryts) *n.* the acts passed by Parliament in 1689 guaranteeing certain rights of English people and limiting the power of the monarch, p. 200

English Civil War (ING glish SIV ul wawr) *n.* the military clash between forces loyal to King Charles I and the forces of Parliament that overthrew the monarchy, p. 199

Enlightenment (en LYT un munt) *n.* a philosophical movement, primarily of the 1700s, that was characterized by reliance on reason and experience, p. 191

excommunication (eks kuh myoo nih KAY shun) *n.* expelling someone from the Church, p. 127

F

feudalism (FYOOD ul iz um) *n.* in Europe, a system in which land was owned by kings or lords but held by vassals in return for their loyalty; in Japan, a system in which poor people were legally bound to work for wealthy landowners, pp. 103, 121

G

Ghana (GAH nuh) *n.* the first West African kingdom with an economy based on the gold and salt trade, p. 45

Great Depression (grayt dee PRESH un) *n.* the worldwide economic downturn of the 1930s, p. 225

Great Plains (grayt playnz) *n.* a mostly flat and grassy region of western North America, p. 83

Great Zimbabwe (grayt zim BAHB way) *n.* a powerful East African kingdom, p. 55

guild (gild) *n.* a medieval organization of crafts-workers or tradespeople, p. 131

H

hieroglyphics (HY ur oh GLIF iks) *n.* the signs and symbols that made up the Mayan writing system, p. 72

Holocaust (HAHL uh kawst) *n.* Nazi Germany's mass killing of Jewish people, p. 227

Holy Land (HOH lee land) *n.* Jerusalem and parts of the surrounding area where Jesus lived and taught; an area considered holy by Christians, Muslims, and Jews, p. 133

humanism (HYOO muh niz um) *n.* a system of thought that focused on the nature, ideals, and achievements of human beings, rather than on the divine, p. 156

Hundred Years' War (HUN drud yeerz wawr) *n.* a series of conflicts between England and France, 1337–1453, p. 143

I

Ile-Ife (EE lay EE fay) *n.* the capital of a kingdom of the West African rain forest, p. 48

imperialism (im PIHR ee ul iz um) *n.* the effort of a nation to create an empire of colonies, p. 216

Incas (ING kuhs) *n.* people of a powerful South American empire during the 1400s and 1500s, p. 62

Industrial Revolution (in DUS tree ul rev uh LOO shun) *n.* the change in the methods of producing goods—from hand tools to machines in factories, 1760s–1860s, p. 205

J

Jerusalem (juh ROOZ uh lum) *n.* a city in the Holy Land, regarded as sacred by Christians, Muslims, and Jews, p. 134

Justinian (jus TIN ee un) *n.* one of the greatest Byzantine emperors, p.12

Mosaic of Justinian

Justinian's Code (jus TIN ee unz kohd) *n.* an organized collection and explanation of Roman laws for use by the Byzantine Empire, p. 13

K

Kilwa (KEEL wah) *n.* one of the many trading cities on the East African coast, p. 52

kiva (KEE vuh) *n.* a round room used by the Pueblo people for religious ceremonies, p. 82

knight (nyt) *n.* a man who received honor and land in exchange for serving a lord as a soldier, p. 118

Kublai Khan (KOO bly kahn) *n.* a Mongol emperor of China, p. 96

Kyoto (kee OH toh) *n.* the capital city of medieval Japan, p. 102

L

labor union (LAY bur YOON yun) *n.* an organization of workers formed to bargain with employers for better pay and working conditions, p. 209

M

Magna Carta (MAG nuh KAHR tuh) *n.* the "Great Charter," in which the king's power over his nobles was limited; agreed to by King John of England in 1215, p. 142

maize (mayz) *n.* corn, p. 71

Mali (MAH lee) a rich kingdom of the West African savanna, p. 45

manor (MAN ur) *n.* a large estate, often including farms and a village, ruled by a lord, p. 121

Mansa Musa (MAHN sah MOO sah) *n.* a king of Mali, p. 44

Mayas (MAH yuhs) *n.* a people who established a great civilization in Middle America, p. 71

Mecca (MEK uh) *n.* an Arabian trading center and Muhammad's birthplace, p. 20

medieval (mee dee EE vul) *adj.* referring to the Middle Ages, p. 119

merit system (MEHR it SIS tum) *n.* a system of hiring people based on their abilities, p. 93

Middle Ages (MID ul AY juz) *n.* the years between ancient and modern times, p. 119

migration (my GRAY shun) *n.* the movement from one country or region to settle in another, p. 36

millennium (mih LEN ee um) *n.* a period of one thousand years, p. 238

Model Parliament (MAHD ul PAHR luh munt) *n.* a council of lords, clergy, and common people that advised the English king on government matters, p. 142

mosque (mahsk) *n.* a Muslim house of worship, p. 21

Mound Builders (mownd BIL durz) *n.* Native American groups who built earthen mounds, p. 78

Mughal Empire (MOO gul EM pyr) *n.* a period of Muslim rule of India from the 1500s to the 1700s, p. 110

Muhammad (muh HAM ud) *n.* the prophet and founder of Islam, p. 18

Muslim (MUZ lum) *n.* a follower of Islam, p. 20

N

Napoleonic Code (nuh poh lee AHN ik kohd) *n.* the French legal system based on Enlightenment ideas, set up during Napoleon's rule, p. 214

nation (NAY shun) *n.* a community of people that shares territory and a government, p. 141

nationalism (NASH uh nul iz um) *n.* a feeling of pride in one's country and a desire for its independence, p. 214

natural rights (NACH ur ul ryts) *n.* rights that belong to all human beings from birth, p. 193

nomads (NOH madz) *n.* people with no permanent home, who move from place to place in search of food, water, or pasture, p. 19

Northwest Passage (nawrth WEST PAS ij) *n.* a sea route through North America, p. 166

O

oasis (oh AY sis) *n.* an area of vegetation within a desert, fed by springs and underground water, p. 19

Omar Khayyam (OH mahr ky AHM) *n.* a Muslim poet, mathematician, and astronomer, p. 26

oral history (AWR ul HIS tuh ree) *n.* accounts of the past that people pass down by word of mouth, p. 40

P

philosophes (fee luh ZOHF) *n.* French thinkers of the Enlightenment, p. 194

pilgrim (PIL grum) *n.* a person who journeys to a sacred place, p. 134

Pizarro, Francisco (pea SAHR oh, frahn SEES koh) *n.* Spanish conquistador who conquered the Incas, p. 182

postwar (POHST wawr) *adj.* after a war; after World War II, p. 230

Protestant (PRAHT us tunt) *adj.* referring to Christian religions that grew out of the Reformation, p. 159

pueblo (PWEB loh) *n.* a Native American stone or adobe dwelling, part of a cluster of dwellings built close together, p. 82

Q

quipu (KEE poo) *n.* a group of knotted strings used by the Mayas to record information, p. 65

Quran (koo RAHN) *n.* the holy book of Islam, p. 22

R

Reformation (ref ur MAY shun) *n.* the effort to change or reform the Roman Catholic Church, which led to the establishment of Protestant churches, p. 158

Reign of Terror (rayn uv TEHR ur) *n.* the period (1793–1794) of the French Revolution during which many people were executed for opposing the revolution, p. 203

Renaissance (REN uh sahns) *n.* the period of the rebirth of learning in Europe between about 1300 and 1600, p. 154

S

Sahara (suh HA ruh) *n.* a huge desert stretching across most of North Africa, p. 37

samurai (SAM uh ry) *n.* Japanese warriors, p. 103

savanna (suh VAN uh) *n.* an area of grassland with scattered trees and bushes, p. 37

schism (SIZ um) *n.* a split, particularly in a church or a religion, p. 14

scientific method (sy un TIF ik METH ud) *n.* a method involving careful observation of nature and, in some sciences, controlled experiments, p. 193

Scientific Revolution (sy un TIF ik rev uh LOO shun) *n.* a time when scientists began to rely on observation of the natural world, p. 192

serf (surf) *n.* a farm worker considered part of the manor on which he or she worked, p. 123

shogun (SHOH gun) *n.* the supreme military commander of Japan, p. 104

Silk Road (silk rohd) *n.* a chain of trade routes stretching from China to the Mediterranean Sea, p. 90

Martin Luther, whose actions sparked the Reformation

slash-and-burn agriculture (slash and burn AG rih kul chur) *n.* a farming technique in which trees are cut down and burned to clear and fertilize the land, p. 71

Song (sawng) *n.* a dynasty that ruled China after the Tang, from 960 to 1279, p. 93

Songhai (SAWNG hy) *n.* a powerful kingdom of the West African savanna in the 1400s and 1500s, p. 47

Strait of Magellan (strayt uv muh JEL un) *n.* the channel linking the Atlantic and Pacific oceans near the southern tip of South America, p. 166

Sufis (SOO feez) *n.* a Muslim mystical group that believed they could draw closer to God through prayer, fasting, and a simple life, p. 30

sultan (SUL tun) *n.* a Muslim ruler in India, p. 108

superpower (SOO pur pow ur) *n.* a powerful country that can influence many other countries, p. 231

Swahili (swah HEE lee) *n.* a Bantu language with Arabic words, spoken along the East African coast, p. 55

T

Taj Mahal (tahzh muh HAHL) *n.* a tomb built by Shah Jahan for his wife, p. 112

Tang (tahng) *n.* a dynasty that ruled China for almost 300 years, from the 600s to the 900s, p. 91

Tenochtitlán (teh nawch tee TLAHN) *n.* capital city of the Aztecs, p. 70

terraces (TEHR us iz) *n.* steplike ledges cut into a slope to make land suitable for farming, p. 66

terrorism (TEHR ur iz um) *n.* causing fear through the threat or use of violence as a way to achieve political goals, p. 242

textile industry (TEKS tyl IN dus tree) *n.* the making of cloth, p. 206

A bedroom at Versailles

trading bloc (TRAYD ing blahk) *n.* a group of countries that agrees to reduce barriers to trade, p. 241

troubadour (TROO buh dawr) *n.* a traveling poet and musician of the Middle Ages, p. 132

tsar (zahr) *n.* the Russian emperor, p. 177

V

Versailles (vur SY) *n.* the palace built for the French king Louis XIV, p. 172

W

World War I (wurld wawr wun) *n.* the first major war of the 1900s (1914–1918), p. 223

World War II (wurld wawr too) *n.* the second major war of the 1900s (1939–1945), p. 226

Index

The *m, g,* or *p* following some page numbers refers to maps *(m)*, charts, tables, graphs, timelines, or diagrams *(g)*, or pictures *(p)*.

Bantu, 36, 38–41, 39*m*, 41*p*
hijra, 21
transportation and, 240
millennium, 238
mill girls, 210–211
Minamoto clan, 104
Mississippian culture, 80*m*, 81
Moctezuma, 75, 75*p*, 180, 181, 181*p*
Model Parliament, 142
Mohawk nation, 84
Mona Lisa (Da Vinci), 157
monarchy, 171
in England, 198–200
of France, 202–203
in Russia, 177
in Spain, 175
monasteries, 129
monasticism, 129
money, 137, 137*p*
Mongols, 176
in China, 96–97, 96*p*, 97*p*
in Japan, 104
Moors, 175
Morse, Samuel F. B., 206
Moscow, Russia, 176, 176*p*
mosque, 21, 46*p*, 52*p*
Mound Builders, 61*m*, 78–81, 78–79*p*, 80*m*
Moundville, 81
movable type, 95
movement, M1, 39*m*. *See also* migration
muezzin, 21
Mughal Empire, 110–112, 110*p*, 111*m*
Muhammad, 18, 20–23
Murphy, Audie, 227, 227*p*
Muscovy, 176
music
of China, 94
jazz, 225
of Muslim civilization, 29
Muslim civilization
architecture of, 28
culture, 28–30, 28*p*, 29*p*, 30*p*
in East Africa, 53
Golden Age of, 26–30
in India, 109–110
literature of, 28, 30
mathematics in, 28, 29, 29*p*
medicine in, 29, 29*p*
music of, 29
science in, 28, 29, 29*p*
spread of Islam, 27–28, 27*m*, 27*p*
trade in, 20, 28, 55
Muslims, 20
beliefs of, 21
business methods, 20
Byzantine Empire and, 15, 15*p*

Golden Age of, 26–30
schism among, 23
in Tombouctou, 50
trade, 20
women, 22
See also Islam
Muslim Turks, 134–136

N

NAFTA. *See* North American Free Trade Agreement
Nagasaki, 227
Napoleon, 213–214, 213*m*, 213*p*, 214*p*
Napoleonic Code, 214
National Assembly, 202, 203
nationalism, 214, 285
industrialization and, 216
nations, 141, 144
Native Americans
Eastern Mound Builders, 78–81, 78–79*p*, 80*m*
encomienda system and, 182
enslavement of, 182
of the Great Plains, 83
horses and, 6, 83
of the Southwest, 81–83, 81*p*, 82*p*, 83*p*
Woodlands, 84, 84*p*
natural law, 193
natural rights, 193
Nazi Party, 226
New Spain, 182, 182*m*
Newton, Isaac, 193, 193*p*
Nicholas, tsar of Russia, 224
Niger River, 45
Nigeria, 258*m*, 265
forest kingdoms of, 48–49, 48*p*, 49*p*
Nok people, 42, 42*p*
nomads, 19, 19*p*, 24–25, 24*p*, 25*p*, 285, M17*p*
Norman Conquest, 142
North America, 2*m*, 248*m*, 250*m*
civilizations of, 61*m*, 78–84, 79*p*, 80*m*, 81*p*, 82*p*, 83*p*, 84*p*
physical map, 253*m*
political map, 252*m*
Vikings in, 121
North American Free Trade Agreement, 241
Northern Renaissance, 156
North Korea, 232, 233*m*
North Vietnam, 232, 233*m*
Northwest Coast people, 84, 84*p*
Northwest Passage, 166, 178–179, 178–179*m*
Notre Dame Cathedral, 128*p*

O

oasis, 19, 37*p*
obas, 49
"Of Swords and Sorcerors" (Hodges and Evernden), 148–151
Olmec people, 71, 71*p*
Omaha people, 83
Oneida nation, 84
onis, 48
Onondaga nation, 84
oral history, 40, 285
Orléans, Battle of, 143
Ottoman Empire, 6*m*, 15

P

Pacific Ocean, 166, 167
Pakistan, 109, 260*m*
papacy, 129
Paris, France, 131, 238*p*
Parliament, 142, 144, 199–201
Paul III, Pope, 160
Pearl Harbor, 226
peasants, 122–123, 123*p*, 131
People's Crusade, 136
Persian Empire, 28
Persian language, 26
perspective, artistic, 157, 186
Peter the Great, 177, 177*p*
Peter the Hermit, 136
Philippines, 167, 216
philosophes, 194–195, 194*p*
phonograph, 206
pilgrims, 134, 286
Pittsburgh, Pennsylvania, 208*g*, 208*p*
Pizarro, Francisco, 67, 182–183
Plains Indians, 83
Plateau of Tibet, 89*m*, 91
poetry
of China, 93, 94
of Japan, 105
of Middle Ages, 132
of Muslim civilization, 28, 30
Persian, 26, 26*p*
Poland, 117*m*, 226
political cartoons, 212*p*
political geography, 6, 6*m*, 6*p*
pollution, 241
Polo, Marco, 97, 97*p*
popes, 129, 140, 142
population
of Dallas, Texas, 236–237, 236*p*, 237*g*
environment and, 241
of Inca civilization, 64
during Industrial Revolution, 208*g*
poverty and, 241

Acknowledgments

Cover Design
Pronk&Associates

Staff Credits
The people who made up *World Studies © 05* team—representing design services, editorial, editorial services, educational technology, marketing, market research, photo research and art development, production services, project office, publishing processes, and rights & permissions—are listed below. Bold type denotes core team members.

Greg Abrom, Ernie Albanese, Rob Aleman, Susan Andariese, **Rachel Avenia-Prol,** Leann Davis Alspaugh, Penny Baker, Barbara Bertell, **Peter Brooks,** Rui Camarinha, John Carle, **Lisa Del Gatto,** Paul Delsignore, Kathy Dempsey, Anne Drowns, Deborah Dukeshire, Marlies Dwyer, **Frederick Fellows,** Paula C. Foye, Lara Fox, Julia Gecha, **Mary Hanisco,** Salena Hastings, Lance Hatch, Kerri Hoar, **Beth Hyslip,** Katharine Ingram, Nancy Jones, John Kingston, Deborah Levheim, Constance J. McCarty, **Kathleen Mercandetti,** Art Mkrtchyan, Ken Myett, **Mark O'Malley,** Jen Paley, Ray Parenteau, **Gabriela Pérez Fiato,** Linda Punskovsky, Kirsten Richert, **Lynn Robbins,** Nancy Rogier, Bruce Rolff, Robin Samper, Mildred Schulte, Siri Schwartzman, **Malti Sharma,** Lisa Smith-Ruvalcaba, Roberta Warshaw, Sarah Yezzi

Additional Credits
Jonathan Ambar, Tom Benfatti, Lisa D. Ferrari, Paul Foster, Florrie Gadson, Philip Gagler, Ella Hanna, Jeffrey LaFountain, Karen Mancinelli, Michael McLaughlin, Lesley Pierson, Debi Taffet

The DK Designs team who contributed to *World Studies © 05* were as follows: Hilary Bird, Samantha Borland, Marian Broderick, Richard Czapnik, Nigel Duffield, Heather Dunleavy, Cynthia Frazer, James A. Hall, Lucy Heaver, Rose Horridge, Paul Jackson, Heather Jones, Ian Midson, Marie Ortu, Marie Osborn, Leyla Ostovar, Ralph Pitchford, Ilana Sallick, Pamela Shiels, Andrew Szudek, Amber Tokeley.

Maps
Maps and globes were created by **DK Cartography.** The team consisted of Tony Chambers, Damien Demaj, Julia Lunn, Ed Merritt, David Roberts, Ann Stephenson, Gail Townsley, Iorwerth Watkins.

Illustrations
Kenneth Batelman: 11; Richard Bonson/Dorling Kindersley: 207; KJA-artists.com: 24, 24–25, 50, 50–51, 51, 76, 76–77, 106, 106–107, 124, 124–125, 125, 168, 168–169, 210, 210–211, 228, 228–229; Trevor Johnston: 197; Jill Ort: 10, 18, 26, 90, 100, 108; Jen Paley: 17, 21, 29, 36, 44, 47, 52, 62, 68, 70, 78, 87, 95, 98, 99, 118, 126, 133, 140, 147, 154, 161, 162, 170, 180, 190, 192, 198, 204, 206, 208, 212, 219, 222, 225, 230, 237, 238; XNR Productions: 240

Photos

Cover Photos
tl, Brian Sytnyk/Masterfile Corporation; **tm,** Firstlight/Heatons; **tr,** Robert Marien/MaXx; Chris Ladd/Getty Images, Inc.

Title Page
Chris Ladd/Getty Images, Inc.

Table of Contents
iv, Max Alexander/Robert Harding World Imagery; **v t,** Chas Howson/The British Museum, London, UK/Dorling Kindersley; **v b both,** Michel Zab/Dorling Kindersley; **vi t,** Gwalior Fort, Madhya Pradesh, India/Bridgeman Art Library; **vi b,** Bridgeman Art Library; **vii,** Francis Speckler/EPA/Sipa Photos; **viii,** Sipa Photos; **ix** Morton Beebe/Corbis; **xi,** David Jones/Alamy Images

Learning With Technology
xiii, Discovery Channel School

Reading and Writing Handbook
RW Michael Newman/PhotoEdit; **RW1,** Walter Hodges/Getty Images, Inc.; **RW2,** Digital Vision/Getty Images, Inc.; **RW3,** Will Hart/PhotoEdit; **RW5,** Jose Luis Pelaez, Inc./Corbis

MapMaster Skills Handbook
M, James Hall/Dorling Kindersley; **M1,** Mertin Harvey/Gallo Images/Corbis; **M2–3 m,** NASA; **M2–3,** (globes) Planetary Visions; **M5 br,** Barnabas Kindersley/Dorling Kindersley; **M6 tr,** Mike Dunning/Dorling Kindersley; **M10 b,** Bernard and Catherine Desjeux/Corbis; **M11,** Hutchison Library; **M12 b,** Pa Photos; **M13 r,** Panos Pictures; **M14 l,** Macduff Everton/Corbis; **M14 t,** MSCF/NASA; **M15 b,** Ariadne Van Zandbergen/Lonely Planet Images; **M16 l,** Bill Stormont/Corbis; **M16 b,** Pablo Corral/Corbis; **M17 t,** Les Stone/Sygma/Corbis; **M17 b,** W. Perry Conway/Corbis

Guiding Questions
1, Christie's Images/Corbis

World Overview
2 l, Buddy Mays/Corbis; **2 tr,** G. Renner/Robert Harding World Imagery; **3 b,** B.S.P.I./Corbis; **3 t,** Pascal Tournaire/Saola/Getty Images, Inc.; **4 t,** Kevin Fleming/Corbis; **4 b,** Conaculta-Inah-Mex. Authorized reproduction by the Instituto Nacional de Antropologia e Historia; **4 ml,** Piers Cavendish/Impact Photos; **5 t, 5 b,** Ted Spiegel/Corbis; **5 mr,** Lowell Georgia/Corbis; **6 t,** Dorling Kindersley; **6 b,** Ed Simpson/Getty Images, Inc.; **7 t,** Dorling Kindersley; **7 b,** Robert Harding World Imagery; **7 ml,** William J. Hebert/Getty Images, Inc.

Chapter One
8–9, Robert Frerck/Woodfin Camp & Associates; **10,** The Granger Collection, New York; **11 t,** Topham/The Image Works; **11 b,** Historical Picture Archive/Corbis; **12 t,** Discovery Channel School; **12 m,** Chas Howson/The British Museum, London, UK/Dorling Kindersley; **12 b,** The Granger Collection, New York; **13,** Robert Frerck/Getty Images, Inc.; **14,** Paul H. Kuiper/Corbis; **15,** Photos12.com-ARJ; **16 t,** Corbis; **16 b,** Jeff Greenberg/The Image Works; **18,** The British Library, London, UK; **19,** Christine Osborne/Agency Worldwide Picture Library/Alamy Images; **20,** Explorer, Paris/SuperStock, Inc.; **21,** Paul Chesley/Stone/Getty Images, Inc.; **22 t,** Latif Reuters New Media, Inc./Corbis; **22 b,** The British Library, London, UK/The Art Archive; **23,** The Granger Collection, New York; **24,** Alan Hills/Dorling Kindersley; **25,** Dorling Kindersley; **26,** Scala/Art Resource, NY; **27,** Archivo Iconografico, S. A./Corbis; **28,** Lauros/Giraudon/Bridgeman Art Library; **29 t, 29 m,** The Granger Collection, New York; **29 b,** Giraudon/Art Resource, NY; **30,** Stuart Cohen/The Image Works; **31 t,** The Granger Collection, New York; **31 b,** Lauros/Giraudon/Bridgeman Art Library

Chapter Two
34–35, M. & E. Bernheim/Woodfin Camp & Associates; **36,** Tim Rock/Lonely Planet Images; **37,** Chris Anderson/Aurora Photos; **38–39,** SuperStock, Inc.; **40,** Walter Bibikow/Jon Arnold Images/Alamy Images; **41 all,** Geoff Dann/Dorling Kindersley; **42,** Werner Forman/Art Resource, NY; **43,** Getty Images, Inc.; **44,** The Granger Collection, New York; **45 t,** Nik Wheeler/Corbis; **45 b,** Ariadne Van Zandbergen/Lonely Planet Images; **46,** David Jones/Alamy Images; **47 both,** Werner Forman/Art Resource, NY; **48,** Lars Howlett/Aurora Photos; **49,** Christie's Images/Corbis; **51,** The Art Archive/Musée des Arts Africains et Océaniens/Dagli Orti; **52,** Marc & Evelyne Bernheim/Woodfin Camp & Associates; **53 t,** David Else/Lonely Planet Images; **53 b,** D. Harcourt-Webster/Robert Harding World Imagery; **54 t,** Dave Bartruff/Corbis; **54 b,** Ariadne Van Zandbergen/Lonely Planet Images; **55 t,** Discovery Channel School; **55 b,** Mitch Reardon/Lonely Planet Images; **56,** I. Vanderharst/Robert Harding World Imagery; **57,** Christie's Images/Corbis

Chapter Three
60–61, SuperStock, Inc.; **62,** Philippe Colombi/Photodisc Green/ Getty Images, Inc.; **63,** The British Museum, London, UK/Dorling Kindersley; **64,** Anthony Pidgeon/Lonely Planet Images; **65 t,** Charles & Josette Lenars/Corbis; **65 b,** The Granger Collection, New York; **66,** Woodfin Camp & Associates; **67,** The British Museum, London, UK/Dorling Kindersley; **69 both,** The Art Archive/Archaeological Museum Lima/Dagli Orti; **70,** Bodleian Library; **71 t,** Angel Terry/Alamy Images; **71 b,** Robert Fried Photography; **72,** Private Collection/Bridgeman Art Library; **73 t,** Discovery Channel School; **73 b,** Robert Frerck/Getty Images Inc.; **74 both, 75,** Michel Zab/Dorling Kindersley; **77,** Werner Forman/Art Resource, NY; **78,** Werner Forman/Art Resource, NY; **79,** Tony Linck/SuperStock, Inc.; **80 t,** Werner Forman Archive/Art Resource, NY; **80 b,** Richard A. Cooke/Corbis; **81,** Dewitt Jones/Corbis; **82–83 t,** George H. H. Huey Photography, Inc.; **82 b,** David Muench/Corbis; **84,** Peter Gridley/Getty Images, Inc.; **85 l,** David Muench/Corbis; **85 r,** Michel Zab/Dorling Kindersley

Chapter Four
88–89, B. Davis/Woodfin Camp & Associates; **90–91 b,** The British Museum, London, UK/Topham-HIP/The Image Works; **91 t,** Werner Forman/Art Resource, NY; **92,** The Granger Collection, New York; **93,** Honolulu Academy of Arts; **94 l,** The Granger Collection, New York; **94 r,** Alan Hills and Geoff Brightling/The British Museum, London, UK/Dorling Kindersley; **95 tl,** The Art